Lecture Notes in Artificial Intelligence 1916

Subseries of Lecture Notes in Computer Science
Edited by J. G. Carbonell and J. Siekmann

Lecture Notes in Computer Science

Edited by G. Goos, J. Hartmanis, and J. van Leeuwen

Berlin
Heidelberg
New York
Barcelona
Hong Kong
London
Milan
Paris
Singapore
Tokyo

Frank Dignum   Mark Greaves (Eds.)

Issues in
Agent Communication

Series Editors

Jaime G. Carbonell, Carnegie Mellon University, Pittsburgh, PA, USA
Jörg Siekmann, University of Saarland, Saarbrücken, Germany

Volume Editors

Frank Dignum
Eindhoven University of Technology
Faculty of Mathematics and Computing Science
P.O. Box 513, 5600 MB Eindhoven, The Netherlands
E-mail: dignum@win.tue.nl

Mark Greaves
The Boeing Company
Mathematics and Computing Technology
Box 3707, MS 7L-43, Seattle, WA 98124-2207, USA
E-mail: mark.t.greaves@boeing.com

Cataloging-in-Publication Data applied for

Die Deutsche Bibliothek - CIP-Einheitsaufnahme

Issues in agent communication / Frank Dignum ; Mark Greaves (ed.). -
Berlin ; Heidelberg ; New York ; Barcelona ; Hong Kong ; London ;
Milan ; Paris ; Singapore ; Tokyo : Springer, 2000
  (Lecture notes in computer science ; Vol. 1916 : Lecture notes in
  artificial intelligence)
  ISBN 3-540-41144-5

CR Subject Classification (1998): I.2.11, C.2.4, D.3, D.2, F.3

ISBN 3-540-41144-5 Springer-Verlag Berlin Heidelberg New York

Springer-Verlag Berlin Heidelberg New York
a member of BertelsmannSpringer Science+Business Media GmbH
© Springer-Verlag Berlin Heidelberg 2000
Printed in Germany

Typesetting: Camera-ready by author, data conversion by PTP-Berlin, Stefan Sossna
Printed on acid-free paper   SPIN: 10722777   06/3142   5 4 3 2 1 0

Preface

In recent years the interest in multi-agent systems (MAS) has grown tremendously. The applications of MAS range from digital libraries through cooperative engineering to electronic commerce. All these applications have one thing in common: the agents operating within these systems have to communicate.

A first attempt to come to a standardised agent communication language (ACL) came forth from the DARPA knowledge sharing project and produced KQML. Up till now KQML is the only ACL that is implemented and (widely) used (at least in the academic world). More recently another effort to come to a standard ACL has started through the FIPA initiative.

Although the above initiatives show that some work has been done on ACL's, there seems to be little consensus on the basics of agent communication. There is no clear understanding of the semantics of individual speech acts or even the basic concepts that should be used to define the semantics. Even less is known about the semantics of conversations and the relations between speech acts and the conversations of which they form a part.

In two separate workshops last year an attempt was made to bring researchers in the field of agent communication together to discuss issues on agent communication languages and conversation policies. The workshop on Specifying and Implementing Conversation Policies (SICP) attracted around 20 papers of which 12 were selected for presentation. The workshop on Agent Communication Languages (ACL) attracted around 25 papers of which 12 were also selected. From these 24 papers two were not selected for this volume, while another two were written by the same set of authors and were so close in content that they were asked to join the papers into one. That leaves 21 contributions in this first volume on agent communication.

After this first successful attempt in organizing a workshop in this area, the organizers decided to join forces for next year such that there will be one international workshop on agent communication that will hopefully serve as the main place for researchers in this area to exchange their ideas.

We believe that the current volume gives an adequate view of the current state of the research in this field. We have added an introduction to highlight a number of issues that play an important role in agent communication in the hope that it will be of use to many researchers and practitioners in the agent community.

July 2000   Frank Dignum (Eindhoven, The Netherlands)
                                              Mark Greaves (Seattle, USA)

Workshops Organization

Organizing Commitee SICP

Mark Greaves   Boeing, Seattle, USA
Jeffrey Bradshaw   Boeing, Seattle, USA

Program Commitee SICP

M. Calisti   École Polytechnique Fédérale de Lausanne (France)
P. Cohen   Oregon Institute of Science and Technolgy (USA)
T. Finin   University of Maryland (USA)
A. Mamdani   Imperial College (UK)
M. Singh   North Carolina State University (USA)
D. Steiner   Siemens AG (Germany)

Organizing Commitee ACL

Frank Dignum   Eindhoven University of Technology,
                           The Netherlands
Brahim Chaib-draa   Laval University, Canada

Program Commitee ACL

J. Allwood   University of Goteborg (Sweden)
M. Barbuceanu   University of Toronto (Canada)
B. Chaib-draa   Laval University (Canada)
P. Cohen   Oregon Institute of Science and Technolgy
                       (USA)
F. Dignum   Eindhoven University of Technology
                       (The Netherlands)
R. Fikes   Stanford University (USA)
T. Finin   University of Maryland (USA)
A. Haddadi   Daimler Benz (Germany)
M. Klusch   DFKI (Germany)
Y. Labrou   University of Maryland (USA)
J.-J. Meyer   Utrecht University (The Netherlands)
P. Noriega   LANIA (Mexico)
D. Sadek   France Telecom (France)
C. Sierra   AI Research Institute (Spain)
M. Singh   North Carolina State University (USA)
D. Steiner   Siemens AG (Germany)
D. Traum   University of Maryland (USA)
H. Weigand   Tilburg University (The Netherlands)
M. Wooldridge   University of Liverpool (England)

Workshops Organization

Organizing Commitee SICP

Mark Greaves	Boeing, Seattle, USA
Jeffrey Bradshaw	Boeing, Seattle, USA

Program Commitee SICP

M. Calisti	École Polytechnique Fédérale de Lausanne (France)
P. Cohen	Oregon Institute of Science and Technolgy (USA)
T. Finin	University of Maryland (USA)
A. Mamdani	Imperial College (UK)
M. Singh	North Carolina State University (USA)
D. Steiner	Siemens AG (Germany)

Organizing Commitee ACL

Frank Dignum   Eindhoven University of Technology,
                          The Netherlands
Brahim Chaib-draa   Laval University, Canada

Program Commitee ACL

J. Allwood	University of Goteborg (Sweden)
M. Barbuceanu	University of Toronto (Canada)
B. Chaib-draa	Laval University (Canada)
P. Cohen	Oregon Institute of Science and Technolgy (USA)
F. Dignum	Eindhoven University of Technology (The Netherlands)
R. Fikes	Stanford University (USA)
T. Finin	University of Maryland (USA)
A. Haddadi	Daimler Benz (Germany)
M. Klusch	DFKI (Germany)
Y. Labrou	University of Maryland (USA)
J.-J. Meyer	Utrecht University (The Netherlands)
P. Noriega	LANIA (Mexico)
D. Sadek	France Telecom (France)
C. Sierra	AI Research Institute (Spain)
M. Singh	North Carolina State University (USA)
D. Steiner	Siemens AG (Germany)
D. Traum	University of Maryland (USA)
H. Weigand	Tilburg University (The Netherlands)
M. Wooldridge	University of Liverpool (England)

Table of Contents

ACL Semantics and Practice

Conversation Policy Description

Conversation Specification

Conversations and Tasks

Issues in Agent Communication: An Introduction

Frank Dignum and Mark Greaves

1 Technology for Agent Communication

Agent technology is an exciting and important new way to create complex software systems. Agents blend many of the traditional properties of AI programs - knowledge-level reasoning, flexibility, pro-activeness, goal-directedness, and so forth - with insights gained from distributed software engineering, machine learning, negotiation and teamwork theory, and the social sciences. An important part of the agent approach is the principle that agents (like humans) can function more effectively in groups that are characterized by cooperation and division of labor. Agent programs are designed to autonomously collaborate with each other in order to satisfy both their internal goals and the shared external demands generated by virtue of their participation in agent societies. This type of collaboration depends on a sophisticated system of interagent communication. The assumption that interagent communication is best handled through the explicit use of an agent communication language (ACL) underlies each of the papers in this collection. In this introduction, we will supply a brief background and introduction to the main topics in agent communication.

Formally, ACLs are high-level languages whose primitives and structures are expressly tailored to support the kinds of collaboration, negotiation, and information transfer required in multi-agent interaction. ACLs exist in a logical layer above transport protocols such as TCP/IP, HTTP, or IIOP. The latter deal with communication issues at the level of data and message transport, while ACLs address communication on the intentional and social level. ACLs themselves are complex structures composed out of different sublanguages that specify the message content, interpretation parameters such as the sender and the ontology, the propositional attitude under which the receiver should interpret the message content, and several other components. Typical ACLs also have a characteristic mentalistic semantics that is far more complex than standard distributed object protocols. This means that ACL design is a delicate balance between the communicative needs of the agent with the ability of receivers to compute (in tractable time) the intended meaning of the message. Further, it is important that the syntax, semantics, and pragmatics of the various components of an ACL be as precise and explicit as possible, so that the agent systems using that ACL can be as open and accessible to developers beyond the original group.

This last point bears some emphasis. Historically, many multi-agent systems have been built using somewhat *ad-hoc* and developer-private communication

F. Dignum and M. Greaves (Eds.): Agent Communication, LNAI 1916, pp. 1–16, 2000.

mechanisms. [1] Although these systems often contain many independent agents and can exhibit impressive accomplishments, the agents involved often rely on a large number of communicative assumptions that are not true of arbitrary agent collections. These assumptions range from the presumption of a shared ontology and problem domain to specific nonstandard meanings for messages (or the absence of a message) that are tailored to particular contexts. These often-undocumented assumptions are made by agent developers for reasons of communication efficiency or developer convenience, and knowledge of them is critical to properly interpret the agent message traffic in these systems. So, while such purpose-built agent collections are important to test and validate different hypotheses and approaches to agent problems, they can be extremely difficult to generalize and extend without extensive interaction with the original developers. The locus of this problem can be traced to these implicit domain-specific assumptions in the agent communication design.

The papers in this collection all address a set of issues in general ACL and agent interaction design. The ACLs that they discuss are intended to have explicit principles surrounding their proper interpretation in a context of use. [2] Further, these ACLs are also designed to be generally applicable to a wide variety of agent interaction types. The combination of explicitness and generality leads to extremely expressive languages with well-defined semantics that are grounded in powerful logics. Thus, these ACLs demand a great deal from the agents that must interpret them: computing the meaning of an arbitrary message may require extensive deductive machinery, and is typically formally intractable. However, using a strong ACL with a consistent semantics that can be precisely known in advance is a great advantage when creating heterogeneous agent systems that are designed to be easily extendible and broadly useful.

The first ACL that was designed to be both standard and general came as a consequence of the DARPA Knowledge Sharing Initiative (KSF) The Knowledge Query and Manipulation Language (KQML) [5] is the subject of several papers in this collection, and was originally devised as a means for exchanging information between different knowledge-based systems. However, because of the generality of its high level primitives and its message orientated structure, KQML was

---

[1] Agents can also communicate with actions other than classically linguistic productions, simply by making observable changes in the environment that have semantic force. For example, an agent that locks a resource for itself might be assumed to communicating to an observer its need for the resource at that time. However, without a general semantic and pragmatic theory of action, it is impossible for other agents to precisely characterize the meaning of such actions, or to understand them as communicative. And, the provision of such a theory simply turns the applicable actions into a *de facto* communication system, albeit one with an unorthodox syntax. For this reason, the papers in this volume concentrate on communication with ACLs.

[2] Although the ACLs described in this volume are very generic, they all make certain assumptions about the agents that use them and/or the environment in which they are used. It is not possible to create an ACL without any assumptions at all; hence the emphasis on making these assumptions explicit.

found to also function well as language for agent communication. KQML is the most widely implemented and used ACL in the agents community.

More recently, an agent standards body called the Foundation for Intelligent Physical Agents (FIPA) has proposed its own ACL, FIPA-ACL.[3] FIPA-ACL was designed to remedy some of the perceived weaknesses of various versions of KQML, and to be a suitable language for the agents community to standardize upon. FIPA-ACL differs from KQML in several ways; some of the more significant ones are the following:

- FIPA-ACL was derived from Arcol [7], and includes a precise semantic model based on a quantified multimodal logic. This semantics makes it possible to describe an agent's communicative acts and their intended effects in an extremely precise way. However, FIPA-ACL's semantic model is so powerful that a FIPA agent cannot in general deduce the intentions of the sending agent from a message received from that agent; thus, agents using FIPA-ACL are forced to employ a variety of semantic simplification strategies (such as conversation polices) to aid in message interpretation. KQML, on the other hand, has a relatively simpler semantics, and can be substantially easier to use in applications where the domain is reasonably restricted.
- KQML includes a number of special administrative and networking message types to make it easier for agent system developers to support registration, brokerage, directory services, streaming data, and the like. In FIPA-ACL these administrative functions have to be performed using the normal REQUEST and INFORM messages and specialized content.
- Because FIPA-ACL is defined and administered by a standards body, the actual ACL is relatively slow to change, and each addition is carefully vetted. KQML has no central administrative body, and so KQML users have developed several incompatible "dialects" by adding individually specialized message types and tinkering with the basic semantics of KQML primitives.

Most of the papers in this collection are based on either KQML or FIPA-ACL.

Finally, we will point out an important area of agent communication and ACL use that the papers in this volume do not emphasize. Successfully using an ACL to communicate between two agent programs is dependent on the proper functioning of a great deal of non-ACL communications infrastructure. This infrastructure involves message ordering and delivery, formatting and addressing, directory services, gateway-style translation, quality-of-service, and other standard networking and communications issues. In practice, implemented agent systems have used both centralized strategies that handle all aspects of messaging between agents (often implemented in KQML through the introduction of a "facilitator" agent), as well as more decentralized systems that devolve this functionality to the communication handlers of the agents themselves (as is typically done in FIPA-ACL). Agent systems exhibit little standardization in this area.

---

[3] FIPA's name for its ACL is technically just "ACL," but to avoid confusion we will refer to it here as "FIPA-ACL."

Further, implementations of ACLs often expose more of the details of this infrastructure than one might strictly like. The safest thing to say is that there are
many deep and difficult problems when designing a general agent communications infrastructure that will be efficient and reliable for different communication
topologies and networking systems, and the papers in this volume do not address
them except in passing.

2   Issues in Agent Communication

In this section we will introduce a set of issues that have been important in
the development of ACLs and agent communication theory generally. Although
we will use KQML and FIPA-ACL as examples and point out a number of
potential problems with them, we do not intend to criticize the effort put into
the design of these languages. Much of our knowledge of these problems came
from the practical experience of researchers applying KQML or FIPA-ACL in
their systems, and we are indebted to the many researchers who have devoted
enormous efforts to these ACLs.

2.1   Theories of Agency

One of the core research issues in the agent communication community involves
the linkage between the semantic underpinnings of the ACL and the theory of
agency that regulates and defines the agent's behavior. In order for the messages
of an ACL to be formally coherent, these two theories must be aligned.

A theory of agency is a general formal model that specifies what actions an
agent can or should perform in various situations. Like the Turing model of com-
putability, it abstracts away from any particular implementation, and functions
as a normative theory that is useful for analysis. Theories of agency for software
agents are usually based on a small set of primitives derived from the propositional attitudes of philosophy (e.g., belief, knowledge, desire, and intention) and
a set of axioms or axiom schema which define their entailment relations. A complete theory of agency also includes accounts of the agent's general reasoning
strategy and deductive model, its theory of action and causality, its account
of planning and goal satisfaction, its system of belief dynamics and revision,
and so forth. An agent need not directly implement its theory of agency, but it
must behave as if it did. Examples of the elements which compose a theory of
agency include Moore's accounts of knowledge and action, Rao and Georgeff's
BDI architectures, Singh's know-how and branching time systems, Cohen and
Levesque's intention theories, and so forth. Different agent systems will combine
different elements to comprise their own theory of agency.

An agent's communicative behavior is among the behaviors regulated by a
theory of agency. Because of this, the semantic theories that define the meaning
of an ACL message must ultimately be linked to the entities provided by the
agent's baseline theory of agency. Current versions of both KQML and FIPA-
ACL handle the linkage between the semantic theory and the theory of agency by

appealing to a simplified version of natural language speech act theory (originally developed in Searle [8] and Grice [3]). In this approach, agent communication is treated as a type of action that affects the world in the same way that physical acts affect the world. Communicative acts are performed in service of intentions, just like any other act. Unlike physical acts, however, the primary effect of a communicative act is to change the beliefs of the parties involved in the communication.[4]

The current semantic theory of FIPA-ACL depends on a theory of agency which supplies a set of BDI-style primitives. The semantics of FIPA-ACL is based on mentalistic notions such as belief and intention, and (because of its speech-act theory component) treats agent messaging as a type of action. Formally, this means that FIPA-ACL's semantic theory is expressed in an extremely powerful quantified multimodal logic involving both belief and intention as primitive operators, as well as a simple theory of action. As a result, agents that aspire to use FIPA-ACL in a semantically coherent way are required to adhere to a BDI-style theory of agency. They also face the somewhat daunting task of acting as if they implemented a reasoning engine for the semantic account.

In contrast to the FIPA-ACL, KQML did not originally assume a full BDI architecture of the agents. Rather, the original KQML semantics were defined in terms of a very simple theory of agency centered on adding and deleting assertions from a virtual knowledge base. The assumptions made about the required behavior of KQML agents were very weak, and the resultant semantics of KQML messages were much more permissive than that of FIPA-ACL. As is now well know, this permissiveness allowed wide latitude in KQML implementations, and the contributed to the proliferation of different and incompatible KQML dialects. Labrou's [5] second-generation semantics for KQML was much more precise, and based on a sophisticated BDI-style theory of agency similar to that of FIPA-ACL. However, Labrou's use of modal logic to specify the preconditions, postconditions, and completion conditions for each KQML communicative act type made the complexity of semantic reasoning for KQML messages comparable to that required by FIPA-ACL.

Mismatches between the theory of agency and the semantic theory can occur when the theory of agency licenses communicative actions that are not expressible in the ACL semantics. The *sincerity* condition on agent ACL usage is one such example. Sophisticated theories of agency often allow agents to act with the intent to deceive if it furthers the agent's goals. This is often cited as a requirement for optimal behavior in electronic commerce applications and adversarial negotiations generally; for example, the revenue-maximizing strategy of an agent might involve deceiving another agent about the first agent's true

---

[4] Certain special classes of acts, parallel to the *explicit performatives* of natural language, can also in some circumstances directly change the properties of objects in the world. For example, a priest can marry a couple by simply pronouncing them husband and wife. In the agent world, there are examples of this when agents register themselves with a matchmaker or broker, or when they grant other agents access rights on a database they manage.

valuation of a good. However, in order to make the message semantics as useful as possible, most ACL semantic theories (such as the KQML and FIPA-ACL theories) require that agents never use that ACL to assert something that they do not themselves believe. This is a strengthening of the analogous principle for humans: we do not typically assume that our interlocutors are lying to us. But it also makes possible the situation that an agent might desire to communicate something that its ACL cannot legally express.

The sincerity condition serves as a simplifying assumption for agent communication. Another such assumption involves the ability of an agent to reliably observe the effects of another agent's actions. Applied to agent communication, this is often taken to mean that the interagent communication channels are error-free. Agent systems routinely assume that all messages eventually arrive to their intended recipients and are not distorted by the environment (or malicious actors) in transit. Often, it is further assumed that the order of the messages that are sent to the same destination does not change during the transportation. Depending on the agent's execution context, these assumptions may not be appropriate. Again, the possibility exists that simplifying assumptions in the ACL could foreclose certain types of desirable or rational behavior relative to the agent's theory of agency.

2.2   ACL Semantics

In order to introduce our discussion of ACL semantics, it will be useful to first look at the simpler domain of programming language semantics. A common method of specifying the semantics of actions in programming languages involves defining the preconditions and postconditions of the corresponding statements. For example, the semantics of $x = 2.1$ might include the precondition that x should be the name of a location able to store a value of type real. The postcondition of this action would be that the value stored in the location denoted by x is 2.1. The precondition of the action is designed to enforce the condition that the action will only be attempted in meaningful situations. So, in case x is an integer variable it will not be possible to assign the real number 2.1 to it. The postcondition tries to capture a kind of minimal effect of the action. The relation between the pre- and postcondition correlates to the intuitive meaning of the action. In the case above, whenever x is the name of a location that can store values of type real, then whatever the value is stored in that location, after the action $x = 2.1$ the value 2.1 will be stored in that location.

The pre- and postconditions of actions in programming languages can be expressed in terms of variables and their values before and after the action, because the relevant types of actions are limited to manipulating the values of variables. However, communicative acts in an ACL do not directly manipulate variables and their values. They are conceived to operate at the higher level of abstraction given by the theory of agency, and refer to the primitives supplied by this theory. Therefore, the preconditions and postconditions for communicative acts are typically expressed in terms of the mental attitudes of the involved agents. For example, the precondition of KQML's TELL message states that the sender believes what it tells and that it knows that the receiver wants to know that the sender believes it. The postcondition of sending the TELL message is that the receiver can conclude that the sender believes the content of the message.[5] The semantics for FIPA-ACL is based on a similar semantic approach that involves specifying a message's feasible preconditions and rationally expected effects.

Although the precondition/postcondition approach can supply a minimal meaning for messages in an ACL, situations occur frequently where it is desirable to overload this minimal meaning with a more precise and context-specific gloss. This leads to a tension in ACL semantic theory. On one hand, we want the semantics to be flexible enough to be applicable in all situations where agents use the ACL. Therefore we formulate very general pre- and postconditions in the formal statement of the semantics. On the other hand, the resulting pre- and postconditions are often so abstract that they are not fully adequate in all situations. Furthermore, it is often very difficult to verify whether the agent's state in fact satisfies the pre- and postconditions. This is partly due to the fact that, although we routinely ascribe mental attitudes to agents, agents are almost never actually programmed using these concepts directly. For example, how would one verify, for agents α and β and a proposition ϕ, that "α knows that β wants to know that α believes ϕ?"

A second distinction between the semantics of agent communication and that of programming languages is the fact that the agents are distributed and (ideally) autonomous pieces of software. For an ordinary program the postcondition of an action can be precisely defined and enforced, because the complete program context is available and the individual elements of the program are not autonomous relative to one another. However, in a multi-agent system the specific postconditions of an action cannot be enforced. This is apparent in the distinction between the actual effect and the intended effect of a speech act for an agent. When an agent tells some information to another agent, it typically does so with the intention that the other agent will at least come to believe that the sending agent believes that information. However, because agents are autonomous, an agent can never *directly* change the beliefs of another agent, and so the effect of a speech act cannot be guaranteed. Agents do not have complete control over the actual effect (in speech act terminology, the *perlocutionary effect*) of their communication.

A final, related point involves the intersection of ACL semantics with the complex social relationships of obligation and commitment that constrain the actions an agent may take. Most of the time, an agent does not just shout in the dark; agents typically perform communicative acts with the expectation of a particular reaction from the receiving agent(s). An agent's communicative behavior is the result of implicit or explicit planning by that agent. For example, a request for information is usually sent with the expectation that the receiving agent will supply the requested information, or will respond to the requesting agent that it

---

[5] KQML also has the notion of a completion condition, which roughly corresponds to the conditions that obtain after the successful performance of the act in a normal and cooperative communicative context.

does not have the information or cannot supply the information. Conversely, an order to perform an action will be sent with the expectation that the receiving agent will perform the ordered action. So, the only reason for an agent to include the performance of a REQUEST in a plan is if it concludes that the response to the REQUEST will further the goals of the plan. At some level, this is a precondition to the use of REQUEST, however this type of pragmatically-inspired precondition is extremely difficult to express in traditional ACL semantic theory. Obligations on the receiving agent are similarly difficult to express.

The above discussion highlights the social aspect of agent communication. This is a facet of agent communication that is only beginning to be addressed. Agent designers have usually assumed that the networks of obligation and power relationships that characterize human social behavior are not relevant to multi- agent systems. In practice, however, idiosyncratic social conventions have ended up being embedded in agent architectures and interaction protocols, with the result that different agent systems exhibit significant incompatibilites in this area. More research is needed into characterizing these fundamental communicative concepts in a multi-agent systems context. This includes concepts such as "commitment," "obligation," "convention," "power" (in the sense of hierarchical relations), and so forth. Once these concepts are clarified, it then becomes possible to build a unified ACL semantics and pragmatics that takes account of these concepts.

2.3   Ontologies

An issue that is closely related to ACL semantics is the proper treatment of ontologies in an ACL. Both FIPA-ACL and KQML include an element that is used to identify the source of the vocabulary used in the message content. This is designed to make these ACLs independent of particular application vocabularies, and to give the message recipient a way to interpret the nonlogical terms in the message content. In the original specification of KQML from the KSE, this element was designed to refer to an ontology specified in Ontolingua. In FIPA-ACL, the semantics of the ontology tag is effectively user-defined.

The way that an agent would make use of the KQML or FIPA-ACL ontology specifier to interpret unfamiliar parts of an ACL message has never been precisely defined. Merely supplying an ontology tag does not solve the problem of how agents acquire and use the common ontological knowledge base that is a prerequisite for successful communication. This is a particularly acute problem in open systems that include agents based in different organizations. The problems associated with learning meanings and reasoning with a new set of terminology are very similar to those in the area of database integration and cooperative information systems: somehow the ontologies that the different agents use have to be "integrated." Of course, ontological integration does not mean that the terminological structures have to actually be unified, but at minimum there must exist translation rules that convert relevant terms from one ontology into the other. Although a human working with representatives of each terminological community can often hash out a satisfactory set of rules, it is almost impossible to construct these rules fully automatically ([6,4]). Consequently, agents can only fully communicate if they already share a common ontology, or if a set of preexisting translation rules is provided.

Although this may seem very restrictive, it has not been so disastrous in reality. For example, standards for product descriptions are very common in trade groups. And, in many open systems the agents communicate initially through some third party that initiates the contact between the agents. This third party will often mandate an ontology that all agents will use, and ontologies thus mandated will typically be built in to the agents by their developers. This is the case in most electronic auctions, where selling agents include specialized code to specify their product using predefined terminology. Nevertheless, the general ontological problem is still the subject of active research.

2.4   Completeness of ACL Message Types

An issue that is closely related to the theory of agency concerns the completeness of the set of message types in the ACL. Because ACLs can be used in arbitrary communicative contexts, one important goal is that their basic set of message types be sufficient to express all possible kinds of agent communicative intent that are allowed by the underlyingi theory of agency. Without a complete message set, agents and their developers may find themselves in situations where they are forced to invent additional *ad hoc* meanings for certain ACL messages, with the attendant decline in interoperability.

An interesting non-agents case of this is the evolution of the X.12 EDI standard. X.12 included a very precise and complete syntactic description of its messages, but had only an informal natural-language description for the message semantics. X.12 began with a limited set of messages that worked in most cases, but has been repeatedly extended over the years when a situation occurred that could not be intuitively captured by simple combinations of the existing message types. Thus, X.12 currently contains message types with overlapping meanings, odd patterns of expressivity, and various other logical problems. This practical but unprincipled approach to X.12 development has given rise to a message set for which it is very difficult, even for humans, to select the correct message type to use in a particular case.

The evolution of KQML and FIPA-ACL has also been involved questions about the completeness of the provided message types. KQML was designed by a loose group of researchers, and its message types were driven by the goals and needs of DARPA's KSE program. The designers of FIPA-ACL patterned their language after KQML, and because they were working in the framework of a formal standards body, they created several processes designed to limit the sorts of problems found with X.12. However, in both ACLs the stock of officially-sanctioned communicative acts is limited to several varieties of directives (*e.g.,* INFORM or TELL) and assertives (*e.g.,* REQUEST or ASK). This means that each ACL is incapable of expressing all agent intentions that are possible in powerful theories of agency, because several classes of performatives (see Searle

[8]) are absent from both. For example, neither ACL can directly express agent commitment, because neither includes commissives like PROMISE. Expressives like WISH also are missing from the standard set of communicative acts supplied in ACLs like KQML or FIPA- ACL. The practical effect of these omissions is limited because both KQML and FIPA-ACL are extensible ACLs: users are free to invent new application-specific performatives as long as they do not overlap or clash with the standard set. However, this freedom encourages the development of different incompatible dialects of these ACLs.

2.5   Conversation Policies

In the preceding sections we have discussed ACL research issues that are primarily related to the generation and interpretation of individual ACL messages. A final topic we will address is how to bridge the gap between these individual messages and the extended message sequences, or *conversations*, that arise between agents. As part of its program code, every agent must implement tractable decision procedures that allow that agent to select and produce ACL messages that are appropriate to its intentions. This is not purely a problem of matching ACL semantics to agent intention: except in the most limited of agent systems, these decision procedures must also take into consideration the context of prior ACL messages and other agent events. Paradoxically, taking this context into account can actually *simplify* the computational complexity of ACL message selection for an agent. By engaging in preplanned or stereotypical conversations, much of the search space of possible agent responses can be eliminated, while still being consistent with the ACL semantics. The specification of these conversations is accomplished via *conversation policies* (CPs).

Because of this computational advantage, virtually all multi-agent systems employ some type of explicit or implicit conversational layer.[6] Theory has lagged practice in this area, however: unlike research in ACL semantics, work on formal accounts of agent conversation remains in its infancy. Terminology and theoretical approaches are still being worked out, formal approaches and metrics are still fairly unsettled, and the role of research in natural language pragmatics and discourse theory is still being evaluated. The wide variety of approaches that are discussed in the papers in the latter parts of this volume testify to the exploratory nature of the research. In this introduction, therefore, we will simply introduce some of the questions that are central to the papers in this collection, and that agents researchers hope to answer in the coming years.

Possibly the overriding theoretical question in the field concerns the linkage between the ACL's semantic theory and its account of conversation. On the one hand, it seems obvious that large-scale properties of agent conversations, such as overall information flow and the establishment of commitments, are a consequence of the individual meanings of the messages that make up the conversation.

---

[6] The original KQML specification had only token support for agent conversations; this shortcoming was noticed as early as 1994 in [2] and has been largely corrected using a variety of methods.

In this view, the ACL semantics is primary, and every conversational property logically derives from the composition of some collection of semantic properties of the individual messages and their sequence. On the other hand, there is a significant thread of research that takes conversational sequences themselves to be semantically primitive, and the precise meaning of the individual messages is nuanced by their role in the overall conversation. In this view, the conversational semantics are primary, and because of the dependence of ACL semantics on context, the same message might have slightly different meanings when used in the context of different agent conversations. Whether one takes conversational semantics or ACL semantics as logically prior will affect their answers to several definitional questions, such as:

- What exactly is (and is not) a conversation policy? What important properties of agent interaction should CPs capture?
- How are CPs individuated? When are two agent conversations instances of the same policy? Are there interesting equivalence classes of CPs? Is there a useful type hierarchy of CPs?

Once one has settled on a basic theoretical perspective on the linkage between CPs and ACL semantics, then there are still a number of technical questions that remain. For example, there are several non-equivalent candidates for a CP specification language, ranging from transition nets like finite state machines and Petri nets, to various types of logic-based specifications, subgoal trees, and network protocol specification systems. These formalisms vary widely in the degree of conversational rigidity they entail, the models of concurrency they support, the computational complexity of their execution, and the availability of tools and techniques to help verify the analytical properties of the represented conversation policy.

Finally, the use of conversation policies to guide agent communicative behavior engenders a host of practical questions. How should conversation policies be implemented in agent systems? Should CPs be downloaded from a common library, prebuilt into the agent's program, or derived from conversational axioms at runtime? How can conversation policies be negotiated, and unfamiliar policies learned? And finally, how can conversation policies be integrated with the other policies, plans, and rules which define an agent's behavior?

3   About This Volume

As the foregoing has indicated, research in agent communication can be placed along a spectrum of maturity, with research in content languages and network protocols being the most developed, research in ACL semantics being somewhere in the middle, and research on conversation policies and agent social obligations being the most exploratory. The papers in this volume clearly reflect this diversity. In our view, this is one of the most exciting aspects of agents research. The contributions in this book were selected from the workshop on *Specifying and*

Implementing Conversation Policies, held in May 1999 jointly with the Autonomous Agents conference in Seattle and chaired by the second author, and the workshop on *Agent Communication Languages: From Speech Acts to Conversations*, held in August 1999 jointly with the International Joint Conference on Artificial Intelligence in Stockholm and chaired by the first author. We decided to join the workshop papers in a single volume because the workshops are very closely related, have different emphasis and together cover most of the research in the field of agent communication.

We have divided the papers into four categories. Section I includes a number of papers concerned with the semantical aspects of agent communication. Section II deals with conversation policy descriptions. Section III concerns itself with fundamental issues surrounding agent conversations. Finally, the papers in section IV consider the relation between agent communication and general agent task planning issues.

ACL Semantics and Practice. Most papers in this describe semantical issues of agent communication. The last paper in this session proposes to use XML as a practical description language for ACLs.

M. Colombetti describes how normative and practical aspects form an integral part of the meaning of agent communication. Although these aspects usually are loosely connected to some of the pre- and postconditions he argues that they also form part of the performance of the speech act (sending the message) itself. He then describes a logic formalism within which the three aspects (semantics, normative aspect and practical aspect) of a message can be described in an integral way. A few consequences for ACL design and conversation protocols are discussed as well.

M. Singh emphasizes the importance of the social aspect of communication in his paper. He uses the theory of Habermas to distinguish different social aspects of communication. With each communicative act correspond three types of validity claims: an objective, a subjective and a practical one. The objective validity claims is based on the truth of the message content. The subjective validity claim is based on the sincerity of the speaker and the practical validity claim is based on the justifiability of the speaker to perform the communicative act. A very important concept in this respect is the social commitment. After a definition of all the concepts in a logic framework he gives some (preliminary) formalizations of the social semantics of speech acts. Finally, some consequences for conversation protocols are discussed.

J. Pitt and A. Mamdani concentrate on one of the validity claims described in Singh's paper. They claim that the sincerity condition that is assumed in all ACLs does not necessarily have to be true at all in non- cooperative settings. They give some examples in which the sincerity condition does not hold in electronic trading. Another important point is that the sincerity condition is hardly verifiable and therefore it is difficult to put it as a precondition on any communicative act. Finally, they show that the claim that agents may be liable to a legal penalty if shown to be non-sincere cannot be sustained. Subsequently they give a new logical formalization of agent communication in which the sincerity condition is not presumed and show the consequences for agent conversations.

Two other papers in this section look at the semantics of ACLs from a different perspective. They use well-known formalisms that were developed for program interaction and see how these formalisms can be applied for agent communication.

K. Hindriks, F. de Boer, W. van der Hoek and J.-J. Meyer use the agent programming language 3APL to describe agents in terms of their beliefs and goals. 3APL is based on a first order language. A number of transition rules describe the operational semantics of an agent. To this formalism two communicative primitives are added (the "ask" and "tell" messages). The semantics of these communicative acts are also described in the form of transition rules within the logic. Logical abduction can be used to obtain proposals in reply to requests, while deduction is used to derive information from received messages. The formalism is illustrated on a multi-stage negotiation protocol.

R. van Eijk, F. de Boer, W. van der Hoek and J.-J. Meyer concentrate on the operational semantics of agent communication. They use a multi-agent programming language based on the well-understood paradigm of object oriented programming. Interaction between the agents takes place by means of a rendezvous mechanism as developed for object-oriented programs. The formal semantics are defined by transition rules for its operational behavior. Because the operational semantics closely follows the syntax of the language, it easily gives rise to an abstract machine to implement it.

The last paper in this section takes a practical view on ACLs and proposes XML as a tool to describe these languages.

B. Grosof and Y. Labrou argue for the use of XML as encoding mechanism for the FIPA ACL. The use of XML facilitates both common parsers for ACLs (synactically linking these ACLs with the WWW world) and also enriches the capability of ACL expressions to link to ontologies. The authors concentrate on a number of business rules that are important as content for the ACLs in electronic commerce settings. These business rules can be encoded in restricted logic programs (called courteous logic programs) that have some desirable properties and can also be described using XML.

Conversation Policy Description

The papers in this section address general issues with conversation policies.

M. Greaves, H. Holmback, and J. Bradshaw is an introduction to the general notion of an agent conversation policy. The authors first identify the major issue in agent communication for which conversation policies are used, and then use this to derive a set of general requirements for any account of conversation policies. With these requirements in hand, they suggest that the current transition-net based approaches to conversation policy specification are misguided, and argue for a more structured and fine-grained approach. Several desiderata for practical conversation policies are also discussed.

L. Phillips and H. Link start by defining an agent conversation specification, which includes the communicative acts to be used by each party and their sequencing. They then argue for an additional level of policy which would supervene on the conversation specification and include various context- dependent high level rules which govern the specific conversation. They describe how such a two-level mechanism might be implemented, and show how this leads to several beneficial properties between the communicating agents.

S. Moore explores the use of Harel's statecharts to represent different classes of conversation policy. He first describes how conversation policies relate to ACLs and to actual conversations, with an emphasis on a speech-act based ACL called FLBC. He next describes several properties of agent conversation and shows with several examples how statecharts can represent these properties. Finally, he speculates on how conversation policies can evolve and spread through the agent community.

J. Pitt and A. Mamdani show how a different type of ACL semantic theory can ameliorate many of the technical problems faced when trying to define and compose conversation policies. First, they briefly describe how the message semantics of a large class of ACLs can be cast as the intention of the receiver to respond. Using this semantics, they define a small sample ACL, and show how the meanings of the messages in this ACL can be made relative to the context of the conversation in which they occur. They discuss various ways that their sample ACL can be extended, and explore the implications for agent conversations.

Conversation Specification

The six papers in this section describe specific formalisms that can be used to capture particular policies.

S. Cost, Y. Chen, T. Finin, Y. Labrou and Y. Peng argue that finite state machines are not sufficient to characterize agent interactions that involve concurrency. They propose Colored Petri Nets (CPNs) as an alternative model to capture conversation specification involving concurrency and multiple conversational roles. They describe CPNs and their implementation in Jackal, and provide several detailed examples.

F. Lin, D. Norrie, W. Shen and R. Kremer also discuss CPNs as a useful description and verification tool for conversation policies. They describe a design methodology based on object-oriented design that links higher-level conversation topics with the actual communicative acts in a conversation. This methodology allows several layers of specification. The authors also show how conversation schemata represented by CPNs can be composed, and how agents can use this formalism and to control their conversational behavior.

M. Nodine and A. Unruh describe the conversation policy mechanism implemented by the agents in MCC's InfoSleuth project. InfoSleuth uses carefully crafted finite-state automata to specify the policies. The authors describe several conversational requirements from the InfoSleuth system, and show how their policy formalism meets the requirements. They also show how their system is able to extend and concatenate different conversation policies, and speculate about how to extend their formalism to address more semantically complex types of conversations, such as multicast and delegation.

M. Barbuceanu and W.-K. Lo describe and analyze the conversational co-ordination language used in the COOL system. The language includes separate notions of conversation plans, conversation rules, and specific execution states. They also address several advanced topics in COOL conversations, including conversation plan composition, the compatibility of conversation plans, group conversations and the application of machine learning technology to support adaptive conversational behavior.

L. Vongkasem and B. Chaib-draa propose to view agent conversations as joint projects (in the same spirit as the paper by R. Elio and A. Haddadi). The conversation is seen as a joint action that has to be coordinated. The agents are put into a social context. They have to figure out not only what is their best action, but also what action (speech act) is expected from them by the other agent(s). The authors conclude that conversations are the basic units of communication and not the speech acts themselves. Therefore, the formal semantics of agent communication should therefore be based on concepts such as joint action, joint intention, etc.

F. Martin, E. Plaza and J. Rodriguez-Aguilar describe their experiences with conversation protocols in IIIA's Fishmarket project. They model the protocols between agents through the use of pushdown transducers, which allows the agents to keep track of nested conversation contexts. The authors also supply a formal analysis of their conversation protocol formalism, concentrating on the notion of protocol compatibility, and discuss issues of conversation protocol negotiation.

Conversations and Tasks

One issue in conversation policy design comes from the interaction of agent communicative behavior with the agent's overall goals. How should we treat the relation between conversation policies and agent tasks or plans? The five papers in this section address this issue.

F. Dignum, B. Dunin-Kęplicz and R. Verbrugge start from a linguistic theory of dialogues to describe conversations. A number of rules are formulated in this theory that describe how a conversation can proceed at each point in time. The rules are formalized in a multimodal logic that also describes the mental state of the agents. Therefore a uniform formalism can be used to describe the complete agent interaction. The theory is applied in the context of team formation, where it is clear which type of conditions should hold after each stage. A rough sketch is given how the postconditions of one stage can be reached using the theory and some simple rules for the agents.

S. Noh and P. Gmytrasiewicz discuss the issue of finding an optimal communicative act. They use a setting of mixed human and artificial agents within a simulated air defense domain. The agents use a decision theoretic framework to compute the communicative act with the highest expected utility. The reasoning is based on a probabilistic frame-based knowledge formalism that represents uncertain information the agents have about their environment. The benefits of this communication strategy are measured and compared to the performance of human subjects under the same circumstances.

R. Elio and A. Haddadi describe a two-level framework for relating agent discourse to the problem-solving methods of the agent. By defining a task space and a discourse space, and showing how the two spaces can be linked via agent intentions, they show how conversation policies can be defined by the interplay between conversation protocols and the recognition of the run-time intentions of the agents in a dialogue. They also explore issues in mixed-initiative dialogues.

T. Wagner, B. Benyo, V. Lesser and P. Xuan describe several scenarios involving multi-agent coordination under complex scheduling models, and address the role of conversation policies in this type of situation. They describe how conversation policies can be represented as extended finite-state machines, and how these can be integrated into a general agent coordination toolkit.

C. Jonker, J. Treur and W. Wijngaards describe some possible interactions between verbal and non-verbal communication. They argue that physical and verbal communication both play an important role, and should be treated in combination rather than being seen as disjunct processes within an agent. They describe a model of an agent that interacts with humans, in which the non-verbal communication influences the content of the verbal communication. In the paper, the authors describe a sample implementation and show some parts of it.

References

1. Cohen, P.R. and Levesque, H.J. Communicative Actions for Artificial Agents. In *Proceedings of the International Conference on Multi-Agent Systems* (ICMAS-95), pp. 65-72, 1995.
2. Finin, T., Labrou, Y. and Mayfield, J. KQML as an Agent Communication Language. In Bradshaw, J. (Ed.), *Software Agents*, MIT Press, Cambridge, 1995.
3. Grice, P.H. Logic and Conversation. In P. Cole and J. Morgan (eds) *Syntax and Semantics, vol.3, Speech Acts*, Academic Press, New York, pp. 41-58.
4. Klusch, M. (ed.) *Intelligent Information Agents*. Springer-Verlag, Berlin, 1999.
5. Labrou, Y. *Semantics for an Agent Communication Language*, Ph.D. thesis, University of Maryland, USA, 1997.
6. Papazoglou, M. and Schlageter, G. (eds). *Cooperative Information Systems: Current Trends and Directions*. Academic Press, 1997.
7. Sadek, M.D. *Attitudes Mentales et Interaction Rationnelle: Vers une Théorie Formelle de la Communication*. Thése de Doctorat Informatique, Université de Rennes I, France, 1991.
8. Searle, J.R. *Speech Acts*. Cambridge University Press, Cambridge, 1969.

Semantic, Normative and Practical Aspects
of Agent Communication

Marco Colombetti

Politecnico di Milano, Piazza Leonardo da Vinci 32
I–20133 Milano, Italy
marco.colombetti@polimi.it

Abstract. Most approaches to agent communication are based on some notion of communicative act. I argue that a satisfactory model of communication should deal with three related but conceptually independent aspects of communicative acts: the semantic aspect, concerning the literal meaning of communicative acts; the normative aspect, concerning the obligations, permissions, and so on, created by performing a communicative act; and the practical aspect, concerning the role of communication in the context of rational action. I propose a definition of the semantics of communicative acts based on modal logic. The approach is extended to treat the normative component through tools of deontic logic. I then argue that the practical side of communication involves general aspects of rational behavior, and is not part of the definition of communicative acts. Finally, I consider some consequences that the proposed approach might have on the design of agent communication languages.

Introduction

In the last few years, the AI community has devoted a great deal of attention to the issue of agent communication. We can distinguish two related but different problems: communication among artificial agents, and communication between humans and artificial agents. In both cases, despite the diversity of models adopted, most proposals are ultimately based on some notion of communicative act, more or less resembling the concept of speech act developed by philosophers of language like Austin (1962) and Searle (1969).

A study of the relevant literature reveals two distinct approaches to the analysis of communicative acts. In the first approach, developed in AI since the late seventies, the key concept is rationality: communicative acts are planned and interpreted under the hypothesis that agents act rationally. The conceptual tools of this line of research have been worked out by Cohen and Perrault (1979), Allen (1983), Cohen and Levesque (1990) and many others, and underlie the definition of agent communication languages like KQML (ARPA, 1993) and FIPA ACL (FIPA, 1997). In the second trend, whose development is more recent, communicative acts are viewed as actions creating obligations. This approach is well exemplified by proposals of programming languages supporting agent communication, like McCarthy's Elephant 2000 (1990) and Shoham's AGENT0 (1993).

Both aspects of communication are important. It seems to me, however, that neither of the two provides for a satisfactory definition of the semantics of communicative acts.

F. Dignum and M. Greaves (Eds.): Agent Communication, LNAI 1916, pp. 17-30, 2000.
© Springer-Verlag Berlin Heidelberg 2000

In fact, I think that a model of communicative acts should consider three different sides: (i) the *semantic* side, which concerns the literal meaning of communicative acts; (ii) the *normative* side, that is, the set of norms specifying which obligations or permissions are created by performing a communicative act; and (iii) the *practical* side, which has to do with the reasons for performing a communicative act as part of rational behavior.

The three aspects of communication, it seems to me, are easily confused. Suppose for example that an agent, a, informs another agent, b, of a proposition represented by a sentence, φ, in a suitable formal language. In such a case, a typical model of communicative acts (like, for example, the one underlying FIPA ACL) requires that at least the following conditions be met:

(1.1) a believes that φ holds, in symbols: $B_a \varphi$.

(1.2) a does not believe that b already believes that φ holds, in symbols: $\neg B_a B_b \varphi$.

But what is the status of these conditions? Are they considered to be semantic (i.e., defining the meaning of informing), normative (i.e., specifying the obligations created by informing), or practical (i.e., specifying rational conditions for an act of informing)? To make the difference clear, let us give three different readings of condition 1.1:

- *the semantic reading*: it is part of the meaning of an act of informing that the sender believes the content of the act;

- *the normative reading*: in the performance of an act of informing, agents ought to be sincere;

- *the practical reading*: it is rational for an agent to be sincere (for example, because this eventually leads to fruitful interactions with other agents).

Analogous readings can be provided for condition 1.2 and, in general, for all conditions used to model communicative acts.

It seems to me that the three aspects of communication, although related, are logically independent. As an example, suppose that agent a is going to manage an electronic auction, and consider the following request from a to b (paraphrased in natural language):

(1.3)   „I request that you let me know whether you intend to participate to the auction,"

to which agent b responds:

(1.4)   „I inform you that I intend to participate to the auction."

Following the normative approach, one is tempted to say that the meaning of 1.4 is to create an obligation of some sort. However, it seems to me that the possible normative effects of 1.4 depend so heavily on the context, that they are not suitable to define the semantics of informing. In fact, depending on the situation, 1.4 might:

- have *no normative effect*, because the responses to 1.3 are going to be used by a only for a rough estimation of the number of participants;

- create an *obligation* for b to take part to the auction;

- create a *permission* for b to take part to the auction, which will not be granted to those agents which did not answer to 1.3.

I think it would be unacceptable to say that „I inform you that ..." has three different meanings in the three situations. I find it preferable to define a uniform literal meaning of informing, and then consider context-dependent normative consequences. Moreover, note that the same normative effects could be achieved by *b* through a different communicative act, with different literal semantics, like:

(1.4') „I promise to take part to the auction."

The same example also shows that both the meaning and the normative effects are distinct from rationality principles. For example, believing that its answer will create no obligation, agent *b* might produce its response even if it is not sure it will actually participate to the auction. But this is, so to speak, part of *b*'s own business, and cannot be regulated by convention.

Another problem with most proposals of agent communication languages, like KQML and FIPA ACL, is that they consider a finite set of primitive communicative act types. Of course, any formal system must be based on primitives at some level, but I think that the level of act types may be the wrong one. A more open and flexible solution would be to consider types of mental states as primitives, and to allow agents to communicate any combination of mental states.

In this paper I shall sketch a formal model of communicative acts that keeps the semantic, normative and practical aspects separate, and does not postulate primitive types of communicative acts. The paper is structured as follows. In Section 2, I investigate the structure of communicative acts, suggest that their semantics can be defined in terms of the mental states expressed by an agent through a communicative act, and propose a formal semantics for the expression of a mental state, thus inducing a semantics on communicative acts. In Section 3, I show how one could deal with the normative component of communication. In Section 4, I comment on the role of rationality in communication. In Section 5, I analyze some questions related to the impact that the approach proposed in the paper may have on the design of agent communication languages. Finally, in Section 6 I draw some conclusions.

It should be noted that, in this paper, I shall be concerned exclusively with communication among artificial agents: my proposal is not intended to be, and should not be interpreted as, a model of human communication. Moreover, I shall not propose a fullyfledged model of communicative acts. Rather, I shall delineate a work plan that I have only started to carry out.

The Semantics of Communicative Acts

Following a wellestablished tradition, I assume that an agent has various types of mental states, like beliefs, desires, and intentions, and that we adopt a formal model of mental states based on modal logic. For example, the modal sentence $B_a\varphi$ will denote that agent *a* believes that φ is the case. A further hypothesis is that the semantics of formal sentences is based on possibleworld models, either of the Kripke or of the ScottMontague type (see for example Chellas, 1980). In general, a *model M* will be made up of a nonempty set *W* of possible worlds, together with the settheoretic apparatus necessary to assign a truth value to every sentence at each possible world. As usual, the notation

$$M,w \models \varphi$$

means that sentence φ is true in model *M* at world *w*.

1.1 Communicating and Expressing

A communicative act typically consists of four components: a type, a sender, one or more addressees, and a content. The content is a *proposition*, represented by a formal sentence φ. A proposition in a model M is conceived as a set $P \subseteq W$ of possible worlds; φ is said to *represent* proposition P in M, if and only if P is the set of worlds at which φ is true in M. It follows that two logically equivalent sentences represent the same proposition in every model. Therefore, replacing the content sentence φ in the symbolic representation of a communicative act with an equivalent sentence ψ will not change the content of the act.

By performing a communicative act, and addressing it to an addressee, the sender *expresses* a mental state, which is a function of the content and of the type of the communicative act. For example:

- by asserting that φ, agent a expresses its belief that φ;
- by requesting that φ, a expresses its desire that φ is brought about through an action performed by its addressee;
- by promising that φ, a expresses its intention to perform an action that brings about φ.

All this is independent of the context in which the communicative act is performed.

This analysis will be reflected in an appropriate notation. I shall make use of a sorted first-order modal language built from:

- *agent expressions*, denoting agents, including *agent constants* (a, b, ...) and *agent variables* (x, y, ...);[1]
- *action expressions*, denoting action tokens, including *action constants* (which will not appear in the rest of this paper) and *action variables* (e, e', ...);
- *proposition, predicate,* and *function symbols*;
- *Boolean connectives* and *quantifiers*;
- *monadic* and *polyadic modal operators*, which take sentences in at least one argument place, and whose semantics will be defined in terms of possible worlds.

Generic sentences will be denoted by the metavariables φ, ψ, and so on. For example, the fact that agent a asserts that φ to b will be represented by the formal sentence:

(2.1) $\exists e\, (Do(e,a) \wedge Address(e,b) \wedge \mathrm{Express}(e, \mathrm{B}_a \varphi))$,

where: a and b are agent constants; e is an action variable; φ is a sentence representing a proposition; the atomic formula $Do(e,a)$ means that action e is performed by agent a; the atomic formula $Address(e,b)$ means that action e is addressed to agent b; and $\mathrm{Express}(-,-)$ is a modal operator whose second argument is a sentence. The sentence:

$\exists e\, \mathrm{Assert}(e,a,b,\varphi)$

will be considered as an abbreviation of 2.1, with the modal operator Assert defined as:

(2.2) $\mathrm{Assert}(e,x,y,\varphi) =_{\mathrm{def}} Do(e,x) \wedge Address(e,y) \wedge \mathrm{Express}(e, \mathrm{B}_x \varphi)$.

---

[1] For the sake of readability, I shall use agent variables also as syntactic metavariables varying on the set of agent expressions. The same will be done with all types of expressions.

The use of the Express operator, combined with a logic of mental states, allows us to represent a wide variety of communicative acts without having to predefine a set of basic communicative act types. Common act types can be defined at any moment as abbreviations. For example, one may want to define „informing that φ' as the act of expressing that the sender believes that φ, and that the sender does not believe that the addressee believes that φ.

(2.3) $\text{Inform}(e,x,y,\varphi) =_{\text{def}}$
$$Do(e,x) \wedge Address(e,y) \wedge \text{Express}(e,B_x\varphi) \wedge \text{Express}(e,\neg B_x B_y\varphi).$$

The problem of defining the semantics of communicative acts is therefore reduced to the problem of defining the semantics of Express. I shall do this in the next subsection.

1.2 The Semantics of Expressing

Coherently with the standpoint advocated in this paper, I define the semantics of expressing independently of any normative or practical aspect.

Let us start from a possible world model, M, of the relevant mental states (e.g., beliefs, desires, and intentions). Individual agents and action tokens will be taken from appropriate domains, respectively denoted by Ag and Act. For the sake of simplicity, I assume that all agents exist at every possible world. On the contrary, a similar assumption is not sensible for actions, given that an action token is understood to „exists" at a possible world if and only if it takes place at that world. The set of actions taking place at a possible world will be specified in M by a function,

$$occur: W \to 2^{Act}.$$

The set of actions occurring at a world may be empty. This implies that our logic will behave as a free logic with respect to quantification over actions; in particular, the scheme:

$$\forall e \varphi \Rightarrow \exists e \varphi$$

is not valid. The agent performing an action is specified in M by a function

$$agent: Act \to Ag.$$

Moreover, the function

$$addressee: Act \to 2^{Ag}$$

specifies the (possibly empty) set of addressees of every action. Assuming that the function [–] returns the interpretation of agent and action expressions, the semantics of the Do and $Address$ predicates is defined by:

$$M,w \models Do(e,x) \qquad \text{iff} \quad [e] \in occur(w) \text{ and } [x] = agent([e]),$$

$$M,w \models Address(e,x) \quad \text{iff} \quad [e] \in occur(w) \text{ and } [x] \in addressee([e]).$$

A communicative act is an action, and as such can take place at a possible world. Moreover, a communicative act expresses something, but this is not true of actions in general (for example, it is not true of opening an umbrella or adding 2 and 3).[2] Therefore I consider a subset Exp of actions,

$$Exp \subseteq Act,$$

---

[2] When human behavior is considered, almost any action can acquire an expressive power if the context is appropriate; for example, opening an umbrella can be used to inform someone that it is raining. I shall not address this problem here.

including all *expressive actions*, that is, all actions which have a semantic content.

A definite meaning can be associated to expressive actions through possible worlds. If we want to keep to traditional methods of modal logic, there are basically two possibilities: we may define models of the Kripke or of the Scott-Montague type. The former class of models would determine a *normal* modal logic on the Express operator, while the latter would determine a weaker *classical* modal logic (see for example Chellas, 1980). Kripke models are more common in AI applications of modal logic. Adopting a normal modal logic for Express, however, would have unpleasant consequences, like the fact that every expressive action would express all tautologies at every world at which it takes place. Therefore, I prefer to take up the perspective of Scott-Montague models. Let us add to M a function

$$express: Exp \rightarrow 2^{2^W},$$

which associates a set of propositions to every expressive action. We can now define:

$$M,w \models \text{Express}(e,\varphi) \text{ iff } [e] \in Exp \text{ and } [\![\varphi]\!] \in express([e]),$$

where $[\![\varphi]\!]$ denotes the set of all possible worlds of M at which φ is true.[3]

We now have a complete semantics of communicative acts. For example, on the basis of 2.3 we see that:

$$M,w \models \text{Inform}(e,x,y,\varphi) \text{ iff}$$

$$[e] \in occur(w) \text{ and } [x] = agent([e]) \text{ and } [y] \in addressee([e])$$

$$\text{and } [\![B_x\varphi]\!] \in express([e]) \text{ and } [\![\neg B_x B_y \varphi]\!] \in express([e]).$$

Note that the use of the *express* function allows us to attribute a meaning to any kind of actions, and not only to acts of speech. For example, we might stipulate that raising one's arm expresses the intention of saying something, or that smiling expresses satisfaction. The approach appears therefore to be very general.

As already remarked, the logic of Express determined by the proposed semantics is very weak. It has no specific axiom and only one modal inference rule, that is:

$$(RE) \quad \frac{\varphi \leftrightarrow \psi}{\text{Express}(e,\varphi) \leftrightarrow \text{Express}(e,\psi)},$$

which is consistent with the assumption on the substitution of equivalent contents made in Section 2.1.

The semantics proposed for Express allows us to explain why assertions like „φ, but I do not believe that φ" sound contradictory, even if the content of the assertion is satisfiable. Indeed, asserting such a proposition implies expressing a mental state of the form $B_x(\varphi \wedge \neg B_x \varphi)$, which is unsatisfiable in any epistemic logic strong at least as KD4. Note that the *express* function returns an empty set of possible worlds as the meaning of a contradictory expressive action.

Even if the modal logic of Express is very weak (indeed, the weakest we can get with a possibleworld approach), it may appear too strong because it does not distinguish between equivalent sentences of different form. This implies, for example, that asserting „φ, but I do not believe that φ" and asserting „φ and not φ" are equivalent. Such a consequence, however, is due to the extensional nature of possibleworld

---

[3] By this definition, the meaning of an expressive action turns out to be independent of the possible world at which the action takes place. If necessary, this limitation can be easily overcome.

methods, and cannot be avoided unless one develops a completely different and truly intensional approach.

We can now proceed with the analysis of the normative aspects of communicative acts.

The Normative Side of Communication

Performing communicative acts may create obligations, prohibitions, permissions and other types of deontic states, which in general will depend on the context of performance. For example, in a given context one may want to adopt the general normative rule that an agent ought to hold all mental state expressed. A more local rule might state that a positive answer to 1.3 implies the obligation for *b* to participate to the auction, or maybe the permission for *b* to do so.

We can deal with obligation, permission and similar notions along the lines of deontic logic (see for example Åqvist, 1984), which offers a rich repertoire of powerful tools (and, unfortunately, also a fair number of open problems.) However, the variety of deontic systems proposed in the literature is so large, that before attempting to choose one we should have clear ideas about our desiderata.

It seems to me that we need a deontic language allowing us to:

- specify different types of *deontic states* (obligations, permissions, etc.) and the conditions under which such states arise;
- at least in some cases, specify which agent bears the *responsibility* of a deontic state (for example, there might be an obligation for agent *a* that agent *b* performs some action);
- distinguish among different *normative systems* (i.e., sets of norms), which may coexist even if they impose different regulations;
- classify possible *violations* of normative systems, and attach to each agent the list of its infractions;
- specify *penalties*, that is, actions that cancel an infraction if they are carried out.

I shall now sketch a possible solution in terms of dyadic deontic logic. In the next subsection I deal with the first three points, while penalties will be considered in Subsection 3.2.

1.3 A Deontic System

I follow here the approach to deontic logic proposed by Tan and van der Torre (1996). Let us first add to our language two monadic modal operators, Nec and Id. Nec is the traditional alethic operator of necessity, and Id is intended to characterize what should ideally be the case (from the point of view of existing norms). The semantic counterparts of Nec and Id will be two accessibility relations on possible worlds, respectively R and $\leq$. R is assumed to be an equivalence relation, and $\leq$ is a partial preorder expressing preference between worlds, such that only Requivalent worlds are related through $\leq$. With the usual definitions for the semantics of $\text{Nec}\,\varphi$ and $\text{Id}\,\varphi$, the logic of Nec is KT5 (or S5), and the logic of Id is KT4 (or S4). The relationship between R and $\leq$ is captured by the axiom

$$\text{Nec}\,\varphi \rightarrow \text{Id}\,\varphi.$$

Nec and Id are then used to define various types of deontic operators. For example, a possible definition of an operator $O(-|-)$ of *conditional obligation* is the following:

$$O(\psi|\varphi) =_{\text{def}} \text{Nec}(\varphi \wedge \psi \rightarrow \text{Id}(\varphi \rightarrow \psi)),$$

where the statement $O(\psi|\varphi)$ can be read as „ψ is obligatory under condition φ.“ The definition of $O(\psi|\varphi)$ says that if φ is true at a world w, then w is ideal with respect to a world at which φ and ψ are both true only if ψ is also true at w.

This deontic system can be used as a starting point to satisfy the requirements given at the beginning of this section. First, I introduce *norm expressions* used to denote different normative systems. For example, the norm expression $sincere(x,y)$, where x and y are agent expressions, can be used to denote a normative system regulating the sincerity of agents with respect to their addressees. Then, I replace the monadic operator Id with a threeplace operator $\text{Id}(-,-,-)$, where the statement $\text{Id}(x,n,\varphi)$ intuitively means „φ is ideal for x with respect to normative system n.“

To define the semantics of $\text{Id}(-,-,-)$ we first add to our models a set *Norm* of normative systems, onto which norm expressions are interpreted by the interpretation function $[-]$. Then, we add to our system a family of preordering relations, so that a given preorder is associated to each pair consisting of an agent and a normative system. The semantics of $\text{Id}(-,-,-)$ is then defined by:

$$M,w \models \text{Id}(x,n,\varphi) \ \text{iff} \ w\leq_{[x][n]}w' \ \text{implies} \ M,w' \models \varphi.$$

We can now define, for example, conditional obligation for a given agent with respect to a specific normative system:

$$O(x,n,\psi|\varphi) =_{\text{def}} \text{Nec}(\varphi \wedge \psi \rightarrow \text{Id}(x,n, \varphi \rightarrow \psi)),$$

where the statement $O(x,n,\psi|\varphi)$ can be read as „normative system n implies that ψ is obligatory for x under condition φ.“ Permissions, prohibitions and the like can be defined in a similar way.

Our deontic logic can now be used to specify the normative effects of communicative acts. For example, here is an axiom stating that, for a generic agent x, there is an obligation of type $sincere(x,y)$ to be sincere about the mental states expressed by x when addressing another agent y:

(3.1) $O(x,sincere(x,y), \varphi|Do(e,x) \wedge Address(e,y) \wedge Express(e,\varphi))$.

Let us now turn to the issue of violations and penalties.

1.4 Violations and Penalties

With its actual behavior, an agent may violate a normative system. This can be expressed, through a predicate $V(x,n)$, by the following axiom:

(3.2) $O(x,n,\psi|\varphi) \wedge \varphi \wedge \neg\psi \rightarrow V(x,n)$.

For example, from 3.1, 3.2 and 2.2 we can derive the theorem:

$$\exists e \ Assert(e,a,b,\varphi) \wedge \neg B_a\varphi \rightarrow V(a,sincere(a,b)),$$

that is: if agent *a* insincerely asserts that *φ* to agent *b*, then *a* violates the norm denoted by *sincere(a,b)*. In a practical application there might be a number of accessory complications; for example, it may be possible for an agent to accumulate several violations of the same norm, and we may want to record this. Adopting a more expressive formalism can easily solve problems of this kind.

We would now like to add that if agent *a* violated the norm *sincere(a,b)*, it can expiate by paying 100 euros to *b*. Before we can say this, however, we have to add to our logic some device for dealing with time. To keep matters as simple as possible, I assume here that time is discrete, and that in all models a function

$$next: W \rightarrow 2^W$$

associates to every possible world the set of all possible worlds that come next. I add to the formal language the modal operator Next, whose semantics is given by:

$$M,w \models \text{Next } \varphi \quad\quad \text{iff} \quad\quad w' \in next(w) \text{ implies } M,w' \models \varphi.$$

We now need to represent two general laws and a specific norm. The general laws are the following:

- a violation persists if there is no associated penalty, or if there is an associated penalty but this is not honored;

- a violation is cancelled if there is an associated penalty, and this is honored.

The specific norm is:

- the penalty for a violation of type *sincere(x,y)* is that *x* pays 100 euros to *y*.

The first general law can be represented easily. I use an atomic formula *Penalty(e,n)* to say that action *e* is a penalty for a violation of norm *n*. We have:

$$V(x,n) \land \neg \exists e \, (Penalty(e,n) \land Do(e,x)) \rightarrow \text{Next } V(x,n).$$

The second law is trickier. In fact, the axiom

$$(3.3) \quad V(x,n) \land \exists e \, (Penalty(e,n) \land Do(e,x)) \rightarrow \text{Next } \neg V(x,n)$$

serves to this purpose only if we can guarantee that agent *x* does not honor the penalty and violate norm *n* again immediately after. If this assumption is not feasible, a more complex version of axiom 3.3 will be necessary, possibly involving a subtler treatment of time.

Finally, let us consider the norm specifying the penalty for being insincere. This can be expressed by the axiom:

$$Pay(e,x,y,100,euro) \rightarrow Penalty(e,sincere(x,y)),$$

where the atomic formula *Pay(e,x,y,100,euro)* says that action *e* is an action by which 100 euros are paid by *x* to *y*.

The Issue of Rationality

A basic tenet of the whole agent-based approach is that agent behavior should not be strictly predetermined, but should be generated on-line according to principles of rationality. This means that an agent has to plan and carry out its actions in order to fulfill its desires, on the basis of its beliefs. To do so, an agent must possess practical reasoning abilities.

As I have already argued, the practical aspect of communication should not be viewed as part of the definition of communicative acts. Rather, practical reasoning will exploit all relevant aspects of communicative acts, including their semantic definitions and the norms regulating their performance. For example, an agent may plan a communicative act taking into account the obligations that descend from its performance, the possibility to honor such obligations, the penalties involved in breaking them, and so on. Processes of this kind will have to be regulated by rationality principles, implemented in suitable computational systems for the formation and execution of action plans.

The idea that the semantics of communicative acts can be defined independently of rationality principles is likely to be controversial. An objection may be based on a comparison between artificial and human communication. Indeed, when dealing with human communication it is not easy to draw a sharp distinction between semantic and practical aspects. For example, Grice's maxims (Grice, 1975) concern practical aspects of communication, but they appear to play an essential role in understanding the *speaker's meaning* of an utterance. However, it seems to me that, at least when dealing with communication among artificial agents, it is possible to single out a *literal meaning* of messages, which can be defined independently of practical aspects. To clarify this point, let me consider an important case of „Gricean communication", that is, indirect requests.

It is well known that human requests are often realized indirectly. For example, a request to close the door may take the form, „Can you close the door?", which is literally a question about an ability of the addressee. Inferring the actual request performed by the speaker is a problem of pragmatics, which can be solved by practical reasoning along the lines drawn by Searle (1969) and implemented in a computational system by Allen (1983). It is by no means obvious, however, that similar forms of communication, which seem to be motivated by reasons of politeness, are going to be interesting for artificial agents. In fact, in order to avoid semantic ambiguity I would strongly suggest that communication among artificial agents be based on the bare literal meaning of messages, which can be defined independently of rationality principles.

On the Design of an Agent Communication Language

Even if it is not my present goal to propose a new agent communication language, it is interesting to analyze some possible consequences that the approach advocated in this paper may have on the design of such languages.

The main tenets of this paper are that: (i) the semantics of communicative acts should be defined independently of the normative and practical aspects of communication; and (ii) that we do not need to predefine a set of basic communicative act types, given that communicative acts can be regarded as „macros" standing for useful combinations of expressed mental states. These two points raise a number of questions, and in this section I shall examine three of them: the choice and definition of basic mental states, the role and use of normative systems, and the relationship with dialogues.

1.5 Defining Mental States

For rational agents, mental states are the causes of action. Even if there is no universal agreement on a specific set of primitive mental states, all models of agents assume mental states of two different types: *epistemic states*, whose function is to represent the agent's environment as it is, and *thelic states*,[4] whose function is to represent the environment as the agent would like it to be. Typical epistemic states are perceptions and beliefs, and typical thelic states are desires and intentions. It is a „tension", or discrepancy, between states of these two types that ultimately leads to action.

A consequence of my approach is that two agents can communicate only if they share some vocabulary of mental states. For example, the definition of assertions involves beliefs; the definition of requests involves desires; and the definition of promises involves intentions. It follows that such basic mental states will have to be defined in a common way, if we want agent interactions to be successful. One has to admit that at the present stage of development a satisfactory definition of mental states is not yet available for all types of mental states involved in the definition of communicative acts. However, this is not a problem only for my approach: if it eventually turns out that we are incapable of providing a satisfactory definition of mental states, the whole idea of designing rational agents may not find a suitable foundation.

It should be noted that principles of rationality might play a role in the definition of mental states. For example, the fact that an agent strives to achieve its desires on the basis of its beliefs is a principle of rationality, but may also be viewed as part of the definition of desires and beliefs.[5] It may seem that there is a problem here: if communicative acts are going to be defined in terms of mental states, and mental states are defined at least partially in terms of rationality principles, how can I claim that the semantics of communicative acts is independent of rationality? However, the difficulty is only apparent. I have argued that rationality conditions can be left out of the definition of communicative acts, because communicative acts can be defined in terms of mental states. In turn, mental states may have to be defined also through rationality principles, but such principles will be relative to action in general, and not specific to communication.

1.6 The Role of Normative Systems

As we have seen, normative systems can be defined by axioms written in a deontic language. In Section 3 I try to give an idea of the kind of things one may want to settle within such a system: normative consequences of acts, penalties for violations, and so on. Normative systems should be common knowledge for all the agents involved in an interaction. From this point of view, normative systems are not different from ontologies, and could be made available to the community of agents in the same way (see for example FIPA, 1998).

---

[4] I propose this term, modeled after the Greek word for will, *thelos*.

[5] I say „may" here, because I am not sure that rationality principles are a necessary component of the definition of mental states. At present, I do not have a definite opinion on this important point.

When two agents exchange messages, it should be clear which normative system regulates their interaction. Given that every normative system has a name, it will be sufficient to include a reference to it in each message, or in a specific message in charge of opening a dialogue. In a language like KQML or FIPA ACL, this may be done through a new `:normative-system` parameter. Moreover, some messages might have the function of proposing, imposing, or accepting a different normative system. Such effects can be obtained by defining a repertoire of suitable actions, with no need to enlarge the set of communicative acts.

1.7 Dialogues

Typically, a communicative act occurs as part of a sequence of similar acts exchanged by two or more agents. Such sequences are called *dialogues* or *conversations*. The structure of dialogues can partly be generated by rationality principles. For example, if agent *a* is notified that an auction of antique musical instruments will take place tomorrow, it may be rational for *a* to request a detailed list of the items that will be put under the hammer.

While its importance in dialogues is obvious, it should be noted that practical reasoning does not account for the whole structure of conversations. In fact, part of this structure depends on rules that are normative rather than practical (see for example the concept of *conversation game* in Airenti, Bara and Colombetti, 1993). In FIPA ACL, such normative rules are expressed through *protocols*. For example, the FIPA-query-if protocol (FIPA, 1997) states that when an addressee, *b*, receives a yes-no query from a sender, *a*, then *b* ought to:

(i)   tell *a* that it did not understand the query, or

(ii)   tell *a* that it cannot produce an answer, giving a reason, or

(iii) tell *a* that it refuses to produce an answer, giving a reason, or

(iv)   answer the query by an act of inform-if.

It seems to me that protocols can be interpreted as sets of conditional obligations for the sender and for the addressee of a message. If they were expressed in a deontic language like the one I have outlined, agents would be able to *reason* on protocols (through deontic logic), and not only to *follow* them. For example, a protocol similar to FIPA-query-if can be represented as follows:

$$O(y, dialogueProtocol(x,y), \text{Next } \exists e' \ \psi \ | \ \text{QueryIf}(e,x,y,\varphi)),$$

where

$$\psi = \text{Assert}(e',y,x,\neg Understood(y,e))$$
$$\lor \text{Assert}(e',y,x,\neg B_y\varphi \land \neg B_y\neg\varphi)$$
$$\lor \text{Assert}(e',y,x,\neg D_y\text{AssertIf}(e,y,x,\varphi))$$
$$\lor \text{AssertIf}(e,y,x,\varphi),$$

where the predicate *Understood(x,e)* means that agent *x* has understood the meaning of *e*, and the modal operator D_y stands for *y*'s desire. Coherently with the approach presented in this paper, the communicative acts involved in the protocol have to be defined in terms of Express. Assert has already been defined by 2.2; then:

AssertIf$(e,x,y,\varphi) =_{def}$
  $Do(e,x) \wedge Address(e,y) \wedge (\text{Express}(e,B_x\varphi) \vee \text{Express}(e,\neg B_x\varphi))$,

QueryIf$(e,x,y,\varphi) =_{def}$
  $Do(e,x) \wedge Address(e,y) \wedge \text{Express}(e,D_x\text{AssertIf}(e,y,x,\varphi))$.

Conclusions

In this paper I have argued that a satisfactory model of communication should consider three related but conceptually independent aspects of communicative acts: the semantic aspect, concerning the literal meaning of communicative acts; the normative aspect, concerning the obligations, permissions, and so on, created by performing communicative acts; and the practical aspects, concerning the role of communication in the context of rational action. To substantiate this claim, I have sketched a formalism, based on modal logic, which can be used to define the semantics and the deontics of communication. Finally, I have argued that the practical aspect is not involved in the definition of communicative acts, but concerns the agents' general ability to reason on all relevant facets of the world – including of course communication.

I am aware of the fact that the present paper suggests an approach, but does not work out a complete alternative to current agent communication languages. Before this can be done, several problems must be solved. Among these are the definition of a satisfactory set of basic mental states and the choice of a suitable deontic system. Moreover, it will be necessary to show that all types of communicative acts introduced by the agent communication languages proposed so far can actually be defined in terms of the Express operator.

Postscriptum

Since this paper was accepted for publication, I have changed my mind about some elements of my proposal. I still believe that the distinction between the semantic, normative, and practical aspects of communication is important, but I am now inclined to draw the boundaries between the semantics and the deontics of communication in a different way. In particular, as far as agent communication is concerned I am now trying to abandon the whole notion of expressing a mental state, and to replace it with a suitable concept of commitment. The idea is that the semantics of messages can be defined in terms of the commitments created by communicative acts. It is then up to normative systems to dictate what is going to happen if a commitment is violated. A technical report on this attempt is currently in preparation.

References

Airenti, G., B. G. Bara and M. Colombetti (1993). Conversation and behavior games in the pragmatics of dialogue. *Cognitive Science*, 17 (2), 197–256.

Allen, J. F. (1983). Recognizing intentions from natural language utterances. In M. Brady and R. C. Berwick, eds., *Computational models of discourse*, MIT Press, Cambridge, MA.

Åqvist, L. (1984). Deontic Logic. In D. Gabbay and F. Guenthner, eds., *Handbook of philosophical logic*, Vol. II, Reidel, 605–714.

ARPA (1993). Specification of the KQLM agent communication language. Working paper, ARPA Knowledge Sharing Initiative, External Interfaces Working Group.

Austin, J. L. (1962). *How to do things with words*, Clarendon Press, Oxford, UK.

Chellas, B. F. (1980). *Modal logic*, Cambridge University Press, Cambridge, UK.

Cohen, P. R., and H. J. Levesque (1990). Rational interaction as the basis for communication. In P. R. Cohen, J. Morgan and M. E. Pollack, eds., *Intentions in communication*, MIT Press, Cambridge, MA, 221–256.

Cohen, P. R., and C. R. Perrault (1979). *Elements of a plan-based theory of speech acts*. Cognitive Science, 3, 177–212.

FIPA (1997). Agent Communication Language. FIPA 97 Specification, Foundation for Intelligent Physical Agents, http://www.fipa.org.

FIPA (1998). Ontology service. FIPA 98 Specification, Foundation for Intelligent Physical Agents, http://www.fipa.org.

Grice, P. H. (1975). Logic and conversation. In P. Cole and J. L. Morgan, eds., *Syntax and semantics, Vol. 3: Speech acts*, Academic Press, New York, 41–58.

McCarthy, J. (1990). Elephant 2000: A programming language based on speech acts. Unpublished manuscript.

Searle, J. R. (1969). *Speech Acts*, Cambridge University Press, Cambridge, UK.

Shoham, Y. (1993). Agentoriented programming. *Artificial Intelligence*, 60, 51–92.

Tan, Y.W., and L. W. N. van der Torre (1966). How to combine ordering and minimizing in a deontic logic based on preferences, *Proceedings of the Third International Workshop on Deontic Logic in Computer Science (Δeon'96)*.

A Social Semantics for Agent Communication Languages

Munindar P. Singh[*]

Department of Computer Science
North Carolina State University
Raleigh, NC 27695-7534, USA

singh@ncsu.edu

Abstract. The ability to communicate is one of the salient properties of agents. Although a number of agent communication languages (ACLs) have been developed, obtaining a suitable formal semantics for ACLs remains one of the greatest challenges of multiagent systems theory. Previous semantics have largely been mentalistic in their orientation and are based solely on the beliefs and intentions of the participating agents. Such semantics are not suitable for most multiagent applications, which involve autonomous and heterogeneous agents, whose beliefs and intentions cannot be uniformly determined. Accordingly, we present a social semantics for ACLs that gives primacy to the interactions among the agents. Our semantics is based on social commitments and is developed in temporal logic. This semantics, because of its public orientation, is essential to providing a rigorous basis for multiagent protocols.

1 Introduction

Interaction among agents is the distinguishing property of multiagent systems. Communications are a kind of interaction that respect the heterogeneity and preserve the autonomy of agents. In this respect, they differ from physical interactions. An agent may have no choice but to physically affect another agent—e.g., to bump into it or to lock a file it needs—or similarly be affected by another agent. By contrast, unless otherwise constrained, an agent need not send or receive communications; if it is willing to handle the consequences, it can maintain silence and deny the requests or even the commands it receives. Consequently, communication is unique among the kinds of actions agents may perform and the interactions in which they may participate.

Our particular interest is in *open* multiagent systems, which find natural usage in modern applications such as electronic commerce. In open multiagent systems, the member agents are contributed by several sources and serve different interests. Thus, these agents must be treated as

---

[*] This research was supported by the NCSU College of Engineering, the National Science Foundation under grant IIS-9624425 (Career Award), and IBM corporation. This paper has benefited from comments by the anonymous reviewers.

F. Dignum and M. Greaves (Eds.): Agent Communication, LNAI 1916, pp. 31–45, 2000.

- *autonomous*—with few constraints on behavior, reflecting the independence of their users, and
- *heterogeneous*—with few constraints on construction, reflecting the independence of their designers.

Openness means that all interfaces in the system, and specifically ACLs, be given a clear semantics. A good ACL semantics must meet some crucial criteria.

- *Formal.* The usual benefits of formal semantics apply here, especially (1) clarity of specifications to guide implementers and (2) assurance of software. In fact, these are more significant for ACLs, because ACLs are meant to be realized in different agents implemented by different vendors.
- *Declarative.* The semantics should be declarative describing what rather than how. Such a semantics can be more easily applied to a variety of settings not just those that satisfy some low-level operational criteria.
- *Verifiable.* It should be possible to determine whether an agent is acting according to the given semantics.
- *Meaningful.* The semantics should be based on some intuitive appreciation of communications and not treat communications merely as arbitrary tokens to be ordered in some way. If it does, we can arbitrarily invent more tokens; there would be no basis to limit the proliferation of tokens.

These criteria, although simple, eliminate all of the existing candidates for ACL semantics. For example, English descriptions of communications (quite common in practice) are not formal, finite-state machines (FSMs) are not declarative or meaningful, mentalistic approaches are not verifiable, and temporal logics (if applied to tokens directly) and formal grammar representations of sequences of tokens are not meaningful. Briefly, we find that an approach based on social commitments (described within) and formalized in temporal logic can meet all of the above requirements.

Organization. The rest of this paper is organized as follows. Section 2 motivates a semantics based on social constructs, and presents our conceptual approach. Section 3 presents a formal social semantics for ACLs, discusses its properties, and shows how it relates to communication protocols. Section 4 concludes with a discussion of our major themes, the literature, and some questions for future investigation.

2   Conceptual Approach

Most studies of communication in AI are based on speech act theory [1]. The main idea of speech act theory, namely, to treat communications as actions, remains attractive. An *illocution* is the core component of a communication and corresponds to what the communication might be designed to (or is meant to) accomplish independent of both how the communication is physically carried out (the *locution*) and the effect it has on a listener (the *perlocution*). For example,

I could request you to open the window (the *request* is the illocution) by saying so directly or hinting at it (these are possible locutions). Whether or not you accede to my request is the perlocution. A proposition can be combined with illocutions of different types to yield different messages. For example, my request to open the window is different from my assertion that the window is open.

It is customary to classify ACL primitives or message types into a small number of categories based on the different types of illocution. Usually these include the following categories—a sample primitive of each category is given in parentheses: *assertives* (inform), *directives* (request), *commissives* (promise), *permissives* (permit), *prohibitives* (forbid), *declaratives* (declare), and *expressives* (wish). The above classification provides sufficient structure for our approach (some alternative classifications could also be used). Each message is thus identified by its sender and receiver, (propositional) content, and type.

Three components of an ACL are typically distinguished: (1) a content sublanguage to encode domain-specific propositions, (2) a set of primitives or message types corresponding to different illocutionary types (e.g., *inform* and *request*), and (3) a transport mechanism to send the messages. Part (2) is the core and the most interesting for the present study.

2.1   Mentalistic Versus Social Semantics

Work on speech act theory within AI was motivated from the natural language understanding perspective and concerned itself with identifying or inferring the "intent" of the speaker. As a result, most previous work on ACLs too concerns itself with mental concepts, such as the beliefs and intentions of the participating agents. In fact, some theories emphasize the mutual beliefs and joint intentions of the agents as they perform their communicative actions. Inferring the beliefs and intentions of participants is essential to determining whether a given illocution occurred: did the speaker make a signal or was he just exercising his arm? However, in ACLs, the message type is explicit and no reasoning is required to determine it. In applications of multiagent systems, such reasoning would usually not be acceptable, because of the difficulty in specifying, executing, and enforcing it in an open environment.

There are a number of objections to using only the mental concepts for specifying ACL semantics; several of these are described in [18]. Although the mental concepts might be suitable for specifying the construction and behavior of the agents, they are not suitable as an exclusive basis for communications. There are a number of objections, but we summarize them in the following major categories.

- *Philosophical.* Communication is a public phenomenon, but the mental concepts are private. Any semantics that neglects the public nature of communication is deeply unsatisfactory. Something obviously takes place when agents interact through language even if they don't have or share the "right" beliefs and intentions.

- *Practical.* Ensuring that only the desirable interactions occur is one of the most challenging aspects of multiagent system engineering. However, the mental concepts cannot be verified without access to the internal construction of the agents. Under current theories of mental concepts, we cannot uniquely determine an agent beliefs and intentions even if we know the details of its construction.

The above evidence supports the conclusion that a purely mentalistic semantics of an ACL cannot be a normative requirement on agents or their designers.

2.2   Language Versus Protocol

To ensure autonomy and heterogeneity, we must specify communications flexibly and without making intrusive demands on agent behavior or design. Traditionally, heterogeneity is accommodated by specifying communication protocols. Traditionally, the protocols are specified by defining the allowed orders in which communicative acts may take place, but no more. Often, this is through the use of FSMs. In particular, FSM protocols are devoid of content. They only state how the tokens are ordered. Thus, the ACL is effectively discarded, and we can just as well choose any arbitrary tokens for the message types. The same holds for other formalisms such as push-down automata, formal grammars, Petri Nets, and temporal logic (when these are applied on tokens), so we won't discuss them explicitly here.

The foregoing indicates how the unsuitability of the traditional semantics forces the protocols to be ad hoc. By contrast, the present paper seeks to develop a nontrivial semantics for an ACL that would also be usable for the construction and verification of protocols.

2.3   Validity Claims

The semantics of ACLs, which concerns us here, relates to the essence of communication. The currently popular approaches to ACL semantics are based on the speaker's intent [8]. Under this doctrine, the illocution is what the speaker believed and intended it to be. This doctrine, championed by Searle and others, however, leads to the philosophical and practical problems discussed above.

In philosophy, another of the best known approaches to communicative action is due to Habermas [9]; short tutorials on Habermas are available in [13] and [23, chap. 2]. The Habermas approach associates three "worlds" or aspects of meaning with communication. These correspond to the three *validity claims* implicitly made with each communication:

- *objective*, that the communication is true.
- *subjective*, that the communication is sincere—in other words, the speaker believes or intends what is communicated.
- *practical*, that the speaker is justified in making the communication.

In conversation, each of the above claims may be challenged and shown to be false. However, even if false, these claims are staked with each communication, which is why they can be meaningfully questioned. The claims involve different aspects of meaning including the subjective, but by fact of being claims in a conversation, they are public and social. If I tell you something, I am committed to being accurate, and you are entitled to check if I am. I am also committed to being sincere, even though you may not be able to detect my insincerity unless you can infer what I believe, e.g., through contradictory statements that I make at about the same time. In general, in open environments, agents cannot safely determine whether or not another agent is sincere.

Perhaps more than his followers in AI, Searle too recognizes the institutional nature of language. He argues that the "counts as" relation is the basis for "constitutive reality" or institutional facts, including definitions of linguistic symbols [15, pp. 152–156] and [16, chap. 4]. But institutions are inherently objective. For example, in an auction, raising your hand counts as making a bid whether or not you have the intention to actually convey that you are bidding. In on-line commerce, pushing the "submit" on your browser counts as authorizing a charge on your credit card irrespective of your intentions and beliefs at that time.

Our proposed approach, then, is simply as follows. We begin with the concept of *social commitments* as is studied in multiagent systems [3] and reasoning and dialogue in general [24]. Our technical definition of commitments differs from the above works in two main respects [19,22]. Our formalization of commitments includes

- the notion of a social context in the definition of a commitment; the social context refers to the team in which the given agents participate and within which they communicate; it too can be treated as an agent in its own right— e.g., it may enter into commitments with other agents.
- metacommitments to capture a variety of social and legal relations.

The different claims associated with a communicative action are mapped to different commitments among the participants and their social context. Consequently, although our semantics is social in orientation, it admits the mental viewpoint.

Social commitments as defined are a kind of deontic concept. They can be viewed as a generalization of traditional obligations as studied in deontic logic. Traditional obligations just state what an agent is obliged to do. In some recent work, directed obligations have also been studied that are relativized to another agent—i.e., an agent is obliged to do something for another agent. Social commitments in our formulation are relativized to two agents: one the beneficiary or creditor of the given commitment and another the context within which the commitment occurs. Further, we define operations on commitments so they can be created and canceled (and otherwise manipulated). The operations on commitments are, however, subject to metacommitments.

In our approach, metacommitments are used to define micro societies within which the agents function. These are intuitively similar to the *institutions* of [14], which however also specify the meanings of the terms used in the given (trading) community.

3 Technical Approach

Communication occurs during the execution of a multiagent system. For this reason, our semantics is based on commitments expressed in a logic of time.

3.1 Background Concepts

Temporal logics provide a well-understood means of specifying behaviors of concurrent processes, and have been applied in areas such as distributed computing. By using classical techniques, such as temporal logic, we hope to facilitate the application of the proposed semantics when multiagent systems are to be integrated into traditional software systems. Computation Tree Logic (CTL) is a branching-time logic that is particularly natural for expressing properties of systems that may evolve in more than one possible way [5]. Conventionally, a model of CTL is a tree whose nodes correspond to the states of the system being considered. The branches or *paths* of the tree indicate the possible ways in which the system's state may evolve.

Our formal language $\mathcal{L}$ is based on CTL. $\mathcal{L}$ builds on a flexible and powerful variety of social commitments, which are the commitments of one agent to another. A commitment involves three agents: the *debtor* (who makes it), the *creditor* (to whom it is made), and the *context* (the containing multiagent system in the scope of which it is made). We include beliefs and intentions as modal operators.

The following Backus-Naur Form (BNF) grammar with a distinguished start symbol L gives the syntax of $\mathcal{L}$. $\mathcal{L}$ is based on a set Φ of atomic propositions. Below, *slant* typeface indicates nonterminals; $\longrightarrow$ and | are metasymbols of BNF specification; $\ll$ and $\gg$ delimit comments; the remaining symbols are terminals. As is customary in formal semantics, we are only concerned with abstract syntax.

L1. $L \longrightarrow$ *Prop* $\ll$atomic propositions, i.e., in $\Phi\gg$
L2. $L \longrightarrow$ $\neg\,L$ $\ll$negation$\gg$
L3. $L \longrightarrow$ $L \wedge L$ $\ll$conjunction$\gg$
L4. $L \longrightarrow$ $L \rightsquigarrow L$ $\ll$strict implication$\gg$
L5. $L \longrightarrow$ A P $\ll$universal quantification on paths$\gg$
L6. $L \longrightarrow$ E P $\ll$existential quantification on paths$\gg$
L7. $L \longrightarrow$ R P $\ll$selecting the real path$\gg$
L8. $P \longrightarrow$ L U L $\ll$until: operator on a single path$\gg$
L9. $L \longrightarrow$ C(*Agent, Agent, Agent, L*)$\ll$commitment$\gg$
L10. $L \longrightarrow$ xB L | xI L $\ll$belief and intention$\gg$

The meanings of formulas generated from L are given relative to a model and a state in the model. The meanings of formulas generated from P are given relative to a path and a state on the path. The boolean operators are standard. Useful abbreviations include false $\equiv (p \wedge \neg p)$, for any $p \in \Phi$, true $\equiv \neg$false, $p \vee q \equiv \neg p \wedge \neg q$ and $p \rightarrow q \equiv \neg p \vee q$. The temporal operators A and E are quantifiers over paths.

Informally, $p\mathsf{U}q$ means that on a given path from the given state, q will eventually hold and p will hold until q holds. $\mathsf{F}q$ means "eventually q" and abbreviates $\mathsf{true}\mathsf{U}q$. $\mathsf{G}q$ means "always q" and abbreviates $\neg\mathsf{F}\neg q$. Therefore, $\mathsf{EF}p$ p will hold on some path. R selects the real path. $\mathsf{RF}p$ means that p will hold on the real path. Although agents can't predict the future, they can make (possibly false) assertions or promises about it.

$M = \langle \mathbf{S}, <, \approx, \mathbf{N}, \mathbf{R}, \mathbf{A}, \mathbf{B}, \mathbf{I}, \mathbf{C} \rangle$ is a formal model for $\mathcal{L}$. $\mathbf{S}$ is a set of states; $< \subseteq S \times S$ is a partial order indicating branching time, $\approx \subseteq S \times S$ relates states to similar states, and $\mathbf{N} : \mathbf{S} \mapsto 2^{\Phi}$ is an interpretation, which tells us which atomic propositions are true in a given state. $\mathbf{P}$ is the set of paths derived from $<$. $\mathbf{PP}$ gives the powerset of $\mathbf{P}$. For $t \in \mathbf{S}$, $\mathbf{P}_t$ is the set of paths emanating from t. $\mathbf{R} : \mathbf{S} \mapsto \mathbf{P}$ gives the real path emanating from a state. $\mathbf{A}$ is a set of agents. $\mathbf{B} : \mathbf{S} \times \mathbf{A} \mapsto \mathbf{S}$, $\mathbf{I} : \mathbf{S} \times \mathbf{A} \mapsto \mathbf{PP}$, and $\mathbf{C} : \mathbf{S} \times \mathbf{A} \times \mathbf{A} \times \mathbf{A} \mapsto \mathbf{PP}$ give the modal accessibility relations for beliefs, intentions, and commitments, respectively.

For p derived from L, $M \models_t p$ expresses "M satisfies p at t" and for p derived from P, $M \models_{P,t} p$ expresses "M satisfies p at t along path P."

M1. $M \models_t \psi$ iff $\psi \in \mathbf{N}(t)$, where $\psi \in \Phi$

M2. $M \models_t p \wedge q$ iff $M \models_t p$ and $M \models_t q$

M3. $M \models_t \neg p$ iff $M \not\models_t p$

M4. $M \models_t p \rightsquigarrow q$ iff $M \models_t p$ and $(\forall t' : M \models_{t'} p \Rightarrow (\forall t'' : t' \approx t'' \Rightarrow M \models_{t''} q))$

M5. $M \models_t \mathsf{A}p$ iff $(\forall P : P \in \mathbf{P}_t \Rightarrow M \models_{P,t} p)$

M6. $M \models_t \mathsf{E}p$ iff $(\exists P : P \in \mathbf{P}_t$ and $M \models_{P,t} p)$

M7. $M \models_t \mathsf{R}p$ iff $M \models_{\mathbf{R}_t,t} p$

M8. $M \models_t x\mathsf{I}p$ iff $(\forall P : P \in \mathbf{I}(x,t) \Rightarrow M \models_{P,t} p)$

M9. $M \models_t x\mathsf{B}p$ iff $(\forall t' : t' \in \mathbf{B}(x,t) \Rightarrow M \models_{t'} p)$

M10. $M \models_t \mathsf{C}(x,y,G,p)$ iff $(\forall P : P \in \mathbf{C}(x,y,G,t) \Rightarrow M \models_{P,t} p)$

M11. $M \models_{P,t} p\mathsf{U}q$ iff $(\exists t' : t \leq t'$ and $M \models_{P,t'} q$ and $(\forall t'' : t \leq t'' \leq t' \Rightarrow M \models_{P,t''} p))$

3.2   Social Semantics

We now present a social semantics for the ACL primitives. Our main purpose with this semantics is to show how the different validity claims can be understood in terms of social commitments and formalized in our framework.

In giving this semantics, we attempt to understand each communication atomically, i.e., as an individual transmission. Clearly communications usually occur in extended protocols. In a strict reading, Habermas too would be against the idea of seeking to understand communications in isolation. However, from a technical standpoint it is simpler if we can characterize the communications individually. Then we can go back to composing them, so that we might, for example, have an explicit acceptance after a request. In a sense, such an acknowledgement is needed to ensure that the receiver becomes committed to carrying out the request. If we are operating in a social context where the receiver's commitment is given, then explicit acceptance is superfluous. We return to this point in analyzing Winograd & Flores' conversation for action protocol in Section 3.2.

Table 1. Social semantics formalized: objective and subjective

Illocution	Objective	Subjective
$inform(x,y,p)$	$C(x,y,p)$	$C(x,y,x\mathsf{B}p)$
$request(x,y,p)$	$C(y,x,\mathsf{RF}p)$	$C(y,x,y\mathsf{IF}p)$
$promise(x,y,p)$	$C(x,y,\mathsf{RF}p)$	$C(x,y,x\mathsf{IF}p)$
$permit(x,y,p)$	$C(x,y,\mathsf{EF}p)$	$C(x,y,\neg x\mathsf{I}\neg\mathsf{F}p)$
$forbid(x,y,p)$	$C(y,x,\neg\mathsf{RF}p)$	$C(y,x,\neg y\mathsf{IF}p)$
$declare(x,y,p)$	$C(x,y,p)$	$C(x,y,x\mathsf{I}p)$

Table 2. Social semantics formalized: practical

Illocution	Practical
$inform(x,y,p)$	$C(x,G,inform(x,y,p)\rightsquigarrow p)$
$request(x,y,p)$	$C(x,G,request(x,y,p)\rightsquigarrow \mathsf{AFC}(y,x,p))$
$promise(x,y,p)$	$C(x,G,promise(x,y,p)\rightsquigarrow \mathsf{RF}p)$
$permit(x,y,p)$	$C(x,G,permit(x,y,p)\rightsquigarrow \neg C(y,G,\neg\mathsf{RF}p))$
$forbid(x,y,p)$	$C(x,G,forbid(x,y,p)\rightsquigarrow C(y,G,\neg\mathsf{RF}p))$
$declare(x,y,p)$	$C(x,G,declare(x,y,p)\rightsquigarrow p)$

Tables 1 and 2 gives the formal semantics of the ACL primitives. (All commitments are relative to G, the context group, which is not shown to reduce clutter; however, G is the creditor of some commitments, which are shown.) This semantics simply captures the objective, subjective, and practical meanings associated with the given primitive. Each aspect of meaning is viewed from the public perspective, because each involves a social commitment. Let's consider each component of the semantics in turn.

Objectively, the sender commits for *inform* that its content is true, for *promise* that its content will be accomplished, for *permit* that its content may be realized, for *declare* that its content is true. For *request*, the sender expects that the receiver will commit to making it true, and for *forbid* that the receiver will commit that its content will not be realized. Although these are not part of the objective meaning, they are related to the practical meaning given below.

Subjectively, the sender commits for *inform* that he believes its content, for *promise* that he intends to carry it out, for *permit* that he does not intend the negation of its content, for *declare* that he intends to bring it about. For *request*, the sender expects that the receiver will commit to intending to make it true, and for *forbid* that the receiver will commit that its content will not be realized. These expectations are not directly incorporated in the semantics.

The practical aspect of the semantics is the most complex. Practically, the sender commits for *inform* that he has reason to know the content, for *promise* that if he promises something he can make it happen, for *permit* that he has the authority to relieve the receiver of any commitment to do otherwise, and for *declare* that his saying so, brings it about. For *request*, the sender commits that the receiver has committed to accepting a request from him. For *forbid*, the sender commits he can cause the receiver to take on a commitment to not let the condition come about. This semantics reflects our intuition that prohibitives such as *forbid* are to be differentiated from directives such as *request*. The requester only has to be committed to the claim that his request will eventually be serviced, whereas the forbidder has to be committed to the claim that his prohibition will immediately commit the receiver to not violating it. The above meanings are naturally phrased as metacommitments to the group. They refer to the communication itself.

Conceivably, even the commitments relating to the subjective expectations might be added here, but we suggest they would be too strong for the basic practical meaning. This is because our goal with this semantics is to specify the objective and the practical components of the semantics for use in the construction and validation of multiagent protocols. This is facilitated when the subjective criteria are not included in the practical meaning.

Notice that any commitment may in principle be broken. However, the breaking of a commitment is typically constrained by some metacommitment, which might prescribe an alternative commitment.

Pragmatic Constraints. What we usually refer to informally as *meaning* is a combination of the semantics and pragmatics. We will treat the semantics as the part of meaning that is relatively fixed and minimal. Pragmatics is the component of meaning that is context-sensitive and depends on both the application and the social structure within which it is applied.

The above semantic validity claims, even the practical claims, are different from pragmatics. Pragmatic claims would be based on considerations such as the Gricean maxims of manner, quality, and quantity [7]. For example, a pragmatic claim basis for *permit* might be that the receiver desires or intends the content that is being permitted. Some of the pragmatic constraints would be the public versions of the expectations listed above in the subjective component of the semantics.

Protocols and Compliance. The limitations of traditional ACL semantics force protocol approaches to fend for themselves and give low-level, procedural characterizations of interactions. Representations based on monolithic finite-state machines are suitable only for the most trivial scenarios. They cannot accommodate distributed execution, compliance testing, or exceptions. However, given a commitment-based semantics for ACLs, an observer of a multiagent system (possibly itself a participating agent) can maintain a record of the commitments being created and modified. From these, the observer can determine the compliance of other agents with respect to the given protocol. This compliance testing would be based on the contents of the messages and the formal public meanings of the ACL primitives used. It would not depend solely on the sequence of events in the system.

However, protocols will continue to be useful even when a social semantics for ACLs is adopted. For example, turn-taking might underlie the specific commitments to ensure that they are created only when they make sense. For instance, a bidder shouldn't make a bid prior to the advertisement, or the commitment content of the bid won't be fully defined. Moreover, protocols supply the requirements through which the communications can be composed. In other words, although the commitment-based semantics can tell us the result of composing some communications, it is the protocols that tell us what composition is appropriate.

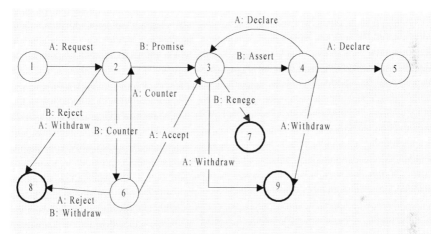

Fig. 1. Conversation for Action [25]

As a simple example, consider the well-known "conversation for action" protocol of Winograd & Flores, which is shown in Figure 1. Commitments can be associated with each state in this protocol. The commitments arise from the basic communication semantics but are enhanced through the metacommitments that are in force in the given organization. This helps us analyze the protocol. For example, if there is a metacommitment that A's requests will be honored, then there is no need to separate states 2 and 3, and in fact, state 6 is eliminated entirely. Conversely, if B makes a promise to A without any explicit request from A, in terms of the commitments, we can see that the protocol effectively begins from state 6. Thus if the applicable metacommitments are captured, the executions are minimally constrained only to satisfy those metacommitments. This we believe is a major advantage of the declarative approach over low-level representations.

As an aside, we observe that as traditionally stated, this protocol is overspecified, because it mixes commitment concerns with coordination requirements. For example, if no metacommitment applies under which A's request must be honored by B, then the purpose of the transition from state 2 to state 8 only helps in announcing that the protocol has terminated, not in changing any commitments among the participants.

3.3   Properties

A formal semantics may be evaluated by showing that it supports the desirable properties. Our semantics satisfies the four criteria of Section 1.

- *Formal.* Our semantics is based on logic.
- *Declarative.* Our semantics involves assertions about commitments, rather than procedures or automata.
- *Verifiable.* Our semantics offers different levels of verifiability. Every commitment to a putative fact can be verified or falsified by challenging that putative fact. Every commitment to a mental state can be similarly verified or falsified, but only through the more arduous route of eliciting the agent's beliefs and intentions. These might be elicited by observing the agent's further communications or other actions. Of course, this elicitation cannot be reliably performed unless significant assumptions about the agent's design and behavior can be made. As a result, the subjective meaning cannot be used in open environments. Mentalist approaches fail because they almost exclusively consider subjective meaning, although the details of their proposals can vary.

    Every commitment to some institutional fact can be verified or falsified by appeal to some external authority. This authority is the context within which the commitments are created. The context essentially defines the institution within which the communication takes place. The context could be defined as just the group of everyone involved, but in distributed computing practice would refer to some sort of a leader, possibly one that was elected.
- *Meaningful.* Every message type has an inherent meaning expressed in terms of commitments, and arbitrary tokens would be rejected.

We consider some additional technical properties. By being based on the commitments of the participating agents, our semantics provides a basis for describing the conversational state of a multiagent system in high-level terms, i.e., using commitments. Thus, the state, defined in terms of commitments, is independent of the *history*, i.e., the steps of a protocol that may have been executed. History-freedom is essential to establishing some important properties of multiagent protocols, which we discuss next.

- *Composition.* Protocols may be combined into larger protocols, as long as one protocol yields a commitment state that the other protocol needs.
- *Digression.* Ad hoc actions, e.g., in response to exceptions or errors, may be interposed without affecting the true meaning of a protocol as long as the commitments were not affected. If the commitments are affected, then we would know there was a fundamental deviation from the protocol, and may repair it or discard the protocol altogether.
- *Optimization.* The agents may directly enter a protocol in execution where the right commitments are defined even though the steps have not been carried out explicitly. Such short-circuiting of the protocols is crucial for optimizing the agents' behavior.

The above properties are essential for enabling opportunistic behavior by the agents while providing all the benefits of protocols in structuring their interactions and individual behavior. Achieving both flexibility and structure is essential for many multiagent applications.

Similarly, the *content* of a message is not only the direct action it connotes, but also the implied actions caused by the discharge of the applicable metacommitments. Thus, if A has a metacommitment that it will honor B's bid, then B's bid will create the commitment to honor it.

4 Discussion

A communication protocol involves the exchange of messages with a streamlined set of tokens. Traditionally, these tokens are not given any meaning except through reference to the beliefs or intentions of the communicating agents. By contrast, our approach assigns *public*, i.e., observable, meanings in terms of social commitments. This leads to the ability to test compliance at a level of abstraction higher than just the ordering of events. It also promises a canonical form of communication protocols, which would give us a meaningful basis for determining where in a protocol execution the agents in a multiagent system are, how to proceed, and how to accommodate exceptions naturally.

4.1 Literature

Social commitments are not to be confused with commitments previously studied in AI. Traditional commitments apply to an agent being in a state where it will persist with a belief or an intention. They do not reflect the agent's social commitments or obligations to other parties. The notion of persistence with a goal provides a basis for the theory of joint intentions due to [11]. Roughly, a joint intention among some agents corresponds to the agents believing that they have persistent goals to achieve the given condition and that they would inform the others if the condition were to be satisfied or become unsatisfiable or if they drop out of the joint intention for any reason. Thus, joint intentions build on mutual beliefs. Roughly, a set of agents mutually believe p iff each of them believes p, and each of them believes that each of them believes p, and so on, *ad infinitum* [6]. In fact, mutual beliefs are used primarily to establish impossibility results for distributed computing protocols. Such results can readily be created for joint intentions as well. Traditional approaches typically assume that mutual beliefs can be achieved easily, sometimes by as little as a single message transmission [21, p. 163]. This is unsatisfactory, because a fairly complex theory is built only to be discarded at the first opportunity where it might be tested.

A number of approaches consider the deontic notion of obligation. Traditional obligations involve what a single agent is obliged to do irrespective of other agents. Traum uses such obligations to state what an agent may be obliged to do in a conversation [21]. Traditional obligations, however, do not capture the subtleties of interactions among agents. More promising are directed obligations of the sort studied by Dignum & van Linder [4]. Dignum & van Linder model agents with an explicit social component (the other components are less relevant here). They model speech acts as affecting the beliefs or obligations of the agents. The classification of speech acts in this approach is a little different from the typical classifications. However, their speech acts can be mapped to the more common kinds of message types. Although some of their constructs are similar to ours, Dignum & van Linder confine themselves to giving the preconditions for various messages, rather than keeping the semantics sensitive to the context of usage as we have sought to do. For example, they assume that the agents will be sincere.

Besides the works referred to in the above, there is a fairly substantial body of literature on ACLs and their semantics. The Foundation for Intelligent Physical Agents (FIPA) has been standardizing an ACL along with a formal semantics. This ACL and its semantics are based on Arcol, which was part of a system for human-computer interaction [2]. Arcol and the FIPA ACL are mentalist in their orientation. FIPA also includes interaction protocols, which are characterized purely operationally. Labrou & Finin present a variant of the knowledge query and manipulation language (KQML) [10]. They offer a semantics stating how the beliefs and intentions of the participants are affected by communications.

Smith & Cohen present an alternative semantics for an ACL, which is based on a theory of joint intentions [20]. The approach treats communication as creating or modifying structures of joint intentions, which are used to describe the agents working as a team. The joint intentions treatment of teams, however, is a mentalist approach to simulate an essentially social phenomenon. It fails to describe teams directly and suffers from all the problems attendant to the mentalist approaches.

A number of approaches have studied communication protocols. Usually, these specify and execute protocols in a representation such as FSMs and Petri Nets. Labrou & Finin present a grammar for constructing conversations or protocols. The grammar is fundamentally of the same style of representation as FSMs, but is more expressive [10]. Smith & Cohen apply their approach on the conversation for action protocol described above [20]. They argue that the different paths in the protocol result in the formation or nonformation of a team. Interestingly they consider the paths in Figure 1 and not the states as we sought to do. Also, because their basic assumptions are strong, they cannot suggest how the protocol may be improved in a nontrivial way.

Singh proposes a semantics that gives the conditions for the "whole-hearted" satisfaction of different communications [17]. Whole-hearted satisfaction depends on the intentions and know-how of the participants. This approach has ingredients relating to the objective and subjective aspects of meaning as described above. However, although whole-hearted satisfaction involved a public stance, it lacks a social perspective as developed here. This approach can state communication constraints for use as inputs into the design of the participating agents.

4.2 Directions

The social semantics developed here treats the social construction of communication as a first class notion rather than as a derivative of the mentalist concepts. Although some previous researchers have discussed the social aspects of communication, they were never quite able to shed the mentalist bias of traditional AI. We hope that by making a fresh start on the semantics, we will be able to produce a semantics that can serve the needs of agents operating and communicating in open environments. Because this work is still in an early stage, some of the details are quite likely to evolve. One of our tasks is to evaluate variations of the above semantics that preserve the social, validity-based theme that we tried to capture above.

Interesting theoretical questions are opened up by the present approach. One of these is the longstanding topic of presuppositions and consensus. *Presuppositions* are essential to understanding and properly interpreting any communication. Potentially, we can interpret the implicit claims behind every communication as presuppositions [24]. If they are not challenged, they become accepted as *consensus*, which corresponds to commitments by the entire group of communicating agents. Consensus might offer a tractable alternative to mutual beliefs, which are used by current theories of dialogue, but which cannot be obtained in realistic environments, e.g., those with unreliable asynchronous communication [6].

References

1. John L. Austin. *How to Do Things with Words*. Clarendon Press, Oxford, 1962.
2. Phillipe Breiter and M. David Sadek. A rational agent as a kernel of a cooperative dialogue system: Implementing a logical theory of interaction. In *ECAI-96 Workshop on Agent Theories, Architectures, and Languages*, pages 261–276. Springer-Verlag, 1996.
3. Rosaria Conte and Cristiano Castelfranchi. *Cognitive and Social Action*. UCL Press, London, 1995.
4. Frank Dignum and Bernd van Linder. Modelling social agents: Communication as action. In *Intelligent Agents III: Agent Theories, Architectures, and Languages*, pages 205–218. Springer-Verlag, 1997.
5. E. Allen Emerson. Temporal and modal logic. In Jan van Leeuwen, editor, *Handbook of Theoretical Computer Science*, volume B, pages 995–1072. North-Holland, Amsterdam, 1990.
6. Ronald Fagin, Joseph Y. Halpern, Yoram Moses, and Moshe Y. Vardi. *Reasoning About Knowledge*. MIT Press, Cambridge, MA, 1995.
7. H. P. Grice. Logic and conversation. In P. Cole and J. L. Morgan, editors, *Syntax and Semantics, Volume 3*. Academic Press, New York, 1975. Reprinted in [12].
8. Paul Grice. Utterer's meaning and intentions. *Philosophical Review*, 1969. Reprinted in [12].
9. Jürgen Habermas. *The Theory of Communicative Action, volumes 1 and 2*. Polity Press, Cambridge, UK, 1984.
10. Yannis Labrou and Tim Finin. Semantics and conversations for an agent communication language. In *Proceedings of the International Joint Conference on Artificial Intelligence*, 1997.

11. Hector J. Levesque, Philip R. Cohen, and Jose T. Nunes. On acting together. In *Proceedings of the National Conference on Artificial Intelligence*, pages 94–99, 1990.
12. Aloysius P. Martinich, editor. *The Philosophy of Language*. Oxford University Press, New York, 1985.
13. Gerald Midgley. The ideal of unity and the practice of plurality in systems science. In Robert L. Flood and Norma R. A. Romm, editors, *Critical Systems Thinking: Current Research and Practice*, chapter 2, pages 25–36. Plenum Press, New York, 1996.
14. Juan A. Rodríguez-Aguilar, Francisco J. Martín, Pablo Noriega, Pere Garcia, and Carles Sierra. Towards a test-bed for trading agents in electronic auction markets. *AI Communications*, 11(1):5–19, 1998.
15. John R. Searle. *The Construction of Social Reality*. Free Press, New York, 1995.
16. John R. Searle. *Mind, Language, and Society: Philosophy in the Real World*. Basic Books, New York, 1998.
17. Munindar P. Singh. *Multiagent Systems: A Theoretical Framework for Intentions, Know-How, and Communications*. Springer-Verlag, Heidelberg, 1994.
18. Munindar P. Singh. Agent communication languages: Rethinking the principles. *IEEE Computer*, 31(12):40–47, December 1998.
19. Munindar P. Singh. An ontology for commitments in multiagent systems: Toward a unification of normative concepts. *Artificial Intelligence and Law*, 1999. In press.
20. Ira A. Smith and Philip R. Cohen. Toward a semantics for an agent communications language based on speech-acts. In *Proceedings of the National Conference on Artificial Intelligence*, pages 24–31, 1996.
21. David R. Traum. A reactive-deliberative model of dialogue agency. In *Intelligent Agents III: Agent Theories, Architectures, and Languages*, pages 157–171. Springer-Verlag, 1997.
22. Mahadevan Venkatraman and Munindar P. Singh. Verifying compliance with commitment protocols: Enabling open web-based multiagent systems. *Autonomous Agents and Multi-Agent Systems*, 2(3):217–236, September 1999.
23. Egon M. Verharen. *A Language-Action Perspective on the Design of Cooperative Information Agents*. Catholic University, Tilburg, Holland, 1997.
24. Douglas N. Walton and Erik C. W. Krabbe. *Commitment in Dialogue: Basic Concepts of Interpersonal Reasoning*. State University of New York Press, Albany, 1995.
25. Terry Winograd and Fernando Flores. *Understanding Computers and Cognition: A New Foundation for Design*. Addison-Wesley, Reading, MA, 1987.

Some Legal Aspects of Inter-agent Communication:
From the Sincerity Condition to 'Ethical' Agents

Jeremy Pitt and Abe Mamdani

Intelligent & Interactive Systems Group, Department of Electrical & Electronic
Engineering
Imperial College of Science, Technology & Medicine, Exhibition Road, London, SW7
2BZ, UK
Email: {j.pitt, e.mamdani}@ic.ac.uk
URL: http://www-ics.ee.ic.ac.uk/

Abstract. The so-called sincerity condition, that an agent believes what
it communicates, is often specified as a semantic condition on performing
a declarative type of speech act in an Agent Communication Language
(ACL). We argue that the sincerity condition should not be part of the
normative standard semantics of an ACL, although it is useful as an
informative guideline for co-operating agents. We need instead to distinguish the meaning of the declarative performative in isolation from its
meaning as used in the context of a conversation or application. As a result, we can begin to appreciate some of the legal implications underlying
agent communications.

1 Introduction

Two commonly used Agent Communication Languages (ACLs) are KQML
[FLM95] and FIPA'97 [FIP97]. They each include a primitive performative for
communicating information in a declarative type of speech act: tell in KQML
and inform in FIPA ACL. Attempts have been made to define the semantics of
the speech act in terms of the intentional stance, i.e. mental attitudes in terms
of beliefs, desires and intentions. In both cases, the meaning of the speech act
specifies a semantic condition that the agent believes the content of the speech
act [LF98,FIP97]. This is the so-called sincerity condition, that an agent believes
what it communicates.

   In this paper, we undertake an analysis of the sincerity condition as a semantic condition for planning and performing a declarative speech act by an agent
in a multi-agent system. This is done specifically with respect to the proposed
semantics for the standard FIPA ACL inform performative. We conclude that
the sincerity condition (as formulated in FIPA ACL) is too strong for a normative specification of a standard semantics. However, there are sound reasons
for a sender to adhere to it, and for a receiver to assume it, in order for two

F. Dignum and M. Greaves (Eds.): Agent Communication, LNAI 1916, pp. 46–62, 2000.
© Springer-Verlag Berlin Heidelberg 2000

agents to co-operate. For this reason, we may seek to include it as part of an informative specification and assimilate it as one behaviour (out of many possible behaviours) of an agent.

In Section 2, we briefly survey the FIPA ACL in general and the semantics of its inform performative in particular, and define the sincerity condition formally. Section 3 presents some 'straw man' arguments in favour of the sincerity condition as part of a normative standard semantics. We counter these on the grounds that the FIPA sincerity condition cannot be verified for compliance in practice, that it is disruptive for certain useful agent applications, and that it cannot provide the assurances demanded of it. In section 4 we investigate the sincerity condition as a prerequisite for co-operation, and consider other axiomatisations which could trigger an inform speech act without an explicitly held belief in the content of that act.

Section 5 is concerned with specifying the sincerity condition as part of an informative specification, allowing it to be strengthened or relaxed according to application and context. We make some concluding remarks in Section 6, where in particular we can begin to appreciate some of the legal implications underlying agent communications.

2   FIPA ACL and the Inform Performative

The FIPA (Foundation for Intelligent Physical Agents) standardisation body has produced a set of specifications outlining a generic model for the architecture and operation of agent-based systems. The FIPA 97 Specification Part 2 is the normative specification of an Agent Communication Language (ACL) which agents use to 'talk' to each other. This is loosely based on speech act theory and defined in terms of a set of performatives or communicative acts. A communicative act occurs whenever one agent sends a message to another.

Each communicative act is given a meaning informally via English descriptions, and a formal semantics in a first order modal logic of mental attitudes and actions, which define feasibility preconditions and rational effects (intended outcomes) of communicative acts, and various agent properties. The logical definitions generally characterise the belief state of the sending agent before performing the communicative act, and the intended belief state of the receiving agent after the act has been performed. Underlying these definitions are a number of properties which an agent can use either to plan a communicative act (i.e. send a message), or to make inferences from 'hearing'/'observing' a communicative act (i.e. receiving a message). These properties are formalised as axioms of the logic.

We are concerned with exploring the formal, (proposed) standard semantics of the FIPA ACL inform performative. This can be summarised below (an explanation of the notation follows):

Performative	Feasibility Preconditions (FP)		Rational Effect (RE)
	inform FP1	inform FP2	
$< s, \mathsf{inform}(r, p) >$	$\mathcal{B}_s p$	$\neg \mathcal{B}_s(\mathcal{B}\mathrm{if}_r p \vee \mathcal{U}\mathrm{if}_r p)$	$\mathcal{B}_r p$

Intuitively, the inform performative is used by some agent s (say) to tell another agent r (say) that some proposition p (say) is true. We will refer to the agent performing the communicative act, in this case S, as the sending agent, and the agent towards whom the act is performed, in this case r, as the receiving agent.

In FIPA, agents either believe propositions or are uncertain about propositions. Belief and uncertainty are indicated by relativised modalities that, for agent s, would be $\mathcal{B}_s$ and $\mathcal{U}_s$ respectively. Belief and uncertainty are mutually exclusive: knowledge in FIPA's logic is an abbreviation for "belief or uncertainty". The abbreviation $\mathcal{B}\mathrm{if}_s p$ is defined as $\mathcal{B}_s p \vee \mathcal{B}_s \neg p$ and $\mathcal{U}\mathrm{if}_s p$ is defined as $\mathcal{U}_s p \vee \mathcal{U}_s \neg p$.

The feasibility preconditions (FP) of a performative are those conditions that need to be true in order for an agent to (plan to) execute a communicative act. The second feasibility precondition (inform FP2) is concerned with only communicating 'new' information, but it is the first condition that concerns us here. The first feasibility precondition, inform FP1, states that an agent performing the speech act, the sending agent s, believes that the proposition p is true. This precondition aims to ensure the so-called **sincerity condition**, and, as it is a precondition, the net effect is that agents believe what they say and only say what they believe.

The full import of the sincerity condition can be best appreciated when considering the FIPA-specified agent properties, two of which define the inferences an agent can make from observing a communicative act. These are called Property 4 and Property 5 and are defined, for all agents i as:

$$\text{Property 4: } \mathcal{B}_i(\mathrm{DONE}(A) \wedge Agent(j, A) \to \mathcal{I}_j \mathrm{RE}(A))$$
$$\text{Property 5: } \mathcal{B}_i(\mathrm{DONE}(A) \to \mathrm{FP}(A))$$

Property 4 states that if an agent i 'sees' that action A has 'just' taken place and agent j did action A, then i can infer that j had the intention to bring about the rational effect of A. Property 5 states that, from the same observation, agent i can infer that the feasibility preconditions of action A (that are unrelated to time) hold. The combined effect of inform FP1 and Property 5 are twofold. Firstly, if agent s believes a proposition p, then s will plan to use the inform performative to (try to) get r to believe p. Secondly, after the speech act agent r may (decide to) not believe p, but by virtue of the axiomatic Property 5, it can infer that agent s does believe p. Agent r is not mandated by the semantics to change its belief state to include a belief in p and correspondingly agent s cannot assume that this is necessarily the result.

3   The Sincerity Condition

The FIPA'97 specification includes a proposed standard ACL, and the semantic specification is proposed as a standard semantics, even if it is not entirely clear whether it is meant to be normative for the agents or informative for the developers. However, it appears to be the case that an agent is expected to at least behave as if it was following the semantic specification, and that all information communicated via an inform speech act was, in some sense, believed to be 'true'. This would be irrespective of whether the agent was implemented as a BDI (Beliefs-Desires-Intentions) agent with explicitly represented beliefs, or whether it was just doing a database look-up.

For some agent developers, the sincerity condition seems to be the cornerstone of an open multi-agent system. They would be satisfied with a specification in which agents could only communicate what they believed to be true, even if it turned out to be false, and otherwise insist on sincerity. A 'straw man' might argue that an agent is responsible for whatever it communicates, and could be held liable if it is found to have knowingly acted upon information it believed not to be true. Furthermore, while humans may lie, there is no reason for FIPA, as a standardisation body, to support (or even allow) agents which lie. Not to exclude lying would imply that it was legal, and that a lying agent was FIPA-compliant. In an electronic commerce application, it can be argued that agents which are insincere should not get the same treatment (i.e. absence of sanction) as those that are not. Since actual contracts and costs will be awarded and accrued to agents in such a multi-agent system, then lying agents should be sanctioned, and declared non-FIPA-compliant. Agents, and their developers, should be responsible for sincerity, and if shown not to be, ought to be held liable (cf. [HW98]).

These are powerful arguments, but we would counter them on the following grounds: (1) that the sincerity condition cannot be verified for compliance in practice, (2) that it is disruptive for certain useful agent interactions, and (3) that it cannot provide the legal assurances demanded of it. We develop each of these counter-arguments in turn (and see also [Sin98]).

3.1   Verification

The issue of verification is particularly thorny [Woo98]. In practice, we expect that it would be extremely difficult to determine whether or not an agent is abiding by the sincerity condition. For example, an unscrupulous agent implementer could work-around the precondition in the following way. Suppose agent s does not believe p but wants to inform r that p. Then s adds p to its database (inform FP1, the sincerity condition, is satisfied), s performs $< s, \mathsf{inform}(r, p) >$ (s tells its lie), and then removes p from its database.

Of course this is a trick, but an agent doing this is still technically complying with the semantic definitions. Furthermore, it is not possible to distinguish between the 'trick' behaviour, and that of any agent with a mental state that is non-monotonic over time, even if all information is time stamped in some way (that is not explicit in the FIPA specification). It is also possible for 'lying' to be created by a straightforward bug in the code, and given all the disclaimers that come with software licenses any legal redress in such cases is likely to be null.

It could however be argued that the agent is actually responsible for its beliefs, and should be held liable if it can be shown to have acted on the negation of a belief. We are then trying to distinguish between, on the one hand, a sincere agent that inadvertently communicated (as being true) something that it believed to be true but was actually false, and, on the other, a malicious agent that willfully communicated (as being true) something it believed to be false (and was actually false). But *showing* this might only be possible with full access to source code and the ability to exactly recreate transient system conditions at the time of the alleged 'lie'.

We would therefore say that since we cannot verify sincerity, there is no point mandating it. Some might say that this is analogous to saying that since we cannot absolutely verify people's intentions, we should not attempt to distinguish between various degrees of criminality. Nevertheless, various legal systems are set up to attempt to infer a person's intentions. Therefore, despite the difficulties, perhaps we should try to infer an agent's intentions.

There are however, limitations associated with this endeavour. On the one hand, it has been commented that Garry Kasparov, when playing Deep Blue 2, admitted to playing better against it when he thought of it as playing with intentions rather than as a state machine. However, Deep Blue 2 was essentially a state machine, albeit a highly optimised one, and certainly had no explicitly represented beliefs, desires, strategy or intentions. The BDI abstraction here was helpful. On the other hand, complex agents may be constructed without using BDI specifications. The 'history' of software engineering has illustrated how hard it is to verify the correct performance of software with respect to its actual requirements, design and specification, so trying to verify behaviour with respect to intended specifications seems to be not so helpful.

Still, at one time animals were tried for crimes [Eva98] and their intentions analysed, so perhaps it is not unreasonable to suppose that one day an agent can be put on trial in the same way. However, the real point is that it is the *owner* of the agent who is ultimately liable, and not for programming an agent to communicate false information, but for programming an agent to communicate false information and thereby seek or achieve gain which causes unlawful loss or damage to another party.

3.2   Agent Interactions

There are certain circumstances where sincerity is certainly desirable, for example commercial activity, but there are others where it is not, e.g. certain role playing games. Examples of the latter include the board-game Diplomacy, where players connive their way to European conquest, and, in an electronic setting, Multi-User Dungeons, where some players act by tricking their way into the confidence of another, before assassinating them. Even in the former case, though, while desirable, sincerity is routinely flouted (only we do not call it lying, we call it 'marketing' or 'advertising').

More seriously, many multi-agent systems are being developed for some kind of electronic commercial activity and underpinning these applications is some notion of negotiation. The idea of sincerity is somewhat compromised under these circumstances. In fact, the FIPA specification specifically notes ([FIP97], p18) a possible extension wherein an agent may intend an action without necessarily intending its precondition. For example, in negotiation an agent may bid some price as its opening bid, but be willing to accept some other price to conclude a deal. To be more precise, much human social activity (and not merely commercial activity) requires the freedom to be "economical with the truth". This is such an important aspect of intelligence that we could say that only the naive and/or unintelligent will always tell the whole truth.

For example, as a first approximation to a formalisation of negotiation by haggling between a buyer and a seller, we have, for the seller of some goods, that it believes (inter alia) that there is:

An offer price (for sale) Y_s
An actual price (known cost) W_s where $W_s < Y_s$
Some intended sale price X_s where $W_s < X_s \leq Y_s$

The seller will sell at Y_s if it can find a 'mug punter' willing to pay 'top whack'. In the final inequality Y_s is strictly greater than W_s on the assumption that the seller wants to make a profit, if it just wants to make a sale (without making a loss) then $X_s \geq W_s$. It is assumed that the seller knows the actual price (i.e. cost to the seller) of the goods being sold.

For the buyer, by contrast, we have the beliefs that there is:

An offer price (to buy) Y_b
A price limit (estimated worth) W_b where $W_b \geq Y_b$
Some intended buying price X_b where $W_b \geq X_b \geq Y_b$

Here we are assuming that the buyer of the goods makes an estimate of their worth via some utility function, and will not pay in excess of this valuation.

The two parties involved in the negotiation are essentially trying to find some value $X_s = X_b$, given the other four values. Ignoring situations where the buyer and seller cannot reach agreement, the buyer-seller system is then in equilibrium (sale occurs) if:

$$\exists X_b.\exists X_s.Y_b \leq X_b = X_s \leq Y_s \land X_b \leq W_b \land X_s > W_s$$

In human terms, a haggle dialogue initiated by the buyer might go something like: buyer — "What is the price of this item?"; seller — "Y_s"; buyer — "I'll give you Y_b"; after which the seller and buyer exchange revised values of Y_s and Y_b, until they converge on and agree a price. While we do not want to be drawn into a complete formal logical analysis of this situation, it seems to us that underpinning the communication of the prices are a number of implicit inferences and entailments that are entirely context dependent. To start with, when the buyer asks "the price", s/he is aiming to know X_b (the actual sale price), is prepared to be told Y_s (an offer sale price), and ideally would find out W_s (the actual price). Whatever was referred to, the seller interprets "the price" to mean Y_s. When the seller states "Y_s" the buyer is supposed to infer firstly, that although she asked for an actual sale price this is in fact the initial offer of a sale price, and secondly, that by haggling the buyer can purchase it more cheaply at the actual sale price.

In an agent system, we could represent, the beliefs ($\mathcal{B}$) and desires ($\mathcal{D}$) of the selling agent s as:

$$\mathcal{B}_s \, offer\_sale\_price(item, Y_s) \wedge price(item, W_s) \wedge W_s < Y_s$$
$$\mathcal{D}_s \exists X_s . actual\_sale\_price(item, X_s) \wedge (price(item, W_s) \rightarrow W_s < X_s))$$

Now while we might formally distinguish between offer sale prices, actual sale prices, and actual prices (worth), humans use short cuts like "price" to refer to all three and context to disambiguate between them. Agents, in contrast, tend to be a little more literal, so that if the buying agent now asked, using FIPA ACL, the question "What is the price of this item?", we might end up with something like:

$$< buying\_agent, \mathsf{query\_ref}(selling\_agent, \iota x : price(item, x)) >$$

The reply to which might be:

$$< selling\_agent, \mathsf{inform}(buying\_agent, x = Y_s) >$$

The question is: has the selling agent told a 'lie'? As we said above, only a naive or unintelligent agent would respond with content $x = W_s$. If an agent asks about price, a not-so-naive selling agent will respond with the *offer_sale_price*, not the actual price. The selling agent will not mind if the buying agent buys at this price, but suppose the buying agent finds out it could have got *item* at a cheaper price. Could we then expect the following dialogue between the respective agent owners:

Buying_agent owner — your agent told my agent the price was Y_s!
Selling_agent owner — yes, but my agent thought your agent meant an offered sale price!

This means that actually the reply to a $\mathsf{query\_ref}$ regarding price should be a refuse (i.e. the selling agent will not reveal the (actual) price, or cost); and to get a usable answer the buying agent must explicitly ask about the offered sale price:

$$< buying\_agent, \mathsf{query\_ref}(selling\_agent, \iota x : offer\_sale\_price(item, x)) >$$

What we are seeing here is that the 'standard' semantics is forcing the agents/developers to make explicit in the content language features of the application which are contextually or even culturally determined. We experienced this also in the MARINER project (see [PM99b]), although we will not develop that here: we shall however return to the situation of haggling agents in Section 5.2 below.

3.3   Legal Assurances

This leads on to our final counter-argument against the sincerity condition being a standard item, which is against the claim that an agent can be liable to a penalty if shown to be non-sincere. We have already discussed the potential practical difficulty of showing an agent to be an insincere, but we would further argue that legal liability for telling a lie is unlikely to be enforceable in practice either. In our opinion, it would be somewhat over-optimistic to implement an agent for electronic commerce in an open environment and expect everyone to be telling the truth, FIPA-compliant or not. The sincerity condition alone, even as part of a standard, is never going to guarantee honest trading. The defence will probably involve some electronic equivalent of the well-established legal precedent of *caveat emptor*, which in some sense requires that the goods exchange in an electronic sale have been fully 'inspected'.

However, it is important to note that different human commercial transactions have developed their own conventions that are also backed by other legal precedents. For example, in the UK, a bid at certain auction houses establishes a verbal contract and the bidder can be liable to pay if the bid is accepted. An offer on a house (to buy it), however, is not binding, nor is the sale price, at any time until contracts have been exchanged. A bet in the UK, on the other hand, even with a betting slip recording the details of the wager, does not constitute a legally binding contract. The bookmaker is not legally obliged to honour a winning bet.

Therefore, other legal mechanisms are required, i.e. digital signatures, enforceable contracts, Quality of Service guarantees, certification authorities, trusted-third parties, and so on. It is these mechanisms which will form the basis of legal agreements in agent-mediated human commerce. In this framework, agents may 'be economical with the truth' to win a contract and should not be sanctioned for this behaviour, but should certainly be sanctioned for breaking the contract if they do so. Again, as with haggling, betting, auctions, buying houses etc., the terms and conditions of winning a contract are domain dependent. For example, there may be certain pre-conditions associated with making a bid or an offer. A bid with a legally-binding, digitally-signed assertion that the agent satisfies the pre-conditions would be fraudulent, and liable to legal action. A bid without such preconditions may be won on the basis of statements that are not sincerely believed. Provided this establishes a binding contract, punishment can be reserved for failing to fulfil the contract – not the insincere belief.

Agents, or at least their developers, should be aware of what their legal commitments are, but this should only apply to external agreements, not internal arrangements. Sincerity is an agent-internal matter. However, in managing the transition to new forms of commerce mediated by agents, FIPA may have a vital role. There are substantial differences between cultures with regard to statutory rights and legal precedents, and so internationally agreed standards are an important tool in regulation and control.

4   The Axiomatisation of Communication

The motivation and requirement for FIPA inform FP1, to our current way of thinking, goes beyond liability. The formalisation of intentional communicative behaviour for an intelligent agent often involves the axiomatisation of the felicity conditions of Searle and the conversational maxims of Grice. The sincerity condition underpinned Grice's analysis of conversational implicatures to support the so-called co-operativity principle. Therefore, from the viewpoint of an agent developer who wants his/her agents to inter-operate co-operatively, the following facts are significant:

 – that the sincerity condition is predicated on the notion of co-operation; and
 – that all speech acts involve the receiver recognizing an intention on the part of the sender.

Therefore, when an agent uses an inform performative in the context of a negotiation protocol for some joint co-operation, the sending agent has to be sincere with respect to its beliefs (i.e. it is pre-disposed to co-operate), otherwise the receiving agent cannot reason (e.g. using FIPA's Property 4 and 5 above) to recognize the sender's intentions in order to co-operate.

The problem with relaxing the sincerity condition is that it pulls down Property 5 with it, because there is an intrinsic asymmetry in the FIPA specification. A FIPA agent is an imperfect witness of perfect integrity: it may communicate incorrect information but at least it believes it to be true. The receiver does not have to believe the content, but it is axiomatic that the sender must have believed it. If, however, whether or not the receiver actually believes the content is a function of trust or reliability of sender, surely then whether or not the receiver actually believes the sender's belief is a similar function of trustworthiness. Put another way: if you don't trust someone to tell you the truth, you don't trust them to believe what they tell you. If an agent s has an inaccurate sense of p it could equally have an inaccurate sense of $\mathcal{B}_s p$.

Furthermore, after $< s, \mathsf{inform}(r, p) >$ the receiving agent r may make no more reliable inferences from $\mathcal{B}_s p$ than it might make from just p. To take an extreme example, there may be a "Baywatch"-type lifeguard whose job it is to stop people swimming if there are sharks in the water. A 'swimmer agent' may have the following rules in its database:

$$no\_sharks \rightarrow safe\_to\_go\_swimming$$
$$\mathcal{B}_{baywatch\_agent} no\_sharks \rightarrow safe\_to\_go\_swimming$$

So after the speech act:

$$< baywatch\_agent, \mathsf{inform}(swimmer\_agent, no\_sharks) >,$$

if *swimmer_agent* is FIPA compliant, it may not believe that there are no sharks, but because of FIPA Property 5, it may infer that it is safe to go swimming. The inference to be made is still unsafe. More generally, if the agent developer codes an agent to make inferences based on other agents' beliefs, s/he may be running the same risks as if the agent just believed the content was true in the first place. As we see in the next section, the receiver's belief in the sender's belief in the content is just as much a matter of trust as the receiver's belief in the content itself.

It follows that FIPA Property 5 is not an axiom: it is just a reasonable assumption that follows from an initial assumption of an intention to co-operate. What we see as a result is the danger of trying to standardise the meaning of a performative in isolation through an axiomatisation that implicitly expects the performative to be used in conversation. In isolation, for example, we could motivate the behaviour of a sincere agent by the behavioural axiom which subsumes the sincerity condition of FIPA inform FP1:

$$\mathcal{B}_s\phi \wedge \mathcal{D}_s\mathcal{B}_r\phi \rightarrow \mathcal{I}_s(\text{DONE}(s, \text{inform}(r, \phi) >))$$

Here $\mathcal{D}$ and $\mathcal{I}$ are respectively the desires (goals) and intends modalities, and DONE is an operator on actions, defined in the FIPA specification as DONE(A) being true when action A has taken place. This axiom therefore states that if the agent s believed ϕ and wanted another agent r to believe ϕ then s would generate the intention to inform r of ϕ.

Alternatively we could define the behaviour of a 'rapacious' agent by the axiom:

$$\mathcal{D}_s\psi \wedge \mathcal{B}_s(\text{DONE}(A) \rightarrow \psi) \rightarrow \mathcal{I}_s(\text{DONE}(A))$$

This axiom states that if s desires (wants) ψ and believes that doing A will achieve ψ, then s will intend to do A. If we let $\psi = \mathcal{B}_r\phi$, then given the rational effect of an inform we get the equivalent communicative action ($A = <$ $s, \text{inform}(r, \phi) >$) but we bypass belief in ϕ altogether. However, it is important to note that with the first axiom the agent is being sincere with respect to its beliefs, and with the second axiom it is being sincere with respect to its desires [CL90].

In the absence of cooperation – for example, a multi-agent system where the agents are in competition – there appears to be no *a priori* reason why a sending agent should believe the content of its inform speech act. The field of DAI (Distributed Artificial Intelligence) has indeed broadly investigated two types of multi-agent system. Firstly, there are those systems in which the agents are prepared to surrender autonomy and sacrifice personal goals for the (pareto) optimality of the entire system. This is generally termed Distributed Co-operative Problem Solving, and, since co-operation is central, sincerity is a not unreasonable assumption. Secondly, there are systems in which the agents are nowadays described as *self-interested*. The assumption of being self-interested is important in open multi-agent systems, wherein the agents have been separately programmed by different parties and each explicitly has the satisfaction of their own goals first and foremost. A good example is the Competing Phone Companies in [RZ98] (companies bid the highest price to win a contract, but need not believe this is the actual price), but the idea is prevalent where there is some kind of computational market being analysed by economic models [WW98].

We would argue that one of the implications of intelligence is that a rational entity possesses the freedom to be as economical with the truth as necessary in order to satisfy its goals. It might therefore be necessary on occasions to make provision for an intelligent agent to act insincerely, and even, on occasions, to lie. However, it can be shown (e.g. [San98]) how to extend game-theoretic and economic modelling techniques and apply them to multi-agent systems, in such a way that the system cannot be manipulated by agents that can act insincerely. In such cases, the safeguard is a property of the system, not a feature of the communication language semantics.

5 Informative Specifications

One way out of this impasse would be to introduce a new performative, inform_without_prejudice, which is still an illocutionary act (rather than simply a locutionary act like assert) because it has intended rational effects. Defining $\mathcal{K}\mathrm{if}_s p$ as $\mathcal{B}_s p \vee \mathcal{B}_s \neg p$, then a semantics for inform_without_prejudice, distinct from the inform performative, is as shown below:

Performative	Feasibility Precondition	Rational Effect
inform_without_prejudice	$\mathcal{K}\mathrm{if}_s p$	$\mathcal{B}_r p$

In other words, the sender does not care whether this is 'new' information or not (there is no concern about the receiver's mental state), the sender still wants the receiver to believe the content (p), but now the receiver can infer nothing about the sender's actual belief in the proposition or its negation (e.g. by FIPA Property 5). The inference that the sender intended the receiver to believe p (e.g. from FIPA Property 4) may still be significant. However, we would like to propose a more general solution.

5.1 'One-off' Speech Acts

In [PM99a] we were concerned with articulating a protocol-based semantics for an ACL. The meaning of a speech act is specified as an intention to reply: the reply itself is conditioned by the inferential effect the content of the speech act has on the information state of the receiver, and the context in which the speech act occurred (i.e. the dialogue or conversation between two agents). We then showed how this could be linked to a BDI-agent architecture, where beliefs and desires triggered intentions, either proactively (to initiate a speech act), or reactively, to select a reply to a speech act. These proactive and reactive behaviours were formalised by what we called plan axiom schemata. Then, for example, we could specify (as above) the proactive behaviour, for a sending agent, for a one-off inform speech act (that is, a speech act that does not occur in the context of a protocol), as the axiom schema:

$$\mathcal{B}_s \phi \wedge \mathcal{D}_s \mathcal{B}_R \phi \rightarrow \mathcal{I}_s(\mathrm{DONE}(< s, \mathsf{inform}(R, \phi, \mathbf{no\_protocol}) >))$$

This states that if s believes p and wants (desires) r to believe p, then s intends to inform r of p, although it will not be using a mutually understood communication protocol.

Additionally, we could specify the reactive behavioural plan, for the actual receiving agent r, as the axiom schema:

$$[S, \mathsf{inform}(r, p, \mathbf{no\_protocol})]\mathcal{B}_r \phi$$

Here, the modal action formula $[a, A]p$ is read 'after agent a does action a, then p holds'. Therefore combination of the two formulas above states that after s informs r that p, r believes p.

These axiom schema would work for a system of trusted and trusting agents. The proactive plan effectively ensures the sincerity condition, and the reactive plan assumes that since the agents will not lie it is safe to believe the content.

However, as the FIPA specification notes [FIP97]: "Whether or not the receiver does, indeed, adopt belief in the proposition will be a function of the receiver's trust in the sincerity and reliability of the sender". Given this, whether or not the receiving agent does or does not believe that the content of an inform is true, should be a function of the trust or reliability that the receiving agent has in the sender. Therefore, in a multi-agent system, we may need some representation of the *trust* relationships between two agents. One agent may come to trust another if there is an agreed commitment to abide by the sincerity axiom for communication via informs. This commitment could be formalised in a legally binding contract.

Then we could put an extra condition on the reactive axiom schema for handling the content of inform speech acts, such that we have a way of believing the content (if the sender is known to be reliable) and believing the sender believes the content (if the sender is trusted, or sincere). For a receiving agent, this could be coded as:

$$[S, \mathsf{inform}(r, \phi, \mathbf{no\_protocol})](\mathcal{B}_r \, reliable(S) \rightarrow \mathcal{B}_r \phi) \land (\mathcal{B}_r \, trust(S) \rightarrow \mathcal{B}_r \mathcal{B}_s \phi)$$

Furthermore, if the trust relationship is mutually known to both sending and receiving agents, then this formula can equally apply to the reasoning of the sending agent, so that it can make inferences about the consequences of its own speech acts. The sending agent can infer that the receiving agent will believe the content, and the receiving agent can safely take the information 'on trust', as it were.

5.2   Haggling: Revisited

We next analyse the meaning of an inform speech act in the context of a conversation, specifically a haggle between a buying agent and a selling agent, as introduced in Section 3.2. We assume that the two agents will use the mutually understood and mutually agreed **haggle** protocol, which is illustrated by the finite state diagram shown in Figure 1.

Figure 1 shows that the conversation is initiated by the prospective buyer performing a query_if (a FIPA performative), which intuitively is inquiring about

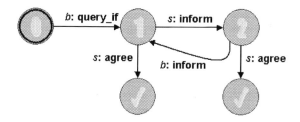

Fig. 1. Haggle Protocol

the price of some goods. After this speech act, the seller and buyer take alternate turns in offering prices using inform speech acts, until the seller agrees to sell or the buyer agrees to buy. The conversation is terminated at that point.

We can now specify the agents behaviour for the negotiation cycle of informs in the context of the haggle protocol between a buyer agent (b) and a selling agent (s). This specification satisfies the formal analysis presented in Section 3.2, and there is no sincerity *a la* sincerity condition in any communication. The basic idea is that after the initial query_if, the seller responds with an initial offer price Y_s. According to its evaluation of the offer, the buyer then responds with a counter-offer Y_b, and so on, until an agreement is reached.

The protocol is initiated by the buyer performing a query_if speech act. This action will be triggered by a combination of beliefs and desires, formally captured by the plan axiom schema:

$$\mathcal{D}_b own(item) \wedge [b, \mathsf{haggle}(s)]mathitown(item) \rightarrow \mathcal{I}_b < b, \mathsf{query\_ref}(s, \iota x :$$
$$price(item, x), \mathbf{haggle}) >$$

The response to this is determined by the reactive behaviour specified for the selling agent, which is encoded by the plan axiom schema:

$$[b, \mathsf{query\_ref}(s, \iota x : price(item, x), \mathbf{haggle})]\mathcal{I}_s < s, \mathsf{inform}(b, x = Y_s, \mathbf{haggle}) >$$

Now, for both buying and selling agent, we can specify the reactive behaviour for responding to an inform from the other agent. For the buyer, we have:

$$[s, \mathsf{inform}(b, x = Y_s, \mathbf{haggle})] \ ((Y_s > W_b) \rightarrow (compute\_offer(Y_s, PrevY_b, W_b, Y_b)$$
$$\wedge \qquad\qquad\qquad\qquad \mathcal{I}_b < b, \mathsf{inform}(s, x = Y_b, \mathbf{haggle}) >))$$
$$\vee$$
$$((Y_s \leq W_b) \rightarrow \mathcal{I}_b < b, \mathsf{agree}(s, x = Y_s, \mathbf{haggle}) >)$$

For the seller, we have:

$$[b, \mathsf{inform}(s, x = Y_b, \mathbf{haggle})] \ ((Y_b \leq W_s) \rightarrow (compute\_offer(Y_b, PrevY_s, W_s, Y_s)$$
$$\wedge \qquad\qquad\qquad\qquad \mathcal{I}_s < s, \mathsf{inform}(b, x = Y_s, \mathbf{haggle}) >))$$
$$\vee$$
$$((Y_b > W_s) \rightarrow \mathcal{I}_s < s, \mathsf{agree}(b, x = Y_b, \mathbf{haggle}) >)$$

The idea of *compute_offer* is to a take an offer from the other agent, the previous offer made by the agent itself, the worth of the goods to the agent (as a limit), and to compute a new offer which will be communicated to the other agent. Provided *compute_offer* is monotonic decreasing for the seller and monotonic increasing for the buyer, then the two parties should iterate toward a mutually satisfactory (equilibrium) sale price. It is straightforward to check that this specification satisfies the formal analysis of Section 3.2.

The protocol and plan specifications can be easily extended to allow for haggling where the two agents cannot reach agreement.

6   Summary and Conclusions

It has been noted that although both KQML and FIPA ACL base their messages on the theory of speech acts the outcome is quite different. The main reason proposed for this difference is the lack of consensus on the semantics of the communication between agents. This paper has identified the sincerity condition as one important item where the consensus is manifestly lacking. We have argued in Sections 3 and 4 of this paper that the sincerity condition is contingent upon the circumstances surrounding the inform speech act, and that it presents difficulties as part of a proposed *standard* semantics for a *standard* ACL. For example, applying the proposed standard for multi-agent systems appears to demand being very explicit in the content language for the semantics to be applicable in the class of computational market applications. We would therefore conclude that the FIPA analysis of sincerity is not sufficiently generic for a standard. However, we would say that sincerity of some kind (for example with respect to one goals) is a desirable agent property, and this might be supported by other analyses. In particular, one approach is to look it at the problem not from the view of sincerity on the speaker's side, but of trust on the receiver's side [JF99].

It has also been noted that although some work has been done on the semantics of individual speech acts, little is known about the semantics of conversations and the relations between speech acts and the conversations of which they form a part. We believe that the general semantic framework outlined by [PM99a] and applied in Section 5 of this paper, is a contribution to the knowledge about the meaning of speech acts and the conversations in which they occur. Furthermore, the occurrence of a speech act actually carries a certain contractual and/or legal weight, depending on the context in which it occurs.

For example, suppose some person arrives in a foreign city, takes a licensed taxi, and asks for an address. The taxi driver verbally agrees, but then drops that person at the wrong location. Who is to blame and what redress does the passenger have, if any? Is the licensing authority at fault for allowing an incompetent navigator with insufficient knowledge to trade as a taxi driver? Is the taxi driver personally responsible? Or is the passenger responsible and have no redress?

Looking in more detail at this scenario, there is an implicit contract between taxi driver and passenger: that the taxi driver will convey the passenger to a specified location in return for money. The taxi driver will use a vehicle that is clearly identified as intended for that purpose and will have a number that licenses him/her to pursue this activity. This licence has been issued by some organization with the authority to do so. Thus we see that the implicit contract has been underwritten by an organization. These situations are very common but vary from situation to situation. For example, in the UK:

- Making an offer to purchase a house: is not binding until a legal contract has been exchanged. After that, if the purchaser pulls out of the deal, s/he .forfeits the deposit, if the vendor pulls out, s/he is liable for the same amount, but needs to be sued through the courts;
- Making a bid in an auction house: establishes a verbal contract which is legally binding. If the bid is accepted and bidder refuses to pay, s/he can be sued through the courts;
- Placing a bet: a bet is not legally enforceable in the UK. Even with a valid betting slip, the bookmaker is not obliged to honour a winning bet.

All of these situations are likely to arise in the different agent societies of the future electronic commerce. Each of them will have different legal implications in the real world. The situated-ness of the electronic society will be an important factor in determining the legal obligations directly or indirectly associated with the 'real' world as a result of social commitments in the agent domain.

Indeed, we can go further by observing that the following rules govern certain human-human communications in UK law:

- If a speaker makes a false statement, knowing it to be false, with the intention that it acted upon by the hearer, who suffers damage, then the speaker will be liable in tort;
- If a speaker makes a false statement without knowing that it is false, then the speaker may be liable for violation of a duty of care to ensure that the information is correct (responsibility for negligent misstatements) under the following conditions: 1. The advice is required for a purpose known to the adviser; 2. The adviser knows that his advise will be communicated to the advisee; 3. It is known that the advice is likely to be acted upon.
- If the speaker makes a false statement, knowing it to be false, and so induces the other party to make a contract, than he will be liable for fraudulent misrepresentation (and the contract will be void).
- If the speaker makes a false statement, without knowing it to be false, and so induces the other party to make a contract, than he will be liable for negligent misrepresentation and the contract can be annulled. Moreover, the speaker will have to pay damages, unless he proves that he had good reasons for his wrong belief.

It may be that it is something like this framework that needs to be formalised to regulate agent–agent communcations.

Therefore, we think there may be something of substance in our analysis of the contention that the sincerity condition has a part to play in the legal conditioning of transactions between agents in a multi-agent system. While we are unconvinced that the sincerity condition itself is an appropriate mechanism for supporting the legal framework required for managing this aspect of a multi-agent system, something of the kind is required. The extent to which, and the mechanisms by which, ACL communications become or contribute to a legally binding and enforceable contract remain, to our minds, open questions, and one that the FIPA standardisation efforts should perhaps address.

We do not see the need for a standard to mandate that agents always live in fear of perjuring themselves. Various applications of multi-agent systems will require that agents are able to be economical with the truth to varying degrees [CTFF99]. A standard should seek more imaginative ways of recommending ethical behaviour of software agents. We are interested and encouraged to note that FIPA organised a symposium on *Intelligent Agents and Ethics* at one of its meetings last year. We are interested in carrying this work further in our future research.

Acknowledgements This paper is a spin-off from a broader analysis of the FIPA ACL semantics [PM99b], and in particular a detailed response to referees' comments we received, seemingly in favour of the sincerity condition. The 'straw man' arguments of Section 3 are therefore theirs. It is our hope that we have not misrepresented them and indeed we have been stimulated to write this paper because of them. For these thoughtful and stimulating comments we would like to acknowledge an intellectual debt.

This work has been undertaken in the context of the UK-EPSRC/Nortel Networks funded Project CASBAh (Common Agent Service Brokering Architecture, EPSRC Grant No. GR/L34440), and support from these funding bodies is also gratefully acknowledged.

We are also highly appreciative of discussions with colleagues, in particular Cristiano Castelfranchi, Andrew Jones, and Giovanni Sartor, the many detailed and constructive comments of the anonymous reviewers, and the help and support of the editors, Frank Dignum and Mark Greaves.

References

[CL90]   P. Cohen and H. Levesque. Rational Interaction as the basis for Communication. In P. Cohen, J. Morgan and M. Pollack (eds.): Intentions in Communication. MIT Press, 1990.

[CTFF99] C. Castelfranchi, Y.H. Tan, R. Falcone and B. Firozabadi (eds.). Deception, Fraud and Trust in Agent Societies. Workshop 7, Autonomous Agents AA'99, Seattle, 1999.

[Eva98]   E. P. Evans. The Criminal Prosecution and Capital Punishment of Animals. New York: E.P. Dutton, 1906. Reprinted The Lawbook Exchange Ltd, 1998. [Finin et al, 1995] T. Finin, Y. Labrou and J. Mayfield. KQML as an Agent Communication Language. In J. Bradshaw (ed.), Software Agents, MIT Press, 1995.

[FIP97]   FIPA, FIPA 97 Specification Part 2: Agent Communication Language. FIPA (Foundation for Intelligent Physical Agents), http://drogo.cselt.stet.it/fipa/, 28th November, 1997.

[FLM95]   T. Finin, Y. Labrou, and J. Mayfield. KQML as an agent communication language. In J. Bradshaw, editor, *Software Agents*. MIT Press, 1995.

[HW98]   C. Heckman and J. Wobbrock. Liability for Autonomous Agent Design. Proceedings Autonomus Agents AA'98, pp392-399, 1998.

[JF99]   A. Jones, and B. Sadighi Firozabadi. On the Characterisation of a Trusting Agent: Aspects of a Formal Approach. To appear.

[LF98]   Y. Labrou, and T. Finin. Semantics for an Agent Communication Language. In M. Singh, A. Rao and M. Wooldridge (eds.), Intelligent Agents IV, LNAI1365, Springer- Verlag, 1998.

[PM99a]   J. Pitt and A. Mamdani. A Protocol-Based Semantics for an Agent Communication Language. Accepted for publication in Proceedings 16th International Joint Conference on Artificial Intelligence, Stockholm, Sweden, to appear (1999).

[PM99b]   J. Pitt and A. Mamdani. Some Remarks on the Semantics of FIPA's Agent Communication Language. Accepted for publication in Journal of Autonomous Agents and Multi-Agent Systems, Kluwer Academic Press, to appear.

[RZ98]   J. Rosenschein and G. Zlotkin. Rules of Encounter. MIT Press, 1998.

[San98]   T. Sandholm. Agents in Electronic Commerce: Component Technologies for Automated Negotiation and Coalition Formation. In M. Klusch (ed.): Cooperative Information Agents, LNAI1435, Springer Verlag, pp.113-134, 1998.

[Sin98]   M. Singh. Agent Communication Languages: Rethinking the Principles. IEEE Computer, pp40-47, December, 1998.

[WW98]   M. Wellman and P. Wurman. Market-aware agents for a multiagent world. Robotics and Autonomous Systems, 24:115-125, 1998.

[Woo98]   M. Wooldridge. Verifiable Semantics for Agent Communication Languages. Proceedings ICMAS-98, Paris, France, 1998.

Semantics of Communicating Agents
Based on Deduction and Abduction

Koen V. Hindriks, Frank S. de Boer, Wiebe van der Hoek, and John-Jules Ch. Meyer

University Utrecht, Department of Computer Science
P.O. Box 80.089, 3508 TB Utrecht, The Netherlands
tel. +31-30-2539267
{koenh,frankb,wiebe,jj}@cs.uu.nl

Abstract. Intelligent agents in the agent language 3APL are computational entities consisting of beliefs and goals which make up their mental state. In this paper, we integrate communication at the agent level into the language 3APL. Communication at the agent level consists of communication between agents of their beliefs and goals. We propose two pairs of communication primitives for agent level communication. The semantics of these primitives is based on two distinct types of reasoning: deduction and abduction. Deduction serves to derive information from a received message. Abduction serves to obtain proposals in reply to requests. We illustrate the use of these communication primitives for agents by an implementation of a multi-stage negotiation protocol. We also discuss the relation of our approach to approaches to communication based on speech act theory.

1   Introduction

Intelligent agents in the agent language 3APL (pronounced "*triple-a-p-l*") are computational entities consisting of beliefs and goals which make up their mental state. 3APL agents use so-called *plan rules* to find plans for their goals (cf. [5]). In this paper, we integrate communication at the agent level into the language 3APL. Communication at the agent level consists of communication between agents of their beliefs and goals. We propose two pairs of communication primitives for agent level communication. The first pair of communication primitives, tell and ask, is used to exchange information between agents. The second pair of communication primitives, req and offer, is used to communicate requests between agents. We provide a clear and formal semantics for these communication primitives. The semantics of the primitives is based on two distinct types of reasoning: deduction and abduction. Deduction serves to derive information from a received message. The use of deduction in the specification of the semantics of information exchange is similar to that of other communication primitives proposed in the literature (cf. [11]). Abduction serves to obtain proposals in reply to requests. A semantics based on abduction is provided for the req and offer primitives.

We illustrate the use of the two communication primitives in a multi-agent meeting scheduling example. The example shows how to implement a multi-stage negotiation protocol in 3APL extended with the new communication primitives. The implementation of the protocol in 3APL is both intuitive and natural, and illustrates the expressive power of the agent programming language and communication primitives.

F. Dignum and M. Greaves (Eds.): Agent Communication, LNAI 1916, pp. 63–79, 2000.

The extension of the single agent language 3APL with communication primitives to a multi-agent language, the idea to use abduction as a semantics for the exchange of a request, and the implementation of a multi-stage negotiation protocol which illustrates the use of the communication primitives are the main contributions of this paper.

We discuss our approach to communication and other approaches based on speech act theory, like KQML ([7]) and FIPA ([4]). We argue that speech act theory should not be viewed as a repository of many different speech acts for which computational equivalents should be provided. Instead, we aim to keep the agent communication language as simple and clear as possible, while maintaining that speech act theory may be useful for the specification and verification of agent systems.

2   The Agent Language 3APL

Intelligent agents in 3APL are entities which represent their environment by means of their beliefs, control this environment by means of actions which are part of their goals or plans, and find plans for their goals using plan rules.

The beliefs of an agent are formulas from a first order language $\mathcal{L}$. We assume that an *entailment relation*, denoted by $\models$, is associated with this language. Moreover, we assume the logical language has associated sets of variables Var, terms T, and atoms At. The free variables from Var in an expression e are denoted by Free(e).

Next we give a formal definition of 3APL goals or plans. 3APL goals are imperative-like programs built from a set of basic goals and the usual imperative constructs, that is, sequential composition and nondeterministic choice.

Definition 1. (goals and basic actions)
Let $\mathcal{B}$ be a set of basic action symbols with typical elements a, a', *and $\mathcal{L}$ be a first-order language. The set of goals* Goal *is defined by: (1) if* a $\in \mathcal{B}$ *and* $t_1, \ldots, t_n \in$ T, *then* a$(t_1, \ldots, t_n) \in$ Goal; *(2)* At $\subseteq$ Goal; *(3) if* $\varphi \in \mathcal{L}$, *then* φ? $\in$ Goal; *and (4) if* $\pi_1, \pi_2 \in$ Goal, *then* $(\pi_1;\ \pi_2), (\pi_1 + \pi_2) \in$ Goal.

The *basic actions* a(t), *achievement goals* $p(t)$, and the *test goals* φ? are the *basic goals* of the agent language. Basic actions are used to achieve the goals of the agent and are interpreted as *update operators* on the belief base. For example, the action ins(*meet(MeetId, Time, Length, Location, Att)*) inserts the fact that a meeting *MeetId* will take place at time *Time* of duration *Length* at location *Location* with attendants *Att* in the belief base. The atomic formulas $p(t)$ of the logical language are also used as an abstraction mechanism to specify that the agent wants to achieve $p(t)$. Plan rules introduced below provide the means to find a plan for an achievement goal. The last type of basic goal, a test goal φ?, can be used to inspect the belief base of the agent to see if a proposition φ follows from it and to compute bindings for free variables in a test (as in logic programming). The complex goals are compositions of basic goals, constructed by using the programming constructs for sequential composition and nondeterministic choice. This allows the specification of a sequence of goals $\pi_1;\ \pi_2$ and disjunctive goals $\pi_1 + \pi_2$ by means of nondeterministic choice.

Next we define the set of plan rules. Plan rules are similar to (recursive) procedures in imperative programming. Plan rules provide for plans which can be used to achieve achievement goals.

Definition 2. (plan rules)
The set of plan rules Rule *is defined by: if* $p(t), \pi \in$ Goal *and* $\varphi \in \mathcal{L}$, *then* $p(t) \leftarrow \varphi \mid \pi \in$ Rule. *If* $p(t) \leftarrow \varphi \mid \pi$ *is a rule, then* $p(t)$ *is called the* head *of the rule,* φ *is called the* guard *of the rule, and* π *is called the* body *of the rule.*

In case the head of a plan rule matches with one of the current achievement goals of the agent, and the guard is entailed by the agents beliefs, then the plan rule can be applied and the achievement goal is replaced by the plan in the body of the rule.

To program an agent means to specify a unique name for the agent, specify its mental state consisting of the beliefs and goals of the agent, and to write a set of plan rules. An agent may have several different goals at the same time. These goals are executed in parallel.

Definition 3. (intelligent agent)
An intelligent agent *is a tuple* $\langle a, \Pi, \sigma, \Gamma \rangle$ *where a is the* name *of the agent,* $\Pi \subseteq$ Goal *is called the* goal base, $\sigma \in \mathcal{L}$ *is called the* belief base, *and* $\Gamma \subseteq$ Rule *is a set of plan rules, also called the* rule base.

A *mental state* is a pair $\langle \Pi, \sigma \rangle$, where $\Pi \subseteq$ Goal and $\sigma \in \mathcal{L}$, consisting of the goals and beliefs at a particular moment during execution. The goal and belief base are the only components of an agent that change during the execution of that agent. The rule base of the agent remains fixed during a computation.

The *operational semantics* of the agent language is defined by a Plotkin-style transition system ([8]). A transition system consists of a set of *transition rules* where each transition rule consists of zero or more premises and a conclusion. A transition system is an inductive definition of a transition relation $\longrightarrow$, where each transition corresponds to a *single computation step*. We use the notion of a *labelled* transition system. Labels are used to distinguish different types of transitions and allow an elegant modelling of communication. A distinction is made between transitions labelled with τ and transitions labelled with communication labels. The label τ is associated with *completed* actions of the agent, while the communication labels are associated with *attempts* to communicate. The transition relation associated with 3APL is a relation defined at several levels of the agent system: (i) at the level of a goal of the agent, (ii) at the level of an agent, and (iii) at the level of a multi-agent system.

The agent level in the language 3APL consists of the mental state of the agent, that is, its goal and belief base. At this level, an agent may execute an action by choosing a goal or plan from its goal base and selecting an action from this plan. An agent may pick any plan in its current goal base that can be executed, execute it, and update its mental state accordingly. Alternatively, an agent may select a plan rule which is applicable to an achievement goal in its goal base and apply the rule to the goal.

In the transition rule below, l denotes a label associated with the transition. The θ denotes a substitution which is computed by executing tests. The substitution θ which is associated with transitions *at the goal level* provides for a parameter mechanism in 3APL similar to that of logic programming. The bindings for variables computed by tests are used to instantiate later occurrences of the variables in a goal. The purpose of the set of variables V is to prevent undesired interaction between variables and is in more detail explained in [5].

Definition 4. (agent level execution)
Let $V = \text{Free}(\pi_i)$ and let θ be a substitution.

$$\frac{\langle \pi_i, \sigma \rangle_V \xrightarrow{l}_\theta \langle \pi'_i, \sigma' \rangle}{\langle a, \{\pi_0, \ldots, \pi_i, \ldots, \pi_n\}, \sigma, \Gamma \rangle \xrightarrow{l} \langle a, \{\pi_0, \ldots, \pi'_i, \ldots, \pi_n\}, \sigma', \Gamma \rangle}$$

An agent is a multi-threaded entity. This means that an agent may have multiple goals at the same time which are executed in parallel. Transition rule 4 reduces a computation step at the *agent level* in the conclusion of the rule to a computation step of one of the goals of the agent (in the premise of the transition rule). The other transition rules in this section deal with transitions *at the goal level* associated with a pair $\langle \pi, \sigma \rangle$ where π is a goal and σ is a belief base.

A basic action is an update operator on the belief base. We assume a specification of the update semantics of basic actions is given by a *transition function $\mathcal{T}$*. For example, the semantics of ins could be defined as follows. For all ground instances of the variables *MeetId, Time, Length, Loc* and *Att*, define:
$$\mathcal{T}(\text{ins}(meet(MeetId, Time, Length, Loc, Att)), \sigma) = \sigma',$$
where $\sigma' = \sigma \wedge meet(MeetId, Time, Length, Loc, Att)$ if σ' is consistent; otherwise, $\mathcal{T}$ is undefined. (We use the convention that capital letters in the examples denote variables.)

A test φ? is used to test whether or not a proposition is believed by the agent and to retrieve information from the belief base. A test computes a set of bindings θ for free variables in the condition φ. These bindings are passed on to other parts of the goal of an agent and used to instantiate other occurrences of the variables for which bindings have been retrieved. The symbol E is used to denote (successful) termination in the transition system. We identify E; π with π and $\Pi \cup \{E\}$ with a goal base Π.

Definition 5. (basic actions)

$$\frac{\mathcal{T}(\text{a}(t_1, \ldots, t_n), \sigma) = \sigma'}{\langle \text{a}(t_1, \ldots, t_n), \sigma \rangle_V \xrightarrow{\tau}_\varnothing \langle E, \sigma' \rangle} \qquad \frac{\sigma \models \varphi\theta}{\langle \varphi?, \sigma \rangle_V \xrightarrow{\tau}_\theta \langle E, \sigma \rangle}$$

The execution of a sequential goal consists in executing the first part of the goal, recording any changes to the belief base, instantiating all variables for which a binding has been computed, and continuing with the execution of the remainder of the goal.

Definition 6. (sequential composition)

$$\frac{\langle \pi_1, \sigma \rangle_V \xrightarrow{l}_\theta \langle \pi'_1, \sigma' \rangle}{\langle \pi_1; \pi_2, \sigma \rangle_V \xrightarrow{l}_\theta \langle \pi'_1; \pi_2\theta, \sigma' \rangle}$$

The execution of a nondeterministic choice goal amounts to selecting one of the subgoals that is enabled, i.e. can be executed, execute this goal, and drop the other goal.

Definition 7. (nondeterministic choice)

$$\frac{\langle \pi_1, \sigma \rangle_V \xrightarrow{l}_\theta \langle \pi_1', \sigma' \rangle}{\langle \pi_1 + \pi_2, \sigma \rangle_V \xrightarrow{l}_\theta \langle \pi_1', \sigma' \rangle} \qquad \frac{\langle \pi_2, \sigma \rangle_V \xrightarrow{l}_\theta \langle \pi_2', \sigma' \rangle}{\langle \pi_1 + \pi_2, \sigma \rangle_V \xrightarrow{l}_\theta \langle \pi_2', \sigma' \rangle}$$

The transition rules presented thus far deal only with the execution of a goal. In the next transition rule, the semantics of plan rules is defined. The application of a rule consists of three steps. First, the head of a rule needs to be unified with a current achievement goal of the agent. Second, it must be checked whether the guard of the plan rule is entailed by the beliefs of the agent. And third, the achievement goal is replaced by the plan in the body of the rule (after instantiating variables in this plan with the bindings obtained in the first two steps).

Definition 8. (application of rules)
Let θ be a most general unifier for $p(t)$ and $p(t')$, and γ be a substitution restricted to the free variables in φ.

$$\frac{\sigma \models \varphi \theta \gamma}{\langle p(t), \sigma \rangle_V \xrightarrow{\tau}_{\theta \gamma} \langle \pi \theta \gamma, \sigma \rangle}$$

where $p(t') \leftarrow \varphi \mid \pi$ is a variant of a rule in the rule base Γ of an agent in which all free variables have been renamed to variables which do not occur in V.

A multi-agent system is a system of multiple agents. Each agent has a unique identity which distinguishes it from other agents. Agents may differ in various respects from each other. They may have different expertise, different planning capabilities, and different tasks.

Definition 9. (multi-agent system)
A multi-agent system is a finite set $\mathcal{M} = \{A_1, \ldots, A_n\}$ of agents $A_1, \ldots, A_n$ such that any two different agents have different names.

The parallel execution of computation steps of agents in a multi-agent system which do *not involve communication* is modelled by the interleaving of such computation steps. In the sequel, we will add a transition rule for computation steps of agents which do involve communication. We remark here that an interleaving semantics is a mathematical abstraction for modelling parallelism which does not exclude true concurrent execution of agents. A multi-agent system is, analogous to a single agent, a multi-threaded system. One of the agents is selected for execution and the multi-agent system is updated accordingly. Note that there is no label associated with the transition of the multi-agent system itself. There is no need to distinguish any transitions at the multi-agent level.

Definition 10. (multi-agent execution)
Let $\{A_1, A_2, \ldots, A_n\}$ be a multi-agent system.

$$\frac{A_i \xrightarrow{\tau} A_i' \text{ for some } i, 0 < i \leq n}{\{A_1, \ldots, A_i, \ldots, A_n\} \longrightarrow \{A_1, \ldots, A_i', \ldots, A_n\}}$$

3   Communication

At the multi-agent level, a new concern of how to manage the interaction of the multiple agents arises. One of the ways to manage the interaction is by means of an *agent communication language*. The exchange of messages between intelligent agents concerns their beliefs and goals. In the agent communication language we propose, the messages that are exchanged between agents are sentences from the same language which the agents use to represent their knowledge.

As will become clear below, our focus is mainly on the *agent receiving a message*. It is the agent which receives a message that has to process this message, and in the formal semantics we want to capture this aspect of the communication of a message (whereas traditional speech act theory is more speaker-oriented, cf. [9]). Other aspects, we believe, can sometimes be *programmed* in the programming language, and for that reason do not have to be incorporated in a formal semantics for communication in an agent programming language.

In this paper, we discuss two types of message exchange. First, we discuss the exchange of a message which is interpreted as *providing an answer to a question*. Secondly, we discuss the exchange of a message which is interpreted as *making a request*. For both types of messages we propose a semantics which we believe captures the successful processing of these messages by the receiver. In the following sections, we will explain what we mean by the *successful processing* of a message. Although we do provide a specific semantics in the formal definitions below for both types of communication, we want to emphasise that these definitions are particular instances of a more general idea: to base a semantics for the exchange of information on deductive reasoning and to base a semantics for the exchange of a request on abductive reasoning. The specific definitions below are illustrations of these ideas. To highlight the fact that a semantics based on deduction and abduction specifies a range of alternatives, we discuss some of the more interesting alternatives to the formal definitions of the semantics.

Corresponding to the two types of message exchange, we introduce two *pairs of communication primitives*. The first set of communication primitives, tell and ask, we use for the exchange of information. The second set of communication primitives, req and offer, we use for the exchange of a request.

Our communication primitives are *synchronous* communication primitives. This means that the agents have to synchronise their communicative actions. Such a simultaneous communicative act of two agents is called a *handshake*. Although synchronous communication primitives may seem to have a number of disadvantages compared with asynchronous communication primitives, these limitations are more apparent than real. For example, asynchronous communication between two agents can be simulated by synchronous communication and a third interface agent which behaves like a buffer. Moreover, for some applications it may be quite natural as is illustrated by the implementation of a multi-stage negotiation protocol in this paper.

Information Exchange. We first introduce two communication primitives for the exchange of information. As mentioned previously, in the formal semantics we want to capture the successful processing of a message by the receiver. In the case of information exchange, from the point of view of the receiving agent, we think it is most important that that agent can *derive an answer to a question from the message* which it received. Therefore, the successful processing of the message is taken to mean that the receiving agent can derive an answer from that message. Because both messages and questions are formulas from a logical language, it is most natural to process a received message by deriving an answer using *logical deduction*. The formal semantics for information exchange therefore is based on *deduction*.

We want to emphasise that our semantics is not intended to capture the much more complicated semantics of a speech act like, for example, informing. Whereas speech act theory is mainly concerned with constraints on the mental state of the speaker, we are interested in the way the hearer (receiving agent) processes the received message.

The communicative action $\text{tell}(b, \varphi)$ is an action to send the message φ to agent b. There are *no* constraints on the sending agent imposed by the semantics; the only constraint is that agent b, to whom the message is sent, accepts the message. The informal interpretation we associate with the action $\text{tell}(b, \varphi)$ is that φ conveys some *information*.

The message φ is required to be a sentence *when* $\text{tell}(b, \varphi)$ *is executed*, since it does not make sense to send indefinite information to another agent when an attempt is made to inform that agent. So, any free variables which occur in a $\text{tell}(b, \varphi)$ action in a plan of an agent must have been instantiated by retrieving bindings for these variables and parameter passing before the formula φ can be communicated. The empty substitution $\varnothing$ is associated with the transition of tell since the sender receives no information. The transition below is labelled with $b!_i\varphi$ to indicate that an attempt of *sending* information φ to agent b is being made. The exclamation mark ! indicates that a message is being sent, while the subscript i indicates the type of communication, namely information exchange.

Definition 11. (transition rule for tell)

$$\frac{\varphi \text{ is closed}}{\langle \text{tell}(b, \varphi), \sigma \rangle_V \xrightarrow{b!_i\varphi}_{\varnothing} \langle E, \sigma \rangle}$$

The transition rule for tell and the transition rule for ask below specify *virtual* or *attempted* computation steps and *do not* specify completed computation steps. Actual communication between agents only occurs when the labels associated with the virtual steps match and the message sent is accepted by the receiving agent; in that case, a handshake occurs. The precise conditions for actual communication are specified in the third transition rule for the exchange of information below.

The communicative action $\text{ask}(a, \psi)$ is an action which specifies a condition for the acceptance of messages sent by a. The condition is that the message sent must entail (an instance of) ψ. The informal interpretation we associate with this action is that ψ is a *question* for which agent a should provide an answer.

The question ψ does not have to be a sentence, but may contain free variables. The free variables in ψ indicate what the question is about. The receiving agent attempts to *deduce* an *answer* θ from a message φ of the sender a and its own beliefs σ. So, an *answer* to a question is a substitution θ such that $\sigma \cup \varphi \models \psi\theta$. Moreover, we require that θ is a *complete* answer, that is, grounds ψ. The receiving agent accepts a message φ only if it is able to compute a complete answer to its question from φ.

In the transition rule for ask, the question mark ? in the label indicates that the asking agent is the receiving agent. The subscript i in the label indicates that the communication concerns information exchange. The substitution θ denotes a possible answer. The fact that there are no restrictions imposed on answers by the transition rule indicates that from the perspective of the receiving agent any answer is acceptable.

Definition 12. (ask)
Let θ be a substitution restricted to the free variables of ψ.

$$\frac{\psi\theta \text{ is closed}}{\langle ask(a, \psi), \sigma \rangle_V \xrightarrow{a?_i\psi\theta}{}_\theta \langle E, \sigma \rangle}$$

Actual communication concerning the exchange of information between two agents occurs when both agents address each other and the sending agent provides the information from which the receiving agent is able to deduce an answer to its question. The computed answer to the question of agent b is implicit in the transition associated with agent b (cf. the transition rule for ask).

Definition 13. (exchange of information)
Let $A = \langle a, \Pi_a, \sigma_a, \Gamma_a \rangle$ and $B = \langle b, \Pi_b, \sigma_b, \Gamma_b \rangle$ be two agents such that $a \neq b$, and let $\mathcal{M}$ be a (possibly empty) multi-agent system such that $A \notin \mathcal{M}, B \notin \mathcal{M}$.

$$\frac{A \xrightarrow{b!_i\varphi} A' , \ B \xrightarrow{a?_i\psi} B' \text{ and } \sigma_b \cup \varphi \models \psi}{\mathcal{M}, A, B \longrightarrow \mathcal{M}, A', B'}$$

As mentioned, we think that a semantics for the exchange of information based on deduction specifies a range of alternatives rather than that it fixes one particular semantics. The semantics in definition 13 provides a useful and simple instance of a semantics based on deduction, but a number of interesting variations on this semantics are possible. For example, one alternative semantics is to update the beliefs of the receiving agent b instead of simply expanding with the message φ in such a way that $\sigma_b \circ \varphi$ remains consistent (where $\circ$ denotes the update operation). The informal interpretation of the exchange of information would be slightly altered into: if agent b *would* believe φ to be true (after updating), the question ψ can be answered.

Example 1. In this example, we illustrate the semantics of definition 13. First, consider two agents John and Roger which are going to a meeting to discuss a paper. A simple question concerning this meeting is where the meeting takes place. The appropriate communicative action for Roger then would be the following: ask(*john, meet(paper, 10 : 00Fri, 1 : 00, Location, [john, roger, mark]*)) The free variable *Location* indicates that the question is about the location of the meeting. Now assume that Roger takes the location of John at 10:00Fri to be definite information as to where the meeting takes place. Rogers beliefs would then imply the proposition *location(john, 10 : 00Fri, Loc) → meet(paper, 10 : 00Fri, 1 : 00, Loc, [john, roger, mark])*. In that case John could send Roger a message concerning his location 10:00Fri from which Roger, given his beliefs, would be able to derive an answer to his question: tell(*roger, location(john, 10 : 00Fri, amsterdam)*). Note that Roger can deduce an answer to his question from Johns message.

Two final remarks are in order. Because we wanted to keep our semantics as simple as possible, we did not include complex conditions on the mental state of agents in our communication semantics. However, it is possible to use the programming language to *program* particular conditions on the mental state of communicating agents. For example, it is possible to define a communication primitive inform by using the primitive tell which only succeeds in case the sending agent believes what it tells (is honest): $\text{inform}(a, \varphi) \stackrel{df}{=} \varphi?;\ \text{tell}(a, \varphi)$. As another example, a credulous agent could also be programmed: after an ask action an agent could update its mental state with the answer it received simply by inserting this information in its belief base (if the answer is consistent with the current beliefs): $\text{ask}(a, \psi);\ \text{ins}(\psi)$.

Requests. The second pair of communication primitives we introduce are used to exchange requests. Again, we are interested in capturing what could be considered as the successful processing of a request by the receiver. The main issue for the receiving agent, we believe, is whether or not the agent is able to compute a goal or plan which would satisfy the request. This is the first issue an agent which receives a request should deal with. Therefore, we take the successful processing of a request to mean that the receiving agent is able to make a proposal that would satisfy the request. Now consider the requirements on such a proposal. First of all, in this paper we only consider declarative proposals and declarative requests, i.e. propositions or statements from $\mathcal{L}$. Given a request φ which specifies a state of affairs to be achieved, for a proposal ψ to satisfy the request, this proposal should entail that a state of affairs such that φ is obtained (given what the agent which makes the proposal currently believes). Now we notice that the problem of finding a proposal ψ such that $\sigma \cup \psi \models \varphi$, that is, a proposal ψ which given the current beliefs σ entails φ, is analogous to an *abductive problem*. This suggests that an appropriate semantics which captures the successful processing of requests by the receiver can be obtained by using an *abductive semantics*.

Abduction is sometimes paraphrased as reasoning from an observation to an explanation, or alternatively, from an effect to a cause. It is the latter explanation which suits our purposes best. In a communication setting, where more than one agent is involved, we think of the agent sending a request as the agent which desires a particular effect to be realised, and of the agent who receives the request as the agent who has to establish a cause which would establish the effect. The basic idea underlying the semantics of the primitives is that abductive reasoning can be used by the receiving agent to compute a proposal that *would* achieve the request of the sender.

Perhaps even more than in the case of the exchange of information we should emphasise that the semantics for req and offer we propose is not intended to capture the much more complicated semantics of the speech act of requesting. We are interested in the way the receiving agent processes a request it receives and in providing an agent with the computational means to do so. We suggest that an abductive semantics is appropriate to model the processing of a request.

The communicative action $\text{req}(b, \varphi)$ is an action to send a message φ to agent b. There are *no* constraints on the sending agent imposed by the semantics; the only constraint is that agent b, to whom the message is sent, is able to offer a proposal which would establish φ. The informal interpretation we associate with the action $\mathsf{req}(b, \varphi)$ is that φ expresses a *request*.

The request φ is required to be definite, i.e. we do not allow the occurrence of free variables in φ when $\mathsf{req}(a, \varphi)$ is executed. The agent which makes the request is not automatically informed of the type of proposal the receiving agent b makes. The sender does not receive any information, which explains the empty substitution $\varnothing$ in the transition rule. The symbol $!_r$ in the label associated with the transition below is used to distinguish between the two types of message exchange, the exchange of a request and the exchange of information. As before the exclamation mark ! indicates that a message is being sent, while the subscript r indicates the type of communication, namely the exchange of a request.

Definition 14. (transition rule for req)

$$\frac{\varphi \ closed}{\langle \mathsf{req}(a, \varphi), \sigma \rangle_V \xrightarrow{a!_r \varphi}_\varnothing \langle E, \sigma \rangle}$$

The communicative action $\mathsf{offer}(a, \psi)$ is an action which specifies a *proposal* ψ to achieve a request of agent a. Informally, the action $\mathsf{offer}(a, \psi)$ could be viewed as advertising that the agent is prepared to offer ψ to agent a; alternatively, the agent offers a *proposal* ψ as a way to achieve a request of agent a.

The proposal ψ may contain free variables which indicate the range of proposals the agent is prepared to make. That is, by offering ψ any instance of the free variables in ψ is offered. The receiving agent needs to process a received request and compute a specific instance of its proposal ψ which would satisfy the request. The process involved, as we suggested, is that of abduction. The receiving agent attempts to *abduce* suitable instances θ for the free variables in ψ such that, given the agents current beliefs σ, the request φ of agent a is entailed by the proposal, i.e. $\sigma \cup \psi\theta \models \varphi$; moreover, the computed proposal $\psi\theta$ must be consistent with the agents beliefs σ, i.e. $\sigma \not\models \neg\psi\theta$.

In the transition rule for offer, the question mark ? in the label indicates that the offering agent is the receiving agent. The subscript r indicates that the communication involves the exchange of a request. The fact that there are no restrictions on the substitution θ by transition rule indicates that the receiving agent in principle is prepared to offer any instance of ψ as a proposal to achieve a request.

Definition 15. (transition rule for offer)
Let θ be a substitution restricted to the free variables of ψ.

$$\frac{\psi\theta \ is \ closed}{\langle \mathsf{offer}(a, \psi), \sigma \rangle_V \xrightarrow{a?_r \psi\theta}_\theta \langle E, \sigma \rangle}$$

Actual communication which involves the exchange of a request between two agents occurs when both agents address each other and the receiving agent is able to abduce a specific proposal which would satisfy the request φ of the sending agent; the receiving agent, moreover, only offers a proposal which is consistent with what it believes to be true. The latter condition prevents the receiving agent from offering too strong proposals like $\perp$ (false) which would satisfy any request. The computed substitution θ to instantiate the proposal is implicit in the transition associated with agent b (cf. the transition rule for offer).

Definition 16. (exchange of a requests)
Let $A = \langle a, \Pi_a, \sigma_a, \Gamma_a \rangle$ and $B = \langle b, \Pi_b, \sigma_b, \Gamma_b \rangle$ be two agents such that $a \neq b$, and let $\mathcal{M}$ be a (possibly empty) multi-agent system such that $A \notin \mathcal{M}, B \notin \mathcal{M}$.

$$\frac{A \xrightarrow{b!_r \varphi} A' , \ B \xrightarrow{a?_r \psi} B' , \sigma_b \not\models \neg\psi, \sigma_b \cup \psi \models \varphi}{\mathcal{M}, A, B \longrightarrow \mathcal{M}, A', B'}$$

The semantics for the exchange of a request in definition 16 is a simple instance of an abductive semantics for this type of communication. Again, there are a number of interesting variations on this type of semantics. A particularly interesting alternative which already is suggested by the use of abduction is to extend the semantics with a *preference relation* on the proposals an agent is prepared to make. In this context, however, the preference relation would not primarily be based on properties of simplicity of the proposal as is usual in the literature on abduction, but would be based on concepts associated with the interests of agents, like efficiency, for example.

Example 2. In this example, we illustrate the semantics of definition 16. Consider again the meeting example concerning agents John and Roger, and suppose that agent John would like to meet to discuss a paper with agent Roger 10:00Fri. Then agent John could use the communicative action req to communicate his request to agent Roger as follows: $req(roger, meet(paper, 10 : 00Fri, 1 : 00, amsterdam, [roger, john]))$. Also assume that agent Roger is prepared to make the following proposal to achieve a request of John by means of the communicative action offer: $offer(john, meet(paper, 10 : 00Fri, 1 : 00, AnyPlace, [roger, john]))$. Here, the free variable *AnyPlace* indicates that Roger is prepared to offer a proposal to meet John at *any place* 10:00Fri in reply to a request of John. We want to emphasise that all agent Roger does by means of the action offer is to try and find a proposal which would satisfy a request of John. There are no conditions on the mental state of the speaker similar to those usually associated with the speech act of requesting, and the actions req and offer are not intended as the equivalents of such a speech act. The action offer provides the receiving agent with the computational means to process a request of another agent in the sense outlined above. In the example, agent Roger uses abduction to compute a specific instance of his proposal that would satisfy the request of John. As is clear in this simple case, the only instance (given that Roger does not believe anything about meetings 10:00Fri) which would satisfy the request is the proposal to meet in Amsterdam.

The example illustrates the use of variables in the proposal of the offering agent. A variable in a proposal ψ means that the proposal is a proposal to satisfy *any specific request* of the requesting agent concerning this parameter in the proposal, as long as this is consistent with the beliefs of the agent. In the example, the agent offers a proposal to meet at any requested place. It does not mean, however, that the agent offers *every* instance of its proposal. That is, it does not offer the universal closure $\forall \psi$ as a way to achieve a request. And neither would the requesting agent be satisfied by such a proposal in the meeting example (it does not even make sense to meet at *all possible* places at a particular time). We assume that the requesting agent would like the other agent to satisfy its request by making a proposal that is as concrete as possible. This explains that the agent computing a proposal abduces a *most specific instance* of its proposal which would satisfy the request.

The distinguishing aspect of the semantics of req and offer is the consistency constraint imposed on any proposals offered to satisfy a request. This constraint can be used to enforce that certain preferences of the receiving agent which computes a proposal are taken into account. The consistency constraint is also used for this purpose in the implementation of the negotiation protocol in the next section. Next we provide a simple example of the use of this constraint. Consider again the example of agent John requesting a meeting with agent Roger. However, in this case, agent John is requesting to meet with agent Roger somewhere, and does not care for any particular place. Agent John could communicate this request by means of the following action: $req(roger, \exists L(meet(paper, 10 : 00Fri, 1 : 00, L, [roger, john])))$. Again, assume that agent Roger is prepared to make the same proposal as before: $offer(john, meet(paper, 10 : 00Fri, 1 : 00, AnyPlace, [roger, john]))$. But in this case, we also assume that agent Roger has a preference to meet in either Utrecht or Rotterdam, and is not prepared to meet in any other place. This type of preference can be coded into the beliefs of the agent. This is achieved by adding a constraint in the belief base of agent Roger as follows: $\forall M, T, D, L, P(meet(M, T, D, L, P) \rightarrow (L = utrecht \lor L = rotterdam))$. Given this preference, the consistency constraint in the semantics makes sure that agent Roger only abduces proposals for meeting in Utrecht or Rotterdam because any instance of his proposal $meet(paper, 10 : 00Fri, 1 : 00, AnyPlace, [roger, john])$ must be consistent with his beliefs. A disadvantage, however, of this way of representing preferences is that if agent John would have requested to meet in Amsterdam, agent Roger would not have been able to compute a proposal which would satisfy this request.

4   Meeting Scheduling

One of the interesting metaphors introduced in agent research, is to view programs as intelligent agents acting on our behalf. For example, intelligent agents may perform routine and tedious information processing activities in organisations on behalf of their users. One of the applications one might consider using agents for is that of meeting scheduling. The problem agents have to solve in this application is to find a meeting time for a meeting that is consistent with all the constraints on meetings associated with the different agents. Although meeting scheduling is a complex problem, some solutions have been proposed in the literature (cf. [10]). One of the solutions proposed, is to implement distributed meeting scheduling by using a multi-stage negotiation protocol ([3]). Below we show how to implement such a multi-stage negotiation protocol in 3APL by using the communicative actions. We design a set of plans for two-agent meeting scheduling. The two-agent case is substantially simpler than the case where more than two agents are allowed. Due to space limitations, however, it is not possible to present a general solution for arbitrary numbers of agents. A solution for the general case can be found in the extended version of this paper [6].

The basic idea of the multi-stage negotiation protocol is to allow agents to negotiate for several rounds to reach an agreement. One agent is designated as the *host agent*; it is the agent who is trying to arrange the meeting with the *invitee*. Every stage of the negotiation protocol consists of two phases. The first phase is the *negotiation phase* in which proposals and counterproposals are exchanged. The second phase is the *evaluation phase* in which the *host* evaluates the proposals made so far.

To guarantee that the negotiation will come to a conclusion, we make a number of assumptions. First of all, we assume that the attendants of a proposed meeting always share a free slot of the appropriate length in their agenda where the meeting can be scheduled. Furthermore, the strategy of the host during the negotiation is to request the invitee to propose the earliest meeting time consistent with its constraints and preferences. Together, these assumptions imply convergence on a solution. Moreover, for ease of exposition, we no longer make any reference to the location of a meeting and in the sequel drop the location argument when the *meet* predicate is used.

Integrity Constraints Associated with Meetings. A number of integrity constraints need to be satisfied for a set of scheduled meetings to be coherent. Here, we restrict ourselves to two constraints. First, the meeting identifiers used as tags to retrieve unique meetings should actually refer to unique meetings. And, secondly, an attendant of one meeting cannot be an attendant of a second concurrent meeting. Of course, agents may have more integrity constraints associated with meetings, in particular concerning the preferences of their users, as was illustrated in example 2. In the sequel, free variables in the beliefs of agents are implicitly universally quantified.

Constraint 1: Meeting Identifiers refer to unique meetings:
$(meet(MeetId, T_1, L_1, Att1) \wedge meet(MeetId, T_2, L_2, Att2)) \rightarrow (T_1 = T_2 \wedge L_1 = L_2 \wedge Att1 = Att2)$

Constraint 2: The attendants of two overlapping meetings are disjoint sets of people:
$(meet(MeetId1, T_1, L_1, Att1) \wedge meet(MeetId2, T_2, L_2, Att2) \wedge T_1 \leq T_2 < T_1 + L_1 \wedge MeetId1 \neq MeetId2) \rightarrow Att1 \cap Att2 = \varnothing$

Two-Agent Meeting Scheduling. In two-agent meeting scheduling, one of the agents is designated to be the host and the other agent is the invitee. Each round begins with a negotiation phase. The negotiation phase is implemented by using the communicative actions req and offer. Intuitively, the agents request each other to meet at particular times, they dont tell each other at which times to meet. Also, the agents which are requested to meet at some time have to come up with some proposal which would satisfy the request and to abduce these meeting times turns out to provide for a suitable and particularly simple implementation in case of the meeting scheduling example. In the implementation, the negotiation phase consists of two steps. In the first step, the host requests the invitee to schedule the meeting at the earliest possible meeting time after some time T consistent with the constraints of the invitee by means of a req action. For this purpose, we introduce the predicate $epmeet(MeetId, PosTime, L, Att, T)$. This predicate is used to express that time $PosTime$ is the earliest time after time T such that the meeting $MeetId$ of Length L and attendants Att can be scheduled (a formalisation can be found in [6]). The invitee computes a meeting time U which would satisfy this request by means of an offer action. In the second step, the roles are reversed and the invitee requests to schedule the meeting at the earliest possible time after time U computed in the first step. Now the host has to compute a meeting time T' which is consistent with its constraints and which would satisfy the request of the invitee. After computing such a meeting time, the host starts the evaluation phase, the second phase in one round of a negotiation. In this phase, the host compares the initial time T with the time T' computed in the second step of the negotiation phase. Because we have $T \leq U$ and $U \leq T'$ (earliest times are requested), in case $T = T'$ an agreement has been reached ($T = U = T'$), and the host sends a message to inform the invitee of this fact by means of a tell action; otherwise, the host starts a new round in the negotiation. The last computed meeting time T' is used as the new initial time in this new round. In the implementation below, we assume that a unique meeting identifier is available to the host, which has not been used to refer to any other meeting to identify the meeting which is being negotiated about.

The plan of the host to negotiate with the invitee is provided by a recursive plan rule in the programming language. The goal to initiate a round of the negotiation is denoted by $invite(Invitee, MeetId, T, L, Att)$ where $Invitee$ is the name the invitee agent, $MeetId$ is the meeting identifier of the meeting being negotiated, T is a time acceptable to the host as a meeting time, L is the length of the meeting, and Att are the attendants of the meeting (in the two-agent case, presumably, the host and the invitee). The plan to achieve the $invite$ goal consists of the body of the plan rule below. The first two steps in the plan which consist of the req and offer actions constitute the *negotiation phase* of the plan. A particular important feature of this implementation is the exploitation of the fact that req and offer are *synchronous* communication primitives. This is used to synchronise the negotiation rounds, and achieved implicitly because the communicative actions have to synchronise, and wait until both agents are ready to communicate. As explained, in the negotiation phase, the host first requests the invitee to meet at the earliest possible time after time T that is consistent with its constraints. The invitee in response computes a proposal for a meeting time U and requests the host to meet at the earliest possible time after this time U. In reply, the host computes a proposal for a meeting time T' (the offer action) which is the earliest possible meeting time at which the host is able to meet and which is later or equal to the time specified in the request of the invitee. The second part of the plan is called the *evaluation phase* of the plan, and as explained, in this phase the host evaluates the proposals. If an agreement has been reached, the host confirms this by means of the tell action; otherwise, the host starts a new round of negotiation by the recursive call $invite(Invitee, MeetId, T', L, Att)$.

```
invite(Invitee, MeetId, T, L, Att) ← true |          reply(Host) ← true |
req(Invitee, ∃T1 · epmeet(MeetId, T1, L, Att, T));   begin
offer(Invitee, meet(MeetId, T', L, Att));               offer(Host, meet(MeetId, U, L, Att));
IF T = T'                                               req(Host,
                                                          ∃U1 · epmeet(MeetId, U1, L, Att, U));
     THEN tell(Invitee, confirm(MeetId, T))             reply(Host)
     ELSE invite(Invitee, MeetId, T', L, Att)           end+
                                                        ask(Host, confirm(MeetId, U))
```

The plan which the invitee uses in the negotiation is provided for by the body of the plan rule for $reply(Host)$. The invitee starts the negotiation with a goal $reply(Host)$ which is achieved by the plan provided by the rule. The invitee first computes a meeting time U in response to a request of the host by means of the offer action. Then, in the second step, the invitee requests the host to meet at the earliest time after U, and prepares for a new round by adopting the goal *reply*(*Host*) again. In case the host confirms that an agreement has been reached, the invitee accepts the confirmation (this is implemented by the ask branch of the nondeterministic plan in the plan). Otherwise, a new negotiation round is started.

5   Approaches Based on Speech Act Theory

The main approaches to agent level communication in the literature like KQML ([7]) or ACL of FIPA ([4]) are based on speech act theory. One of the basic insights of speech act theory is that the communication of a message not only consists in making a statement, but in a more broader sense constitutes a communicative action: making a promise, begging, informing, etc. are all different kinds of communicative actions. In speech act theory, communicative actions are decomposed into locutionary, illocutionary and perlocutionary acts.

Our approach is based on the view that agent level communication should be based on a well-defined and clear semantics and at the same time should be kept as simple as possible. Moreover, our focus has been more on the hearer than on the speaker. Therefore, we take a somewhat different perspective as to how speech act theory could be of use in the design and development of agents. Our view is that speech act theory may provide a useful set of *abstract descriptions* of communicative actions for agents which can be used to *specify* and *verify* the behaviour of agents. Speech acts thus would play a role in the *proof theory* associated with the agent programming language. In the associated programming logic, the speech acts could be derived just like, for example, the mental attitude of belief would be derived from the program text and its semantics. Instead of *defining* a set of communication primitives corresponding to all kinds of subtle distinctions related to speech acts, we propose to *derive* what kind of speech act has been performed by an agent from the characteristics of the content proposition and the mental state of the agent. The arguments are similar to, but not the same, as some of those put forward in [1] (cf. also [2]). In [1] a *logical* approach to modelling speech acts is discussed. In our case, we argue that a distinction should be made between actions provided for in a *programming language* and actions which are defined in a *logic*. Moreover, we do introduce a number of communication primitives in contrast with the approach in [1]. We think that speech act theory should not be viewed as a repository of all kinds of different communicative acts for which *computational equivalents* should be provided in an agent communication language, as is done in KQML or ACL. Also, it is hard to see how the *logical semantics* for either KQML or ACL relates to any existing *programming languages*.

The view outlined has a number of advantages. First of all, the agent communication language is kept simple. This prevents all kinds of confusions on the part of the programmer as to what kind of communication primitive he should use in a particular case. Second, the idea to derive speech acts from the semantics of the agent (communication) language seems to provide for a more principled approach than the approach which is used to provide semantics for KQML or FIPA. It prevents unnecessary complications in the semantics and precludes the tendency to incorporate everything into the semantics of speech acts.

6   Conclusion

In this paper, we integrated communication into the agent programming language 3APL and extended the language into a multi-agent language. We illustrated and introduced two pairs of communication primitives. Our focus has been mainly on the hearer or the receiving agent in the communication. We argued that an appropriate semantics for the exchange of information and a request from the perspective of the hearer can be based on deduction and abduction, respectively. The semantics of tell and ask is based on deductive reasoning and are used for information exchange. The semantics of req and offer is based on abductive reasoning and are used to abduce feasible proposals which would satisfy a request. We believe the semantics provided captures important aspects of the processing of a message received by the hearer. Both deduction and abduction are well-understood, and provide a clear and expressive semantics for communication primitives.

We illustrated the use of the communication primitives by an implementation of a multi-stage negotiation protocol for meeting scheduling agents. The implementation illustrates the expressive power of the communication primitives, and shows that the agent programming language 3APL is a natural means for programming personal assistants. We argued that our approach is a viable alternative to approaches based on speech act theory, while maintaining that speech act theory may be useful in the proof theory of an agent programming language.

Acknowledgements. We would like to thank Yves Lespérance and Hector Levesque for many constructive and helpful discussions.

References

1. Philip R. Cohen and Hector J. Levesque. Rational Interaction as the Basis for Communication. In Philip R. Cohen, Jerry Morgan, and Martha E. Pollack, editors, *Intentions in Communication*. The MIT Press, 1990.
2. Marco Colombetti. Semantic, Normative and Practical Aspects of Agent Communication. In *Issues in Agent Communication*. Springer-Verlag, 2000.
3. Susan E. Conry, Robert A. Meyer, and Victor R. Lesser. Multistage Negotiation in Distributed Planning. In Alan H. Bond and Les Gasser, editors, *Readings in Distributed Artificial Intelligence*, pages 367–384. Morgan Kaufman, 1988.
4. FIPA. FIPA 97 Specification, Part 2, Agent Communication Language, October 1998.
5. Koen V. Hindriks, Frank S. de Boer, Wiebe van der Hoek, and John-Jules Ch. Meyer. Agent Programming in 3APL. *Autonomous Agents and Multi-Agent Systems*, 2(4):357–401, 1999.
6. Koen V. Hindriks, Frank S. de Boer, Wiebe van der Hoek, and John-Jules Ch. Meyer. Semantics of Communicating Agents Based on Deduction and Abduction. Technical Report UU-CS-1999-09, Department of Computer Science, University Utrecht, 1999.
7. Yannis Labrou and Tim Finin. A semantics approach for KQML - a general purpose communication language for software agents. In *Third International Conference on Information and Knowledge Management (CIKM94)* . 1994.
8. G. Plotkin. A structural approach to operational semantics. Technical report, Aarhus University, Computer Science Department, 1981.
9. John R. Searle. *Speech acts*. Cambridge University Press, 1969.

10. Sandip Sen and Edmund Durfee. A Contracting Model for Flexible Distributed Scheduling. *Annals of Operations Research*, 65:195–222, 1996.
11. Rogier M. van Eijk, Frank S. de Boer, Wiebe van der Hoek, and John-Jules Ch. Meyer. Information-Passing and Belief Revision in Multi-Agent Systems. In J. P. M. Müller, M. P. Singh, and A. S. Rao, editors, *Intelligent Agents V (LNAI 1555)*, pages 29–45. Springer-Verlag, 1999.

Operational Semantics for
Agent Communication Languages

Rogier M. van Eijk, Frank S. de Boer,
Wiebe van der Hoek, and John-Jules Ch. Meyer

Utrecht University, Department of Computer Science
P.O. Box 80.089, 3508 TB Utrecht, The Netherlands
{rogier, frankb, wiebe, jj}@cs.uu.nl

Abstract. In this paper, we study the operational semantics of agent communication languages. We develop a basic multi-agent programming language for systems of concurrently operating agents, into which agent communication languages can be integrated. In this language, each agent has a mental state comprised of an informational component and a motivational component; interaction between the agents proceeds via a rendezvous communication mechanism. The language builds upon well-understood concepts from the object-oriented programming paradigm as object classes, method invocations and object creation. The formal semantics of the language are de ned by means of transition rules that describe its operational behaviour. Moreover, the operational semantics closely follow the syntactic structure of the language, and hence give rise to an abstract machine to interpret it.

1   Introduction

The research on agent-oriented programming has yielded a variety of programming languages for multi-agent systems, each of which incorporates a particular mechanism of agent communication. Many of these communication mechanisms are based on *speech act theory*, originally developed as a model for human communication. A speech act is an action performed by a speaker to convey information about its mental state with the objective to in uence the mental state of the hearer. This notion has been fruitfully adopted in agent communication languages as KQML [10] and FIPA-ACL [11], which prescribe the syntax and semantics of a collection of speech act-like messages. Such a message is comprised of a performative, a content and some additional parameters as the sender and receiver of the message; e.g., there is a message to inform a receiving agent that the sender believes a particular formula to be true, and a message to request a receiving agent to perform some particular action. Both agent communication languages assume an underlying communication mechanism that proceeds via asynchronous message-passing.

As was indicated by Cohen and Levesque (cf. [4]) communicative acts should be considered as *attempts* of the sending agent to get something done from the receiving agent. An important consequence of this view is that there is no guarantee that the receiving agent will actually act in accordance with the purposes the sending agent has attributed to the message. That is, it is possible that a receiving agent will simply ignore

F. Dignum and M. Greaves (Eds.): Agent Communication, LNAI 1916, pp. 80–95, 2000.
© Springer-Verlag Berlin Heidelberg 2000

the message or will do the opposite of what it is requested for. Hence, in giving semantics to messages one should not confuse the *effects* that a message has on the receiving agent with the subsequent *reactions* taken by the receiver that it brings about. For instance, one could easily be tempted to describe the meaning of an $ask(\varphi)$ message as that upon its reception, the receiving agent should respond with a $confirm(\varphi)$ message in the situation it believes the formula φ to be true, and with a $disconfirm(\varphi)$ message if it this is not the case. In our opinion however, the reactions towards a message are not part of the semantics of the message, but rather are consequences of the characteristics of the receiving agent. The point we advocate in this paper is to describe the semantics of messages solely in terms of the effects they have on the mental state of the receiving agent, without giving any references to the possible subsequent reactions. For instance, the meaning of an $ask(\varphi)$ message would be that upon its reception the receiving agent registers that it is asked whether it believes φ to hold. It will be on the basis of its altered mental state that the agent will subsequently decide what actions to perform. This behaviour is however not considered to be part of the semantics of the message. Moreover, we give an *operational* semantics of agent communication (in contrast for instance with the approach of Colombetti [5], which is based on modal logic).

Types Of Communication. In the research on intelligent agents, it is common practice to think of an agent as an entity having several different mental attitudes. These attitudes are divided into a category of *information attitudes*, which are related to the information an agent has about its environment such as belief and knowledge, and secondly, a class of *pro-attitudes* which govern the actions that the agent performs in the world and hence, concern the agent's motivations. Examples of the latter category of attitudes are goals, intentions and commitments (cf. [16]). Our previous work on communication in multi-agent systems has been centred around the agents' information attitudes (cf. [6,8,7,9]). A central topic in this study is the development of a communication mechanism that allows for the *exchange of information*. In this report, we consider communication that concerns the agents' pro-attitudes; that is, we study the communication of *actions and programs to be executed*. In particular, we will focus on the motivations that directly stem from communication, and refer the reader to [13] for details on non-communicative motivations.

We distinguish between two different types of interaction. First of all, there is communication that concerns *properties* of the agent system, which are not considered as to give information about the current agent system but rather as *speci cations* of a pursued con guration of the agent system. An example of a communicative act that falls in this category is the KQML message **achieve**(i, j, φ), which denotes a request of the agent i to the agent j to accomplish a state in which φ is true. This type of communication typically involves planning of actions, which is an issue that we will not address here.

Secondly, there is communication that involves executable programming code to change the agent system; i.e., the communication concerns implementation rather than speci cation, or in other words, is procedural of nature instead of declarative. An example of a communicative act in this category is the FIPA-ACL message $\langle i, \text{request}(j, a)\rangle$, which denotes a request of the agent i directed to the agent j to execute the action a. This type of interaction is similar to that of *higher order communication,* studied in the eld of concurrency theory. In this paradigm, programs themselves constitute rst class communication data that can be passed among the processes in the system (cf. [15]). Upon reception of a program, the receiving process integrates it in its own program and subsequently resumes its computation. Although communication of mobile code gives rise to a very powerful computation mechanism, it also gives rise to a wide range of problems especially with respect to safety and security issues in computer systems, like the unauthorised access to and manipulation of sensitive data and services.

In this paper, we will not follow the road of higher order communication, but adopt a more traditional communication mechanism that has been fruitfully employed in various distributed programming paradigms. It amounts to the idea that rather than accepting and executing arbitrary programs, a process speci es a collection of programs that other processes can request it to execute.

Rendezvous and Remote Procedure Call. In the eld of concurrency, there is the classical notion of a *rendezvous*, which constitutes a communication mechanism in which one process j executes one of its procedures on behalf of another process i (cf. [2]). In particular, a rendezvous can be viewed upon as to consist of three distinct steps. First, there is the call of a procedure of j by i. This is followed by the execution of this procedure by j, during which the execution of the calling process i is suspended. Finally, there is the communication of the result of the execution back to i, which thereupon resumes its execution. It follows that a rendezvous comprises two points of synchronisation. First, there is the call with the exchange of the actual procedure parameters from the caller to the callee and secondly, there is the communication of the results back from the callee to the caller

The notion of a rendezvous is almost equal to that of a *remote procedure call* (RPC) (cf. [3]). The difference between the two notions lies in the fact that for an RPC an entirely new process is created that takes care of the call, whereas in the case of a rendezvous the call is handled by the called process itself (cf. [2]). This implies that in the former case different procedure calls can be handled simultaneously, whereas in the latter case the calls are taken one at a time.

The rendezvous communication mechanism has for instance been adopted in the concurrent programming language POOL (cf. [1]), which constitutes a semantically well-understood programming language for systems of concurrently operating *objects*. In this paper, we outline a framework for agent communication that builds upon the object-oriented features of languages like POOL. The most important aspect we have to take into account is that in agent-oriented programming computations are not performed relative to a *local state* that maps variables to their associated values but by to *mental state* that consists of attitudes as beliefs and goals.

The remainder of this paper is organised as follows. In Section 2, we de ne a general multi-agent programming language for systems of agents that interact with each other by means of a rendezvous communication scheme. In Section 3, develop an operational model of the programming language by means of a transition system. We study the relation of the framework with the existing agent communication languages KQML and FIPA-ACL in Section 4. Finally, we round off in Section 5 by suggesting several issues for future research.

2   Syntax

In this section, we define a general programming language for multi-agent systems that covers the basic ingredients to describe the operational semantics of agent communication languages. In particular, we assume that a multi-agent system consists of a dynamic collection of agents in which new agents can be integrated, and where the interaction between the agents proceeds via a rendezvous communication scheme. Each agent is assigned a mental state comprised of a belief state and a goal state that can be inspected and updated. Additionally, an agent is assumed to be an instance of an agent class that defines the methods the agent can invoke itself as well as can be called by other agents in the system. Finally, the behaviour of an agent is governed by a program consisting of the standard programming constructs of sequential composition, non-deterministic choice, parallel composition and recursion.

Definition 1 *(First-order language)*

- A *signature* $\mathcal{L}$ is a tuple $\langle \mathcal{R}, \mathcal{F} \rangle$, where $\mathcal{R}$ is a collection of predicate symbols and $\mathcal{F}$ a collection of function symbols. The 0-ary function symbols are called *constants*. We assume a set *Ident* of constants to represent agent identifiers with typical elements i, j and k.
- We assume a set *Var* of logical variables with typical elements x, y and z.
- The set *Ter* (typical element t) of terms over $\mathcal{L}$ is the smallest set that satisfies *Var* $\subseteq$ *Ter* and secondly, if $t_1, \ldots, t_k \in$ *Ter* and $F \in \mathcal{F}$ of arity k then $F(t_1, \ldots, t_k) \in$ *Ter*. A term is *closed* if it contains no variables from *Var*.
- The set *For* (typical element φ, ψ) is the smallest set that contains a set *ForVar* of formula variables (typical element X) and additionally satisfies: if $t_1, t_2, \ldots, t_k \in$ *Ter* and $R \in \mathcal{R}$ of arity k then $(t_1 = t_2)$, $R(t_1, \ldots, t_k) \in$ *For* and if $\varphi, \psi \in$ *For* and $x \in$ *Var* then $\neg\varphi, \varphi \wedge \psi, \exists x\varphi \in$ *For*.

We define a mechanism of inferring conclusions from first-order information stores, which accounts for conclusions that contain free variables (cf. [9]). The idea of the derivation of a formula $?\mathbf{x}\psi$ from an information store φ is that the free occurrences of the variables $\mathbf{x}$ (we use boldface notation to denote *sequences*) are substituted for in ψ by a closed term such that the resulting formula becomes a consequence of φ.

Definition 2 *(Ground substitutions)* A ground substitution Δ is modeled as a finite conjunction of equalities of the form $x = t$, where $x \in$ *Var* and t is a closed term in *Ter*. We require that Δ binds each variable to at most one term. Moreover, we will use $dom(\Delta)$ to denote the variables for which Δ is defined.

For all formulae φ and substitutions Δ, we define $\varphi \oplus \Delta$ to be the formula φ in which all free occurrences of the variables of $dom(\Delta)$ have been substituted for by their corresponding value in Δ.

Definition 3 *(Ground unifiers)* Given the formulae $\varphi, \psi \in$ *For* and the sequence $\mathbf{x}$ of variables, a substitution Δ is called a *ground unifier* for the pair $(\varphi, ?\mathbf{x}\psi)$, if $dom(\Delta) = \mathbf{x}$ and $\varphi \vdash (\psi \oplus \Delta)$, where $\vdash$ denotes the standard first-order entailment relation.

We will use the notation $\varphi \vdash_\Delta \psi$ to denote that Δ is a ground unifier for (φ, ψ). For instance, the substitution $x = a$ is a ground unifier for (φ, ψ), where φ is given by $\forall x(P(x) \rightarrow Q(x)) \land P(a) \land P(b)$ and ψ equals $?xQ(x)$, and so is the substitution $x = b$. This shows that ground unifiers are not necessarily unique.

We assume a set $Func$ of functions that map formula variables to formulae, with typical element θ. We assume a function $\cdot$ such that $\varphi \cdot \theta$ yields the formula φ in which all formula variables have been replaced by the formula given by the function θ. Additionally, we use the notation $\theta\{\varphi/X\}$ to denote a function that yields φ on the input X and the value yielded by the function θ on all other inputs. For instance, we have that $\exists x(x = a \land X_1 \land X_2) \cdot \theta$ where $\theta = \theta'\{P(a)/X_2\}\{\neg Q(a)/X_1\}$, is defined to be the formula $\exists x(x = a \land \neg Q(a) \land P(a))$.

We assume a set $Class$ of agent classes with typical element C, a set $Meth$ of methods with typical element m and an operator $\circ$ to update belief states. Additionally, the set $Goal$ is comprised of goal states with typical element G. A goal state is a set of elements of the form $m(\varphi) \Rightarrow i$, denoting a goal to execute the method m with actual parameter φ (we consider methods with only one parameter, the generalisation to methods with more than one parameter is obvious). The constant i denotes the agent to which the result of the execution is to be sent back.

Definition 4 *(Syntax of programming language)*

$$a ::= X \leftarrow \varphi \mid X \leftarrow a \mid \mathsf{query}(?\mathbf{x}\varphi) \mid \mathsf{update}(\varphi) \mid m(\varphi) \mid \mathsf{integrate}(C, S) \mid$$

$$\mathsf{request}(\iota x.\psi, m(\varphi)) \mid \mathsf{accept}(\mathbf{m}) \mid \mathsf{handle}(\mathbf{m})$$

$$S ::= a; S \mid S_1 + S_2 \mid S_1 \,\&\, S_2 \mid \mathsf{skip}$$

$$A ::- \langle i, S, (\psi, G), \theta \rangle$$

If an *action* a is of the form $X \leftarrow \varphi$ it denotes the assignment of the formula φ to the formula variable X, while an action of the form $X \leftarrow a$ stands for the assignment of the result of executing the action a to X. The action $\mathsf{query}(?\mathbf{x}\varphi)$ denotes the query whether the formula φ follows from the agent's belief state modulo a ground substitution of the variables $\mathbf{x}$, while the action $\mathsf{update}(\varphi)$ represents the update of the belief state with φ. An agent executes the action $\mathsf{request}(\iota x.\psi, m(\varphi))$ to send an agent x that satisfies the formula ψ a request to execute the method m with actual parameter φ. An agent executes the action $m(\varphi)$ to invoke its method m with parameter φ. The action $\mathsf{accept}(\mathbf{m})$ denotes the acceptance of a request to execute a method in $\mathbf{m}$, while the action $\mathsf{handle}(\mathbf{m})$ is employed to select and execute an invocation of one of the methods $\mathbf{m}$ from the goal state. The difference between both actions is that the former fills the goal state whereas the latter empties it. Finally, the action $\mathsf{integrate}(C, S)$ is used to integrate an instance of the agent class C in the agent system, which thereupon will start to execute the statement S. A *class* is defined as a collection of method declarations of the form $m(\varphi) :- S$, where m is the name of the method, φ denotes its formal parameter and S is its body statement.

A *statement* is either the sequential composition $a; S$ of an action and a statement, the non-deterministic choice $S_1 + S_2$ between two statements, the parallel composition S_1 & S_2 of two statements or an empty statement skip.

An *agent* A consists of an identifier i that distinguishes it from all other agents, a program S that governs its behaviour, a mental state (for which we will use the symbol Λ) consisting of a belief state φ and a goal state G. For technical convenience we also include in the agent configuration an auxiliary function θ that is used to map formula variables to formulae. Implicitly, we assume that each agent is an instance of an agent class, which means that the methods the agent can invoke are those that are defined in its class. Finally, a *multi-agent system* $\mathcal{A}$ is a set of agents.

3   Operational Semantics

An elegant mechanism of defining the operational semantics of a programming language is that of a transition system. Such a system, which was originally developed by Plotkin (cf. [14]) constitutes a means to formally derive the individual computation steps of a program. In its most general form a *transition* looks as: $P, \sigma \longrightarrow P', \sigma'$ where P and P' are two programs and σ and σ' are some stores of information. The transition denotes a computation step of the program P which changes the store of information σ to σ', where P' is identified to be the part of the program P that still needs to be executed. Transitions are formally derived by means of *transition rules* of the form:

$$\frac{P_1, \sigma_1 \longrightarrow P'_1, \sigma'_1 \quad \cdots \quad P_n, \sigma_n \longrightarrow P'_n, \sigma'_n}{P, \sigma \longrightarrow P', \sigma'}$$

Such a rule denotes that the transition below the line can be derived if the transitions above the line are derivable. Sometimes, we will write transition rules with several transitions below the line. They are used to abbreviate a collection of rules each having one of these transitions as its conclusion. A rule with no transitions above the line is called an *axiom*. A collection of transition rules defines a *transition system*.

The advantage of using transitions systems is that they allow the operational semantics to closely follow the syntactic structure of the language. As an effect, if we view the configurations P, σ as an abstract model of a machine then the transitions specify the actions that this machine can subsequently perform. In fact, this machine would act as an interpreter for the language.

The transition system for our programming language derives transitions of the form: $\mathcal{A} \longrightarrow \mathcal{A}'$. Usually, we will omit from notation the agents in $\mathcal{A}$ that do not affect nor are affected by the transition. Additionally, besides agent configurations of the form $\langle i, S, \Lambda, \theta \rangle$, we will employ configurations that are of the form $\langle i, a, \Lambda, \theta \rangle$ and $\langle i, \varphi, \Lambda, \theta \rangle$ in which the second element is not a statement but an action a or a result φ of executing an action.

Definition 5 *(Transition for the substitution of formula variables)*

$$\langle i, a, \Lambda, \theta \rangle \longrightarrow \langle i, a \cdot \theta, \Lambda, \theta \rangle$$

where $a \cdot \theta$ denotes the obvious extension of the operator $\cdot$ to atomic actions: e.g., $(X \leftarrow \varphi) \cdot \theta = X \leftarrow (\varphi \cdot \theta)$ and $\mathsf{query}(\varphi) \cdot \theta = \mathsf{query}(\varphi \cdot \theta)$.

In the transition rule all formula variables that occur in a formula in the action a are replaced by their associated value given by the function θ.

Definition 6 *(Transitions for assignment)*

$$\frac{\langle i, a, \Lambda, \theta\rangle \longrightarrow \langle i, \varphi, \Lambda', \theta'\rangle}{\langle i, X \leftarrow a, \Lambda, \theta\rangle \longrightarrow \langle i, X \leftarrow \varphi, \Lambda', \theta'\rangle} \qquad \langle i, X \leftarrow \varphi, \Lambda, \theta\rangle \longrightarrow \langle i, \varphi, \Lambda, \theta\{\varphi/X\}\rangle$$

The first rule states how the transition for $X \leftarrow a$ can be derived from the transition for a, viz. the result φ of executing a is assigned to the formula variable X. The second rule shows that the assignment $X \leftarrow \varphi$ results in an update of θ such that it yields φ for the input X. We take the result of executing $X \leftarrow \varphi$ to be φ in order to model nested assignments as for instance $X' \leftarrow (X \leftarrow \varphi)$, which assigns φ to both X and X'.

Definition 7 *(Transition for query)*

$$\langle i, \mathsf{query}(?\mathbf{x}\psi), (\varphi, G), \theta\rangle \longrightarrow \langle i, \psi', (\varphi, G), \theta\rangle,$$

where we distinguish the following options for ψ':

> (1) a substitution Δ, where $\Delta \in \mathcal{S}$
> (2) a formula $\psi \oplus \Delta$, where $\Delta \in \mathcal{S}$
> (3) the formula $\bigwedge_{1 \leq i \leq n}(\psi \oplus \Delta_i)$

and $\mathcal{S} = \{\Delta_1, \ldots, \Delta_n\}$ denotes the set of distinct ground unifiers for $(\varphi, ?\mathbf{x}\psi)$.

The choices above model different interpretations of querying the agent's belief state. The first is one in which the result of the query is a ground unifier (provided that such a unifier exists). It is either the empty substitution denoting that the formula ψ is a classical consequence of the belief state, or a non-empty substitution defining a value for the variables $\mathbf{x}$. For instance, the following transition is derivable:

$$\langle i, \mathsf{query}(?xP(x)), \Lambda, \theta\rangle \longrightarrow \langle i, x = a, \Lambda, \theta\rangle$$

where $\Lambda = (P(a) \wedge P(b), G)$. Note that this transition is not necessarily unique, as shown by the following transition that is derivable as well:

$$\langle i, \mathsf{query}(?xP(x)), \Lambda, \theta\rangle \longrightarrow \langle i, x = b, \Lambda, \theta\rangle$$

The second option is to apply the derived substitution to φ and yield this formula as the result of the query. In this case, the transition looks like:

$$\langle i, \mathsf{query}(?xP(x)), \Lambda, \theta\rangle \longrightarrow \{\langle i, P(a), \Lambda, \theta\rangle\}$$

Finally, there is the option to yield an exhaustive description comprised of all instances of the formula φ. The transition is then given by:

$$\langle i, \mathsf{query}(?xP(x)), \Lambda, \theta\rangle \longrightarrow \langle i, P(a) \wedge P(b), \Lambda, \theta\rangle$$

We refer to the first option as the *substitution* interpretation, while the latter two are called the *derive-one* and the *derive-all* interpretations, respectively. Unless indicated otherwise, we will in this paper assume that the derive-one interpretation is in force.

De nition 8 *(Transition for update)*

$$\langle i, \mathsf{update}(\psi), (\varphi, G), \theta \rangle \longrightarrow \langle i, true, (\varphi \circ \psi, G), \theta \rangle$$

The transition for updates amounts to the incorporation of the formula ψ in the agent's belief state, where it is required that ψ does not contain any formula variables. We will not go into the details of the operator $\circ$, we assume it to be a parameter of the framework (see [12] for more details). We take the formula $true$ as the result of the update.

De nition 9 *(Transition for sending a request)* If $\varphi_1 \vdash_{x=i_2} \psi$ and $m \in \mathbf{m}$ then:

$$\langle i_1, \mathsf{request}(\iota x.\psi, m(\varphi)), \varLambda_1, \theta_1 \rangle, \langle i_2, \mathsf{accept}(\mathbf{m}), \varLambda_2, \theta_2 \rangle \longrightarrow$$
$$\langle i_1, \mathsf{wait}(i_2), \varLambda_1, \theta_1 \rangle, \langle i_2, true, \varLambda_2', \theta_2 \rangle$$

where $\varLambda_1 = (\varphi_1, G_1)$ and $\varLambda_2 = (\varphi_2, G_2)$ and $\varLambda_2' = (\varphi_2, G_2 \cup \{m(\varphi) \Rightarrow i_1\})$.

In the classical notion of a rendezvous, the computation step of the agent i_2 that follows the rst synchronisation, would be the execution of the method invocation $m(\varphi)$. However, as mentioned before, a crucial characteristic of agent-oriented programming is that computations are performed relative to a mental state. Hence, the decision when to execute the method invocation should be based upon this state rather than that it is executed without any regard for the agent's current beliefs and goals. This is why the invocation $m(\varphi)$ is not executed immediately but added to the agent's goal state, along with the identi er i_1 representing the agent that the result of the invocation is to be sent back to. The construct $\mathsf{wait}(i_2)$ is used in the operational semantics to mark that the execution of this thread in i_1 is *blocked* until the result from i_2 has been received (see also de nition 12). We remark that in order to keep things simple here, we assume that i_1 cannot concurrently invoke (in another thread) any other method of i_2.

Finally, the construct $\iota x.\psi$ denotes a witness for x that satis es the formula ψ. The condition that $x = i_2$ is a ground uni er for $(\varphi_1, ?x\psi)$ requires this witness to be i_2. For instance, we have $Agent(i_2) \vdash_{x=i_2} ?x\, Agent(x)$, where $Agent(x)$ is used to express that x is an agent in the system (see also de nition 13).

De nition 10 *(Transition for method invocation)* If m is declared as $m(X) :- T$ then:

$$\langle i, m(\psi), \varLambda, \theta \rangle \longrightarrow \langle i, S \Rightarrow i, \varLambda, \theta \rangle,$$

where S equals $T[\psi/X]$, which denotes the body statement T of m in which the actual parameter ψ has been substituted for the formal parameter X.

Note that in comparison with standard concurrent programming, the parameter-passing mechanism in our framework is rather high-level, as formulae themselves constitute rst-class values with which methods can be invoked. The construct $S \Rightarrow i$ denotes that the result of executing the statement S should be sent back to the agent i.

De nition 11 *(Transition for handling goals)*
If m is declared as $m(X) :- T$ and $m \in \mathbf{m}$ then:

$$\langle i, \mathsf{handle}(\mathbf{m}), \varLambda, \theta \rangle \longrightarrow \langle i, S \Rightarrow j, \varLambda', \theta \rangle,$$

where $S = T[\psi/X]$ and $\varLambda = (\varphi, G \cup \{m(\psi) \Rightarrow j\})$ and $\varLambda' = (\varphi, G)$.

The presence of goal states yields the need for a mechanism of controlling the selection and execution of goals, which is a mechanism that is not present in the traditional concurrent language POOL. The above transition reflects a straightforward approach in which one of the invocations of a method m (if present) is taken from the goal state and identified to be subsequently executed.

Definition 12 *(Transitions for returning the result)*

$$\langle i_1, \mathsf{wait}(i_2), \Lambda_1, \theta_1 \rangle, \langle i_2, \varphi \Rightarrow i_1, \Lambda_2, \theta_2 \rangle \longrightarrow \langle i_1, \varphi, \Lambda_1, \theta_1 \rangle, \langle i_2, true, \Lambda_2, \theta_2 \rangle$$

$$\langle i, \varphi \Rightarrow i, \Lambda, \theta \rangle \longrightarrow \langle i, \varphi, \Lambda, \theta \rangle$$

If a computation of a method invocation has terminated with a result φ then the second synchronisation of the rendezvous takes place, in which this result is communicated back to the agent i_1. The second rule deals with the case the invocation has been executed on behalf of the agent itself.

Definition 13 *(Transition for integration)*

$$\langle i, \mathsf{integrate}(C, S), \Lambda, \theta \rangle \longrightarrow \langle i, Agent(j), \Lambda, \theta \rangle, \ \langle j, S, (true, \{\}), \bot \rangle,$$

where $j \in Ident$ is a *fresh* agent identifier and $\bot$ denotes the totally undefined function.

The transition rule defines the integration of an instance of the agent class C. It shows how the agent system is expanded with a new agent j that starts its execution with the statement S where its initial mental state is defined to be the empty one. The methods that the integrated agent can invoke are given by the methods of C.

The result of the integration is formulated by the information $Agent(j)$, which expresses that the agent with identifier j is part of the multi-agent system.

Definition 14 *(Transition rules for the construct $S \Rightarrow j$)*

$$\frac{\langle i, S, \Lambda, \theta \rangle \longrightarrow \langle i, S', \Lambda', \theta' \rangle}{\langle i, S \Rightarrow j, \Lambda, \theta \rangle \longrightarrow \langle i, S' \Rightarrow j, \Lambda', \theta' \rangle} \qquad \frac{\langle i, S, \Lambda, \theta \rangle \longrightarrow \langle i, \varphi, \Lambda', \theta' \rangle}{\langle i, S \Rightarrow j, \Lambda, \theta \rangle \longrightarrow \langle i, \varphi \Rightarrow j, \Lambda', \theta' \rangle}$$

The transition for the construct $S \Rightarrow j$ can be derived from the transition for the statement S. The first transition rule deals with the case that S does not terminate after one computation step: S' denotes the part of S that still needs to be executed, while the second rule deals with the case that S terminates with a result φ.

Definition 15 *(Transition rule for sequential composition)*

$$\frac{\langle i, a, \Lambda, \theta \rangle \longrightarrow \langle i, \varphi, \Lambda', \theta' \rangle}{\langle i, a; S, \Lambda, \theta \rangle \longrightarrow \langle i, S, \Lambda', \theta' \rangle}$$

The transition for the sequential composition of an action a and a statement S can be derived from the transition for the action a. Note that the result φ of executing a is simply ignored, because (possibly) it has already been processed in Λ' and θ'. For instance, we can derive the transition $\langle i, (X \leftarrow \varphi); S, \Lambda, \theta \rangle \longrightarrow \langle i, S, \Lambda, \theta\{\varphi/X\} \rangle$.

De nition 16 *(Transition rules for non-deterministic choice)*

$$\frac{\langle i, S_1, \Lambda, \theta\rangle \longrightarrow \langle i, S_1', \Lambda', \theta'\rangle}{\begin{array}{l}\langle i, S_1 + S_2, \Lambda, \theta\rangle \longrightarrow \langle i, S_1', \Lambda', \theta'\rangle\\ \langle i, S_2 + S_1, \Lambda, \theta\rangle \longrightarrow \langle i, S_1', \Lambda', \theta'\rangle\end{array}} \qquad \frac{\langle i, S_1, \Lambda, \theta\rangle \longrightarrow \langle i, \varphi, \Lambda', \theta'\rangle}{\begin{array}{l}\langle i, S_1 + S_2, \Lambda, \theta\rangle \longrightarrow \langle i, \varphi, \Lambda', \theta'\rangle\\ \langle i, S_2 + S_1, \Lambda, \theta\rangle \longrightarrow \langle i, \varphi, \Lambda', \theta'\rangle\end{array}}$$

The transition for the non-deterministic choice $S + T$ between two statements can be derived from the transition of either S or T. The second rule deals with termination.

De nition 17 *(Transition rules for internal parallelism)*

$$\frac{\langle i, S_1, \Lambda, \theta\rangle \longrightarrow \langle i, S_1', \Lambda', \theta'\rangle}{\begin{array}{l}\langle i, S_1 \& S_2, \Lambda, \theta\rangle \longrightarrow \langle i, S_1' \& S_2, \Lambda', \theta'\rangle\\ \langle i, S_2 \& S_1, \Lambda, \theta\rangle \longrightarrow \langle i, S_2 \& S_1', \Lambda', \theta'\rangle\end{array}} \qquad \frac{\langle i, S_1, \Lambda, \theta\rangle \longrightarrow \langle i, \varphi, \Lambda', \theta'\rangle}{\begin{array}{l}\langle i, S_1 \& S_2, \Lambda, \theta\rangle \longrightarrow \langle i, S_2, \Lambda', \theta'\rangle\\ \langle i, S_2 \& S_1, \Lambda, \theta\rangle \longrightarrow \langle i, S_2, \Lambda', \theta'\rangle\end{array}}$$

The internal parallel composition $S \& T$ of two statements is modeled by means of an interleaving of the computation steps of S and T.

De nition 18 *(Transition rule for skip statement)*

$$\langle i, \text{skip}, \Lambda, \theta\rangle \longrightarrow \langle i, true, \Lambda, \theta\rangle$$

The statement skip does not effect Λ and θ and yields the result $true$.

Example. Let $\mathcal{A}$ be an agent system (used in a library, for instance) consisting of a client agent i and additionally two server agents j and k. Consider the situation that the client i is looking for a biography on Elvis Presley and hence, asks the serving agent j for it.
 The methods of the servers j and k are de ned as follows:

$$answer :- \quad (\text{accept}(ask) + \text{handle}(ask)); answer$$
$$ask(X) :- \quad \text{query}(X) + \text{request}(\iota x.Server(x), ask(X))$$

The method *answer* is a recursive procedure in which in each round either a new *ask*-message is accepted or an *ask*-message is selected from the goal state and subsequently executed. Additionally, the method *ask* corresponds to a choice between querying the private information store (belief state) for an appropriate document and passing the question on to another server. We assume that the mental state Λ_2 of agent j is given by $(\neg P(a) \wedge Server(k), \{\})$ and the mental state Λ_3 of k is given by $(P(b), \{\})$, where we use the predicate P to denote that a document is a biography of Elvis Presley. Consider the initial con guration of the agent system $\mathcal{A}$:

$$\langle i, X \leftarrow \text{request}(j, ask(?xP(x))); \text{update}(X), \Lambda_1, \bot\rangle,$$
$$\langle j, answer, \Lambda_2, \bot\rangle,$$
$$\langle k, answer, \Lambda_3, \bot\rangle,$$

The agent i thus asks the agent j for the information $?xP(x)$ and subsequently will add the result of the query to its belief state. The following then constitutes a sequence of transitions (computation) starting with the above con guration.

$\longrightarrow$
$\langle i, X \leftarrow \mathsf{request}(j, ask(?xP(x))); \mathsf{update}(X), \Lambda_1, \perp \rangle,$
$\langle j, (\mathsf{accept}(ask) + \mathsf{handle}(ask)); answer, \Lambda_2, \perp \rangle,$
$\langle k, answer, \Lambda_3, \perp \rangle \longrightarrow$

$\langle i, X \leftarrow \mathsf{wait}(j); \mathsf{update}(X), \Lambda_1, \perp \rangle,$
$\langle j, answer, \Lambda'_2, \perp \rangle,$
$\langle k, answer, \Lambda_3, \perp \rangle \longrightarrow$
where $\Lambda'_2 = (\neg P(a) \wedge Server(k), \{ask(?xP(x)) \Rightarrow i\})$

$\langle i, X \leftarrow \mathsf{wait}(j); \mathsf{update}(X), \Lambda_1, \perp \rangle,$
$\langle j, (\mathsf{accept}(ask) + \mathsf{handle}(ask)); answer, \Lambda'_2, \perp \rangle,$
$\langle k, answer, \Lambda_3, \perp \rangle \longrightarrow$

$\langle i, X \leftarrow \mathsf{wait}(j); \mathsf{update}(X), \Lambda_1, \perp \rangle,$
$\langle j, (\mathsf{query}(?xP(x)) + \mathsf{request}(\iota x.Server(x), ask(?xP(x))) \Rightarrow i); answer, \Lambda_2, \perp \rangle,$
$\langle k, answer, \Lambda_3, \perp \rangle \longrightarrow$

$\langle i, X \leftarrow \mathsf{wait}(j); \mathsf{update}(X), \Lambda_1, \perp \rangle,$
$\langle j, (\mathsf{query}(?xP(x)) + \mathsf{request}(\iota x.Server(x), ask(?xP(x))) \Rightarrow i); answer, \Lambda_2, \perp \rangle,$
$\langle k, (\mathsf{accept}(ask) + \mathsf{handle}(ask)); answer, \Lambda_3, \perp \rangle \longrightarrow$

$\langle i, X \leftarrow \mathsf{wait}(j); \mathsf{update}(X), \Lambda_1, \perp \rangle,$
$\langle j, (\mathsf{wait}(k) \Rightarrow i); answer, \Lambda_2, \perp \rangle,$
$\langle k, answer, \Lambda'_3, \perp \rangle \longrightarrow$
where $\Lambda'_3 = (P(b), \{ask(?xP(x)) \Rightarrow j\})$

$\langle i, X \leftarrow \mathsf{wait}(j); \mathsf{update}(X), \Lambda_1, \perp \rangle,$
$\langle j, (\mathsf{wait}(k) \Rightarrow i); answer, \Lambda_2, \perp \rangle,$
$\langle k, (\mathsf{accept}(ask) + \mathsf{handle}(ask)); answer, \Lambda'_3, \perp \rangle \longrightarrow$

$\langle i, X \leftarrow \mathsf{wait}(j); \mathsf{update}(X), \Lambda_1, \perp \rangle,$
$\langle j, (\mathsf{wait}(k) \Rightarrow i); answer, \Lambda_2, \perp \rangle,$
$\langle k, (\mathsf{query}(?xP(x)) \Rightarrow j); answer, \Lambda_3, \perp \rangle \longrightarrow$

$\langle i, X \leftarrow \mathsf{wait}(j); \mathsf{update}(X), \Lambda_1, \perp \rangle,$
$\langle j, (\mathsf{wait}(k) \Rightarrow i); answer, \Lambda_2, \perp \rangle,$
$\langle k, (P(b) \Rightarrow j); answer, \Lambda_3, \perp \rangle \longrightarrow$

$\langle i, X \leftarrow \mathsf{wait}(j); \mathsf{update}(X), \Lambda_1, \perp \rangle,$
$\langle j, (P(b) \Rightarrow i); answer, \Lambda_2, \perp \rangle,$
$\langle k, answer, \Lambda_3, \perp \rangle \longrightarrow$

$\langle i, X \leftarrow P(b); \mathsf{update}(X), \Lambda_1, \perp \rangle,$
$\langle j, answer, \Lambda_2, \perp \rangle,$
$\langle k, answer, \Lambda_3, \perp \rangle \longrightarrow$

$\langle i, \mathsf{update}(X), \Lambda_1, \{P(b)/X\} \rangle,$
$\langle j, answer, \Lambda_2, \perp \rangle,$
$\langle k, answer, \Lambda_3, \perp \rangle \longrightarrow$

$\langle i, true, (P(b), \{\}), \{P(b)/X\} \rangle,$
$\langle j, answer, \Lambda_2, \perp \rangle,$
$\langle k, answer, \Lambda_3, \perp \rangle \longrightarrow$

4 Related Work

The research on multi-agent systems has resulted in the development of various agent communication languages, none of which however has yet been assigned a satisfactory formal semantics. And it is this lack of a clear semantics that in our opinion constitutes one of the major hindrances for an agent communication language to become widely accepted. In this section, we discuss the relation of our framework with two of these languages, viz. the agent communication languages KQML and FIPA-ACL.

KQML. The Knowledge Query and Manipulation Language (KQML) provides a language for the exchange of knowledge and information in multi-agent systems (cf. [10]). It de nes the format of a collection of messages that are exchanged between communicating agents. The main constituents of a KQML message are a *performative* that indicates the purpose of the message, its *content* expressed in some representation language and nally , the *identities* of the sender and the receiver.

The semantics of a KQML message are given by the following three ingredients: (1) a *precondition* on the mental states of the sender and receiver before the communication of the message, (2) a postcondition that should hold after the communication and (3) a *completion* condition that should hold after the conversation of which this message was a constituent, has terminated. The language in which these conditions are expressed consists of logical combinations of the following v e operators: $bel(i, \varphi)$ denoting that φ is in the knowledge base of i and $know(i, \varphi)$, $want(i, \varphi)$ and $intend(i, \varphi)$, expressing that i knows φ, wants φ and is committed to φ, respectively. Finally, $process(i, m)$ denotes that the message m will be processed by the agent i.

An important feature of the framework is that the communication of a message is not an action that occurs in isolation, but it takes place in the context of a conversation comprised of a sequence of communications. In this wider context, the semantics of the KQML messages can be thought of de ning correct conversations. That is, the precondition of a message determines the collection of messages that are allowed to precede the message, while the postcondition lays down the messages that are permitted to succeed the message. Additionally, in case the completion condition is a logical consequence of the postcondition, the conversation can be identi ed to have successfully terminated.

For instance, the following sequence of messages constitutes a typical conversation:

$$\mathbf{advertise}(i, j, \mathbf{ask\text{-}if}(j, i, \varphi)), \quad \mathbf{ask\text{-}if}(j, i, \varphi) \text{ and } \mathbf{tell}(i, j, \varphi)$$

Let us examine the constituents of this conversation in more detail. First, the pre-, post- and completion conditions for a message $\mathbf{advertise}(i, j, m)$ are as follows, where in this case m is given by $\mathbf{ask\text{-}if}(j, i, \varphi)$:

(1) $intend(i, process(i, m))$
(2) $know(i, know(j, intend(i, process(i, m)))) \wedge$
     $know(j, intend(i, process(i, m)))$
(3) $know(j, intend(i, process(i, m)))$

The intuitive meaning of the message $\mathbf{advertise}(i, j, m)$ amounts to letting the agent j know that i has the intention to process the message m. Additionally, the fact that the completion condition coincides with the postcondition, implies that this message constitutes a conversation by itself.

In our framework, we have a slightly different mechanism: there is the primitive of the form accept(m), which re ects the agent's intention to accept a message that is in the collection m. It has the advantage above the KQML message $\mathbf{advertise}(i, j, m)$ that it is very e xible as it speci es the messages that will *currently* be accepted; a subsequent occurrence of the primitive in the agent program might specify a sub-, super- or even a completely disjoint set.

Secondly, the conditions for a message $\mathbf{ask\text{-}if}(j, i, \varphi)$ are as follows:

(1) $\bigvee_{\psi \in \Gamma}(want(j, know(j, \psi))) \wedge$
     $know(j, intend(i, process(i, m))) \wedge$
     $intend(i, process(i, m))$
(2) $\bigvee_{\psi \in \Gamma}(intend(j, know(j, \psi))) \wedge$
     $know(i, \bigvee_{\psi \in \Gamma}(want(j, know(j, \psi))))$
(3) $\bigvee_{\psi \in \Gamma}(know(j, \psi))$

where m is given by $\mathbf{ask\text{-}if}(j, i, \varphi)$ and Γ equals $\{bel(i, \varphi), bel(i, \neg\varphi), \neg bel(i, \varphi)\}$.

The intuitive meaning of the message $\mathbf{ask\text{-}if}(j, i, \varphi)$ amounts to letting the agent i know that j wants to know whether i believes φ, believes $\neg\varphi$ or does not believe φ. The second and third conjunct of the precondition re ect the requirement that the message is to be preceded by an $\mathbf{advertise}(i, j, m)$ message. Additionally, the completion condition indicates that the conversation of which this message is a constituent, has not successfully terminated until the agent j knows one of the formulae in k. As KQML abstracts away from the content language of messages, it is not clear to us why the formula $bel(i, \neg\varphi)$ is an element of the set Γ, as it refers to an operator $\neg$ in the content language (which in principle, does not need to be present at all). In particular, if the agent j wants to know whether i believes $\neg\varphi$ it can use the message $\mathbf{ask\text{-}if}(j, i, \neg\varphi)$.

Thirdly, the conditions for the message $\mathbf{tell}(i, j, \varphi)$ are as follows:

(1) $bel(i, \varphi) \wedge know(i, want(j, know(j, bel(i, \varphi)))) \wedge$
     $intend(j, know(j, bel(i, \varphi)))$
(2) $know(i, know(j, bel(i, \varphi))) \wedge know(j, bel(i, \varphi))$
(3) $know(j, bel(i, \varphi))$

The intuitive meaning of the message is to let the agent j know that i believes the formula φ to be true. The rst conjunct of the precondition states that i should indeed believe the formula φ, where the second and third conjunct should indicate that the message is to be preceded by a message of the form **ask-if**(j, i, φ). Here we see why it is so important to have a formal framework to give semantics to a language: mistakes are easily made. The postcondition $\bigvee_{\psi \in \Gamma}(intend(j, know(j, \psi)))$ where $\Gamma = \{bel(i, \varphi), bel(i, \neg\varphi), \neg bel(i, \varphi)\}$ of the $ask\text{-}if$ message, does not entail the precondition $intend(j, know(j, bel(i, \varphi)))$ of the $tell$ message. Hence, with this semantics the reception of an **ask-if**(j, i, φ) message is not suf cient to be able to send a **tell**(i, j, φ) message. Additionally, the nesting of knowledge operators seems to be quite arbitrary: it is unclear why the nesting of knowledge operators in the postcondition is restricted to depth two, and for instance does not include $know(j, know(i, know(j, bel(i, \varphi))))$.

Our concern with de ning the semantics of communication in the manner as employed for KQML, is that it still does not yield an exact meaning of agent communication. The KQML semantics is de ned in terms of operators for which the semantics themselves remain unde ned. For instance, the exact difference between the operators $want$ and $intend$ remains unclear.

Moreover, in contrast to the approach employed in this paper, there is a gap between the syntactic structure of the language and its semantics, which is due to the use of rather high-level operators. In our framework however, the operational semantics closely follow the syntactic structure of the language, which opens up the possibility of developing an interpreter for the language on the basis of this operational description. This is due to the fact that the con gurations of an agent system can be seen as an abstract model of a machine, where its transitions de ne the actions that it can perform. In fact this machine would act as an interpreter for the language.

Thirdly, we believe that the KQML semantics impose too strong requirements on the agents with respect to their reactions towards incoming messages. We believe that these reactions are agent-dependent and hence should not be part of the semantics of messages. For instance, in our framework, consider three agents each having one the following de nitions of the method $ask(X)$:

$$ask(X) :- \quad \mathsf{query}(X) + \mathsf{query}(\neg X)$$
$$ask(X) :- \quad X' \leftarrow \mathsf{query}(X); X'' \leftarrow \neg X'$$
$$ask(X) :- \quad \mathsf{request}(\iota x. Agent(x), ask(X))$$

The rst agent tests its belief state and checks whether it entails the formula X or its negation. This corresponds to the reaction imposed by the KQML semantics for the **ask-if**(X) message. On the other hand, the second agent checks whether its belief state entails X and subsequently delivers the negation of what it believes to hold (note that the result of the sequential composition of two actions is given by the result of the second action). In KQML this reaction is simply ruled out. However, in our opinion this reaction is not a result of the semantics of the message but of the characteristics of the receiving agent. We believe that any reaction should be allowed, as for instance shown by the third agent, which simply passes the message along to another agent and delivers the result that it receives from this agent.

FIPA-ACL. Besides the language KQML there is a second proposal for a standard agent communication language, which is developed by the organisation FIPA. This language, which we will refer to as the FIPA-ACL, also prescribes the syntax and semantics of a collection of message types (cf. [11]). The format of these messages is almost equal to that of KQML, while their semantics are given by means of (1) a *precondition* on the mental state of the sender that should hold prior to the dispatch of the message and (2) the expected *effect* of the message.

There are four primitive messages; viz. $\langle i, \mathsf{inform}(j, \varphi)\rangle$ and $\langle i, \mathsf{confirm}(j, \varphi)\rangle$ in which the agent i tells the agent j that it believes the formula φ to hold and a message $\langle i, \mathsf{disconfirm}(j, \varphi)\rangle$ in which the agent i tells the agent j that it believes the negation of φ to hold. The difference between the inform and con rm message is that the former is employed in case agent i has no beliefs about the beliefs of j concerning φ, i.e., it does not believe that j believes φ or its negation or is uncertain about φ or its negation, whereas the latter is used in case i believes that j is uncertain about φ. Thirdly, the discon rm message is used for situations in which i believes the negation of φ and additionally that j believes φ or is uncertain about φ. The expected effect of informing φ, con rming φ and discon rming $\neg\varphi$ is the same: the receiver believes φ.

The fourth primitive message is of the form $\langle i, \mathsf{request}(j, a)\rangle$ in which i requests the agent j to perform the action a. The condition for this message is that i believes that the agent j will be the only agent performing a and that it does not believe that j has already an intention of doing a. Additionally, the part of the precondition of a that concerns the mental attitudes of i should additionally hold.

All other messages are de ned in terms of these primitives together with the operators ; for sequential composition and | for non-deterministic choice. An example of a composite message is $\langle i, \mathsf{query\text{-}if}(j, \varphi)\rangle$, which is an abbreviation for the construct $\langle i, \mathsf{request}(j, \langle j, \mathsf{inform}(i, \varphi)\rangle \mid \langle j, \mathsf{inform}(i, \neg\varphi)\rangle)\rangle$. Analogous to KQML, there remains a gap between the syntax of the communication language and the semantic description given in terms of high-level modal operators as those for (nested) belief and uncertainty. We think however that the operational model outlined in this paper, could act as a rst step in the development of an operational description of the FIPA-ACL.

5 Future Research

In this paper, we have outlined a basic programming language for systems of communicating agents that interact with each other via a rendezvous communication scheme. In subsequent research, we will study the extension of the framework with a notion of agent expertise in the form of a vocabulary or signature together with the incorporation of object-oriented features as subtyping and inheritance. Inheritance would then not be restricted to the inheritance of methods but could also involve the inheritance of expertise. Another issue is the study in what way the current framework could be used to develop an operational semantic model for existing agent communication languages.

References

1. P.H.M. America, J. de Bakker, J.N. Kok, and J. Rutten. Operational semantics of a parallel object-oriented language. In *Conference Record of the 13th Annual ACM Symposium on Principles of Programming Languages*, pages 194–208, St. Petersburg Beach, Florida, 1986.
2. G.R. Andrews. *Concurrent Programming, Principles and Practice*. The Benjamin/Cummings Publishing Company, Inc., Redwood City, California, 1991.
3. A. D. Birrell and B. J. Nelson. Implementing remote procedure calls. *ACM Transactions on Computer Systems*, 2:39–59, 1984.
4. P. Cohen and H. Levesque. Communicative actions for arti cial agents. In *Proceedings of the First International Conference on Multi-Agent Systems*, 1995.
5. M. Colombetti. Semantic, normative and practical aspects of agent communication. *In this volume*.
6. R.M. van Eijk, F.S. de Boer, W. van der Hoek, and J.-J.Ch. Meyer. A language for modular information-passing agents. In K. R. Apt, editor, *CWI Quarterly, Special issue on Constraint Programming*, volume 11, pages 273–297. CWI, Amsterdam, 1998.
7. R.M. van Eijk, F.S. de Boer, W. van der Hoek, and J.-J.Ch. Meyer. Systems of communicating agents. In Henri Prade, editor, *Proceedings of the 13th biennial European Conference on Arti cial Intelligence (ECAI-98)*, pages 293–297, Brighton, UK, 1998. John Wiley & Sons, Ltd.
8. R.M. van Eijk, F.S. de Boer, W. van der Hoek, and J.-J.Ch. Meyer. Information-passing and belief revision in multi-agent systems. In J. P. M. Müller, M. P. Singh, and A. S. Rao, editors, *Intelligent Agents V — Proceedings of 5th International Workshop on Agent Theories, Architectures, and Languages (ATAL'98)*, volume 1555 of *Lecture Notes in Arti cial Intelligence*, pages 29–45. Springer-Verlag, Heidelberg, 1999.
9. R.M. van Eijk, F.S. de Boer, W. van der Hoek, and J.-J.Ch. Meyer. Open multi-agent systems: Agent communication and integration. In *Intelligent Agents VI, Proceedings of 6th International Workshop on Agent Theories, Architectures, and Languages (ATAL'99)*, Lecture Notes in Arti cial Intelligence. Springer-Verlag, Heidelberg, 2000.
10. T. Finin, D. McKay, R. Fritzson, and R. McEntire. KQML: An Information and Knowledge Exchange Protocol. In Kazuhiro Fuchi and Toshio Yokoi, editors, *Knowledge Building and Knowledge Sharing*. Ohmsha and IOS Press, 1994.
11. Foundation For Intelligent Physical Agents. Fipa'97 speci cation part 2 – agent communication language. Version dated 10th October 1997.
12. P. Gärdenfors. *Knowledge in ux: Modelling the dynamics of epistemic states*. Bradford books, MIT, Cambridge, 1988.
13. K.V. Hindriks, F.S. de Boer, W. van der Hoek, and J.-J.Ch. Meyer. A formal semantics for an abstract agent programming language. In M.P. Singh, A. Rao, and M.J. Wooldridge, editors, *Proceedings of Fourth International Workshop on Agent Theories, Architectures and Languages (ATAL'97)*, volume 1365 of *LNAI*, pages 215–229. Springer-Verlag, 1998.
14. G. Plotkin. A structured approach to operational semantics. Technical Report DAIMI FN-19, Computer Science Department, Aarhus University, 1981.
15. B. Thomsen. A calculus of higher order communicating systems. In *Conference Record of the 16th Annual ACM Symposium on Principles of Programming Languages*, pages 143–153, 1989.
16. M. Wooldridge and N. Jennings. Intelligent agents: theory and practice. *The Knowledge Engineering Review*, 10(2):115–152, 1995.

An Approach to Using XML and a Rule-Based Content Language with an Agent Communication Language

Benjamin N. Grosof[1] and Yannis Labrou[2]

[1] IBM T.J. Watson Research Center,
P.O. Box 704, Yorktown Heights, NY 10598, USA
grosof@us.ibm.com (alt.: grosof@cs.stanford.edu),
http://www.research.ibm.com/people/g/grosof/
[2] Electrical Engineering and Computer Science Department
University of Maryland, Baltimore County, Baltimore, MD, 21250, USA
jklabrou@cs.umbc.edu,
http://www.cs.umbc.edu/~jklabrou

Abstract. We argue for an XML encoding of FIPA Agent Communication Language (ACL), and give an alpha version of it, called Agent Communication Markup Language (ACML), which we have implemented. The XML approach facilitates: (a) developing/maintaining parsers, integrating with WWW-world software engineering, and (b) the enriching capability to (hyper-)link to ontologies and other extra information. The XML approach applies similarly to KQML as well. Motivated by the importance of the content language aspect of agent communication, we focus in particular on business rules as a form of content that is important in e-commerce applications such as bidding negotiations. A leading candidate content language for business rules is Knowledge Interchange Format (KIF), which is currently in the ANSI standards committee process. We observe several major practical shortcomings of KIF as a content language for business rules in e-commerce. We argue instead for a knowledge representation (KR) approach based on Courteous Logic Programs (CLP) that overcomes several of KIF's representational limitations, and argue for this CLP approach, e.g., for its logical non-monotonicity and its computational practicality. CLP is a previous KR that expressively extends declarative ordinary logic programs cf. Prolog; it includes negation-as-failure plus prioritized conflict handling. We argue for an XML encoding of business rules content, and give an alpha version of it, called Business Rules Markup Language (BRML), which we have implemented. BRML can express both CLP and a subset of KIF (i.e., of first-order logic) that overlaps with CLP. BRML expressively both extends and complements KIF. The overall advantages of an XML approach to content language are similar to those for the XML approach to ACL, and indeed complements the latter since content is carried within ACL messages. We have implemented both ACML and BRML/CLP; a free alpha prototype of BRML/CLP, called IBM CommonRules, was released on the Web in July of 1999.

F. Dignum and M. Greaves (Eds.): Agent Communication, LNAI 1916, pp. 96–117, 2000.
© Springer-Verlag Berlin Heidelberg 2000

1   Introduction

The concept of an Agent Communication Language (ACL) has its origins in the work of the Knowledge Sharing Effort (KSE). The KSE work gave birth to Knowledge Query and Manipulation Language (KQML) in the early 1990's, which in turn influenced the Foundation for Intelligent Physical Agents (FIPA standards body) ACL[1]. (Terminology: In this paper, by "ACL" we mean either KQML (which has now several variants) or FIPA ACL. Since then the problem of an adequate semantics of an ACL has dominated the debate on ACL's. Despite the substantial amount of work on this problem, the issue of an agent's conformance with the ACL semantics is as thorny as ever [20] and moreover puts into question the degree of usefulness of semantic accounts. But even worse, the emphasis on ACL semantics has drawn attention away from other issues that are perhaps even more important to the success of ACL's: (1) how do agents find one another and manage to establish a "conversation"; (2) having achieved that, what is the "content" about which they actually talk; and (3) the relationship between ACL's and WWW technologies. We are interested in the latter two issues. [2]

KQML and FIPA ACL have evolved at a considerable distance from the mainstream of Internet technologies and standards. No Internet standardization organization has ACL's in their agenda. With the exception of the Artimis project (France Telecom), no major industry player has committed major resources to depend upon, or to develop, ACL's, although there are some plans for future work that will take advantage of FIPA technologies, as they become available. At the same time the WWW is a huge repository of information and agents are almost always referred to in conjunction with the WWW. ACL's are driving a great part of the agent work (FIPA ACL is the centerpiece of the FIPA effort); it is thus reasonable to suggest that ACL work ought to integrate easily with the WWW and to be able to leverage WWW tools and infrastructure. This motivates us to give (and to advocate) an Extensible Markup Language (XML) encoding of ACL messages, as a first step towards this kind of integration.

Agents, while conversing, exchange their information content; specifically we focus on the language used to describe it, i.e., the *content language* in ACL terminology. An ACL message's content layer, which contains descriptions in the content language, is distinct from the *propositional-attitude* layer which contains the (speech act type of) primitive of the ACL message. (Terminology: In this paper, by an ACL communication "primitive", we mean what KQML calls a "performative" and what FIPA ACL calls a "communicative act".) The KSE developed the Knowledge Interchange Format (KIF) as a general-purpose content language. However, it is important for ACL's to support multiple, e.g., special-purpose, content languages. We are particularly interested in representing business rules for e-commerce applications of communicating agents. For this purpose, we observe that KIF has significant shortcomings, notably, its inability to represent logical non-monotonicity. Accordingly, we give a new con-

---

[1] http://www.fipa.org
[2] We do not deal with the first issue in this paper. See [13] for such a discussion.

tent language for business rules: an extended form of logic programs, with deep declarative semantics, encoded moreover in XML. This language, called Business Rules Markup Language (BRML), overcomes several limitations of KIF, yet broadly overlaps with KIF both syntactically and semantically; it thus extends and complements KIF.

Next, we give an outline of the remainder of this paper. In Section 2, we argue for the advantages of encoding ACL messages in XML and then present ACML, an XML language for that purpose. In Section 3 we review the content language concept and some existing content languages, then discuss our focus on business rules for e-commerce applications such as bidding negotiations. In Section 4, we review KIF and critique its shortcomings as a representation for business rules. In Section 5, we give a business rules content language, called *Courteous Logic Programs (CLP)*, that extends and complements KIF, while addressing several of KIF's shortcomings. In Section 6 we present BRML, the XML encoding of CLP. In Section 7, we describe our implementation. A free alpha prototype of BRML/CLP, called IBM *CommonRules*, was released on the Web in July of 1999. Current and future work directions are discussed in appropriate spots throughout the paper but we summarize them in Section 7.

2   XML Embodiment of FIPA ACL

In this section, we give an encoding of FIPA ACL messages in XML, and observe that using XML has several advantages. This leads us to suggest that in future industry practice, the preferred encoding for ACL messages should be XML rather than pure ASCII. (We are focusing on FIPA ACL but the same arguments and approach would apply to KQML too.) Finin, Labrou, and Grosof together first advocated this idea to FIPA during the FIPA meeting in Dublin, in July 1998. Although other groups of researchers have been considering a XML encoding for FIPA ACL, this paper is (to the the best of our knowledge) the first published treatment of this issue. As we will detail in Section 6, we advocate using XML also for the content of the ACL message itself, for similar reasons. Keep in mind, however, that the content need not be in XML even if the ACL message is in XML, or vice versa.

2.1   Brief Review of XML

XML is a language for creating markup languages that describe data. XML is a machine-readable and application-independent encoding of a "document", e.g., of a FIPA ACL message including its content.

In contrast to HTML which describes document structure and visual presentation, XML describes data in a human-readable format with no indication of how the data is to be displayed. It is a database-neutral and device-neutral format; data marked up in XML can be targeted to different devices using, for example, eXtensible Style Language (XSL). The XML source by itself is not primarily intended directly for human viewing, though it is human-understandable. Rather, the XML is rendered using standard available XML-world tools, then browsed, e.g., using standard Web browsers or specialized other browsers/editors. (Netscape and Microsoft already are supporting XML in the latest versions of their Web browsers, for example.) One leading method for rendering is via XSL, in which one specifies a stylesheet.

XML is a meta- language used to define other domain- or industry-specific languages. To construct a XML language (also called a "vocabulary"), one supplies a specific *Document Type Definition (DTD)*, which is essentially a context-free grammar like the Extended BNF (Backus Naur Form) used to describe computer languages. In other words, a DTD provides the rules that define the elements and structure of the new language. For example, if we want to describe employee records, we would define a DTD which states that the <NAME> element consists of three other elements called <FIRST>, <MIDDLE>, and <LAST>, in that order. The DTD would also indicate if any of the nested elements is optional, can be repeated, and/or has a default value. Any browser (or application) having an XML parser could interpret the employee document instance by "learning" the rules defined by the DTD.

2.2   Review of ACL

The core semantics of an ACL is defined as the *"deep"* semantics (i.e., semantics in the sense of declarative knowledge-representation) of its (communication) primitives. This semantics are expressed in some knowledge representation language: SL in the case of FIPA ACL. This semantics only takes into account the *speaker*, the *hearer* (in *speech act* terminology) and the content of the communicative act. The speaker, the hearer and the content correspond to the :sender, the :receiver and the :content of the *syntactic* representation of the ACL. The previous canonical syntactic form of the ACL message (for both KQML and FIPA ACL) is a Lisp-like ASCII sequence.

The (previous) canonical ACL message syntax (both in FIPA ACL and KQML) further includes additional message parameters whose semantics go beyond that of the primitives. These parameters are unaccounted for in the deep semantics but are essential to the processing of an ACL message. In other words, the ACL includes several *"pragmatic"* (i.e., operational) aspects, in addition to the primitives aspect. One pragmatic aspect is parsing in and out of the ACL, i.e., digesting and composing well-formed ACL syntax (which is Lisp-like) to extract or insert message parameters. A second pragmatic aspect is queuing (and de-queuing) ACL messages for delivery through TCP or some other network protocol.

Further pragmatic issues being dealt with in the context of ACL efforts include the agent naming scheme, and the conventions for finding agents and initiating interaction; although, in our view, these issues are actually outside of the ACL's scope. Actually, the various APIs for KQML and FIPA ACL provide nothing (as expected) regarding the actual processing of ACL messages (depending on the primitive), since respecting the deep semantics of the primitives is the responsibility of the application that makes use of those API's. Such API's today mainly take care of the parsing and queuing tasks mentioned above. Performing these tasks is what using KQML (or FIPA ACL, for that matter) has come to mean. For all intents and purposes, compliance with the ACL's specification means compliance with all these pragmatic conventions. Such conventions are not part of the standard (to the extent that the ACL semantics is standardized) and the subtle (or not so subtle) discrepancies amongst their implementations account in large part for the situation today in which there is often a lack of interoperability between systems using the same ACL. [3]

2.3   Introducing ACML

Next, we give an alpha-version specification of FIPA ACL in XML, which we call **Agent Communication Markup Language (ACML)**. To begin with, we need to define a DTD for ACML [4]. We have indeed defined an alpha-version DTD for ACML, and have a running prototype implementation of ACML that uses this DTD.

We begin with an example of a XML encoding of a FIPA ACL message. Figure 1 shows an example FIPA ACL message, in the previous (ASCII, Lisp-like) syntax. Figure 2 shows the same FIPA ACL message encoded in XML, i.e., in ACML. The content is a KIF expression which is not encoded in XML in this example. The DTD for ACML is shown in Figure 3. This is an alpha version.

The deep semantics of the communication primitives in ACML is simply taken to be the same as previously. This semantics is not affected by encoding in XML instead of the previous ASCII; it is defined independently of the choice of syntactic encoding.

By XML-ifying the syntactic representation we enhance (i.e., extend) the (previous) canonical (pure ASCII) syntactic representation by introducing mark-up for parsing (the "tags", in XML terminology). This markup significantly facilitates the development effort needed for parsing in and out.

---

[3] The differences in sets of primitives used and their intended meaning constitute a second-in-order interoperability barrier that is not confronted due to these more mundane "lower-level" obstacles.

[4] The same will be done for the content language (see Section 6).

```
(inform
   :sender    jklabrou
   :receiver  grosof
   :content   (CPU libretto50 pentium)
   :ontology  laptop
   :language  kif)
```

Fig. 1. A FIPA ACL message.

```
<?xml version="pre-1.0"?>
<!DOCTYPE fipa_acl SYSTEM "fipa_acl.dtd">
<message>
  <messagetype>
     inform
  </messagetype>
  <messageparameter>
     <sender link="http://www.cs.umbc.edu/~jklabrou">
     jklabrou
     </sender>
  </messageparameter>
  <messageparameter>
     <receiver link="http://www.research.ibm.com/people/g/grosof/">
     grosof
     </receiver>
  </messageparameter>
  <messageparameter>
     <ontology link="http://www.cs.umbc.edu/~jklabrou/
                                      ontology/laptop.html">
     laptop
     </ontology>
  </messageparameter>
  <messageparameter>
     <content>
     (CPU libretto50 pentium)
     </content>
  </messageparameter>
  <messageparameter>
     <language link="http://www.stanford.edu/kif.html">
     kif
     </language>
  </messageparameter>
</message>
```

Fig. 2. An example of a FIPA ACL message encoded in XML, i.e., expressed in ACML. Notice that the XML encoding carries additional information as compared to the canonical ASCII encoding: in particular, links (as well as parsing information).

The XML representation also facilitates introducing pragmatic/operational elements that go beyond what the pure ASCII previous syntax did: notably, via *links* (in a similar sense as does HTML compared to ASCII). And we indeed introduced such extras in our alpha DTD and example. For example, the ACL message of Figure 2 includes information beyond what is equivalent to that in Figure 1. Here (Figure 2), the receiver is not just some symbolic name but is also a URL that points to a particular network location which could provide additional information about the receiver agent's identity (e.g., how to contact its owner, its network ports, etc.).

```
<?xml version="pre-1.0" encoding="US-ASCII"?>

<!ENTITY % messagetp "accept-proposal | agree | cancel |cfp |
confirm | disconfirm | failure | inform | inform-if |
inform-ref | not-understood | propose | query-if | query-ref |
refuse | reject-proposal | request | request-when |
request-whenever | subscribe">

<!ELEMENT message (messagetype, messageparameter* )>
<!ELEMENT messagetype (%messagetp;)>


<!ELEMENT messageparameter (sender | receiver | content |
reply-with | reply-by| in-reply-to | envelope | language |
ontology | protocol | conversation-id)>

<!ELEMENT sender (agentname)>
<!ATTLIST sender link CDATA #REQUIRED >

<!ELEMENT receiver (agentname)>
<!ATTLIST receiver link CDATA #REQUIRED >

<!ELEMENT content (#PCDATA)>
<!ATTLIST content link CDATA #REQUIRED >

<!ELEMENT reply-with (#PCDATA)>
<!ELEMENT reply-by (#PCDATA)>
<!ELEMENT in-reply-to (#PCDATA)>
<!ATTLIST in-reply-to link CDATA #REQUIRED >

<!ELEMENT envelope (#PCDATA)>
<!ELEMENT language (#PCDATA)>
<!ATTLIST language link CDATA #REQUIRED >

<!ELEMENT ontology (#PCDATA)>
<!ATTLIST ontology link CDATA #REQUIRED >

<!ELEMENT protocol (#PCDATA)>
<!ATTLIST protocol link CDATA #REQUIRED >

<!ELEMENT conversation-id (#PCDATA)>

<!ELEMENT agentname (#PCDATA)>
```

Fig. 3. A DTD for ACML. The DTD is in draft form.

2.4   Advantages of XML Approach

Encoding ACL messages in XML offers some advantages that we believe are potentially quite significant.

(1) The XML-encoding is **easier to develop parsers for** than the Lisp-like encoding. The XML markup provides parsing information more directly. One can use the off-the-shelf tools for parsing XML — of which there are several competent, easy-to-use ones already available — instead of writing customized parsers to parse the ACL messages. A change or an enhancement of the ACL syntax does not have to result to a re-writing of the parser. As long as such changes are reflected in the ACL DTD, the XML parser will still be able to handle the XML-encoded ACL message. In short, a significant advantage is that the process of *developing or maintaining* a parser is much simplified.

Indeed, we have first-hand experience that this parsing advantage is significant. In our own implementation efforts, we have developed parsers for FIPA ACL and for content languages (both KIF and logic programs), both for ASCII encoding and for XML encoding.

(2) More generally, XML-ifying makes ACL more "**WWW-friendly**", which **facilitates Software Engineering** of agents. Agent development ought to take advantage and build on what the WWW has to offer as a software development environment. XML parsing technology is only one example. Using XML will facilitate the practical integration with a variety of Web technologies. For example, an issue that has been raised in the ACL community [5] is that of addressing security issues, *e.g.* authentication of agents' identities and encryption of ACL messages, at the ACL layer. The WWW solution is to use certificates and SSL. Using the same approach for agent security considerations seems much simpler and more intuitive than further overloading ACL messages and the ACL infrastructure to accommodate such a task.

As we mentioned earlier, the operational semantics of the pragmatic aspects of ACL can differ subtly between implementations or usages, and there is today a practical problem of interoperability. XML can help with these pragmatics, by riding on standard WWW-world technologies: to facilitate the engineering, and as a by-product to help standardize the operational semantics, thereby helping make interoperability really happen.

(3) Because XML incorporates links into the ACL message, this takes a significant step toward addressing the problem (or representational layer) of specifying and sharing the **ontologies** used in an ACL message's content. The values of the ACL parameters are not tokens anymore, but links that can point to objects and/or definitions. Although the `ontology` slot has been present since the inception of ACLs, the ACL community has not been very clear on how this information is to be used by the agent. This vagueness, further compounded by the scarcity of published ontologies, can be addressed by "interfacing" the ACL message to the knowledge repository that is the WWW.

(4) More generally, **links may be useful for a variety of other purposes**. For example, the `receiver` parameter might have a link to network location

---

[5] Private communication at FIPA meetings

that provides information about the **agent's identity**: e.g., its owner, contact and administrative information, communication primitives that the agent understands, network protocols and ports at which it can receive messages, conversation protocols it understands, *etc.*. This type of information is necessary for a establishing an extended interaction with another agent and has to somehow be available to an agent's potential interlocutors. The same argument can be made about the other message parameters.

3   ACL Content Languages, e.g., for Business Rules

3.1   Layered Approach of Knowledge Sharing Effort

Our and many other current efforts in inter-agent communication approaches are influenced by the pioneering approach of the Knowledge Sharing Effort [15, 16] (KSE)[6] The KSE was initiated as a research effort circa 1990 with encouragement and relatively modest funding from U.S. government agencies (DARPA especially). The KSE was highly active for roughly five years thereafter, and enjoyed the participation of dozens of researchers from both academia and industry. Its goal was to develop techniques, methodologies and software tools for *knowledge sharing and knowledge reuse* between *knowledge-based (software) systems*, at *design, implementation,* or *execution* time. Agents, especially intelligent agents, are an important kind of such knowledge-based systems (other kinds include expert systems or databases, for example). The central concept of the KSE was that knowledge sharing requires communication, which in turn, requires a common language; the KSE focused on defining that common language.

In the KSE model, agents (or, more generally, knowledge-based systems) are viewed as (virtual) knowledge bases that exchange propositions using a language that expresses various *propositional attitudes*. Propositional attitudes are three-part relationships between: (1) an agent, (2) a content-bearing proposition (*e.g.,* "it is raining"), and (3) a finite set of propositional attitudes an agent might have with respect to the proposition (*e.g.,* believing, asserting, fearing, wondering, hoping, *etc.*). For example, $< a, fear, raining(t_{now}) >$.

The KSE model includes three **layers** of representation: (1) specifying propositional attitudes; (2) specifying propositions (i.e., "knowledge") — this is often called the (propositional) **content** layer; and (3) specifying the *ontology* [12] (i.e., vocabulary) of those propositions. The KSE accordingly includes a component (with associated language) for each of these: Knowledge Query and Manipulation Language (KQML) for propositional attitudes, **Knowledge Interchange Format (KIF)** [4][7] for propositions, and Ontolingua [3] (which had supporting software tools) for ontology.

Within the KSE approach, the three representational layers are viewed as mainly independent of another. In particular, the language for propositional

---
[6] http://www.cs.umbc.edu/kse/

[7] http://logic.stanford.edu/kif/ and http://www.cs.umbc.edu/kif/

content (i.e., the *content language*) can be chosen independently from the language for propositional attitudes. In other words, in the KSE approach, the role of an ACL such as FIPA's is only to capture propositional attitudes, regardless of how propositions are expressed, even though propositions are what agents will be "talking" about.

In a similar spirit, the approach of the technical committee that worked on FIPA ACL is that the content language should be viewed as orthogonal to the rest of the ACL message type.

The KSE focused especially on developing one general-purpose content language: KIF. However, the KSE also recognized that it is important to support multiple special-purpose content languages, since some are more expressive or more convenient for a particular purpose. Indeed, the KSE also included a fourth component effort (abbreviated "KRSS") devoted to defining a special-purpose content language for "description logics" (a.k.a. "terminological logics", descended from KL-ONE).

We agree with the view that it is important to support multiple content languages. Beyond the KSE, a number of important specialized content languages have been developed which are particularly good at describing certain fields. For example, STEP (Standard for the Exchange of Product Model Data) [12] is an ISO standards project working towards developing mechanisms for the representation and exchange of a computerized model of a product in a neutral form. SGML is an example of a language, which is designed to describe the logical structure of a document. There are special languages for describing workflow, processes, chemical reactions, etc. SQL and OQL are somewhat more general content languages: for relational and object databases.

3.2 Business Rules in E-Commerce as Focus

Motivated by the importance of the content language aspect of agent communication, we focus in particular on rules as a form of content that is important in e-commerce applications such as bidding negotiations, i.e., "business rules". We are particularly interested in this kind of application, and have been developing techniques for it [10] [17] (to describe these is beyond the scope of this paper, however).

In bidding negotiations, agents exchange requests for bids, (i.e., proposals), make proposals, make counter-proposals, until agreeing or giving up. Rules are useful to represent the contents of these proposals and requests for proposals: e.g., to describe the products/services, prices, quantities, delivery dates, customer service agreements, contractual terms & conditions, and other surrounding agreements that together constitute the content of a bid. Rules are also useful to represent relevant aspects of business processes, e.g., how to place an order, respond to an RFQ, return an item or cancel a delivery.

The usefulness of rules for the overall area of agent communication, particularly for such e-commerce applications is based largely on their following advantages relative to other software specification approaches and programming languages. First, rules are at a relatively high level of abstraction, closer to human understandability, especially by business domain experts who are typically non-programmers. Second, rules are relatively easy to modify dynamically and by non-programmers.

Rules provide an expressive yet automatically executable form for the substance of these specifications. Rules with deep declarative semantics[8] are valuable because they help enable business rules to be specified dynamically, i.e., at runtime, and relatively easily by business domain experts who are non-programmers.

There are a number of different rule representations in wide deployment today. A major challenge in communicating content between e-commerce agents is thus the heterogeneity of rule representations (within agents/applications) to be integrated, e.g., during negotiation. In translating content via a common rule representation, deep semantics (in the sense of declarative KR) is desirable. However, one can only hope to obtain deep semantics for expressive *cores*, i.e., for the expressive cases that overlap between the source and target rule KR's. Beyond the cores, translation must be performed with superficial semantics.

To begin with, we are focusing on three broad families of rule representations that are currently commercially important for business rules in e-commerce. These are both executable and practically important in the software world at large. One family is logic programs (LP's): including, but not limited to, Prolog. Logic programs have a general, declarative sense; they can be forward-chaining as well as backward-chaining, and need not be a general-purpose programming language in the manner of Prolog. Baral & Gelfond [1] gives a useful review of declarative logic programs as a KR. Another family is production rules: descendants of OPS5 [2], e.g., the public domain system Jess[9]. A third (relatively loose) family is Event-Condition-Action (ECA) rules. Both logic programs and ECA rules are important in commercial databases[19] [18] and related standards (including SQL). Rules in these three families are to be found, for example, in object-oriented applications and worfklows, as well.

4   KIF and Its Shortcomings for Business Rules Content

A leading candidate content language for rules is KIF. KIF is currently well along in the ANSI standards committee process. Supporting or endorsing KIF is also being considered informally in several other standards efforts relevant to agent communication, e.g., FIPA.

KIF has pioneered the concept of a KR content language for agent communication. That said, there are some important differences between (1) the goals of the KIF effort and (2) our goals for a business rules content language (for practical e-commerce agents' communication). The KIF effort's goals were initially to facilitate exchange among research systems rather than commercial systems. Also, it aimed to help at least somewhat with exchange of many forms of knowledge beyond just rules. It was designed with an orientation towards knowledge

---

[8] in the sense of declarative knowledge representation, in which a set of premises entails a set of conclusions, independent of the inferencing procedure, e.g., whether it is forward or backward direction, what its control strategy is, *etc.*.

[9] http://herzberg.ca.sandia.gov/jess/ . Jess is written in Java and is an update of CLIPS (http://www.ghg.net/clips/CLIPS.html).

as a non-executable specification as much or more than towards knowledge as executable. Finally, the KIF effort has focused more on a highly inclusively expressive representation than on ease of developing translators in and out of that representation.

KIF is a prefix[10] version of first-order predicate calculus (i.e., first-order classical logic) with extensions to support the "quote" operator (thus enabling additional expressiveness akin to that of classical higher-order logic) and definitions. The language description includes a specification not only for its syntax but also for its semantics. Its deep semantics is based on classical logic, which is logically monotonic. Its primary focus (in terms of deep semantics) is on first-order logic, which is highly expressive and computationally intractable for the general case (as well as logically monotonic).

KIF can express a broad class of rules. However, it has several important shortcomings as a content language for business rules in e-commerce. In particular, it has two shortcomings of its fundamental knowledge representation.

(1) KIF is a *logically monotonic* KR. KIF cannot conveniently express rules that are **logically non-monotonic**, e.g., rules that employ **negation-as-failure** or **default rules**. Thus it cannot conveniently express **conflict handling**, e.g., where some rules are subject to **override by higher-priority conflicting rules**, e.g., by special-case **exceptions**, by more-recent **updates**, or by higher-authority sources. Most commercially important rule systems employ non-monotonic reasoning as an essential, highly-used feature. Typically, they employ some form of negation-as-failure. Often they employ some form of prioritized override between rules, e.g., the static rule sequence in Prolog or the computed rule-activation sequence/"agenda" in OPS5-heritage production rule systems.

Early in the KIF effort, incorporating logical non-monotonicity was considered seriously. However, no technical agreement could be reached on an approach, largely because of its ambitions for great expressive generality in the direction of full classical logic. The current ANSI draft proposal of KIF is logically monotonic.

(2) KIF is a *pure-belief* KR. KIF cannot conveniently express "**procedural attachments**": the association of procedure calls (e.g., a call to a Java method ProcurementAuthorization.setApprovalLevel) with belief expressions (e.g., a logical predicate such as approvalAuthorizationLevel). Procedural attachments are crucial in order for rules to have actual effect beyond pure-belief inferencing, i.e., for actions to be invoked/performed as a result after rule conclusions are inferred. While procedures can of course be invoked by an application based on KIF premises or conclusions, KIF provides no way to express this, and its semantics do not treat the connection to such invocations, i.e., to such procedural attachments.

---

[10] The current draft ANSI specification of KIF (http://logic.stanford.edu/kif/dpans.html) also includes an infix version of KIF intended for human consumption rather than automated exchange.

5   A Logic Program Based Business Rule Content KR

5.1   Overall Approach: Ordinary, Courteous, and Situated LP's

We identified two fundamental shortcomings of KIF as a KR for business rules content: logical non-monotonicity and procedural attachments. In this paper, we focus on selecting a business rules content KR to remedy the first shortcoming only. We select a business rules content KR to enable logical non-monotonicity, including two steps. (1) Negation-as-failure, a basic form of non-monotonicity, is the first step. (2) Prioritized override between conflicting rules (i.e., prioritized default rules and conflict handling) is the second step.

Our approach is to use ordinary Logic Programs to provide the first step. By Logic Program, we mean in the declarative sense, e.g., cf. [1][11]. Inferencing for LP's can be run forward or backward, using a variety of control strategies and algorithms; Prolog, by contrast, does backward-only inferencing, using a particular control strategy. Ordinary LP's (OLP's) offer several other significant advantages beyond enabling non-monotonicity, including: computational tractability, wide practical deployment, semantics shared with other practically important rule systems, relative algorithmic simplicity, yet considerable expressive power.

Our approach is then to use **Courteous Logic Programs (CLP's)**, an expressive extension of ordinary Logic Programs, to provide the second step. Courteous Logic Programs [6] [9] [7] provide a computationally low-overhead, semantically-clean capability for prioritized handling of conflicts between rules. CLP's permit classical negation; syntactically they also permit optional rule labels which are used as handles for specifying prioritization.

In current work, we are also enabling procedural attachments as well — in a semantically clean manner (i.e., declaratively in a particular well-defined sense). Our approach to enabling procedural attachments is based on **Situated Logic Programs**, another expressive extension of ordinary logic programs. Situated Logic Programs [5] [11] hook beliefs to drive procedural API's. Procedural attachments for testing conditions (sensing) and performing actions (effecting) are specified as part of the knowledge representation: via sensor and effector link statements. Each sensor or effector link associates a predicate with an attached procedure.[12]

5.2   Ordinary LP's: Core & Advantages

Our point of departure for the business rules content KR is pure-belief ordinary LP's. "Pure-belief" here means without procedural attachments.

OLP's include negation-as-failure and thus support basic non-monotonicity. Yet they are relatively simple, and are not overkill representationally. OLP's are also relatively fast computationally. Under commonly-met restrictions (e.g., no

---

[11] They call an ordinary LP: a "general" LP. This is also known in the literature as a "normal" LP, and also sometimes as (declarative) pure Prolog.

[12] Note that "link" here does not mean in the sense of an XML or HTML hypertext link.

logical functions of non-zero arity, a bounded number of logical variables per rule), inferencing (i.e., rule-set execution) in LP's can be computed in (worst-case) polynomial-time. By contrast, under similar restrictions, first-order-logic (cf. KIF) inferencing is (co-)NP-hard.

To obtain deep semantics that is/will-be shared widely among heterogeneous rule systems, however, the core must be an expressively restricted case of OLP's. Our alpha-version choice of this expressive restriction is: "predicate-acyclic" (pure-belief) OLP's — below, we discuss this in more detail. This core has a deep semantics that is useful, well-understood theoretically and highly declarative. Moreover, this semantics reflects a consensus in the rules representation community beyond just the LP community: this semantics is widely shared among all three of the rule system families we mentioned in subsection 3.2.

This core is also relatively computationally efficient, in the sense we described above.

The unrestricted case of declarative OLP's, with unrestricted recursion/cyclicity (in a sense explained below) interacting with negation-as-failure, has problems semantically, is more complex computationally and, perhaps even more importantly, is more difficult in terms of software engineering. It requires more complicated algorithms and is not widely deployed.

OLP's have been widely deployed practically, in contrast to full first-order-logic which has not been. Moreover, there is a large population of software developers who are familiar with Prolog and OLP's, in contrast to general first-order-logic theorem-proving for which there is not.

5.3 Ordinary LP's: Semantics & Recursion

Ordinary LP's have been well-studied, and have a large literature (reviewed, for example, in [1]). For several broad but restricted expressive cases, their (declarative) semantics is uncontroversial.[13] However, OLP's have problematic semantics for the unrestricted case, due essentially to the interaction of recursion with negation-as-failure. "Recursion" here means that there is a *cyclic* (path of syntactic) dependency among the predicates (or, more generally, among the ground atoms) through rules. [14]

There is a lack of consensus in the research community about which semantics to adopt for the fully general case of OLP's: e.g., well-founded semantics versus stable semantics, etc.; these semantics coincide for the uncontroversial restricted cases but diverge beyond that. Under the well-founded semantics, probably the currently most popular semantics, the unrestricted case is tractable.

---

[13] e.g., for the predicate-acyclic, stratified, locally stratified, and weakly stratified cases; these form a series of increasing expressive generality

[14] In each rule, the predicate(s) appearing in the consequent/head of the rule has a directed dependency arc to each of the predicates appearing in the antecedent/body of the rule. Accumulating such dependency arcs for a whole rule set, and taking their transitively closed paths, defines which predicates are dependent on which others for a given LP.

Our approach for an initial practically-oriented LP-based business rules content KR is to keep to expressively restricted cases that have uncontroversial (i.e., consensus) semantics; these have other virtues as well: e.g., they are algorithmically and computationally simpler. More precisely, our approach is to define/expect deep semantics (including for translation between agents) only for these restricted cases.

Our starting choice for such an expressive restriction is: **predicate-acyclic**, i.e., where there are no cycles of (syntactic) dependency among predicates. This expressive restriction can be checked syntactically with a relatively simple algorithm and with relatively low computational cost. Inferencing for the predicate-acyclic case is also simpler algorithmically and computationally than for the expressively unrestricted case.

In our XML embodiment (next section) of the LP-based content language, we define an alpha-version DTD that is syntactically inclusive: it permits unrestricted OLP's. It is thus useful there to have an optional tag to indicate which semantical variant of LP's is intended: the DTD accordingly defines an optional "documentation" link which can be used to specify the intended semantics (e.g., well-founded versus stable). For the alpha-version, our approach is to choose the well-founded semantics to be the default semantics for the expressively unrestricted case.

5.4   Courteous Logic Programs

Courteous LP's expressively generalize OLP's by adding the capability to conveniently express prioritized conflict handling, i.e., where some rules are subject to override by higher-priority conflicting rules. For example, some rules may be overridden by other rules that are special-case exceptions, more-recent updates, or from higher-authority sources. Courteous LP's facilitate specifying sets of rules by merging and updating and accumulation, in a style closer (than ordinary LP's) to natural language descriptions.

Courteous LP's also expressively generalize ordinary LP's and permit **classical negation** to appear in head (i.e., consequent) or body (i.e., antecedent) literals (negation-as-failure must appear outside, not inside, the scope of classical-negation). They also permit rules to have optional labels, which are used as handles for specifying priorities. A syntactically-reserved (but otherwise ordinary) predicate *overrides* is used to specify prioritization. Priorities are represented via a fact comparing rule labels: *overrides*($lab1, lab2$) means semantically that a rule having label $lab1$ has higher priority than another rule having label $lab2$. If two such rules conflict, then the rule with the higher priority will win the conflict; the lower priority rule's head will not be concluded.

The prioritization specified is a partial ordering, rather than a total ordering. Classical negation is enforced: p and classical-negation-of-p are never both concluded, for any belief expression p.

In the alpha-version business rules content KR (BRML) given here, the Courteous LP KR is also expressively restricted in two further regards cf. [6]: (1) priority is specified via ground facts only, and (2) priority is specified to be a strict partial order. Elsewhere [7] [9] [8] [10], we give an expressively generalized version of Courteous LP's and BRML that relaxes these restrictions and the predicate-acyclicity restriction, and adds several further expressive generalizations, notably to permit conditional pairwise mutual exclusion constraints (*mutex*'s) that specify the scope of conflict handling.

Courteous LP's have several virtues semantically and computationally. A Courteous LP is guaranteed to have a **consistent**, as well as unique, set of conclusions. Priorities and merging behave in an intuitively natural fashion. Execution (inferencing) of courteous LP's is **fast**: only relatively low computational overhead is imposed by the conflict handling.

From a software engineering viewpoint as well, CLP's are a relatively straightforward extension of OLP's. A CLP can always be **tractably compiled into a semantically equivalent OLP** — indeed, we have implemented CLP's using such a *"courteous compiler"* [7] [9] [8] [10].

Detailed computational complexity analysis for courteous LP inferencing and the courteous compiler is given in [6] [7] [8] [10]; next, we summarize that analysis. The complexity of courteous compilation is worst-case cubic, both in time and in output size. Suppose the input LP, having size n, is either ground or Datalog (no logical functions of more than zero arity), and has an upper bound v on the number of logical variables appearing in any rule. As we mentioned earlier, the worst-case time complexity of inferencing in OLP's under these restrictions is tractable (i.e., polynomial). Courteous LP inferencing then has the same worst-case time and space complexity as: OLP inferencing where the bound v on the number of variables per rule has been increased to $v + 2$.

There are several other formalisms for prioritized LP's that have similar syntax to Courteous LP's but different semantics in regard to conflict handling (see [6] [7] for a review). A direction in our current work is to explore this dimension of heterogeneity.

5.5   Relationship to KIF; Discussion

In this subsection, we discuss how the alpha-version business rules content KR, i.e., CLP cf. [6] encoded in XML as BRML, relates to KIF.

Syntactically, the alpha CLP adds two (optional) features to OLP: classical negation and rule labels. KIF permits classical negation but not negation-as-failure. Also KIF remarkably lacks rule labels (or rule names/id's), even though this is rather routine as a basic naming/scoping mechanism in rule specification systems and many programming languages. Syntactically, the alpha CLP thus adds two (optional) features to KIF: negation-as-failure and rule labels.

Syntactically, OLP and first-order-logic/KIF overlap to a considerable degree: OLP without negation-as-failure is logically monotonic[15]. Syntactically and semantically, such monotonic OLP is simply Horn and is thus a restricted case of first-order logic/KIF. Semantically, OLP entailment/inferencing is sound but

---

[15] when one interprets lack of membership in the minimal/least model of the OLP as corresponding to classical non-entailment rather than to classical falsity

incomplete when compared to first-order-logic (FOL). The incompleteness can be described as: an OLP's entailed conclusions are equivalent to a set of ground atoms.

Syntactically, CLP and FOL/KIF overlap to an even more considerable degree: CLP without negation-as-failure is logically monotonic. Such monotonic CLP with its labels omitted or ignored is thus syntactically a restricted case of FOL/KIF. Semantically, a monotonic CLP may contain conflict; we say it is "classically consistent" or "conflict free" when it is consistent when viewed as FOL. Semantically, a consistent monotonic CLP is sound but incomplete when compared to FOL. The incompleteness is similar to that of OLP; it can be described as: a CLP's entailed conclusions are equivalent to a set of ground classical literals.

6   XML Embodiment: Business Rules Markup Language

Just as we have defined an XML encoding for ACL messages in Section 2.3, we have defined an XML encoding for CLP rulesets. We refer to this language as **Business Rules Markup Language (BRML)**. BRML inherits the deep semantics of CLP.

Figure 4 gives an example of a single-rule CLP ruleset, in BRML. See the IBM CommonRules release package (`http://alphaworks.ibm.com`) for an extensive collection of examples, including about price discounting, targeted ads/promotions, refunds, creditworthiness, etc.. Figure 5 gives the (alpha) BRML DTD. The XML encoding extends the pure ASCII syntactic representation of CLP (not shown here for reasons of space and focus) with parsing information (and eventually with various optional links). The optional `documentation` attribute in the BRML DTD could point to a link which has information such as the semantical variant of the language.

In the draft DTD shown, we do not yet allow a predicate (or another token such as a logical constant or function, *etc.*) to have an associated link, because here we are focused on specifying the basic XML encoding of CLP. However, we plan to permit such links: e.g., the `loyalCustomer` predicate, for example, could then point to a URL containing a document that provides an account in natural language of what the particular company considers a loyal customer. Or, in the case of the example of Figure 2, the particular laptop for sale could include a linked picture and a URL with the full natural-language description of the laptop's technical specification.

The **advantages of an XML encoding** for business rules content are similar to those for ACL that we discussed in Section 2. As compared to plain ASCII text, XML is easier to automatically parse, generate, edit, and translate: because there are standard XML-world tools for these tasks. The hyper-text (i.e., links) aspects of XML are also useful. For example, a rule set may via XML have some associated URL's which point to documents describing that rule set's knowledge representation or authors or application context. Or it may have associated URL's which point to tools for processing that rule set, e.g., to

Let C_1 be a simple example CLP ruleset that contains the single rule
`giveDiscount(percent5 , ?Cust) <- shopper(?Cust) and`
`loyalCustomer(?Cust).`
, shown here in ASCII encoding. This rule says to give a 5% discount to loyal
customers. The CLP ruleset C_1 can be expressed in BRML as follows:

```
<?xml version="1.0"?>
<!DOCTYPE brml SYSTEM "brml.dtd">
<clp>
  <erule rulelabel="emptyLabel">
    <head>
      <cliteral predicate="giveDiscount">
        <function name="percent5"/>
        <variable name="?Cust"/>
      </cliteral>
    </head>
    <body>
      <and>
        <fcliteral predicate="shopper">
          <variable name="?Cust"/>
        </fcliteral>
        <fcliteral predicate="loyalCustomer">
          <variable name="?Cust"/>
        </fcliteral>
      </and>
    </body>
  </erule>
</clp>
```

Fig. 4. An example of a single-rule CLP ruleset expressed in BRML.

execute it, edit it, analyze it, or validate it (syntactically or semantically). Particularly useful for our nearer-term purposes is that an associated URL may point
to documents describing the semantics and algorithms for translator services or
components, as well as to translator tools and examples. Representing business
rules in XML has a further advantage: it will complement domain-specific ontologies (i.e., vocabularies) available in XML. Many such ontologies exist already,
and many more are expected to be developed in the next few years, including in
e-commerce domains.

Further discussion of our DTD: Actually, our BRML DTD permits a
syntactic superset of our alpha expressive core, i.e. a superset of CLP cf. [6]. Applications using the BRML need to perform additional *"validation"*, i.e., checking
of syntactic restrictions, beyond what is furnished by XML parsers that validate
with respect to the DTD. However, such additional syntactic validation would
be necessary even if the DTD was as "tight" as XML made possible; various
other conditions such as predicate-acyclicity are impractically difficult (if not
impossible) to capture in a DTD.

```
<?xml version="1.0" encoding="US-ASCII"?>

<!ENTITY % bool "yes|no">

<!ELEMENT clp (erule*, mutex*)>
<!ATTLIST documentation link CDATA #IMPLIED>

<!ELEMENT erule (head, body?)>
<!ATTLIST erule rulelabel CDATA #IMPLIED>

<!ELEMENT mutex (cliteral, cliteral)>

<!ELEMENT head (cliteral | and)>

<!ELEMENT body (fcliteral | and | or)>

<!ELEMENT cliteral ( (function|variable|string)* )>
<!ATTLIST cliteral predicate CDATA #REQUIRED>
<!ATTLIST cliteral cneg (%bool;) #IMPLIED>

<!ELEMENT fcliteral ( (function|variable|string)* )>
<!ATTLIST fcliteral predicate CDATA #REQUIRED>
<!ATTLIST fcliteral cneg (%bool;) #IMPLIED>
<!ATTLIST fcliteral fneg (%bool;) #IMPLIED>

<!ELEMENT and ((cliteral|fcliteral|and|or),
               (cliteral|fcliteral|and|or)+)>

<!ELEMENT or ((fcliteral|and|or), (fcliteral|and|or)+)>

<!ELEMENT function ((function|variable|string)*)>
<!ATTLIST function name CDATA #REQUIRED>

<!ELEMENT variable EMPTY>
<!ATTLIST variable name CDATA #REQUIRED>

<!ELEMENT string EMPTY>
<!ATTLIST string value CDATA #REQUIRED>
```

Fig. 5. A DTD for BRML. The DTD is in draft form.

As a syntactic convenience, we permit the OR connective and nested sub-expressions to appear in the body, and we permit the AND connective to appear in the head. This does not change the essential expressiveness of OLP or CLP (see, e.g., [14]) [16].

---

[16] though in the worst-case depending on inferencing engine implementation this may cost exponential time/space caused by converting to the representation without OR's

It appears fairly straightforward to extend our DTD in stages so as to express full first-order logic and then full KIF. A direction for future work is to create a DTD, maximally compatibly with BRML, that expresses full KIF.

7 Discussion: Implementation; Future Work Summary

We have a **running prototype implementation** of ACML, and of BRML and Courteous LP's as a Java library. Based on the DTD's we gave earlier, this includes encoding and parsing in/out in both XML and ASCII (including KIF for the content). It also includes translators to two other ASCII rule representations in the logic program family, used by previously existing OLP inferencing engines built by others and implemented in C. One is backward-direction: XSB, by David Warren *et al*, http://www.cs.sunysb.edu/~sbprolog/ . The other is exhaustive forward-direction: Smodels (first version), by Ilkka Niemela and Patrik Simons, http://saturn.hut.fi/html/staff/ilkka.html . All the encoding, parsing, and translating preserves the deep semantics of the alpha core that we described in Section 5. The implementation further includes a courteous compiler, and a rule inferencing/execution engine.

The prototype implementation of BRML and Courteous LP's, called **IBM CommonRules** was released free on the Web in July of 1999: at http://alphaworks.ibm.com. As of Nov. 10 1999, there have been more than 2000 downloads of CommonRules. Overviews of CommonRules, with e-commerce examples, are given in [9] [10], and its courteous compiler algorithms are given in [7] [8]. The XML DTD's are under ongoing (non-radical) revision; see the authors' websites and CommonRules for updated versions.

Future work includes extending this XML content language expressively in multiple directions. One such direction is to cover full KIF; another is to incorporate semantically-clean procedural attachments, cf. the existing Situated Logic Programs KR; a third is to expressively generalize the Courteous LP conflict handling aspects .

Acknowledgments. Hoi Y. Chan (IBM), Michael Travers (IBM), and Xiaocheng Luan (of UMBC, while at IBM), contributed to the current implementation of the CLP KR, BRML, and the associated translators. Michael Travers' contributed especially to the XML embodiment, using his Skij tool. Hoi Y. Chan and Miao Jin (UMBC) contributed to the XML DTD's. Tim Finin (UMBC) contributed to the formulation of our ideas for the XML embodiment of the FIPA ACL, which he first presented at the FIPA meeting in Dublin, in July 1998.

References

1. Chitta Baral and Michael Gelfond. Logic programming and knowledge representation. *J. Logic Programming*, 19,20:73–148, 1994. Includes extensive review of literature.

2. Thomas Cooper and Nancy Wogrin. *Rule-based Programming with OPS5*. Morgan Kaufmann, San Francisco, CA, 1988. ISBN 0-934613-51-6.
3. Adam Farquhar, Richard Fikes, and James Rice. The ontolingua server: A tool for collaborative ontology construction. In *KAW96*, Nov. 1996.
4. M. Genesereth and R. Fikes et. al. Knowledge interchange format, version 3.0 reference manual. Technical report, Computer Science Dept., Stanford Univ., 1992.
5. Benjamin N. Grosof. Building Commercial Agents: An IBM Research Perspective (Invited Talk). In *Proc. 2nd Intnl. Conference and Exhibition on Practical Applications of Intelligent Agents and Multi-Agent Technology (PAAM97)*, Practical Application Company Ltd., P.O. Box 137, Blackpool, Lancashire, FY2 9UN, UK. http://www.demon.co.uk./ar/PAAM97, Apr. 1997. Held London, UK. Also available as IBM Research Report RC 20835.
6. Benjamin N. Grosof. Prioritized Conflict Handling for Logic Programs. In Jan Maluszynski, editor, *Logic Programming: Proceedings of the International Symposium (ILPS-97)*, MIT Press, Cambridge, MA, USA, 1997. http://www.ida.liu.se/~ilps97. Extended version available as IBM Research Report RC 20836.
7. Benjamin N. Grosof. Compiling Prioritized Default Rules Into Ordinary Logic Programs. IBM Research Report RC 21472, 1999.
8. Benjamin N. Grosof. A Courteous Compiler from Generalized Courteous Logic Programs To Ordinary Logic Programs (Preliminary Report). Technical report, IBM T.J. Watson Research Center, included as documentation in the IBM CommonRules 1.0 alpha prototype Web release of July 30, 1999 at http://alphaworks.ibm.com . This is a supplementary followon to IBM Research Report RC 21472. Revised version forthcoming as another IBM Research Report.
9. Benjamin N. Grosof. DIPLOMAT: Compiling Prioritized Default Rules Into Ordinary Logic Programs, for E-Commerce Applications (extended abstract of Intelligent Systems Demonstration). In *Proceedings of AAAI-99*, Morgan Kaufmann, San Francisco, CA, USA, 1999. Extended version available as IBM Research Report RC21473, May 1999.
10. Benjamin N. Grosof, Yannis Labrou, and Hoi Y. Chan. A Declarative Approach to Business Rules in Contracts: Courteous Logic Programs in XML. In Michael P. Wellman, editor, *Proceedings of 1st ACM Conference on E-Commerce (EC-99)*, New York, NY, USA, 1999. ACM Press. `http://www.ibm.com/iac/ec99/` or `http://www.acm.org`. Held Denver, CO, USA, Nov. 3–5, 1999. Extended version to be available as an IBM Research Report.
11. Benjamin N. Grosof, David W. Levine, Hoi Y. Chan, Colin P. Parris, and Joshua S. Auerbach. Reusable Architecture for Embedding Rule-Based Intelligence in Information Agents. In *Proceedings of the ACM Conference on Information and Knowledge Management (CIKM-95) Workshop on Intelligent Information Agents*, `http://www.cs.umbc.edu/iia/`, December 1995. Held Baltimore, MD. Paper also available as IBM Research Report RC 20305.
12. Thomas R. Gruber. A translation approach to portable ontology specifications. *Knowledge Acquisition*, 2:199–220, 1993.
13. Yannis Labrou, Tim Finin, and Yun Peng. Agent communication languages: the current landscape. *IEEE Intelligent Systems*, May 1999.
14. J. W. Lloyd. *Foundations of Logic Programming, 2nd ed.*. Springer, Berlin, Germany, 1987.
15. R. Neches, R. Fikes, T. Finin, T. Gruber, R. Patil, T. Senator, and W. Swartout. Enabling technology for knowledge sharing. *AI Magazine*, 12(3):36–56, Fall, 1991.

16. Ramesh S. Patil, Richard E. Fikes, Peter F. Patel-Schneider, Don McKay, Tim Finin, Thomas Gruber, and Robert Neches. The DARPA knowledge sharing effort: Progress report. In Michael Huhns and Munindar Singh, editors, *Readings in Agents*. Morgan Kaufmann, 1997. (reprint of KR-92 paper).
17. Daniel M. Reeves, Benjamin N. Grosof, Michael Wellman, and Hoi Y. Chan. Toward a Declarative Language for Negotiating Executable Contracts. In *Proc. AAAI-99 Workshop on Artificial Intelligence in Electronic Commerce (AIEC-99)*, 1999. Proceedings published by AAAI/MIT Press (http://www.aaai.org) as Technical Report, also available at AIEC website `http://www.cs.umbc.edu/aiec/`. Also available as IBM Research Report RC 21476.
18. Jeffrey D. Ullman. *Principles of Database and Knowledge-Base Systems, volume 1*. Computer Science Press, Rockville, Maryland, 1988.
19. Jeffrey D. Ullman and Jennifer Widom. *A First Course in Database Systems*. Prentice-Hall, 1997.
20. Michael Wooldridge. Verifiable semantics for agent communication languages. In *International Conference on Multi-Agent Systems (ICMAS'98)*, Paris, France, 1998.

What Is a Conversation Policy?

Mark Greaves, Heather Holmback, and Jeffrey Bradshaw

Mathematics and Computing Technology
The Boeing Company
P.O. Box 3707 MS 7L-43
Seattle, WA 98124-2207
{mark.t.greaves, heather.holmback,
jeffrey.m.bradshaw}@boeing.com

Abstract. In this paper we define the concept of *conversation policies:* declarative specifications that govern communications between software agents using an agent communication language. We discuss the role that conversation policies play in agent communication, and suggest several subtypes of conversation policy. Our reasoning suggests, contrary to current transition net approaches to specifying conversation policies that conversation policies are best modeled as sets of fine-grained constraints on ACL usage. These constraints then define the computational process models that are implemented in agents.

1. The Roots of Conversation Policies

The dream of agent interoperability is commonly thought to rest on three main characteristics shared by the interoperating agents:

1. They would be able to access a set of shared infrastructure services for registration, reliable message delivery, agent naming, and so forth (*i.e.,* there must be *structural* interoperability);
2. They would share (possibly through translation) a common content ontology, truth theory, and method of binding objects to variables (*i.e.,* there must be *logical* interoperability); and
3. They would agree on the syntax and semantics of a common agent communication language (ACL) in which to express themselves (*i.e.,* there must be *language* interoperability).

In the last few years, international standards bodies (*e.g.,* OMG, FIPA) and government-sponsored research efforts (ESPRIT, DARPA CoABS) have attempted to address these three aspects of agent interoperability. A surprising thing that all of this work has shown is the incompleteness of this list of interoperability characteristics: it is not difficult to construct a group of agents which satisfies all of them, and yet which cannot usefully interoperate. One common problem occurs because the above characterization of language interoperability is not broad enough. Specifically, for logically powerful and expressive ACLs like KQML [6] and the FIPA ACL [14], language interoperability requires more than simply that the agents agree on the for

F. Dignum and M. Greaves (Eds.): Agent Communication, LNAI 1916, pp. 118-131, 2000.

mat and meaning of the various primitive ACL messages. As a practical matter, agents must also agree on the range of possible sequences and contents of messages when they are interpreted in the context of larger goal-directed interagent dialogues, or *conversations*.

Why aren't existing ACL specification techniques sufficient for this task? Current methods for defining ACLs are built around complex and technically arcane methods for making precise the syntax and semantics of each message type. In the most advanced of these, the semantics are also formally compositional, in that there are well-defined ways to derive the meaning of a sequence of two or more messages from the meanings of the constituents [5]. However, compositional semantic theories for ACLs often do not uniquely specify the actual content and sequencing of agent messages needed to achieve to a given communicative goal. This gives rise to a significant ambiguity problem for agents that need to interact using a powerful ACL, which we will call the *Basic Problem:*

> Modern ACLs, especially those based on logic, are frequently powerful enough to encompass several different semantically coherent ways to achieve the same communicative goal, and inversely, also powerful enough to achieve several different communicative goals with the same ACL message.

Put another way, the Basic Problem states that for powerful ACLs, there is a many-to-many mapping between the externally visible messages an agent produces and the possible internal states of the agent that would result in the production of the message. This would be a significant but manageable problem, except that agent interaction does not consist of agents lobbing isolated and context-free directives to one another in the dark. Rather, the fact that problems of high communicational complexity may be delegated to agents dictates that those agents must participate in extended interactions. Because agents are autonomous, they will need to independently optimize their own utility functions in these interactions, and hence they must use their beliefs about the probable goals of the other participants in order to determine the best next message to generate. And, because knowledge of the semantics of ACL messages provides only an imperfect guide to these goals (due to the Basic Problem), it is nearly impossible for an agent to reliably infer the intentions and goals underlying another agent's use of a particular ACL message.

The Basic Problem is not limited to agent communication; indeed, it is a prime characteristic of human communication in natural language. There are an infinite number of ways to express a given meaning and communicative intent in a natural language such as English, and the same English utterance can be used to achieve an infinite, or at least large, number of communicative functions. In fact, a large part of speech act theory is concerned with explaining how a certain communicative intention can be expressed by a certain utterance in a certain context, given the expressive power of natural languages. The Basic Problem is not a prohibitive one in human communication because the use of language is always situated in some context and humans are in general well equipped to use that context to interpret linguistic utterances.[1] Communication breakdowns in natural language conversations are largely due to the lack of sufficient shared context in which to interpret an utterance, not the

---

[1] In fact, the compactness of expression that the Basic Problem entails is one of the features that allows natural languages to be learnable.

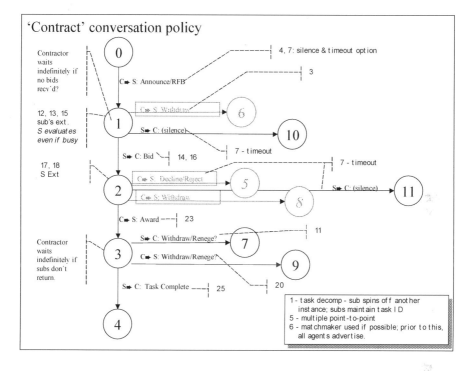

Fig. 1. A sample KAoS notation for Contract Net

lack of syntactic and semantic knowledge with which to interpret the utterance itself.
These breakdowns are resolved by reestablishing the shared context of facts and inference mechanisms. However, lacking both human inferential skills and the rich
shared context of human interaction, agents lack the means to directly overcome the
Basic Problem in the way that humans do.

In order to address this problem, designers of ACLs like FIPA [14] and KAoS [2]
have included elements in the ACL specification which further specify some of the
different types of stereotypical interactions into which agents using that ACL could
enter. Essentially, these elements function as templates to limit the form, content, and
ordering of the possible message sequences which could be used to accomplish a
communicative goal. For example, the current version of the KAoS specification of
conversation types is based on a form of finite state machine (see figure 1). FIPA's
interaction protocols are both somewhat more ambitious (*e.g.*, including a description
of several different auction types) and considerably more vague [14]. By providing
these templates, ACL designers have hoped to circumvent the Basic Problem by providing additional context information beyond that supplied by the bare form of a
message. This context information at minumum includes shared expectations about
the possible and required conversational moves between two agents. For example, a
template might specify that a **REQUEST** will be followed by an **ACCEPT** or a **RE-**

JECT.[2]   However, ACL designers have also included many other important types of context information in these templates, such as canonical mappings between ACL message types and the goals of the agent which generated the messages. For example, if an agent **A** knows that agent **B** sent a **INFORM** message in the context of a KAoS *INFORM* conversation policy, then **A** can conclude that **B**'s use of **INFORM** was intended to get **A** to do something – to adopt a particular belief – and furthermore that **B** expects only a limited range of replies from **A**.[3]   Because of the explicit policies which govern this type of KAoS conversation, **A** does not have to perform a lengthy piece of reasoning evaluating all the possible communicative goals **B** might be using the **INFORM** to achieve (*e.g.*, **B** could be using this message to indirectly get **A** to adopt a particular goal), and based on this evaluation select an appropriate response from among the universe of all of **A**'s syntactically legal responses.[4]

Unfortunately, there is no agreement in the agents community on the status of these conversation templates in the specification of agent communicative behavior, or on their standing within ACL specification practice. Different agent architectures disagree on what to call these templates (Bradshaw [2;4] uses *conversation policies*, which is the term we adopt in this paper), whether they are optional or mandatory, what formalism should be used to specify them, what conversational properties they should capture, and what their exact relationship should be to the actual message sequences that agents produce. The goal of this paper is to sort out some of these questions, and locate conversation policies within a more general model of agent communicative behavior.

2. First Principles for Conversation Policies

Our basic account of conversation policies is based on an observation that is commonplace in linguistic pragmatics and somewhat less so in ACL circles: at a fundamental level, the use of language by an agent is no different from any other action that an agent might take. Like other actions, an agent's production of a message is always the result of a plan to bring about some identified state in the world. This characteristic is the reason we use the theoretical framework of speech *acts* (and their intended *perlocutionary effects*) when we think about agent communicative behavior. In this style of theoretical framework, every agent message is driven by a strategy to achieve the agent's current goals. Of course, this process of planning and goal satisfaction may be completely implicit in any particular agent: an agent may be unreflectively executing some prebuilt procedure or state machine, and not performing any explicit deliberation at all. Nevertheless, if an agent can be coherently analyzed as having

---

[2] Note that the requirement for these responses is not a consequence of the semantics of the **REQUEST** message under most ACL semantic theories.

[3] Of course, much of this reasoning might be implicit in the logic of **A**'s program, but nevertheless this is an accurate model of **A**'s ideal behavior.

[4] For example, **B** could send an **INFORM** to **A** stating that **B** requires help on some action *a*. The KAoS conversation policy for **INFORM** forbids **B**'s goal in sending this message to be to get **A** to adopt a goal to help **B** with *a*; **B**'s direct goal in sending this message can only be to get **A** to form a belief about **B**'s capabilities for *a*.

goals and acting to bring about those goals, then our account will apply. For many researchers, the ability to take such an intentional stance is one of the prime characteristics of agenthood [1]. We implicitly adopt this stance in this paper.

Another important observation is that, unlike other types of agent actions, such as turning on a piece of machinery or booking a travel itinerary, interagent messages are fundamentally limited in the type of effects they can directly bring about. The only possible direct effect of producing an interagent message is to change the internal state of the recipient agent so that it comes to have a particular belief about the sending agent.[5] Therefore, reasoning about the proper ACL message to generate next in a conversation necessarily involves reasoning about the beliefs, goals, and abilities of other agents, both in understanding what was intended by a received message and in projecting what the perlocutionary effects of a sent message are likely be. Indeed, the only reason we have ACLs and conversation policies in the first place is because agents do not have direct access to the beliefs and goals of other agents. And, because reliable logical reasoning about the private beliefs and goals of others is technically extremely difficult, and especially so in light of the necessity for ACLs and the Basic Problem, implemented agent systems typically must employ various *ad hoc* simplifying assumptions.[6]   Differing simplifying assumptions about the mapping between the received ACL messages and the inferred goals of the sending agent are at the root of the agent interoperability problem outlined in the first section.

Given that agents using powerful ACLs are required to (at least implicitly) perform this type of reasoning, and given that the Basic Problem applies to using these ACLs, we can make the following broad claim:

> Conversation policies are necessary in powerful ACLs in order to simplify the process of inferring another agent's relevant beliefs and goals from that agent's public messaging behavior.

After all, if it were straightforward to figure out what a sending agent intends with a message and the range of appropriate responses, then recipient agents would have no need for the additional information which conversation policies provide. This is the case in very simple and inexpressive agent communication languages, where only a limited range of interaction is possible. Agents whose interaction is bounded in this way do not require conversation policies. An example of this would be a simple agent command language in which there is only one way to express any command type. On the other hand, an agent with a high-powered reasoning engine and the luxury of time might in principle be able to entirely reason its way through a complex conversation, where every message is the result of an exhaustive analysis about its possible effects (*cf.* [12]). Such an agent might not need a conversation policy to help interpret the behavior of others. However, given that time and reasoning power are typically in short supply for contemporary agents, public conversation policies serve a critical logical function in limiting the scope of what the agent must consider [2]. Conversely, when an agent reasons about its next conversational move, public conversation policies can directly constrain the set of possible responses to consider, and (by limiting the agent's range of communicative action) indirectly limit the possible

---

[5] This admittedly ignores the possibility that an agent could use an ACL message to "drown out" or otherwise make unintelligible another ACL message.

[6] These simplifying assumptions can be seen as explicitly inducing a type of context into agent communications.

goals the agent can achieve with a response. So, we can make the following claim as well:

> Conversation policies are necessary in powerful ACLs in order to simplify an agent's process of generating interagent messages that support achieving a particular set of goals.

If the two claims above are correct, we can conclude that the central role of conversation policies is to attack the Basic Problem by constraining the possible interagent messages that can appear on the wire, and in this way artificially restrict the expressive power of the ACL in use. By agreeing to use a conversation policy, an agent effectively makes public important information about how it is binding itself, and thereby makes both the reasoning and modeling task easier for all agents with which it is communicating. Specifically, conversation policies limit the possible ACL productions that an agent can employ in response to another agent, and they limit the possible goals that an agent might have when using a particular ACL expression. In the extreme case, the constraints provided by a conversation policy are so strong that the many-to-many mapping between agent states and possible ACL productions is driven down to a one-to-one mapping. That is, for a given agent goal or goal type, the conversation policies which govern an interaction will in the limiting case define a unique sequence of messages for the agents participating in the interaction to follow. In this way, the use of public conversation policies can be seen to provide a less *ad hoc* set of shared simplifying assumptions of the sort mentioned above.

We therefore view the functional role of conversation policies as publicly shared *constraints* on the potentially unbounded universe of possible semantically coherent ACL message sequences which could be used to achieve a goal. By constraining ACL usage so that the necessary communicative reasoning about beliefs and goals becomes tractable or even trivial, shared conversation policies allow agent designers to concentrate their resources on optimizing the agent's non-communicative actions – *i.e.,* the sort of actions for which we write most agents in the first place. We can state this more forcefully:

> Any public declaratively-specified principle that constrains the nature and exchange of semantically coherent ACL messages between agents can be considered a conversation policy. A given agent conversation will typically be governed by several such policies simultaneously. Each policy constrains the conversation in different ways, but there is no requirement that every policy be relevant or active in every interaction.

Our account of conversation policies presents them essentially *fine-grained* – the individual constraints are presumed to only address a single feature of a particular conversation. This stands in contrast with current conversation policy description mechanisms, which attempt to regulate every relevant property of a conversation within a single policy (*e.g.,* the conversation policy shown in figure 1). We have come to believe that different conversation types should be governed by different *clusters* of policies, with some policies shared by virtually all agent conversations, such as those regulating question/answer or high level timing, and others which are applicable only to certain specific conversation types like contracting or brokering. Moreover, individual conversation policies still must take the logical power of the underlying ACL into account, because they will be closely linked to the expressive

124 M. Greaves, H. Holmback, and J. Bradshaw

power of that ACL. Finally, this approach to conversation policies still agents to address the Basic Problem. By agreeing in advance that a particular interaction will be bound by a given set of public constraints on ACL use, each interacting agent is able to simplify their conversational modeling task, and more easily determine the appropriate next conversational production.

Fine-grained accounts of conversation policies have an important advantage over traditional accounts. Traditional models of conversation policies (*i.e.,* transition nets) encode large numbers of individual policy decisions in a single formalism, making it difficult for both agents and agent designers to be precise about exactly which assumptions about agent communication a given model incorporates. For example, figure 1 combines policies about timing, withdrawing, sequencing, and other properties into a single complex diagram. In contrast, by conceptually separating the individual policies from the transition net computational models in which they are typically embedded, fine-grained accounts gain great flexibility about the types of policy which can be specified and the range of conversation types over which they will be valid. For example, we are now able to consider several important assumptions about the character of agent interactions that have typically been left implicit in the various extant ACL conversation policy descriptions, and separate them from the sequencing constraints which make up the traditional subject matter of a conversation policy:

1. *Termination.* It is a typical, if unstated, assumption of most agent conversation design work that agent conversations can be depended on to eventually terminate. Certain applications have stricter termination conditions, such as limits on the number of total messages that can be sent or a strict time limit on the overall length of the conversation. Other assumptions will govern the nature of acceptable termination for specific conversation types – *e.g.,* that an offer-type conversation will terminate when the offer is accepted, rejected, or withdrawn. In any case, though, there are several principles which address why individual agent conversations can come to an end, and these principles should be encoded explicitly as policies.
2. *Synchrony.* Different basic assumptions about the nature of agent conversational turn-taking, possible concurrency of messaging, interruption possibilities, and the like are often implicit in the formalisms with which current conversation policies are specified. Yet, precise knowledge of these is critical to an agent or agent designer's reasoning about how to produce messages with proper sequencing and timing.
3. *Uptake acknowledgment.* Whether or not an agent must send a message indicating successful receipt of another message, and the possible range of contents of this uptake message (*i.e.,* simple **ACK**, or some more complex message from which uptake can be inferred) is a common property of many different kinds of agent conversations. It is also a conversation policy decision, as the requirement to send an uptake messages is not typically a logical consequence of ACL message semantics. Fine-grained conversation policies can make this kind of policy explicit.
4. *Exception handling.* Exception or error conditions are always possible in real agent conversations. This means that the transition nets that have traditionally been used to specify agent conversations have had to be decorated with enormous numbers of little-used error handling transitions, often to the extent that the preferred conversational flow in the net is completely obscure. Further, many of these basic exception handling strategies are common across different types of agent

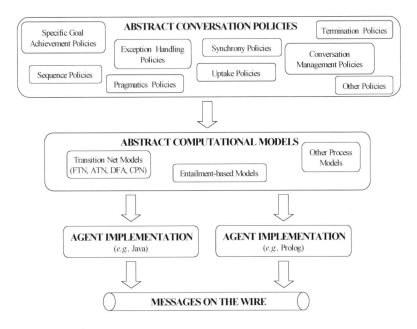

Fig. 2. A Model of Conversation Policies

conversations. A fine-grained account of conversation policies promises to be flexible enough to account for conversational exceptions in a satisfactory way.

5. *Pragmatics.* There may be several semantically equivalent messages which can be used to achieve the same communicative goal [9;13]. Agreement between agents on the preferred way to express a given communicative act in an ACL is an important way in which conversation policies can address the Basic Problem.

This is obviously only a partial list of the kinds of implicit assumptions which regulate agent inter-action, but it illustrates our motivation for proposing an account of conversation policies focused around mixing and matching fine-grained policies in order to regulate an agent's usage of its ACL.

3. Agent Conversation Redux

Thinking about conversation policies as these sorts of fine-grained constraints on semantically coherent ACL usage is a powerful idea, and it fits well with the use of deterministic finite automata (DFA) and other formalisms which have traditionally specified conversation policies. We model agent communication with four layers, each providing a different level of abstraction (see figure 2). The direct inspiration for this approach is from Manna and Pnueli's work on reactive systems verification [ref], but this type of four-layered model of analysis is common in other parts of computer science. For example, in order to analyze how a computer performs a piece of mathematics, we need to explain how an abstract mathematical theory (the constraints) can be reflected in one or more abstract algorithms (the computational models) and implemented in different actual programming languages and execution models (the agents).

At the top of the hierarchy is the set of conversation policies for an ACL, which are the different fine-grained constraints which agent message production in an interaction must not violate. These policies are public, shared, abstract, and normative, and can combine in different ways. When agents agree to abide by specific conversation policies for an interaction, they are agreeing to let their ACL usage be governed by a specified subset of these constraints. Further, we believe that these constraints will fall naturally into different packages: *e.g.,* general conversation management constraints, clusters of constraints relative to the use of specific communicative acts, constraints that govern message sequencing for particular kinds of goal-directed interactions, and so on. All of these constraints are sensitive to the semantic model and expressive power of the target ACL. Agent designers (or sophisticated agents), when presented with the need to interact with other agents in the service of a particular goal, will select the governing conversation policies for that interaction from the larger set of possible conversation policies for the ACL.

The set of policies that are in force for a particular agent interaction will together define a set of abstract *computational models* for that interaction. The computational models induced by a set of policies might include, for example, several different types of state transition network, but it might also range over more logically-based computational models, such as those based on entailment relations in a situation calculus or dynamic logic. The computational models are extensionally defined by the requirement that their semantics must satisfy the composition of the policy constraints that are in force; hence, these models are only normative to the extent that they accurately reflect the constraints that define them.[7] Thus, these computational models have a type-token relationship to the actual agent conversations. Also, while policies must be shared between agents, the specific computational models induced by these policies need not be – one agent might include code implementing a DFA, while another might be running a Petri net. Nevertheless, if the agents agree on conversation policies, then the computational models used by the agents should allow them to communicate within the limits of the constraints that they agree upon.[8] This approach allows for a wide latitude of agent implementations, and guarantees that certain properties of the conversation will hold even when sophisticated agents are communicating with simpler ones.

It is important to note that there is no requirement that the computational model chosen by an agent or designer to implement a particular set of policies regulate every aspect of an agent's messaging behavior. Models which are induced by a very tight set of policy constraints might indeed do so; but it is also possible (and indeed likely) that many aspects of messaging behavior might be unspecified by the computational model. Most commonly, computational models will provide on very general constraints on message content, and while they might include some global timing pa-

---

[7] In general, the choice of a computational model will fix many more properties of an agent's interaction behavior than are accounted for by the chosen set of policies. This is not a problem; presumably, agents who converse under this set of conversation policies will be able to deal with the variations.

[8] We note that it is logically possible that agents could agree on a set of constraints that are incompatible: *i.e.,* that there is no computational model that could satisfy all the constraints.

rameters, they will typically leave open the timing of individual message exchanges. More interestingly, though, a model might not specify the exact sequencing of messages required to achieve a particular state – it might specify only that a set of communicative states must be achieved in a particular sequence. This type of higher-level computational model would correspond to the agents agreeing on only a very weak set of policies to govern their interaction.

For example, a model such as the one described above might only describe a relative sequence or partial order of conversational *landmarks* (*e.g.*, that an offer has been made; that an offer has been accepted) in a conversation of a given type. Each landmark would be characterized by a set of properties that must be true of the agents involved at that point in the conversation. Consider the *CONTRACT* conversation policy shown in figure 1. The initial segment involves an announcement made by some agent **C** immediately followed by an bid (or decline) by some other agent **S**. While it is reasonable to think of announcing and bidding as typically being a two-step process, this might not always be the case: between **C**'s announcement and **S**'s bid, **S** might ask **C** for a clarification about payment, or if a partial bid is acceptable, or whether multiple bids will be accepted. There might be any number of contract-related exchanges between **C** and **S** until the acceptance (or nonacceptance) of the original announcement. A loose set of conversation policies might not specify the number and exact sequence of messages in advance, but rather would constrain the ACL usage to attempting to achieve certain high-level states, given certain other restrictions (*e.g.*, turn-taking).

In our view, the traditional methods for specifying conversation policies [2; 6] have *not* specified policies *per se,* but rather have attempted to specify these computational models directly, typically by using automata or transition net formalisms. The individual policy decisions that traditional conversation policies are designed to capture are only implicit in these formalisms. This has lead to a significant problem in existing conversation policy design practice – how to guarantee that existing policies are interoperable or composable, how to modify them, and how to model and verify the expected effects of following these policies.

Once a set of computational models is defined, an agent designer will implement a specific choice of computational model in a particular agent for conversation of a particular type using a particular ACL. One agent might include a set of rules that simulate a DFA, while another agent whose computational model involves entailment over a particular axiom set might contain a theorem prover. A third agent might implement an interpreter for a DFA language, and download specific DFAs for a conversation from a server. The designer's choice of implementation model for an agent's communication behavior will governed by the requirements on the sophistication of an agent's conversation, performance requirements on the agent, interaction with other parts of the agent's architecture, and so on. However, the fact that all the computational models for the conversation type will encode the same chosen constraints on ACL usage will guarantee that each agent's production of ACL messages will be limited in a consistent way. Hence, agents implementing these models will be able to minimize the Basic Problem to the extent to which their conversation policies allow.

4. Objectives for Conversation Policies

Viewing conversation policies as general constraints on semantically coherent ACL messaging behavior is a powerful idea. Besides being consistent with the general goal of addressing the Basic Problem by limiting the possible usage of the ACL, it allows us to bind together many of the classic arguments for using conversation policies to govern agent communication:

1. *Conversation policies should allow us to cleanly separate policy from mechanism in our theories of agent behavior, thus dividing public policies from private implementations.* Many authors have pointed out that the use of explicit conversation policies in agent interaction facilitates the separation of policy and mechanism – i.e., the policy must be independent of the program used to implement it. This is desirable because it enables conversation policy reuse, metareasoning over conversation policies, and off-line analysis of the implications of various conversation policy choices [8]. Viewing conversation policies as sets of interacting constraints which can induce a variety of computational models is entirely consistent with this idea, as it provides a level of analysis that is independent of the model with which the conversation policies are implemented in an agent. Explicit implementation-independent conversation policy representation also makes practical the development of consistent agent-system-wide exception handling mechanisms: unless we can unambiguously and declaratively describe expected agent behavior and the constraints by which it is bounded, we can neither detect, facilitate, nor repair problems when they arise [4; 10].

2. *Conversation policies should provide a level of abstraction that allows us to identify equivalence classes of conversations across different specification formalisms.* An important objective for any theory of conversation policies is that it provide criteria for identifying identical conversation policies across different agent implementations. If one agent is executing a theorem prover and another is running a Petri net, it should nevertheless be possible for them to have common policies governing their conversation. This means that the conversation policies themselves need to apply at a level beyond the computational models that the agents implement. Our account provides a natural way to express this.

3. *Conversation policies should be compositional, so that different pieces can be mixed and matched to govern different domain-specific conversations.* We found in our KAoS work that we were constantly tinkering with the DFAs that expressed KAoS's conversation policies. KAoS conversations have certain common features, such as the way that question/answer loops and exceptions are handed, and we wanted to be able to flexibly integrate these with our existing DFAs. However, without a precise way to describe the critical properties of the original DFAs that we needed to preserve, we could not guarantee that the modified DFAs expressed the same ideas about conversation design as the original ones. Policies expressing certain kinds of pragmatic constraints were difficult to express as pure DFAs (e.g., timing, abnormal termination, and general turn-taking constraints) and we found ourselves extending the representation in ad hoc ways to reflect these concerns rather than applying a more systematic approach. Essentially, we found that the

nature of the conversations we were designing required fine-grained policies that could be combined to yield larger composite policy entities. The present framework allows us to do that.

4. *Conversation policies should be flexible enough to allow agents of different levels of sophistication to interoperate, and should therefore allow for conversational control at different levels.* The successful agent-based ensembles of the future will include agents created by different vendors with widely varying degrees of sophistication and reasoning ability, operating under many different kinds of resource constraints, and interacting with each other at many different levels [3;4]. Many agents will be small and simple, some will have medium-scale reasoning abilities, and relatively few will exhibit complex and explicit reasoning on beliefs and goals. All will have to communicate with each other, at least to advertise their services and autonomously negotiate for resources they need. This kind of extreme heterogeneity entails that agents will need to tailor their use of the ACL to match the capabilities of the interacting agents – the highly restricted language necessary to interact with a simple database agent wrapper is too inexpressive to handle, e.g. complex distributed planning problems. By expressing individual ACL constraints at a level above the composite computational models, agents and agent designers can reason about how precisely to manage the ACL tradeoffs that the Basic Problem requires, and match these tradeoffs to the capabilities of the agents that are conversing.

5. Conclusion

We realize that the approach to conversation policies sketched out in the above text will require a great deal of formal work to make it precise and convincing. We are currently engaged in research which we believe will do just that. Specifically, we are looking at:

1. Formal languages for representing conversational constraints and computational models
2. Deductive techniques which will allow us to verify that a computational model meets a specification.
3. The relationship and boundaries between ACL semantic theories and the account of conversation policies given here.

Though agent designers who have not been dealing with conversations in any formal way may worry that the kinds of approaches discussed in this paper will just add unnecessary complexity to their implementations, we assert precisely the contrary. We believe that the combination of powerful offline conversation analysis tools, with the resultant systematically constructed conversation policies, policy facilitators, enforcement mechanisms, and exception handling facilities will actually simplify the online reasoning task for agents and help guarantee a level of robustness and responsiveness to pragmatic considerations that has been lacking in deployed agent systems [4].

Our hope is to move the analysis of agent conversations up a level, and make explicit all of the fine-grained policies which have hitherto been implicit in the conversations we have designed. In this way, the view that we are advocating is not substantially different from many other types of formally-based scientific work. It is always important to bring out the relations between the abstract theories which provide our intellectual touchstones, the process models which allow us to combine our theories into constructive procedures, the artifacts in which our theories are implemented, and the results of allowing these artifacts to interact in the world. Our account of conversation policies is a step in this direction.[9]

6. Acknowledgments

The authors thankfully acknowledge support from the DARPA CoABS program (Contract F30602-98-C-0170); the Aviation Extranet joint-sponsored research agreement between NASA Ames, The Boeing Company, and the University of West Florida (Contract NCA2-2005); and the Agency for Health Care Policy Research (Grant R01HS09407).

References

1. Bradshaw, J. M. (1997). An introduction to software agents. In J. M. Bradshaw (Ed.), *Software Agents.* pp. 3-46. Cambridge, MA: AAAI Press/The MIT Press.
2. Bradshaw, J. M., Dutfield, S., Benoit, P., and Woolley, J. D. (1997). KAoS: Toward an industrial-strength generic agent architecture. In J. M. Bradshaw (Ed.), *Software Agents.* pp. 375-418. Cambridge, MA: AAAI Press/The MIT Press.
3. Bradshaw, J. M., Gawdiak, Y., Cañas, A., Carpenter, R., Chen, J., Cranfill, R., Gibson, J., Hubbard, K., Jeffers, R., Kerstetter, M., Mathé, N., Poblete, L., Robinson, T., Sun, A., Suri, N., Wolfe, S., and Bichindaritz, I. (1999). Extranet applications of software agents. *ACM Interactions.* Forthcoming.
4. Bradshaw, J. M., Greaves, M., Holmback, H., Jansen, W., Karygiannis, T., Silverman, B., Suri, N., and Wong, A. (1999). Agents for the masses: Is it possible to make development of sophisticated agents simple enough to be practical? *IEEE Intelligent Systems* (v. 14:2, March 1999), pp. 53-63.
5. Cohen, P. R., and Levesque, H. (1997). Communicative actions for artificial agents. In J. M. Bradshaw (ed.), *Software Agents.* pp. 419-436. Cambridge, MA: The AAAI Press/The MIT Press.
6. Finin, T., Labrou, Y., and Mayfield, J. (1997). KQML as an agent communication language. In J. M. Bradshaw (ed.), *Software Agents.* pp. 291-316. Cambridge, MA: The AAAI Press/The MIT Press.
7. Greaves, M., Holmback, H., and Bradshaw, J. M. (1999). Agent conversation policies. In J. M. Bradshaw (ed.), *Handbook of Agent Technology.* Cambridge, MA: AAAI Press/The MIT Press. Forthcoming.

---

[9] We are currently working on a more complete account of conversation policies to appear in [7].

8. Greaves, M. T., Holmback, H. K., and Bradshaw, J. M. (1998). CDT: A tool for agent conversation design. *Proceedings of 1998 National Conference on Artificial Intelligence (AAAI-98) Workshop on Software Tools for Developing Agents.* pp. 83-88. Madison, WI, Menlo Park, CA: AAAI Press.

9. Holmback, H., Greaves, M., and Bradshaw, J. M. (1999). A pragmatic principle for agent communication. J. M. Bradshaw, O. Etzioni, and J. Mueller (ed.), *Proceedings of Autonomous Agents '99* Seattle, WA. New York: ACM Press. Forthcoming.

10. Klein, M., and Dellarocas, C. (1999). Exception handling in agent systems. J. M. Bradshaw, O. Etzioni, and J. Mueller (ed.), *Proceedings of Autonomous Agents '99,* Seattle, WA. New York: ACM Press. Forthcoming.

11. Manna, Z. and Pnueli, A. (1995). *Temporal Verification of Reactive Systems: Safety.* New York: Springer-Verlag.

12. Sadek, M. D., Bretier, P., and Panaget, F. (1997). Artimis: Natural Dialogue Meets Rational Agency. *Proceedings of the 1997 International Joint Conference on Artificial Intelligence (IJCAI-97),* Palo Alto: Morgan Kaufmann.

13. Smith, I. A., Cohen, P. R., Bradshaw, J. M., Greaves, M., and Holmback, H. (1998). Designing conversation policies using joint intention theory. *Proceedings of the Third International Conference on Multi-Agent Systems (ICMAS-98).* pp. 269-276. Paris, France. Los Alamitos, CA: IEEE Computer Society.

14. Steiner, D., (ed.) *FIPA 97 Specification Vesion 2, Part 2: Agent Communication.* http://www.fipa.org/ spec/FIPA97.html.

The Role of Conversation Policy in Carrying Out Agent Conversations

Laurence R. Phillips and Hamilton E. Link

Sandia National Laboratories
MS 0445
Albuquerque, NM 87185
lrphill@sandia.gov , helink@sandia.gov

Abstract. Structured conversation diagrams, or conversation specifications, allow agents to have predictable interactions and achieve predefined information-based goals, but they lack the flexibility needed to function robustly in an unpredictable environment. We propose a mechanism that dynamically combines conversation structures with separately established policies to generate conversations. Policies establish limitations, constraints, and requirements external to specific planned interaction and can be applied to broad sets of activity. Combining a separate policy with a conversation specification simplifies the specification of conversations and allows contextual issues to be dealt with more straightforwardly during agent communication. By following the conversation specification when possible and deferring to the policy in exceptional circumstances, an agent can function predictably under normal situations and still act rationally in abnormal situations. Different conversation policies applied to a given conversation specification can change the nature of the interaction without changing the specification.

1 Introduction

A: *An argument is a connected series of statements intended to establish a proposition.*
B: *No, it isn't!*
A: *Yes, it is! It isn't just contradiction!*
            Policy discussion, Monty Python,
            Argument Clinic Sketch

Software agents communicate while they pursue goals. In some cases, agents communicate specifically in order to accomplish goals. We restrict our interest in this paper to goals that can be described as information states, that is, *information goals*. We discuss agents that intend to accomplish information goals by communicating.

Although individual speech acts have been well-characterized, consensus on higher-order structured interactions has not been reached. There is little or no discussion in the

F. Dignum and M. Greaves (Eds.): Agent Communication, LNAI 1916, pp. 132-143, 2000.
© SpringerVerlag Berlin Heidelberg 2000

literature of how to constrain the behavior of an agent during communication in response to a dynamic environment.

When a set of communication acts among two or more agents is specified as a unit, the set is called a *conversation*. Agents that intend to have a conversation require internal information structures that contain the results of deliberation about which communication acts to use, when to use them, whom the communications should address, what responses to expect, and what to do upon receiving the expected responses. We call these structures *conversation specifications*, or specifications for short. We claim that specifications are inadequate for fully describing agent behavior during interaction.

Consider two agents who are discussing the location of a surprise party for a third agent, who is not present. When that agent enters the room, all discussion of the party suddenly ceases. The cessation occurs because the first two agents understand that the third agent cannot receive any information that such a party is being considered. Conversely, suppose that the conversation is about a party in honor of the third agent and all three agents know the third agent is aware of it. Now, when the third agent enters the room, the conversation continues.

Are the first two agents having the same conversation in both cases? We claim the answer is "Yes, but they're operating under different policies." In both cases, they are having a conversation whose essence is organizing the party. The conversation might roughly be specified to contain information exchange components (e.g., to establish a set of possible locations), allocation components ("I'll call these two restaurants, and you call this other one"), and a continuationscheduling component ("I'll call you tomorrow with what I find out and we'll take it from there"). These are all matters that we expect to find in a conversation specification. On the other hand, the decision of whether to stop talking when a specific third party enters the room is based on a mutually understood policy and might reasonably be applied to any number of conversations, for example, negotiations about the price of a commodity on which the third agent is bidding.

Historically the agent communication literature has used the word "policy" to refer to the description of the structure of interaction between a number of agents, generally two but sometimes more (Bradshaw et al. 1997). The dictionary, however, defines "policy" as "a highlevel overall plan capturing general goals and acceptable procedures." This coincides with what we expect of a conversation policy: an agent using a conversation *policy* would operate within certain constraints while attempting to satisfy general informationbased goals. When discussing procedures and constraints of interaction beyond the basic structure of a conversation, the word "policy" has connotation that we feel is more appropriately bound to the procedures and constraints rather than to the basic structure. For the latter, then, we will instead use the word "specification," and use the word "policy" to refer to the former.

2 Policies for Interaction

The focus of our work is to create a mechanism for combining specifications with policies that constrain the behavior of an agent in order to generate conversations among agents.

We have begun to design a mechanism that uses the specification's description of input states and actions based on them and the policy's description of constraints, limitations, and requirements together to determine an agent's response to a message. Given a suitable mechanism, the specification and the policy can be implemented as data objects. The specification defines the structure for the conversation, and the policy defines the acceptable procedures, rules, and constraints for the conversation.

We can interact with and speak of agents as intentional systems (Dennett 1987). We assume that agents are able to emit illocutions and that illocutions can have perlocutionary effect on other agents that "hear" them (Searle 1969). (We follow Searle in using *illocution* to mean an utterance intended to affect the listener and *perlocution* to mean the production of effect on the listener). This means that an agent can emit information with the intent of altering the information state of some other agent, that the information can be received by some other agent, and that receipt of this information can cause the recipient to be in an information state intended by the emitter. The emitter desires the recipient to be in a certain state because the emitter believes that this either is or assists in achieving one or more of its goal states.

Conversation specifications are distinctly similar to KAoS conversation policies (Bradshaw et al. 1997). The specification dictates the transitions and outputs made by the agent in response to input. A conversation policy is a set of constraints on the conversation specification that limit the behavior of an agent beyond the requirement of following the procedures and structures of the conversation specification. The policy object is used by the mechanism to make decisions about acceptable courses of action when the conversation specification fails to completely determine a course of action. Lynch and Tuttle said it well: "Our correctness conditions are often of the form 'if the environment behaves correctly, then the automaton behaves correctly.'" (Lynch and Tuttle, 1989) This stems from the constraint that IOA's cannot block inputs, the automaton is permitted to exhibit arbitrary behavior when "bad" or unexpected inputs occur. What happens when the environment *doesn't* behave "correctly?" This is where policy applies.

Policy differs from specification in that specifications describe individual patterns of interactions, while policies are sets of highlevel rules governing interactions. It is possible for a class of conversation policies to have subclasses. For one policy to be a subclass of another, the subclass must be more strict (more constraining) in at least one attribute and no less constraining in any.

Our new mechanism combines the policies and specifications to determine the set of conversations that can be generated. When policies change in the midst of a conversation, the goal may become infeasible. In our formulation, the conversation policy does not specify the types of messages that can occur. It is made up of constraints on who can participate, and under what circumstances, whether subconversations can be initiated within an existing open conversation, whether equivalent conversations can take place in parallel with the same participating entities (e.g., an agent can't carry on two price negotiation conversations with the same entity w.r.t. the same object). We claim that issues of specification are orthogonal to issues of policy; specifications define the structure of interactions, while policies govern the way interactions are carried out.

3 Methods

We developed our current agent conversation mechanism using the Standard Agent Architecture (SAA) developed by the Advanced Information Systems Lab (Goldsmith, Phillips, and Spires 1998) at Sandia National Laboratories. The SAA provides a framework for developing goalbased reasoning agents, and we are currently using a distributed object system that enables agents to send each another simple objects or sets of information. We are using the Knowledge Query and Manipulation Language (KQML) (Labrou and Finin 1997) as our message protocol.

Interacting with an agent first requires that the agent be able to correctly identify and respond to illocutionary messages. A situated agent in pursuit of goals must be able to answer two questions: To which, if any, of its current goals does new information relate, and what actions, if any, should it execute based on new information that relates to a given goal? In the SAA, the primary structure that enables this is the agent's stimulus response table (SRT). An agent anticipating input of a certain type puts an entry into its SRT, which maps stimuli (by class or instance) to the appropriate action. Our system currently requires messages to contain an explicit reference to the context within which the SRT entry was created. The reference is realized as the object identifier (OID) of the current conversation object that gave rise to the message.

When an input arrives, the appropriate SRT entry is retrieved and its goal is undeferred (having previously been deferred, presumably awaiting relevant input), which activates the goal. The agent now determines how the new information in the context affects the goal and either marks it satisfied, failed, or deferred or continues to attempt to satisfy the goal. When satisfaction of the goal requires a speech act, the agent creates an utterance, delineates the context, embeds the context signature in the utterance, attaches the goal to the context, places the entry in the SRT, defers the goal, and executes the utterance. In short, illocution is a deliberate act that creates an utterance and sets up an expectation of the response that the recipient will make.

To engineer a conversation, the entire set of context descriptors of interest is laid out as a set of subgoals, each of which is satisfied by gathering specific information. We have automated the construction of an utterance from a context, the updating of the context to reflect the new information conveyed by the input, and the connectivity that enables the utterance and the input to refer to the same context. Specialized code is written to construct goals, execute side effects, maintain the SRT, and so on.

Composing speech acts in a theoretically predictable fashion is more difficult; this is the motivation for creating a structured way of merging specification and policy at run time to get a structured interaction that is forced to remain within certain operational boundaries.

In our current mechanism, policy is embedded in the conversation mechanism as part of the design. A policy change, for example, that an agent should institute a timeout and ignore all messages responding to a particular request after the timeout expires, would require reengineering the conversation. The mechanism would be much more maintainable given an explicit policy object that could just be changed to reflect the fact that there's now a timeout. Our essential thesis is that policies and conversation specifications should be independent so that conversations could be switched under the same policy and policies could be changed without changing existing conversations.

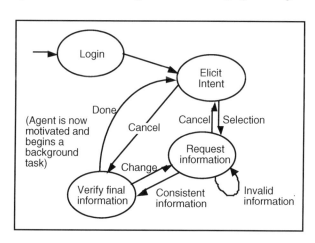

Fig. 1. A conversation specification that does not specify a variety of potential constraints on the agent's activities

4 Conversation Policy

Consider the conversation in Figure 1. It describes a session allowing agent A to determine agent B's identity, offer B a choice of services and ascertain B's selection, and perform a task based on the selection. Describing the conversation is generally simple for such things: when a request or assertion comes in, the agent deliberates, returns information to the initiator, and anticipates the continuation. The two participants are responding to one another in turn, barring interruption, retransmission, or communication failure. There is no representation of what happens when the conversation is interrupted or when an agent retransmits a message. These issues are matters of policy that must be dealt with separately.

KAoS conversation "policies" enable definite courses of action to be established and failstop conditions to be dealt with (Bradshaw et al. 1997). They also imply mechanisms for initiating and concluding conversations. Specifications play the crucial role in agent communication of providing structure, but they do not, for example, describe whether a discussion can be postponed, or, if so, under what conditions or for how long. Indeed, KAoS conversation "policies" appear to concern matters of conversation *specification*, fundamentally how to respond to input given the current information state, rather than matters of conversation *policy*, such as what to do when interrupted, whether the conversation can be postponed, or whether there is a time constraint on reaching an end state.

Policy issues are important. One constraint imposed by the policy in Figure 1 is that it requires turntaking. If agent A receives several messages in a row, it may respond to each in turn without realizing that, say, B's third message was sent before A's second response. If agent A cannot detect the violation of the turntaking policy, it might consider the second and third messages in an outdated context. A similar situation could occur if several agents were communicating and one were speaking out of turn. Without policy, designing a mechanism to deal with these violations means that a conversation specification that enforced turntaking and one that merely allowed it would be two different things that would need to be maintained separately and activated separately by the agent. Furthermore, designing them into a system that had no notion of turntaking would require that every state/action pair of every conversation specification be examined to see what should now happen if turntaking is violated. At worst, accommodating a single policy issue doubles the number of conversation specifications an agent might be called upon to employ.

Examining constraints immediately leads to ideas for policies that replicate familiar patterns of interaction, such as a forum policy or a centralpointofcontact policy. Different classes of states, changes in context, and the particular protocol of communication used are independent of the conversation policy, although some make more sense in one policy or another. The web page and informationstate context, for example, make the most sense in a 1:1 turntaking policy when dealing oneonone with a number of individual humans. KQML, in contrast, has many performatives that support broadcasting to a group of agents involved in the same conversation. In practical terms we may end up having to constrain which policies can be upheld based on communication details.

An explicit representation of policy also enables an agent to express the policy under which it is operating. It is easy to transmit, say, a policy message outlining the level of security required for any of several possible upcoming conversations for which the recipient already has the specifications. In contrast, without policy, the "secure" version of each conversation specification needs to be transmitted anew. If two agents agree on a policy at the beginning of a conversation, the amount of communication required to determine a course of action once a violation has occurred can be minimized.

The structure of the conversation depends thus on the nature of the information and how this changes the state of the conversation. By abstracting to the policy level, we enable a set of constraints to support the execution of several conversations, as long as they have the same *kinds of states* and the same *kinds of transitions*, i.e., the nature of information in a state does not matter as long as there is a common means of mapping input and state to another state in the conversation. If the conversation can be described as a collection of states with transitions between them, then the conversation policy should be describable as a *form* of transition function operating on the current perceived state of the world and the communications the agent is receiving.

This abstraction is powerful because the individual conversation policies can be combined with specifications to create several classes of conversations, all similarly constrained. The constraints the framework imposes are then the conversation policy; and specializations of the conversation policy framework methods are implementations of particular transition functions, which operate on particular classes of conversations. These conversation policies would support transformations by our mechanism, each of which defines a range of possible specializations within the high-level constraints. Radically different behavior between two sets of conversations would imply radically different frameworks, just as the difference between context-free grammars and regular languages implies a greater difference in both the nature of states and the transition function forms of finite automata and stack machines.

5   Example

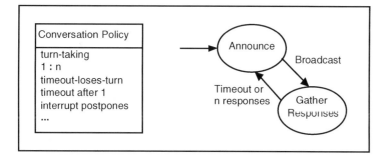

Fig. 2. Policy and specification as seen by the announcer. The policy allows conversations to be postponed, which the conversation specification need not explicitly state.

Consider the specification in Figure 2. Agent A_1, the announcer, broadcasts a message to a group of agents $A_2 \ldots A_n$ and gathers responses from the group before continuing. By itself, however, this specification leaves many questions unanswered—for example, if some agent doesn't respond at all, or responds more than once in a cycle, what should agent A_1 do? These questions may be asked of many specifications, and may have different answers even from one interaction to the next.

The policy in Figure 2 provides answers to some questions of this sort. The policy enforces turn-taking, meaning that agents in the group have only one opportunity to respond to each broadcast. If they do not respond within one minute of each broadcast, they lose the chance to do so during that turn. This might be the case if broadcasts were frequent. If more pressing matters come up during a session, the discussion is postponed (perhaps leaving messages in the announcer's queue to be dealt with later), but it can be expected that the session will resume at some future time.

How might we tailor policies to get usefully different behavior? For policies concerned with faulttolerance, the same policies could be used in many conversations to handle the same expected problems, but policy can also be used to control conversations during the course of normal interaction as well.

Suppose we combine the specification above with a policy that does not enforce turn taking, but rather says that newer messages from an agent take precedence over older messages. The announcer is forbidden from sharing message data among group members, and the time allowed for responses to each broadcast is 24 hours. Combining the policy and specification with a sales announcer produces a silent auction. If the policy were replaced with one that had a time limit of a few minutes and required the announcer to rebroadcast new information to the group, the same specification could be used to produce an English auction. Using different policies with the same specification as a foundation can produce a variety of desirable behaviors with minimal changes to the agent's code.

6 The Impact of a Policy Mechanism

In this section we discuss the relationship between conversation specifications, policies, and an operational mechanism. We show how policy information can be used to direct the action of an agent without reference to the conversation that agent is having.

Consider a set of state/action pairs with the property that when an agent perceives the world to be in a given state and executes the corresponding action, the world state that results is described by the "state" component of one of the pairs (I/O automata fall conveniently close to this). States with no corresponding actions are end states. Such a set embodies no notion of intent, but an agent can commit to achieving one of the end states by executing the actions. The point of an action specification is to explicate a series of acts that will result in one of a known set of states.

A conversation specification is such a set of state/action pairs; the specified states are information states and the specified actions are speech acts. A conversation specification explicates a series of speech acts and their triggering states that will result in a one of a known set of information states. An end state may be a goal state, i.e., a state whose achievement is the agent's intent, or a state in which the desired state is known or believed to be either no longer desirable or unachievable.

The conversation specification may specify states and actions that are never realized; e.g., failuredenoting states or errorcorrecting actions. All actions and states are only partially specified, in the sense that none specify the entire state of the world, because the number of features that might be observed at execution time is infinite, and only a few of these are perceived at specification design time as having any material effect on movement towards the goal.

For example, a plan that includes forming a team might specify neither who is to fill every role on the team, though a specific agent must be cast in each role, nor in what order the roles are to be filled, because the specific order has no effect on the goal state.

Neither the conversation specification nor the policy controls the thread of conversation; the specification specifies the invariant part of the conversation's course, and policy specifies constraints on behavior, not the behavior itself. Control falls to the mechanism that combines the specification object and the policy object to arrive at an executable action at deliberation time. In the remainder of this section, we examine team formation with respect to what is determined by the conversation specification and what is determined by policy.

Assume that an agent is in a state where will listen until it receives a message from another agent. When a message arrives, the agent's policy is to select and commit to achieve one of the end states of a particular conversation specification; in other words, the agent's policy is to have a conversation when contacted. Leaving aside for the moment the question of how the agent makes the selection, assume the agent receives a message asking it to commit to achieving a goal and that it selects a conversation specification wherein it will inform the requester that it has committed if it commits and that it will not commit if it doesn't. This could be a matter of policy; suppose there were many agents available and this was known to the agent. The agent might reason that the best policy would be to report only when it could commit and to keep silent otherwise, in order not to use bandwidth.

Now what happens when an agent achieves a goal to which it has committed? Should the agent report satisfaction to the requester, when there is one? If this were a matter of policy, it could be turned on or off as overarching issues (security, priority, traffic levels, etc.) dictated and overridden as needed by specific policy overrides from the requester.

What should the agent do when it is asked to achieve a goal it believes it cannot achieve by itself? It might be the agent's policy to refuse to commit and to so report. An alternative policy would be to attempt to acquire commitments from other agents to assist. This would begin the team formation phase.

When the agent has acquired commitments from agents whose combined effort it believes can achieve the goal, it builds the team roster of agents $\{A_1, \dots, A_n\}$, marks the team formation goal satisfied, and ends the team formation phase (this ignores the issue of whether everyone on the team must believe the team can achieve the goal in order to commit). It might be the case that the agent must form the team within a given time period; what the agent should do when it does not receive sufficient commitments within the allotted time is a matter of policy. A reasonable policy would be to report to the original requester that the goal is unsatisfiable. This can be enforced at a high level, that is, *whenever* the agent has committed to achieving a goal, and the source of that goal is another agent, the agent must notify the source agent as to the achievement or non achievement of that goal. The agent holding a team roster for a given goal constructs a joint persistent goal (JPG) (Cohen and Levesque 1991), allocates the subgoals (assume the goal is linearizeable so that allocation is deterministic) and sends each subgoal and the JPG to the appropriate team member. The JPG contains a statement of the original goal and the team roster. When an agent A_i has achieved its subgoal, it multicasts this fact to the rest of the team using the roster in the JPG. Here, policy to notify only the requester must be overridden by JPG-specific policy. Every team member now believes A_i has achieved its subgoal. Once A_i believes that every team member has achieved its subgoal, it believes that the JPG has been satisfied and it multicasts this fact to the rest of the team. At this point, A_i believes that every team member believes that the JPG has been satisfied and is free to leave the team.

7 Conclusions

A conversation policy must be established so that the communicating agents (who may have differing languages) have a common logical and contextual structure for communicating. This allows each agent to establish predictive models of one another's behavior in response to information and to plan and reason about the outcome of conversations with the other agent. Each agent can establish this model based on information that another agent can perform a certain conversation specification while conforming to certain requirements.

We advocate a separate conversation policy structure that embodies the constraints that will be enforced while a conversation is going on—using a conversation specification as a template or model. A participant in a conversation must have some means of determining whether events that transpire during the conversation bear on the realization of its goals. It is relatively straightforward to specify the normative events in a conversation; the speaker intends to have engendered a specific state in the listener, and the normative response types are limited. On the other hand, it is not generally possible to specify all the exceptions. Even if we could, the necessary responses depend on states of the environment, not states of the conversation. To take the state of the environment into consideration, a policy must be able to constrain the behavior of virtually any conversation specification to which it is applied.

8 Future Developments

It would be useful to define and prove certain formal properties of policies when combined with specifications, for example,
1. Is the question of whether a conversation conforms to a given conversation policy decidable, and if so, how can this be tested?
2. Does conversation X conform to some conversation policy, and if so, which one?
3. What is the maximally confining policy to which a set of conversations conforms?

4. Will the conversation generated from a specification terminate when following a particular policy?
5. Under certain circumstances, a policy may render given specifications impossible. What is the minimal set of constraints that can be established that will still allow a set of conversations to take place?
6. Given a policy that has the potential to render a conversation impossible, what should an agent do?

Consider for a moment the agent as an I/O automaton (IOA) (Lynch and Tuttle, 1989). The IOA's I/O table specifies the agent's behavior. The IOA's input column describes agent's information states. These states can be entered as an agent internalizes information in messages it has received (i.e., as those messages have perlocutionary effect). The agent then executes the specified internal and external actions specified by the righthand side of the automaton's I/O table. This formalism has some appeal because it makes a very clear distinction between actions under control of the automaton and those under control of the environment and allows a readable and precise description of concurrent systems.

Analyzing collections of speech acts in terms of I/O automata would be possible if it were not for the dependency of the proofs about the IOAs on their being inputenabled. Agents that filter their stimuli before taking action or replying do not meet this requirement, so the applicability of the IOA theory is questionable.

A formal theory that establishes conversation semantics, describes how the semantics of individual speech acts contribute to conversation, and allows us to demonstrate certain characteristics of combinations of specifications and policies may or may not be useful. When discussing a system whose purpose is to deal with the unexpected, it may be more reasonable to engineer a policy that provides some reasonable capstone when an unanticipated problem arises. Engineering conversations that meet certain requirements, dynamically generating policies and specifications based on beliefs and intentions, and modifying conversations based on changing constraints may allow productive agent behavior even in the absence of a complete theoretical description.

9 In Context

Throughout these papers we see two common issues being addressed: by what means can an agent intend to have, and then have, a conversation, and by what means can an agent manage the process of having conversations in a dynamic environment? Two recurring subproblems are declaring behavioral models for an agent's own use and transmitting these models to other agents; agents need to be able to express the following in both internal and external settings: "This <conversation_spec> is the conversation I want to have" and "This <conversation_policy> is the policy I want to follow." In this paper we have labeled these structures *conversation specifications* and *conversation policies*, respectively.

A primary question roughly separates the papers in this volume into two categories: Are issues of specification and policy to be addressed by a single structural form that unifies specification and policy (Category 1), or by two separate structural forms, one for specification and one for policy, that are somehow composed during the conduct of a conversation (Category 2)? We are in category 2, having explicitly proposed a *policy object* to be communicated among conversing agents.

An essential question, approached by some authors, but not genuinely disposed of, is: what, exactly, is gained by having two structures? Although efficiency, complexity, and realizeablility have been used as motivators, we'd like to see a formal approach that enables decisions of where a particular aspect of discourse should be represented and, in particular, how such decisions are realized when policies and specifications are composed during a conversation.

10 Acknowledgements

This work was performed at Sandia National Laboratories, which is supported by the U.S. Department of Energy under contract DEAC0494AL85000.
Regina L. Hunter made numerous valuable comments on the manuscript.

References

1. Bradshaw, J.; Dutfield, S.; Benoit, P.; and Wooley, J. 1997. "KAoS: Toward an IndustrialStrength Open Agent Architecture," in Software Agents, AAAI Press/MIT Press.
2. Cohen, P. R., and Levesque, H. J. 1991. Confirmation and Joint Action. In Proceedings of the 12th Annual International Joint Conference on Artificial Intelligence.pp 951959, Menlo Park, CA, Morgan Kaufmann
3. Dennett, D.C. 1987. The Intentional Stance. Cambridge, MA: MIT Press.
4. Goldsmith, S.; Phillips, L.; and Spires, S. 1998. A multiagent system for coordinating international shipping. In Proceedings of the Workshop on Agent Mediated Electronic Trading (AMET'98), in conjunction with Autonomous Agents '98, Minneapolis/St. Paul, MN, USA
5. Labrou, Y. and Finin, T 1997. A Proposal for a new KQML Specification, Technical Report, CS9703, Dept. of Computer Science and Electrical Engineering, University of Maryland, Baltimore County
6. Lynch, N. A. and Tuttle, M. R. 1989. An Introduction to Input/Output Automata, Technical Memo, MIT/LCS/TM373, Laboratory for Computer Science, Massachusetts Institute of Technology
7. Searle, J. 1969. Speech Acts, Cambridge, UK: Cambridge University Press.

On Conversation Policies and the Need for Exceptions

Scott A. Moore

University of Michigan Business School
701 Tappan, Ann Arbor, MI 48109-1234
samoore@umich.edu

Abstract. The author describes a system for defining conversation policies that allows conversants to exchange explicit representations of how they use messages to get things done. This system allows conversation policies to be defined for one or more conversation partners. It does not require that every partner be aware of the other's conversation policies; however, it does provide more capabilities if partners have this information. It also does not require that conversing agents have the same capabilities. Most importantly, its use of modular conversation policies, acceptance of deviations from them, and its method of dynamically combining the policies encourages constructing policies that are relatively simple to interpret and manage.

1 Introduction

Recent research in agent communication languages (ACLs) has focused on the semantics of messages (FIPA's ACL [3], FLBC [12], KQML [6]). Much of this research has focused on languages whose semantics are expressed in terms of the beliefs, desires, and intentions (BDIs) of the participants in the exchange—or at least the computerized simulation of such states. Neither researchers nor the marketplace have come to any kind of agreement about what messages should mean nor how they should be interpreted. The reasons for this failure are deep and will not be going away soon; for example, one basis for this disagreement is the diversity of agent models. Agents are built for different purposes and need correspondingly simpler or more complex agent models.

In this paper I present a means of modeling conversations composed of messages in an ACL. This is an area fraught with trade-offs because of competing criteria. On the one hand, companies want to have models that are not complex to interpret (to ease maintenance) or to execute (to increase response time and decrease technology investment). On the other hand, they also want to have flexible conversation models that can both handle many alternative responses and integrate unexpected responses. If it were possible to implement such a system, it would benefit those who use and deploy agents in several ways. First, the ability to share models would make it easier to get started. Organizations could build on the expertise and experiences of others instead of having to start from scratch when building communicating agents. Second, focusing on and explicitly

F. Dignum and M. Greaves (Eds.): Agent Communication, LNAI 1916, pp. 144–159, 2000.
© Springer-Verlag Berlin Heidelberg 2000

specifying how messages are being used to *do* things would make it clearer than current practice allows how a message should be interpreted and responded to. Finally, changing from an inference-based interpretation system—such as that used by FLBC and FIPA's ACL—to one based more directly on convention should simplify and speed up the interpretation of frequently used messages. However, care will have to be taken to keep the system flexible so that it can meaningfully respond to messages from a wide variety of partners. This is something that, I propose, KQML has not been able to do.

In this paper I define what I mean by "conversation policy." I then develop a solution to a general, but relatively simple, communication problem. Through this analysis I progressively reveal an approach to implementing conversation policies. I conclude by discussing the benefits and drawbacks of the proposal.

2   Conversation Policies

In this section I present my views on conversation policies. As a basis for understanding that presentation, I first discuss my assumptions regarding agents, ACLs, and conversations.

Researchers have deployed many types of agents. These agents have been built to accomplish many different tasks and have widely differing capabilities. This situation shows no signs of stabilizing. One of the main differences relates to mobility. As discussed by Labrou et al. [7], the current situation is so bad that researchers of mobile and (non-mobile) agents even mean different things when referring to agent interoperability. For mobile agents it means being able to make remote procedure calls on its current host. For (non-mobile) agents it generally means being able to exchange messages in some ACL. Other differences, while less dramatic, offer similarly difficult obstacles to overcome if agents of all types are to ever to cooperate or interoperate. The point of this work is to describe a means for allowing—in the sense used by the (non-mobile) agent community—agents, mobile or not, to communicate with each other so that one can get information from another or get the other agent to do something for it.

In this paper I assume as little as possible about agent architecture and communication language so as to increase the chances that the framework might be widely applied. An underlying assumption is that if a fully formal specification for both responding to messages and handling conversations in a heterogeneous environment were specified, it would be difficult, if not impossible, to completely verify the conformity of any random agent to that specification. One important impediment would be the political reality of the verification process: Does a third party handle the verification? Do they have to look at the code that makes up the agent? A second impediment would be to determine what is meant by verification. Would it mean that an agent is able to reply to a message in that ACL or all messages in the ACL? Would it mean that the agent is able to generate a response to a message no matter how simplistic that message might be (e.g., replying "yes" to all messages)? Another impediment is determining what the specification looks like. Would it be a static document? Would it change every time a new type of message were defined, every time a new message were defined, or not at all? To summarize, I assume that if all agents were able to conform, then that would imply that either 1) the specification was so simple as to be of limited benefit to those who are deploying systems, or 2) the specification was so complex and had so many exceptions that it could not be usefully, easily, or meaningfully deployed.

What I am going to assume is that developers can understand a formal specification and can implement it *in whatever way they see fit* given the needs of their application. For example, in FLBC the standard effects of a `request` message are that 1) the hearer believes that the speaker wants the hearer to do something, and 2) the hearer believes that the speaker wants the hearer to want to do that same something [12, Appendix B, D]. Some agents might implement these effects within a defeasible belief system that models its own and others' beliefs. Other agents might not have such sophisticated technology, might not model the beliefs of speakers, and might focus on the second standard effect and simply do what it is that the requesting agent asked. I assume that agents can have any capabilities (e.g., use a belief system, have deontic reasoning). I base the examples in this paper on a specific language but the principles should be applicable to a wide range of languages.

In order to communicate with other agents, some particular ACL must be used. For the purposes of discussing conversation policies in this paper, the specifics of any one language are mostly irrelevant. It should be possible to add these facilities for describing and managing conversations to almost any ACL, though the benefits of such an addition may vary from one language to the next. That said, in this paper I refer periodically to FLBC (see [10,11,12], among others; more information can be found at the Web site http://www-personal-.umich.edu/~samoore/research/flbc/). FLBC is a language similar to KQML. Its message types are based on speech act theory; in contrast with KQML, this set of types has not needed frequent additions.

An FLBC message is an XML document [1,8] and has deep foundations in speech act theory. The `flbcMsg` XML DTD is located at http://www-personal-.umich.edu/~samoore/research/flbcMsg.dtd. An FLBC message has the basic form shown in Fig. 1.This message's interpretation is fairly straight-forward. This is a message, identified by M, from A to B in reply to a message identified by V. Speech act theory hypothesizes that all utterances have the form F(P) where F is the *illocutionary force* of the message (e.g., `inform`, `request`, `predict`) and P is the propositional content of the message (what is being informed, requested, or predicted). In conformance with the theory, the structure all FLBC messages is F(X). The content X is written using the language L and the ontology N.

When using FLBC, a message's sender constructs and sends a message knowing that he cannot know, but can only predict, how it will be interpreted. The message's recipient receives the message, interprets it, and then uses it as a basis for inferring how he should respond. The "standard effects" of a message are those specific to the message type; for example, the standard effects of all `request` messages are those defined above. The "extended effects" are those ef-

```
<?xml version="1.0" encoding="UTF-8" standalone="no"?>
<!DOCTYPE flbcMsg SYSTEM
  "http://www-personal.umich.edu/~samoore/research/flbcMsg.dtd">
<flbcMsg msgID="M">
  <simpleAct speaker="A"  hearer="B">
    <illocAct force="F"  vocab="N" language="L">
      X
    </illocAct>
  </simpleAct>
  <context>
   <resources>
    <actors>
     <person id="A"/><person id="B"/>
    </actors>
   </resources>
   <respondingTo message="V"/>
  </context>
</flbcMsg>
```

Fig. 1. Form of an FLBC message

fects that depend on the message's content (the *propositional content* in speech act terms) and context. Part of the context is the conversation to which the message belongs. This separation increases the probability that an agent will be able to usefully interpret a message it has not received before since 1) each agent developer knows the definition of the standard effects of each message type, 2) the standard effects contain a significant portion of the meaning of any particular message, and 3) the set of currently-defined message types covers a significant portion of the messages that agents need to say.

A conversation among agents is an exchange of messages made toward the accomplishment of some task or the achievement of some goal. In its simplest form it is a sequence of messages in which, after the initial message, each is a direct response to the previous one. More complicated structures occur when subdialogs are needed. Linguistics and philosophers have not come to any consensus about subdialogs, but several types consistently appear [9,12,13]: subordinations, corrections, and interruptions. A message begins a *subordinate* conversation when it elaborates on a point made in a previous message. This message should be about the previous message, probably as a clarification of some fact. A message that begins a *correction* subdialog indicates that the message somehow corrects a previous message in the conversation. A message *interrupts* the current conversation when it is neither an expected nor the standard reply to the previous message. This should be used only if the other two do not apply.

A conversation policy (CP) defines 1) how one or more conversation partners respond to messages they receive, 2) what messages one partner expects in response to a message it sends, and 3) the rules for choosing among competing courses of action. These policies can be used both to describe how a partner will respond to a message (or series of messages) it receives and to specify the procedure the partner actually executes in response to that message (or those messages). The policy is a template describing an agent's reactions to an incoming message, its expectations about upcoming messages, and the rules it applies to determine its own reactions. In a linguistic sense, it moves the conversation from an inference-based process to a convention-based one. Inference acts now as a backup, providing a more computationally expensive way of understanding unfamiliar messages for which CPs have not been defined.

A CP is said to be *well-formed* if it does not contain contradictory directions for what a partner should do. (The following discussion is similar to that concerning compatibility semantics given by Martin, Plaza, & Rodríguez-Aguilar in this volume.) These rules may assume any underlying agent model but, clearly, cannot assume more capabilities than the associated agent actually has. A specific CP is invoked upon receipt of a message and specifies a series of actions that usually, but not always, includes sending messages related to the received message. Two dimensions of this approach differ when a CP specifies actions for all the partners in a conversation (instead of simply one of them), specifically well-formedness and differing agent models. In addition to the requirement above, a well-formed multi-agent CP specifies a coherent set of actions that does not lead the conversation to a *deadlock*—a situation in which each agent waits for the other. These two meanings of well-formedness are related to Elio & Haddadi's concepts of local and global coherence (elsewhere in this volume). As for agent models, just as no specific one is required for a single-agent CP, a multi-agent CP does not require that all agents share the same model; thus, the rules for picking alternate courses of actions for one agent might be based on that agent's beliefs, another agent might have rules that automatically reply to all incoming messages (the degenerate case), and another might look at the status of environmental variables (such as indications of whether a machine is on).

The ACL actually used should not much matter; however, there is a specific, and to the point of this paper, quite relevant way in which FLBC and KQML differ—how each treats a response to a message. (This difference applies to the version described in [2] but not in [5].) As I have previously argued [11, p. 216], information about discourse structure should not define a speech act. If we were to go down this path, agents might need, in addition to `reply`, acts for `reply-request` (if a message is replying to a question but is asking for more information) and `reply-request-reply` (if a message is replying to a question that was asked in response to a question) and so on. These are not what we want. I propose that discourse information, as much as possible, be represented in a message's context term, separate from the speech act (illocutionary force and content) itself.

3   Proposal

In the following I describe my proposal for how agents should handle and how ACLs should represent conversation policies.

Agents should work with conversation policies that are represented using the statechart formalism defined by Harel [4]. This is a graphical language which developers would find easier to work with than the underlying XML representation which the agents themselves use. Harel states [4], more clearly than I could, why statecharts were developed and why I think they are appropriate:

> "A reactive system... is characterized by being, to a large extent, event-driven, continuously having to react to external and internal stimuli. ... The problem [with specifying and designing large and complex reactive systems] is rooted in the difficulty of describing reactive behavior in ways that are clear and realistic, and at the same time formal and rigorous, sufficiently so to be amenable to detailed computerized simulation. The behavior of a reactive system is really the set of allowed sequences of input and output events, conditions, and actions, perhaps with some additional information such as timing constraints." [pp. 231–2]. "Statecharts constitute a *visual formalism* for describing states and transitions in a modular fashion, enabling clustering, orthogonality (i.e., concurrency) and refinement, and encouraging 'zoom' capabilities for moving easily back and forth between levels of abstraction." [p. 233].

Everything that Harel states about reactive systems applies to agent communication systems; thus, statecharts are an appropriate technology to investigate for modeling CPs.

Every CP begins with a message being either sent or received. An agent maintains a database of both CPs it can use and a set of currently executing CPs. Figure 2 contains a sample statechart representation of a conversation policy. The whole statechart is labeled advertise with broker. It has six states: advertise with broker, msg with broker, broker knows we sell, broker sent description, not a broker, and broker has description. Transition labels have the form t(c)/g, each part of which is optional. When the event represented within the trigger t occurs, then, if the condition c is met, the transition between states is made. If the g is present on the transition, then the event g is generated as the transition is taken.

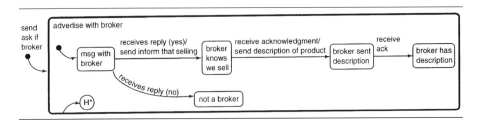

Fig. 2. A sample statechart representation of a conversation policy

To interpret the statechart in Fig. 2, start at the left, think of the broker as some external agent, and think of these figures as representing our agent's CPs.

When the send ask if broker event is generated somewhere within the system (that is, when a message asking if someone is a broker is sent), then this statechart is invoked. No condition (c) or generated event (/g) is on this transition. The transition is taken and this statechart is invoked because that event is the trigger for this statechart. The system's decision rules will favor specificity so it will choose the CP whose trigger provides the most specific match with the event that occurred. Specificity of triggers grouped by the type of the message provides one way of hierarchically organizing CPs. The unlabeled arrow with a dot on the end signifies that the system should start in the msg with broker state by default. The system stays in this state until a reply to this message is received. If the reply is "no", then the system takes the transition to the not a broker state. If the reply is "yes", then the transition to broker knows we sell is taken. When this is taken, the send inform that selling event is generated (that is, the system sends a message informing the broker that we sell some particular product). The system stays in this state until it receives acknowledgment. As it takes the transition to the broker sent description state, it generates the event send description of product. The system stays in this state until it receives an acknowledgment of this message. At that point it takes the transition to the broker has description state.

In the figures and body of this paper I informally represent the triggers, conditions, and generated events. I think of this as being the business analyst's view of the statecharts. This could be universally shared. Again, an XML DTD for statecharts could define the interchange vocabulary for describing statecharts that agents would be able to send, receive, and process. I envision that the tool supporting the definition of these statecharts would also contain more formal (even executable) specifications more appropriate for the system designer's needs. These formal descriptions could provide a more detailed and clear definition of the statecharts for all who see them; however, I do not believe that it is realistic to expect that this formal specification would be universally executable. The most that might be expected is to have a certain core set of operators (see those defined by The Open Group [14] and Table 1) that are shared by all and that have a shared semantic meaning.

Table 1. A sample of the operators defined by The Open Group

Event	Occurs when
entered(S)	State S is entered
exited(S)	State S is exited
true(C)	The value of condition C is set to true
false(C)	The value of condition C is set to false

I expect that CPs will be stored in a public repository that people can browse. The process of publishing a CP would assign it a unique identifier. After finding an appropriate CP in such a repository, the person could download it and subsequently adapt it or its implementation (depending on the programming language the agent is written in, etc.) so that his or her agent could use it. The more modular it is, the smaller it is, and the more it uses just the core statechart operators, then the simpler this adaptation process will be.

As for using this CP, when the agent is following a publicly-available CP, it would include the CP's name in any related message's context. This would have varying effects on the message recipient. First, if the recipient is not aware of that CP and does not want to change, then this information would simply be ignored. Because of the default standard effects in FLBC, an agent can usefully reply to many messages without being aware of the structure of the sending agent's CP. Second, the recipient may not have this CP implemented but may have noted that it has received many messages that use this CP. This could lead the agent designer to add this CP—or, more appropriately, a CP that could be used to interact with or respond to messages under that CP—to the agent's set of CPs. Third, if the recipient is aware of the CP, it may have already implemented a CP that it uses to interact with messages from that CP. If so, the receiving agent could simply invoke the appropriate CP, knowing that this is the most efficient and effective way both to handle the incoming message and to respond to the reason or goal underlying that message.

The statechart in Fig. 2 describes a process in which an agent confirms that another agent is a broker, tells the broker that it sells a product, and then descri-bes that product. This process could be represented by different statecharts—for example, the statecharts in Fig. 3. This pair of statecharts is equivalent to Fig. 2 except that two separate statecharts are composed to accomplish what, pre-viously, one statechart accomplished. In the top statechart in Fig. 3, when the system generates the send inform that selling event, the inform broker about product we sell state is entered. The bottom statechart in this figure has this same name and is invoked with this same event. Benefits of the representation in Fig. 3 are that 1) the function of the advertise with broker statechart is more apparent because of the new, descriptive state, and 2) the inform broker about product we sell statechart can be used separately from the advertise with broker statechart. As Greaves, Holmback, & Bradshaw also point out in this issue, this modularization should be applicable to a wide variety of procedures.

An alternate representation of the bottom statechart in Fig. 3 is the state-chart shown in Fig. 4. Though it is close, it is *not* equivalent to the original re-presentation. The system no longer waits for the receipt of the acknowledgment message before transitioning to the broker sent description state. It also eliminated the need for the broker has description state by dropping the last receive ack trigger.

This raises one of the general difficulties with specifying conversation policies that are not shared by all conversants: each conversation partner may handle the same message in different ways. In this instance, the bottom CP in Fig. 3 assumes that the partner returns an acknowledgment. If the partner does not return this message, then the conversation never progresses without some sort of external intervention (e.g., sending an email to the partner and asking him or her to send an acknowledgment—clearly not the solution we're looking for). The alternate representation shown in Fig. 4 removes the requirement that the

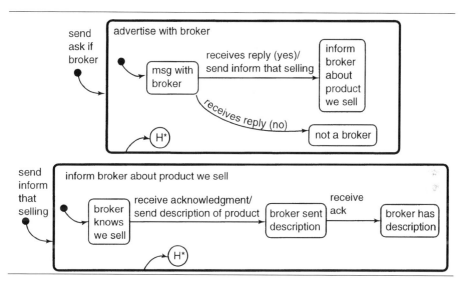

Fig. 3. A sample statechart representation of a conversation policy using composition (this is equivalent to Fig. 2)

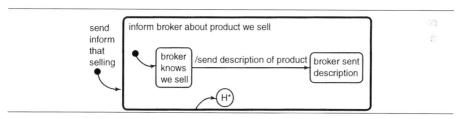

Fig. 4. A statechart representation of a conversation policy that leaves a few messages out compared with the bottom statechart in Fig. 3

partner send acknowledgment messages but also no longer specifies how these messages would fit into the conversation were they actually sent. This is where the proposed method really shines. The following shows how this would work.

To this point I have ignored the process of how a statechart used to describe a CP becomes a statechart used both to define a set of executable activities and to monitor and control their execution. I describe that process here. Suppose both that the agent has just sent a message to another agent asking if that agent is a broker for a certain kind of product (i.e., send inform that selling) and that our agent uses the CP depicted in Fig. 4. When the system determines that it is going to use this statechart, it puts it inside a state that has a unique (random and meaningless) conversation identifier. The original statechart (in Fig. 4) is a normative specification for how the conversation should proceed. This new outer state (in Fig. 5) is used to individuate this conversation among the set of all other conversations (not shown) this agent is currently (or has been) involved in. This allows the agent to carry on simultaneously multiple conversations that use the same CP.

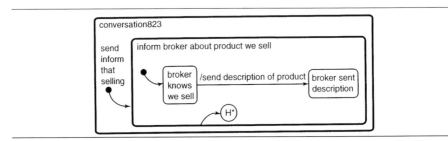

Fig. 5. A statechart representation of a current conversation

Now, suppose that the broker agent informs our agent (via an inform message) that it received our message that we sent informing it that we sell a product (i.e., send inform that selling). The message our agent receives contains a term that indicates the message is a reply to the original inform message our agent sent. This term tells our system that the reply should be part of this conversation (conversation823 in Fig. 5); thus, the CP should specify how the system should respond to it. Given all this, the figure clearly *does not* specify how to handle this message since there is no trigger receive inform in the figure. However, there is more to the system than has been described and there actually *is* a defined procedure for responding to this message. It simply is not shown. To that we now turn. Recall that the agent has a database of CPs. For FLBC the database contains a CP for the standard effects of each message type; these CPs are invoked only when other, more specific CPs do not apply. Thus, for every incoming message, a procedure can unambiguously choose one appropriate statechart.

Suppose our agent has just received this message—informing it that the broker agent received the original message—that the CP does not specify how to handle. Further, suppose that our agent has the statechart depicted in Fig. 4 in its database of normative CPs. The system follows a procedure such as the following:

1. It looks for an appropriate CP. In this case it chooses standard effects for inform. See the bottom portion of the statechart in Fig. 6.
2. The system draws a transition from the state immediately following the transition containing the message that the incoming message says it is a reply to. In this case, the message is a reply to the send inform that selling message on the left of the inform broker about product we sell state. The state immediately following this one is the broker knows we sell state. The transition is drawn from this state to the statechart representing the CP identified in the previous step (standard effects for inform). This transition should be labeled with a description of the reply. This label is descriptive—so as to show what caused the system to take this transition—and restrictive—so as to keep the

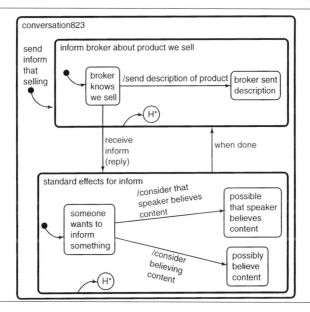

Fig. 6. A statechart representation of a conversation policy with an unplanned-for subdialog

system from taking it again after the system returns to the inform broker about product we sell state (described below). In Fig. 6 this is represented by the transition labeled receive inform (reply).

3. The system now draws a transition from the CP chosen in the first step. The transition is drawn from this state back to the original CP. This transition is labeled when done to indicate that this transition should be taken when the standard effects for inform state is completed. Not shown is that each statechart contains a definition of the conditions that must hold for it to be completed.

The new statechart is now joined to the old statechart within the context of this conversation. This dynamic joining is similar to what Nodine & Unruh accomplish (elsewhere in this volume) when they extend conversations. In terms of the statechart, this means that the system has finished joining the original statechart to the statechart for the standard effects; this is all shown in Fig. 6. Now that they are joined, the system can execute the appropriate steps: The send inform that selling message was sent (before these two statecharts were joined) and conversation823 was begun. The inform broker about product we sell state was entered. The default state broker knows we sell was entered. Because it was entered, the transition to its immediate right is taken and the event send description of product is generated. This takes it to the broker sent description state. At some later time (or even concurrently with the last transition) the system receives the reply to the first message, joins the statecharts as described above, and enters the standard effects for inform state. The default state is entered which immediately causes the system to take both transitions and generate their associated events. The system then determines that the statechart standard effects for inform is done and takes the when done transition back to the original statechart.

This is where the H* (history) node is useful. This signals that the statechart should restart in the node it last finished. In this case, since the transition was immediately taken into the last state, this statechart has already been completed so the system does not re-enter it. If the transition had not been taken because a trigger had not been fired or because a condition had not been met, then the system would go back into the broker knows we sell state.

Figure 6 is possibly incomplete in two ways. First, later messages might add further subconversations. At some later time the broker might send something back in response to the send description of product message. Second, the CP does not plan for all contingencies. For example, if the agent had been informed that the broker does not sell the product, then a message (the send description of product message) would be erroneously sent. This might happen if the broker receiving our inquiries employed the CP depicted in Fig. 7. The inform broker about product we sell CP, as it is currently constructed, essentially assumes that the broker is not going to say anything that would convince the agent to not send the product description. If this were a common occurrence and if the sending of the product description were expensive, the CP inform broker about product we sell should certainly be refined.

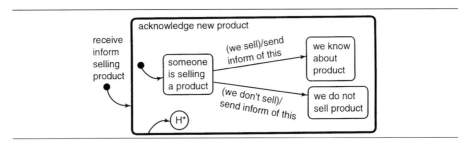

Fig. 7. A statechart that describes the process of acknowledging a new product

The above discussion has mostly applied to the actions, messages, decisions, and conversation policies for one participant in a conversation. Using FLBC as a communication language, this agent cannot know what the other does with this message. The sending agent can only know that the receiving agent knows what the sender wants the hearer to consider believing as a result of the message. Consider the message send inform that selling that the agent sends to the broker. The broker agent—not our agent, but the broker agent—may have a CP defined like the one shown in Fig. 7 or it may simply use the standard effects for inform. The sending agent simply does not know which one the broker uses. This incomplete knowledge is highly applicable to many circumstances since agents need not be cooperative, friendly, or trustworthy. It is unreasonable to expect that these types of agents should be required to share specifications of the effects of messages or that they would even have to believe this information were they told it. However, even under these circumstances it should be possible for one agent to effectively communicate with another. Further, even if a CP is not defined, the FLBC standard effects provide a "fail soft" mechanism. If a CP is not defined, then the system would be able to do something useful with the message and not always require manual intervention.

Some situations call for less uncertainty. In these situations communication partners can get together and define multi-agent CPs. Figure 8 contains an example of such a policy. The dotted line is the statechart feature that expresses concurrency and, for CPs, also separates the actions taken by separate conversation partners. The idea behind these multi-agent CPs is that each participant is committing to making public the messages it *generally* sends in a conversation and the rules it employs in choosing among alternatives. The exposure of these messages and rules are expected to result in CPs that have fewer unexpected subdialogs (as shown in Fig. 6). This would certainly be more effort than defining a single-agent CP and would, therefore, only be attempted with conversation partners with whom many messages are exchanged and who have special needs.

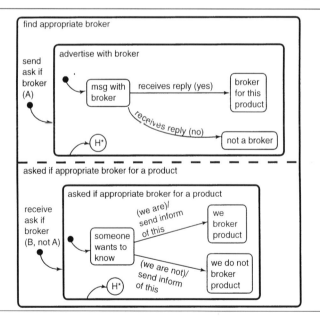

Fig. 8. A statechart that describes the activities of both parties in a conversation

Defining a multi-agent conversation policy does not bind the partners to never sending a message that does not conform to the CP. In fact, it opens up new ways in which the partners can deviate from the CP—for example, with subordinations, corrections, and interruptions. Consider the following situation in which two agents, A and B, use the CP shown in Fig. 8. Agent A uses the top of the CP while Agent B uses the bottom.

1. Agent A has started the CP by sending a message asking Agent B if it is a broker for disk drives (top half of the figure). It asserts that this message is part of a new conversation identified by conv874.
2. Agent B receives this message (bottom half of the figure) and tries to determine an answer to the question. Now, Agent B is only a broker for disk drives of a certain price range. In order to answer Agent A's question, Agent B sends a question back to A starting a subordinate conversation (identified by conv921) to determine the price of the disk.
3. Agent A receives this message that is a question and which states that it is related to conversation conv874 in that it is starting a conversation subordinate to it. Agent A composes a response that states the price of the disk drive, adds the information that it is a reply to another message and is part of conversation conv921, and sends it back to Agent B.
4. Agent B receives this message and determines that it has completed the subordinate conversation. It returns to executing the original conversation. In this CP it is in state someone wants to know. It attempts to make a transition out of it. Agent B's knowledge base now contains the information necessary to determine that it does sell the product so it takes the top transition and generates the event send inform of this.
5. And so on. . .

The question Agent B sent in step 2 is not part of the CP but was sent as part of the process of answering Agent A's question. The way the CP is defined suggests that Agent A's question is not a common one. If it were, then these two agents should probably get together and refine this CP.

4   Conclusion

In this paper I have described at a moderate level of detail the needed capabilities of an agent communication system that implements conversation policies. In developing this approach I guarded against several pitfalls that would limit its applicability. First, conversation partners do not have to specify down to the last detail every possible outcome that might result from sending a message. This is unreasonable and would discourage people from undertaking the application of the technology. Second, these CPs are not inflexible. They should allow different agents to implement features in different ways and should allow deviations (in specified ways that are not overly restrictive) from defined CPs. Third, agents have only minimal requirements placed on their architecture in order to use these CPs. Fourth, and finally, these CPs are effective under various levels of cooperation. Agents are able to apply a CP without another agent's cooperation but, if that other agent chooses to cooperate in the use of a multi-agent CP, agents gain benefits from cooperation.

I envision agents that use this system of managing conversations as a system that will evolve. The core of the system for agents that use the FLBC is the set of CPs for the standard effects associated with each message type. These CPs are the only context-free portion of the system and are, thus, the most widely applicable. This core is shared by every agent. What will happen next as the agents are used more is that the developers for each agent will develop CPs for those messages that the agent receives frequently. If it is a generally useful CP, then the developer would post it to a public repository so that others could use it. Other CPs will develop that are domain specific and still others will develop that are conversation partner specific. Each of these will have their place in the agent's repertoire of conversation management tools. Further, not only will the population of CPs grow but CPs themselves will evolve. Nuances and special cases will be added to the CPs that weren't foreseen when the CP was originally defined. Thus, when initially deployed, an agent will have a small set of simple CPs. Over time the agent will gain more CPs, and those CPs will be more complicated and more specialized for specific tasks. If all goes well, they will still be composed of reusable modules that can be shared among different agents and different agent developers.

There is much that needs to be tested and refined concerning this system. The XML DTD for statecharts must be defined. The set of core operators on statecharts must be defined. A set of scenarios must be defined that would test the capabilities of and demonstrate the effectiveness of this approach—and then a system must be built to actually operate within those scenarios. The usefulness of a single-agent CP and default standard effect CPs (both single- and multi-agent) must be demonstrated. A system for publishing and naming CPs must be developed. Further, this system must allow CPs to evolve but at the same time must synchronize the version of a CP among conversation partners. The usefulness of allowing communication among agents of differing capabilities must be carefully examined to determine how those differences effect what is said and how it is interpreted.

Even given all these needs, the promise of this system is encouraging, pointing to a future in which cooperation and knowledge-sharing might be more easily realized.

References

[1] Robin Cover. Extensible markup language (XML). Accessed at http://www.sil-.org/sgml/xml.html, June 22, 1998.
[2] DARPA Knowledge Sharing Initiative External Interfaces Working Group. Specification of the KQML Agent-Communication Language. http://www.cs.umbc-.edu/kqml/kqmlspec.ps, June 15, 1993. Downloaded on July 14, 1997.
[3] Foundation for Intelligent Physical Agents. FIPA 97 specification part 2: Agent communication language, November 28, 1997. Geneva, Switzerland.
[4] David Harel. Statecharts: A visual formalism for complex systems. *Science of Computer Programming*, 8:231–274, 1987.

[5] Yannis Labrou. *Semantics for an Agent Communication Language*. PhD thesis, University of Maryland, Computer Science and Electrical Engineering Department, August 1996. UMI #9700710.

[6] Yannis Labrou and Tim Finin. A proposal for a new KQML specification. Downloaded from `http://www.cs.umbc.edu/kqml/` in January 1998 (Technical Report CS-97-03), February 3, 1997.

[7] Yannis Labrou, Tim Finin, and Yun Peng. The interoperability problem: Bringing together mobile agents and agent communication languages. In Jr. Ralph Sprague, editor, *Proceedings of the 32nd Hawaii International Conference on System Sciences*, Maui, Hawaii, January 5–8, 1999. IEEE Computer Society.

[8] Richard Light. *Presenting XML*. SAMS.net Publishing, 1st edition, 1997.

[9] Diane J. Litman and James F. Allen. A plan recognition model for subdialogues in conversations. *Cognitive Science*, 11:163–200, 1987.

[10] Scott A. Moore. *Saying and Doing: Uses of Formal Languages in the Conduct of Business*. PhD thesis, University of Pennsylvania, Philadelphia, PA, December 1993.

[11] Scott A. Moore. Categorizing automated messages. *Decision Support Systems*, 22(3):213–241, March 1998.

[12] Scott A. Moore. A foundation for flexible automated electronic commerce. Working paper at the University of Michigan Business School, July 1998.

[13] Livia Polanyi. A formal model of the structure of discourse. *Journal of Pragmatics*, 12:601–638, 1988.

[14] The Open Group. Statechart specification language semantics. `http://www-.opengroup.org/onlinepubs/9629399/chap8.htm`, downloaded February 5, 1999. Chapter 8 of *CDE 1.1: Remote Procedure Call*, 1997.

Communication Protocols in Multi-agent Systems:
A Development Method and Reference Architecture

Jeremy Pitt and Abe Mamdani

Intelligent & Interactive Systems Group, Department of Electrical & Electronic
Engineering
Imperial College of Science, Technology & Medicine, Exhibition Road, London, SW7
2BZ, UK
Email: {j.pitt, e.mamdani}@ic.ac.uk
URL: http://www-ics.ee.ic.ac.uk/

Abstract. The meaning of a communicative act in a multi-agent system
can be characterised at a number of different levels. We argue that only
one level of meaning is common across all applications: what we call the
action-level semantics given by protocols or conversation policies. We define a general semantic framework for specifying the semantics of a class
of Agent Communication Languages (ACLs) based on protocols. We then
introduce sACL, a small ACL, and show how the action-level semantics
of this language can be integrated with an intentional semantics. This
enables us to specify the meaning of an individual communicative act in
the context of the conversation in which it occurs, and to customise sACL
for different application domains. We describe a development method for
defining an ACL for a particular application, and give a reference architecture for the method using the Beliefs-Desires-Intentions (BDI) agent
architecture.

1 Introduction

The meaning of a communicative act in a multi-agent system can be characterised at a number of different levels. In the FIPA'97 specification [FIP97], for
example, of a proposed standard Agent Communication Language (ACL), each
performative is given a meaning in two ways. Firstly, the semantics is given informally via an English description of the intuitive meaning. Secondly, a formal
semantics is defined in a first order modal logic of mental attitudes and actions,
i.e. an intentional semantics with various axioms. However, we find that:

- it is not clear how the semantics and axioms should be used: whether they
  are guidelines for the developers or requirements that the agents themselves
  are responsible for satisfying;

F. Dignum and M. Greaves (Eds.): Agent Communication, LNAI 1916, pp. 160–177, 2000.
© Springer Verlag Berlin Heidelberg 2000

- the information states of both sender and receiver are being updated, and, according to context, more axioms are needed to fully characterise the changes in state;
- the performatives and protocols are not exhaustive, and different applications may require variations on the agent behaviour and the performative semantics.

We argue that only one level of meaning is common across all applications: what we call the action-level semantics given by protocols or conversation policies (cf. [BDBW97,SCB+98,Sin98]) It has been our experience that protocols are a very useful tool in the development of Multi-Agent Systems. The advantages are that: the protocol specification is considerably less complex than the intentional description; interoperability of separately developed components via a protocol-based semantics is improved; reuse of recurrent interchanges is enabled; and verification of compliance with the standard is made easier. We therefore propose that an alternative approach to formulating the semantics of an ACL is to concentrate on the protocols and the performatives.

In this paper, we define a general semantic framework for specifying the semantics of a class of ACLs. based on protocols. We then introduce sACL, a small ACL, and show how the action-level semantics of this language can be integrated with an intentional semantics. This enables us to specify the meaning of individual communicative acts in the context of the conversation in which it occurs, and to customise sACL for different application domains. Furthermore, these descriptions can also be used as reference implementation models, which can be linked to a reference architecture (in our case, the Beliefs-Desires-Intentions (BDI) architecture). This leads onto a general development methodology for defining an ACL for a particular application. We are then in a position to offer some insight on certain issues in agent conversation policies.

2   The General Semantic Framework

Consider the situation illustrated in Figure 1. It shows two agents, embedded in an environment which they can partially sense, and parts of what they can individually sense overlap. However, rather than communicating by changing the environment, they can communicate by using speech acts and the ACL protocols.

We would argue that there are three layers of semantics here:

i the content level semantics, which is concerned with interpreting and understanding the content of a message, and is internal to an agent;
ii the action level semantics, which is concerned with replying in appropriate ways to received messages, and is external to the agents;
iii the intentional semantics, which is concerned with making a communication in the first place, and with replying, and again is internal to the agent.

We would argue that the current FIPA ACL semantics for example, is level 3. This is internal to an agent, and so its usefulness in standardisation has

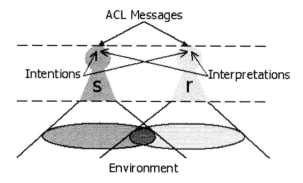

Fig. 1. Communicating Agents

been questioned [Woo98,Sin98]. The only part of the communication that is amenable to standardisation is the observable tip of the iceberg: namely the communication itself. Note that this properly includes ontologies, so that there may be a standard interpretation, but the actual interpretation of the content of the message is once again internal to the agent.

We are therefore inclined (as are many others, e.g. [LF98,SCB+98,Sin98]) to take a more protocol-oriented view of the ACL semantics. From this point of view, the communication between two (or more) agents can be viewed as a conversation. Individual speech acts therefore take place in the context of a conversation. We then specify the meaning of performatives by describing an input-output relationship. In our case, we define the meaning of a speech act (as input) to be the intention to perform another speech act (as output). The performative used in the output speech act will be determined and constrained by the context (i.e. the conversation state) in which the input speech act occurred, while the content of the output speech act will be determined by the context (the agent's information state) in which the input was received.

We therefore base this input-output relation on how the object-level content of a message induces a change in the information state of the receiver, and how the meta-level action descriptor of a message (the performative) induces a response from the receiver. Our proposal is that the semantics of performatives can be characterised in these terms, and that this is the semantics that should be specified for a standard agent communication language. This means specifying, for the content, what it 'means' for an agent (receiving a message) to add its interpretation of that content to its current information state, and for the speech act, the space of possible responses an agent may make, one of which it is obliged to make. We require that agents use agreed protocols to communicate, and that agents involved in a conversation are behaving according to a protocol (i.e. a conversation policy), and maintain the history of the ongoing dialogue (cf. [BDBW97]).

An agent s communicates with (and communicates information to) an agent r via a speech act. This is represented by:

$$< s, \mathsf{perf}(r, (C, L, O, p, i, t_{snd})) >$$

This is saying that s does (communicates with) performative perf with content C in language L using ontology O, in the context of a conversation identified by i which is following protocol p, at the time of sending t_{snd}. Define a function f which for any speech act sa returns the performative used in that speech act.

For the specification that follows in this section, let c and σ be sets of integers, and let Δ, *content_meanings*, and *speech_acts* be, respectively, possibly infinite sets of agent information states, the agent's interpretation of the content of a message, and speech acts.

Then an ACL is defined by a 3-tuple <Perf, Prot, *reply*> where Perf is a set of perfomative names, Prot is a set of protocol names, and *reply* is a partial function given by:

$$reply : \mathsf{Perf} \times \mathsf{Prot} \times \sigma \mapsto \wp(\mathsf{Perf})$$

Note we include a null performative null which is a 'do nothing' (no reply) performative (cf. *silence* as used in Smith *et al.* [SCB+98]), and require an empty protocol **no_protocol**: agents can communicate using one-shot speech acts irrespective of a particular protocol (see below).

Each element of Prot names a finite state diagram. Then *reply* is a (partial) function from performatives, protocols and protocol states to the power set of performatives. This states for each perfomative, 'uttered' in the context of a conversation following a specific protocol, what performatives are acceptable replies. The *reply* function can be constructed from inspection of the protocol state diagrams, and vice versa, although more formal characterizations are possible (e.g. [KIO95]).

This 3-tuple is standard for all agents using the ACL. To fully characterise the semantics, we need three further functions which are relative to an agent a, and specify what an agent does with a message, not how it does it:

$$add_a : \mathsf{Perf} \times \mathsf{Prot} \times content\_meanings \times \Delta \to \Delta$$
$$select_a : \wp(\mathsf{Perf}) \times \Delta \to speech\_acts$$
$$conv_a : c \mapsto \sigma$$

Here, add_a is agent a's own procedure for computing the change in its information state from the content of an incoming message using a particular performative 'uttered' in the context of a particular protocol. add_a then converts a's (a-type) information state into a new (a-type) information state. $select_a$ is agent a's own procedure for selecting a performative from a set of performatives (valid replies), and from its current information state generating a complete speech act for this performative which will be its (intended) reply. Finally, we require that agents keep track of the state of each conversation in which it is involved, and uniquely identify each conversation with some identifier, i.e. an agent may be involved in more than one conversation and uses the identifier to distinguish between them. $conv_a$ then maps a conversation identifier onto the current state of the protocol being used to conduct the conversation. (Note that FIPA ACL has message attributes (`reply-with`, `in-reply-to` and `conversation-id`) to serve such purposes, but they are not accommodated in the formal semantics.)

The meaning of a speech act is then given by:

$$[\![< s, \mathsf{perf}(r, (C, L, O, p, i, t_{snd})) >]\!] = \mathcal{I}_r < r, sa >$$

$$\text{such that } f(sa) \in reply(\mathsf{perf}, p, conv_r(i))$$

This defines the meaning of the speech act by sender s to be an intention of receiving agent r to perform some other speech act. The performative used in the speech act as the response is selected from $reply(\mathsf{perf}, p, conv_r(i))$, i.e. it is constrained to be one of the performatives allowed by the protocol. The speech act is generated from r's information state at the time of selection $\Delta_{r,t_{now}}$ and the state of the conversation i according to the protocol p, using r's $select_r$ function:

$$sa = select_r(reply(\mathsf{perf}, p, conv_r(i)), \Delta_{r,t_{now}})$$

where $\Delta_{r,t_{now}}$ is given by:

$$\Delta_{r,t_{now}} = add_r(\mathsf{perf}, p, L_r[\![C]\!]_{L,O}, \Delta_{r,t_{rcv}})$$

This states that r's information state after receiving the message is the result of adding, using r's own procedure add_r, r's own interpretation (content meaning) of the content C in language L using ontology O to its database at the time of receipt, $\Delta_{r,t_{rcv}}$.

3   sACL: A Small Agent Communication Language

This general semantic framework can now serve to give meaning to a class of ACLs. This is demonstrated in this section by the definition of sACL, a small Agent Communication Language. We begin with core-sACL, which comprises just three basic speech acts, declarative (statement), interrogative (question), and directive (command), and no protocols. We will use the undefined symbol $\perp$ to indicate that there is no conversation involved in one off communications, and so of course the $reply$ function returns no state.

Let core-sACL be the 3-tuple <Perf, Prot, $reply$> where:

$$\text{Perf} = \{inform, query, command\}$$
$$\text{Prot} = \{\textbf{no\_protocol}\}$$

$$reply(\mathsf{inform}, \textbf{no\_protocol}, \perp) = \{\mathsf{null}\}$$
$$reply(\mathsf{query}, \textbf{no\_protocol}, \perp) = \{\mathsf{inform}\}$$
$$reply(\mathsf{command}, \textbf{no\_protocol}, \perp) = \{\mathsf{inform}, \mathsf{null}\}$$

This defines the action level semantics of core-sACL, i.e. a semantics at level 2 in Figure 1 above. We next define an intentional semantics (a semantics at level 3). We do this using a BDI (Beliefs-Desires-Intentions) logic, where there are modal operators $\mathcal{B}$, $\mathcal{D}$ and $\mathcal{I}$ for respectively the beliefs, desires (goals) and intends modalities. The notation in the following includes: $\mathcal{K}_s$ denotes 'knowledge' and is defined by $\mathcal{K}_s p \leftrightarrow \mathcal{B}_s p \vee \mathcal{B}_s \neg p$; DONE is an operator on actions, which is true after action A has taken place; and $[a, A]$ is an agent-action modality, so that the formula $[a, A]p$ is read "after agent a does action A, then p holds". For any agent i, $\mathcal{I}_i < i, A >$ is logically equivalent to $\mathcal{I}_i < A >$ (i.e. the agent intends to do action A itself). For clarity of presentation, we have omitted the language, ontology and conversation identifier parameters. The protocol parameter is also omitted but it is **no_protocol** in all cases.

Table 1 shows, in rows 1-3, a possible axiomatic combination of beliefs and desires that trigger the intention to perform each of the three specified speech acts, for a given sending agent s and an intended receiving agent r. Rows 4-6 are then a logical specification of the add_r and $select_r$ functions for the receiving agent r. These specifications determine which performative to use in a reply in order to comply with the semantic definition, the extra information that is required to parameterise the performative to turn it into a speech act, and how the information state of the receiving agent changes after the speech act.

Note, however, that this is a 'non-binding' specification only, and other agents may respond differently provided they comply with the action level semantic definition. This is why we describe the 3-tuple as specifying *the* action level semantics, as all agents 'talking' core-sACL should comply with this specification. The specification in Table 1 is *an* intentional semantics as different agents may act and re-act in different ways (i.e. it will depend on how each one has its *add* and *select* functions implemented).

Communication rarely takes place in isolation. It is more likely to occur in the context of a conversation and/or a social situation. Therefore we extend core-sACL to sACL by adding in protocols and new performatives. Let sACL be the 3-tuple $<$ Perf, Prot, *reply* $>$ given by specifying:

Perf = {inform, query, command, acknowledge, end, request, agree, cancel, fail, null}

Prot = {*yesno_query*, *confirmation*, *commitment*, *datasync*, **no_protocol**}

The finite state diagrams for the four protocols are illustrated in Figure 2. The corresponding extension to the *reply* function can be constructed from the finite state diagrams.

Table 1: Speech Acts and Intended Actions for One-shot Communications

	Comment	
1	$\models \mathcal{B}_s p \wedge \mathcal{D}_s \mathcal{B}_r p \to \mathcal{I}_s < \mathsf{inform}(r, p) >$	s believes p and wants (desires) r to believe p, then s intends to inform r of p
2	$\models \mathcal{D}_s \mathcal{K}_s p \wedge \mathcal{B}_s \mathcal{K}_r p \to \mathcal{I}_s < \mathsf{query}(r, p) >$	s wants to know p and believes r knows p, so s intends to query r about p
3	$\models \mathcal{D}_s \mathrm{DONE}(A) \wedge \mathcal{B}_s \, capable(r, A) \to \mathcal{I}_s < \mathsf{command}(r, A) >$	s wants action A done and believes r is capable of A, then s intends to command r to do A
4	$\models [s, \mathsf{inform}(r, p)]\mathcal{B}_r p$	after s informs r that p, r believes p
5	$\models [s, \mathsf{query}(r, p)](\mathcal{B}_r p \to \mathcal{I}_r < \mathsf{inform}(s, \mathbf{true}) >) \vee (\mathcal{B}_r \neg p \to \mathcal{I}_r < \mathsf{inform}(s, \mathbf{false}) >)$	after s queries r about p, then either r believes p and intends to inform s that it is true, or r does not believe p and intends to inform s that it is false
6	$\models [s, \mathsf{command}(r, A)]\mathcal{I}_r < A > \wedge [r, A](\mathrm{DONE}(A) \to \mathcal{I}_r < \mathsf{inform}(s, \mathrm{DONE}(A)) >)$	after s commands r to do A, then r should intend to do A, and after doing A, if $\mathrm{DONE}(A)$ is true, r should intend to inform s that $\mathrm{DONE}(A)$ is true. (We are assuming that action A is always completed successfully.)

The notation used in Figure 2 is as follows. States are numbered, and arcs are labelled with the speech act that causes the transition between states. The state with the heavy border (state 0) is the start state. States labelled with a tick or cross are end states, with the conversation terminating successfully or not respectively. The different shading on each state indicates which agent's turn it is to continue the dialogue, so here we are specifying turn-taking conversations between only two agents. The notation needs to be extended to accommodate conversations involving multiple participants and/or sequences from one agent. There are other extensions that could also be envisaged: for example, making 'terminate' and 'interrupt' available from any state. These would be a sort of

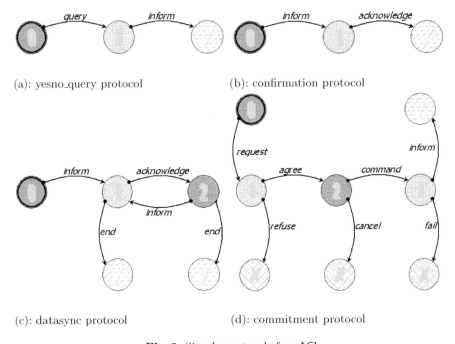

(a): yesno_query protocol   (b): confirmation protocol

(c): datasync protocol   (d): commitment protocol

Fig. 2. Simple protocols for sACL

meta-performative which respectively end or change the state of the conversation.

These protocols can be used by one agent to communicate with another in order to:

- query another agent about the value of some proposition (note this is protocol instance of the expected behaviour for one shot query speech acts);
- inform an agent of some proposition and receive an acknowledgement (of belief and/or receipt);
- synchronize data with another agent about the value of some proposition;
- ask an agent if it will undertake some action, and, if it is agreeable, to tell (command) it to do that action. The final communication will be the result of doing the action (if it succeeds or fails).

It is now straightforward to construct the actual *reply* function from the finite state diagrams. Furthermore, each protocol can be supplemented by an additional specification (which may be intentional) of a version of the *add* and *select* functions which have been implemented by an agent in order to comply with this action level semantics. However, agents are not constrained to implement this specification. Each agent may have its own way of doing things and can do that, provided that its behaviour (in terms of responses to received messages) complies with the action level semantics.

4   A Reference Agent Architecture

In this section, we discuss an operational model of the BDI agent architecture as suggested in [KGB+95], enhanced to accommodate BDI-reasoning about agent–agent communication protocols based on the semantics described in the previous section.

4.1   The BDI Architecture

Kinny *et al.*'s [KGB+95] BDI-agent architecture consists of the modules illustrated in Figure 3. Here, the belief database contains facts about 'the world'; the desires module contains goals to be realized; the plan library consists of plans, which are sequences of actions which achieve goals; and the intention structures contains instances of those plans chosen for execution (and currently being executed). The interpreter executes intentions, updates beliefs, modifies goals, and chooses plans.

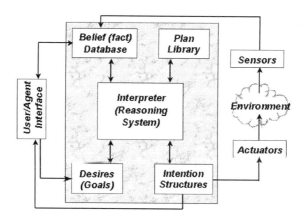

Fig. 3. BDI Agent Architecture

The interpreter execution cycle is as follows: At time t: certain goals are established, and certain beliefs are held. Event(s) occur that alter the beliefs or modify goals, and the new combination of goals and beliefs trigger action plans. One or more action plans are selected and placed on the intention structures. An executable plan is selected and one step is executed, whereby the agent performs the action. Performing the action changes the environment and may establish new goals and beliefs, and so the interpreter execution cycle starts again.

The way we envisaged this architecture working in conjunction with the protocol-based semantics of sACL discussed in the previous two sections is based on the following ideas:

- that the protocols are plans, and the appropriate representation is stored in the Plan Library;
- that a conversation is an instance of a plan, and all the conversations the agent is currently engaged in are stored in the Intention Structures;
- that beliefs and desires are used to trigger plans, i.e. to initiate a conversation by starting an instance of the appropriate protocol;
- that the *select* and *add* functions are used to determine how to progress a conversation according to the plan (i.e. within the remit of the *reply* function).

4.2   The Semantics in Operation

Ignoring for now issues like language, time, ontology and protocol, an agent designer could specify an agent a's behaviour for reacting to an inform message with content ϕ from an agent s using the *datasync* protocol to be:

$$add_a(\text{inform}, datasync, \phi, \Delta_a) = \Delta'_a, \text{where}$$

$$\phi \in \Delta_a \to \Delta'_a = \Delta_a$$
$$\phi \notin \Delta_a \to \Delta'_a = \Delta_a \cup \{\phi, \mathcal{D}_a\mathcal{B}_s\mathcal{B}_a\phi\}, \text{if } \Delta_a \cup \{\phi\} \text{ is consistent}$$
$$\to \Delta'_a = \Delta_a \cup \{\phi^c, \mathcal{D}_a\mathcal{B}_s\phi^c\}, \text{if } \Delta_a \cup \{\phi\} \text{ is inconsistent}$$
$$\phi^c \in \Delta_a \to \Delta'_a = \Delta_a - \{\phi^c\} \cup \{\phi, \mathcal{D}_a\mathcal{B}_s\mathcal{B}_a\phi\}, \text{if } belief\_revise_a(\Delta_a, \phi, \phi^c) = \phi$$
$$\to \Delta'_a = \Delta_a \cup \{\mathcal{D}_a\mathcal{B}_s\phi^c\}, \text{otherwise}$$

This is only an exemplary specification in a semi-formal notation. Note the formula ϕ^c denotes the complement of formula ϕ. It treats each of the three cases: when the content of the inform is already known, new, or contradictory. The function $belief\_revise_a$ is a gloss on a's belief revision for contradictory statements (cf. [Gal92]), and we are not saying how the agent ensures its database is consistent (but there are algorithms for doing this, e.g. forward chaining).

This intentional reading of informing agent a of some information can be paraphrased informally as follows, noting that the new combination of beleiefs and desires will be influntial in determining a reply that will be consistent with the ACL semantics:

> *If you tell me something I already know, then I'll stay as I am;*
> *If you tell me something I don't know, then*
> * if it is consistent with my database Δ, I'll add it to Δ and want you to believe I believe it*
> * else if it is inconsistent with Δ, I'll want you to believe I believe the opposite;*
> *If you tell me something that I disagree with, then*
> * if I prefer your version, I'll revise Δ and acknowledge it*
> * else if I prefer my version, I'll keep Δ as it is and inform you otherwise*

This is of course just one formulation: the treatment of new and contradictory information may not be treated in the same way, for example. It is also easy to refine such a specification to incorporate elements of trust. Furthermore, since the sincerity condition is predicated on the notion of co-operation; and all speech acts involve the receiver recognizing an intention on the part of the sender, agents are free (but not forced) to make further inferences about the other agent's beliefs and intentions. Different inferences may be more appropriate for particular types of agents in different kinds of application.

However, we can now appreciate the potential utility of intentionality for individual agents. Suppose we encoded, for agent s, the following axioms in its Plan Library:

$$\mathcal{B}_s\phi \wedge \mathcal{D}_s\mathcal{B}_A\phi \to \mathcal{I}_s < s, \mathsf{inform}(A, p, datasync) >)$$

$$[A, \mathsf{inform}(s, \phi, datasync)]\mathcal{B}_s\phi \wedge \mathcal{D}_s\mathcal{B}_A\mathcal{B}_s\phi \to \mathcal{I}_s < s,$$
$$\mathsf{acknowledge}(A, \phi, datasync) >$$

$$[A, \mathsf{inform}(s, \phi, datasync)]\mathcal{B}_s\phi^c \wedge \mathcal{D}_s\mathcal{B}_A\phi^c \to \mathcal{I}_s < s, \mathsf{inform}(A, \phi^c, datasync) >$$

Note that these are plan axiom schema, and can be instantiated for any agent R and proposition ϕ. Furthermore, suppose agent r has identical axioms in its plan library, except substituting r for s. Then these axioms state, respectively that: firstly, if s wants (desires) that both itself and some other agent r believe to believe some proposition p, and believes that after successfully "doing" the *datasync* protocol it will achieve this goal, then it will form the intention to do the first action which will initiate that protocol (plan). Secondly, that after some agent informs it of a proposition ϕ using the dataysnc protocol, if it believes it and wants the sender to believe it, then it will form the intention to acknowledge it. Otherwise, if it believes the opposite, it will form the intention to inform the sender of that.

For the sending agent s, there are facts, such as p, q, etc. (implictly $\mathcal{B}_s p, \mathcal{B}_s q$, etc.) and more modal action schema. These states the beliefs that an agent will hold after performing or witnessing an action. For example, for agent s, we might have:

Belief Database: $\mathcal{B}_s$

p	fact p
$[A, \mathsf{acknowledge}(s, \phi, \_)]\mathcal{B}_A\phi$	after A acknowledges ϕ, A believes ϕ
$[s, \mathsf{acknowledge}(A, \phi, \_)]\mathcal{B}_A\mathcal{B}_s\phi$	after s acknowledges ϕ, A believes that s believes ϕ

The post-condition of these modal action schemas specify the intended rational effects of the action which the agent *believes* will result after doing the action. (Note that these are still *beliefs* of s. They may not be the *actual* results, in which case the agent will have to do belief revision.) The formulas here concern the acknowledge performative, irrespective of the protocol it is used in. The first case is for when agent s is the receiver of the message, the second case for when it is the performer of the speech act.

In the desires database of s, there are goals, for example:

Goals: $\mathcal{D}_s$

$\mathcal{B}_r p \wedge \mathcal{B}_r\mathcal{B}_s p$	the goal of s is for r to believe p and that s believes p

The combination of beliefs and desires is now used to trigger a plan, or protocol. In this case, it is the intention to execute the *datasync* protocol, in effect a joint plan with r. This is achieved by sending the first message which initiates the protocol, in this case an inform. Thus, in this case, for s we get:

Belief Database: $\mathcal{B}_s$	Desires (Goals): $\mathcal{D}_s$	Intentions: $\mathcal{I}_s$
p	$\mathcal{B}_r p$	$< \mathsf{inform}(r, p, datasync) >$
$[A, \mathsf{acknowledge}(s, \phi, \_)]\mathcal{B}_A\phi$		
$[s, \mathsf{acknowledge}(R, \phi, \_)]\mathcal{B}_A\mathcal{B}_s\phi$		

The database of agent r, the intended recipient of the speech act, might be entirely empty, except that it will have its versions of the axiom schema in its belief database and plan library, viz:

Beliefs: $\mathcal{B}_r$
$[A, \mathsf{acknowledge}(r, \phi, \_)]\mathcal{B}_A\phi$
$[r, \mathsf{acknowledge}(A, \phi, \_)]\mathcal{B}_A\mathcal{B}_r\phi$
Plan Library:
$\mathcal{B}_r\phi \wedge \mathcal{D}_r\mathcal{B}_A\phi \rightarrow \mathcal{I}_r < s, \mathsf{inform}(A, \phi, datasync) >)$
$[A, \mathsf{inform}(r, \phi, datasync)]\mathcal{B}_r\phi \wedge \mathcal{D}_r\mathcal{B}_A\mathcal{B}_r\phi \rightarrow \mathcal{I}_r < r,$
$\mathsf{acknowledge}(A, \phi, datasync) >$
$[A, \mathsf{inform}(r, \phi, datasync)]\mathcal{B}_r\phi^c \wedge \mathcal{D}_r\mathcal{B}_A\phi^c \rightarrow \mathcal{I}_r < r, \mathsf{inform}(A, \phi^c, datasync) >$

After it receives the incoming message, r runs its add_r procedure on the content. If implemented as above, the new belief $\mathcal{B}_r p$ and goal $\mathcal{D}_r\mathcal{B}_s\mathcal{B}_r p$ are added (p is not present in the belief database and adding it is consistent). Then the axiom schema in the plan library which is triggered after receiving the event is the second one, triggering the intention to acknowledge the inform. Thus the following beliefs, desires and intentions are added:

Beliefs: $\mathcal{B}_r$	Desires: $\mathcal{D}_r$	Intentions: $\mathcal{I}_r$
p	$\mathcal{B}_s\mathcal{B}_r p$	$< r, \mathsf{acknowledge}(A, \phi, datasync) >$

Now we see that the meaning of a speech act (at the action level) is indeed an intention to reply with a valid performative in the context of the protocol. Furthermore, after r executes the intention, by sending the message, the axiom schema in its belief database $[r, acknowledge(A, \phi, \_)]$ is instantiated (with $A = s$ and $\phi = p$), with the conclusion $\mathcal{B}_s\mathcal{B}_r p$. This achieves the goal which is duly discharged.

When s receives this message, the other axiom schema ($[A, acknowledge$ $(s, \phi, \_)]$) concerning acknowledge in its belief database is instantiated in turn, with the conclusion $\mathcal{B}_r p$. This achieves s's original goal, which is in turn discharged.

4.3   A Reference Implementation

If any instance of an axiom schema in the Plan Library becomes true, then this combination of beliefs and desires will trigger a protocol as an action plan. An instance of this protocol will be instantiated with the conversation respondent, a new unique conversation identifier (e.g. c_1471 in Figure 4 below), and possibly some maintenance goals (i.e. these are goals, which if they become untrue, will cause the interpreter to abandon the plan/conversation). This situation is illustrated in Figure 4. (Note that it is the integer part of the conversation identifier (e.g. 1471) which is used in the *conv* function, the $c\_$ part is for human readability only.)

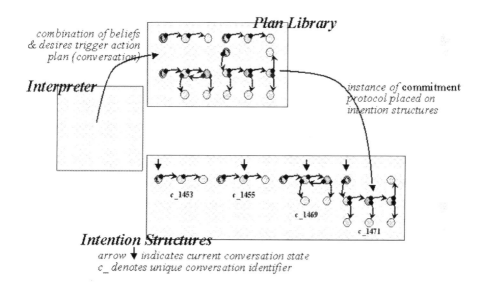

Fig. 4. BDI Architecture with Protocols as Plans

Figure 4 also illustrates the idea that other conversations are going on at the same time as the new conversation is initiated and enacted. Note that not all these conversations may have been initiated by agent s, in some cases, other agents will have started a conversation with s.

Each conversation is identified by a unique identifier, which is part of the ACL message syntax, and each message is similarly identified by a unique message identifier. These are standard parameters, for example, in the syntax of FIPA ACL [FIP97]. Here, though, it is used in the implementation of $conv_a$ to map a particular conversation identifier onto the protocol state in order to determine the set of valid replies for the $select_a$ function.

Now, in the next round of the interpreter execution cycle, the agent may choose to perform one of the communicative acts available to it. Note that in some ongoing conversations, it may be waiting to receive a message (i.e. a speech act) from another agent. When such a message is received, the conversation identified by conversation identifier is advanced to the next state according to the performative and the protocol. Any conversation state variables are updated and the content of the message acted upon. These actions can all be specified and implemented as part of its *add* function. Note, however, that each agent could chose to implement things differently.

When an agent has a choice of possible performatives from the new protocol state, its *select* function determines which of these performatives is actually used. Again the *select* function may be different for different agents. It is only necessary to comply with the protocol description. Whatever way two agents implement their *add* and *select* functions, then the specification of the protocol semantics should ensure that they can interoperate at the action level. Of course, there has also to be common agreement on syntax, ontology, etc., for interoperability at level 1, and this is another matter entirely.

5   Method and Tool Support

The definition of a particular ACL by a 3-tuple $<$ Perf, Prot, *reply* $>$ effectively defines a set of finite state diagrams with arcs labeled by performatives and states labeled by which agent's turn it is to 'speak' in the conversation. It is relatively straightforward to do this for, for example, the FIPA ACL, which has a relatively small set of primitive communicative acts and a small number of given protocols, most of which have fewer than 10 states. Some attention needs to be paid to protocols where there are more than two participants, the sequence of speech acts is not simple turn-taking, there are timing constraints which affect which actions that may be taken, and so on. It may also be that a protocol, if not infinite, may nevertheless have a 'very large' number of states. Therefore a further generalisation of the specification may be required, by defining rules for generating speech acts between two players (i.e. a game). A further generalisation would be possible if we identify the actual Searle speech act category [Sin98].

However, in general our approach allows us to define a class of ACLs, rooted on core-sACL. We envisage starting from a set of core performatives and protocols (i.e. performatives whose intended meaning is intuitively clear and protocols from some common functions). This would be the 'standard' ACL, the root of this class of ACLs, which could then be extended within the same semantic framework for particular applications. There are three directions in which core-sACL could be extended, as illustrated in Figure 5:

- *generalization.* New performatives and new protocols can be defined to create a new ACL where there were general interactions not covered by the standard. For example, auction protocols are a common requirement in some multi-agent systems, and new protocols could be added for the particular type of auction demanded by an application (Dutch, English, etc.);
- *specialization.* Additional constraints can be added to transitions, and/or richer description of states can be specified. For example, in the development of a FIPA'97-compliant multi-agent system for real-time load control [PP98], we required some interactions to be 'timed out'. Also, a state could be associated with a set of conversation variables that determine the conversation

state, and there could be a complex interaction of state changes according to certain transitions given a particular conversation state;

- *instantiation.* The specific decision-making functionality for deciding which reply from a set of allowed replies can also be specified. For example, the same protocol may be used in quite different application domains. The decision-making that characterises whether to reply with performative X or performative Y from the same state may then be dependent on very different functions. In principle, application designers can take an ACL "off the shelf", if it contains a protocol that serves the task required, and specify the application-specific functions which the system developers can then implement.

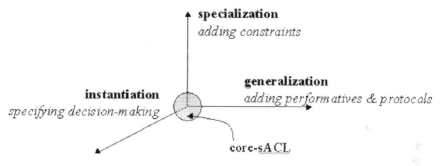

Fig. 5. Framework for Extending core-sACL

We are currently working on the development of tool support to assist in the ACL development process, and a middleware extension that we call *brown pages* that enable one agent to publish a 'non-standard' protocol and other agents to discover how to use this protocol (cf. [BDBW97]).

6   Comments and Conclusions

Our research programme in agent–agent communication is focused on:

- specifying a general semantic framework for characterising the semantics of a speech act as an action occurring in the context of a conversation, and therefore proscribing a valid set of action as replies. These stylised interactions can be formalised as protocols and, we believe, are generic across all applications, although not all applications will need all protocols;
- specifying the semantics of the content and intentional aspects of a speech act relative to an individual agent, according to social context, agent information state (including conversation state), and application requirements. These we believe are specific to individual applications;
- providing a library, method and tool to develop a class of reusable and/or extensible ACLs, containing commonly recurring performatives and protocols, which can be customised for particular applications and systems.

In this paper, we have defined a general semantic framework for specifying the semantics of a class of Agent Communication Languages (ACLs) based on protocols. We then introduced sACL, a small ACL, and showed how the action-level semantics of this language can be integrated with an intentional semantics, using the BDI architecture as a reference. This enabled us to specify the meaning of individual communicative acts in the context of the conversation in which it occurs. We can then customise sACL for different application domains, by generalising sACL with new performative and protocols, specialising the language with additional constraints and richer conversation states, and instantiating the ACL with the particular decision making required.

Conversation policies and protocols, in our framework, are concerned with meaning as actions and inducing (an intention) to reply, while the individual messages are concerned with inducing a change in information state of both sender and receiver. The latter can vary according to context (i.e. information state, conversation state, application domain, etc.), while the former are commonly recurring structures in many application domains. Like the original conversation policies of KAoS [BDBW97], this means we specify the form of a conversation but leave open the content. Note that this means we are specifying some extra semantics on the receiver's side: while we can- not stipulate the change in information state for the receiver of a message, we can stipulate that in the context of a protocol, it is appropriate to produce a certain type of reply.

This approach allows us to define the semantics of ACL performatives relative to their use in a protocol. We would expect the meaning of a conversation policy to be composed from the meaning of its component performatives. However, to make a conversation policy useful and re-usable there has to be a way of tailoring the semantics and pragmatics to the context of use and the type of agent using it. We argue that this what our framework and method begins to provide. The informal and formal (logical) descriptions in Table 1 can be interpreted as reference implementation models, but are informative specifications in the sense that they can be specialised in two ways. Firstly, that there can be other 'triggers' for initiating speech acts, and secondly, that there may be other implementations of reacting to speech acts which subsume the reference model.

For example, we have already seen an example of generalization in our framwork, in the extension of core-sACL in our framework. We illustrate our method further with two brief examples of specialization. Firstly, consider again the yesno query protocol. Basically, after the query performative, there is only one possible type of speech act allowed as a reply. Whatever the content of the reply it will still be labelled by an inform. Thus we have only one arc which covers both the cases, i.e. whether the replying agent (r say) believes p or : p. Normally, then, the BDI specification of the agent behaviour for sACL might mirror that of row 5 in Table 1, i.e.:

$$\models [s, \mathsf{query}(r, p, yesno\_query)]$$

$$(\mathcal{B}_r p \rightarrow \mathcal{I}_r < \mathsf{inform}(s, \mathbf{true}, yesno\_query) >) \vee$$

$$(\mathcal{B}\neg \rightarrow \mathcal{I}_r < \mathsf{inform}(s, \mathbf{false}, yesno\_query) >)$$

However, it might well be the case that in another type of application the recipient does not in fact know the answer, i.e. : $\neg\mathcal{B}_r(p \vee \neg p)$, and the closed world assumption does not apply. In this case we can specialise sACL by specifiying the behaviour to be:

$$\models [s, \mathsf{query}(r, p, yesno_q uery)]$$

$$(\mathcal{B}_r p \to \mathcal{I}_r < \mathsf{inform}(s, \mathbf{true}, yesno\_query) >)\vee$$

$$(\mathcal{B}_r \neg \to \mathcal{I}_r < \mathsf{inform}(s, \mathbf{false}, yesno\_query) >)\vee$$

$$\neg\mathcal{B}_r(p \vee \neg) \to \mathcal{I}_r < \mathsf{inform}(s, \bot, yesno\_query) >)$$

The open questions then are how an agent makes it clear that it is 'talking' this systematically specialised dialect of sACL, and how another agent can learn and use this new dialect.

For a second example, we revisit the contract-net protocol, which we used in both the EU GOAL and EU MARINER projects. In the EU GOAL project, we developed an agent-based system for distributed document review [PAC96]. In the MARINER project, we are developing an agent-based system for load control in Intelligent Networks [PP98]. The same basic pattern of interaction was common to both systems. However, in GOAL, the deadline for responses to the initial call-for-proposals was potentially days, in MARINER, potentially seconds. Thus this deadline is enormously domain-dependent. This is why we allow the possibility of specialising a protocol to suit the particular application requirements with application-dependent constraints.

Furthermore, the contract net as used in these two projects provides us with an illustration of instantiation in our framework. Each application required the agents to make a decision on whether to bid in response to the call for proposals. However, the specification of the logic behind the decision-making is very different, even if the 'stub' remains the same. While we would argue that our framework and method offer a very powerful approach to designing communication protocols and conversation policies for multi-agent systems, a number of open questions remain. Firstly, although this work bears a number of similarities to that of [SCB + 98], the property of compositionality enjoyed by the joint intention theory used in that work is lost here. Secondly, while the semantics provides the developer with a useful guide, some abstract analysis may also be required. Therefore, it might be necessary to show that a conversation policy is deterministic, correct, consistent and complete, which presupposes some fairly powerful tools. Thirdly, it is not certain that finite state diagrams with states labelled by numbers are sufficient, and we have begun to explore how to represent the conversation state by structured information that is altered by the transitions between states. Finally, the issue of multi-party conversations needs to be addressed. Thus, it is clear that we have taken only the first few steps at the start of a programme of research and development.

Acknowledgements. This research has been undertaken in the context of the UK EPSRC/Nortel Networksjoint funded project CASBAh (GR/L34440), and the EU-funded ACTS project MARINER (AC333), and we are grateful for all this support. We also appreciate the many constructive comments of the three anonymous reviewers, and the help and support of the editors, Mark Greaves and Frank Dignum.

References

[BDBW97] J. Bradshaw, S. Dutfield, P. Benoit, and J. Woolley. KAoS: Toward an industrial-strength open agent architecture. In J. Bradshaw, editor, *Software Agents*. AAAI/MIT Press, 1997.

[FIP97] FIPA. FIPA'97 specification part 2: Agent communication language. FIPA (Foundation for Intelligent Physical Agents), http://drogo.cselt.stet.it/fipa/, 1997.

[Gal92] J. Galliers. Autonomous belief revision and communication. In P. Gardenfors, editor, *Belief Revision*. Cambridge University Press, 1992.

[KGB+95] D. Kinny, M. Georgeff, J. Bailey, D. Kemp, and K. Ramamohanarao. Active databases and agent systems: A comparison. In Proceedings Second International Rules in Database Systems Workshop. 1995.

[KIO95] K. Kuwabara, T. Ishida, and N. Osato. AgenTalk: Describing multiagent coordination protocols with inheritance. In Proc. 7th IEEE *International Conference on Tools with Artificial Intelligence* (ICTAI '95), pages 460–465. 1995.

[LF98] Y. Labrou and T. Finin. Semantics and conversations for an agent communication language. In M. Huhns and M. Singh, editors, *Readings in Agents*, pages 235–242. Morgan Kaufmann, 1998.

[PAC96] J. Pitt, M. Anderton, and J. Cunningham. Normalized interactions between autonomous agents: A case study in inter-organizational project management. *Computer-Supported Cooperative Work*, 5:201–222, 1996.

[PP98] J. Pitt and K. Prouskas. Initial specification of multi-agent system for realisation of load control and overload protection strategy. MARINER Project (EU ACTS AC333) Deliverable D3, http://www.teltec.dcu.ie/mariner, 1998.

[SCB+98] I. Smith, P. Cohen, J. Bradshaw, M. Greaves, and H. Holmback. Designing conversation policies using joint intention theory. In Y. Demazeau, editor, *Proceedings ICSMAS98*. IEEE Press, 1998.

[Sin98] M. Singh. Agent communication languages: Rethinking the principles. *IEEE Computer*, pages 40–47, 1998.

[Woo98] M. Wooldridge. Verifiable semantics for agent communication languages. In Y. Demazeau, editor, Proceedings ICMAS98. *IEEE Press*, 1998.

Using Colored Petri Nets for Conversation Modeling

R. Scott Cost, Ye Chen, Tim Finin, Yannis Labrou, Yun Peng

Department of Computer Science and Electrical Engineering
University of Maryland Baltimore County
Baltimore, Maryland 21250
cost@acm.org, {yechen,finin,jklabrou,ypeng}@cs.umbc.edu

Abstract. Conversations are a useful means of structuring communicative interactions among agents. The value of a conversation-based approach is largely determined by the conversational model it uses. Finite
State Machines, used heavily to date for this purpose, are not sufficient
for complex agent interactions requiring a notion of concurrency. We propose the use of Colored Petri Nets as a model underlying a language for
conversation specification. This carries the relative simplicity and graphical representation of the former approach, along with greater expressive
power and support for concurrency. The construction of such a language,
Protolingua, is currently being investigated within the framework of the
Jackal agent development environment. In this paper, we explore the use
of Colored Petri Nets in modeling agent communicative interaction.

1 Introduction

Conversations are a useful means of structuring communicative interactions
among agents, by organizing messages into relevant contexts and providing a
common guide to all parties. The value of a conversation-based approach is
largely determined by the conversational model it uses. The presence of an underlying formal model supports the use of structured design techniques and
formal analysis, facilitating development, composition and reuse. Most conversation modeling projects to date have used or extended finite state machines
(FSM) in various ways, and for good reason. FSMs are simple, depict the flow of
action/communication in an intuitive way, and are sufficient for many sequential interactions. However, they are not adequately expressive to model more
complex interactions, especially those with some degree of concurrency. Colored
Petri Nets (CPN) [17, 18, 19] are a well known and established model of concurrency, and can support the expression of a greater range of interaction. In
addition, CPNs, like FSMs, have an intuitive graphical representation, are relatively simple to implement, and are accompanied by a variety of techniques and
tools for formal analysis and design.

We have explored the use of model-based conversation specification in the
context of multi agent systems (MAS) supporting manufacturing integration [26].
Agents in our systems are constructed using the Jackal agent development platform [8], and communicate using the KQML agent communication language

F. Dignum and M. Greaves (Eds.): Agent Communication, LNAI 1916, pp. 178–192, 2000.

(ACL) [13]. Jackal, primarily a tool for communication, supports conversation-based message management through the use of abstract conversation specifications, which are interpreted relative to some appropriate model. Conversation specifications, or protocols, can describe anything from simple acknowledged transactions to complex negotiations.

In the next section, we present a motivation for using conversations to model and organize agent interaction. Next, we present CPNs, the model we propose to use, in more detail. Following this, we discuss the implementation of these ideas in a real MAS framework. Finally, we present two examples of CPN use: the first, specification of a simple KQML register conversation, and the next, a simple negotiation interaction.

2   Conversation-Based Interaction Protocols

The study of ACLs is one of the pillars of current agent research. KQML and the FIPA ACL are the leading candidates as standards for specifying the encoding and transfer of messages among agents. While KQML is good for message-passing among agents, directly exploiting it in building a system of cooperating agents leaves much to be desired. After all, when an agent sends a message, it has expectations about how the recipient will respond to the message. Those expectations are not encoded in the message itself; a higher-level structure must be used to encode them. The need for such conversation policies (CP)is increasingly recognized by the KQML community, and has been formally recognized in the latest FIPA draft standard [14, 10].

It is common in KQML-based systems to provide a message handler that examines the message performative to determine what action to take in response to the message. Such a method for handling incoming messages is adequate for very simple agents, but breaks down as the range of interactions in which an agent might participate increases. Missing from the traditional message-level processing is a notion of message context.

A notion growing in popularity is that the unit of communication between agents should be the conversation. This is evidenced by the advent of a conversation policies workshop at the 1999 Autonomous Agents Conference. A conversation is a pattern of message exchange that two (or more) agents agree to follow in communicating with one another. In effect, a conversation is a communications protocol, albeit one that may be initiated through negotiation, and may be short-lived relative to the way we are accustomed to thinking about protocols. A conversation lends context to the sending and receipt of messages, facilitating interpretation that is more meaningful. The adoption of conversation-based communication carries with it numerous advantages to the developer. There is a better fit with intuitive models of how agents will interact than is found in message-based communication. There is also a closer match to the way that network research approaches protocols, which allows both theoretical and practical results from that field to be applied to agent systems. Also, conversation structure can be separated from the actions to be taken by an agent engaged in the conversation, facilitating the reuse of conversations in multiple contexts.

Until recently, relatively little work has been devoted to the problem of conversation specification and implementation for mediated architectures. Strides must be taken in the toward facilitating the construction and reuse of conversations. An ontology of conversations and conversation libraries would advance this goal, as would solutions to the problems of specifying conversations, sharing these specifications, and aggregating them into meaningful 'APIs'.

2.1   Conversation Specification

A specification of a conversation that could be shared among agents must contain several kinds of information about the conversation and about the agents that will use it. First, the sequence of messages must be specified. Traditionally, deterministic finite-state automata (DFAs) have been used for this purpose; DFAs can express a variety of behaviors while remaining conceptually simple. For more sophisticated interactions, however, it is desirable to use a formalism with more support for concurrency and verification. This is the motivation for our investigation of CPNs as an alternative mechanism. Next, the set of roles that agents engaging in a conversation may play must be enumerated. Many conversations will be dialogues; however conversations with more than two roles are equally important, representing the coordination of communication among several agents in pursuit of a single common goal. For some conversations, the set of participants may change during the course of the interaction.

DFAs and roles dictate the syntax of a conversation, but say nothing about the conversation's semantics. The ability of an agent to read a description of a conversation, then engage in such a conversation, demands that the description specify the conversation's semantics. To be useful though, such a specification must not rely on a full-blown, highly expressive knowledge representation language. We believe that a simple ontology of common goals and actions, together with a way to relate entries in the ontology to the roles, states, and transitions of the conversation specification, will be adequate for most purposes. This approach sacrifices expressiveness for simplicity and ease of implementation. It is nonetheless perfectly compatible with attempts to relate conversation policy to the semantics of underlying performatives, as proposed for example by [5].

These capabilities will allow the easy specification of individual conversations. To develop systems of conversations though, developers must have the ability to extend existing conversations through specialization and composition. Development of these two abilities will entail the creation of syntax for expressing a new conversation in terms of existing conversations, and for linking the appropriate pieces of the component conversations. It will also demand solution of a variety of technical problems, such as naming conflicts, and the merger of semantic descriptions of the conversations.

2.2   Conversation Sharing

A standardized conversation language, as proposed above, dictates how conversations will be represented; however, it does not say how such representations are shared among agents. Agents must know how to map conversation names to specifications, how to communicate the identity of a conversation being used, and how to determine what conversations are know to other agents in their environment. While the details of how conversation sharing is accomplished are more mundane than those of conversation representation, they are nevertheless crucial to the viability of dynamic conversation-based systems.

2.3   Conversation Sets as APIs

The set of conversations in which an agent will participate defines an interface to that agent. Thus, standardized sets of conversations can serve as abstract agent interfaces (AAIs), in much the same way that standardized sets of function calls or method invocations serve as APIs in the traditional approach to system-building. That is, an interface to a particular class of service can be specified by identifying a collection of one or more conversations in which the provider of such a service agrees to participate. Any agent that wishes to provide this class of service need only implement the appropriate set of conversations. To be practical, a naming scheme will need to be developed for referring to such sets of conversations, and one or more agents will be needed to track the development and dissolution of particular AAIs. In addition to a mechanism for establishing and maintaining AAIs, standard roles and ontologies, applicable to a variety of applications, will need to be created.

There has been little work on communication languages from a practitioner's point of view. If we set aside work on network transport protocols or protocols in distributed computing (e.g., CORBA) as being too low-level for the purposes of intelligent agents, the remainder of the relevant research may be divided into two categories. The first deals with theoretical constructs and formalisms that address the issue of agency in general and communication in particular, as a dimension of agent behavior (e.g., AOP [29]). The second addresses agent languages and associated communication languages that have evolved somewhat to applications (e.g., TELESCRIPT [30]). In both cases, the work on communication languages has been largely part of a broader project committed to a specific architecture.

Agent communication languages like KQML provide a much richer set of interaction primitives (e.g., KQML's performatives), support a richer set of communication protocols (e.g., point-to-point, brokering, recommending, broadcasting, multicasting, etc.), work with richer content languages (e.g., KIF), and are more readily extensible than any of the systems described above. However KQML lacks organization at the conversation level that lends context to the messages it expresses and transmits. Until recently, limited work has been done on implementing and expressing conversations for software agents. As early as 1986,

Winograd and Flores [32] used state transition diagrams to describe conversations. The COOL system [2] has perhaps the most detailed current FSM-based model to describe agent conversations.

Other conversation models have been developed, using various approaches. Extended FSM models, which, like COOL, focus more on expressivity than adherence to a model, include Kuwabara et al. [20], and Elio and Haddadi [11]. A few others have chosen to stay within the bounds of a DFA, such as Chauhan [6], Nodine and Unruh [24], and Pitt and Mamdani [27]. Lin et al. [22] demonstrate the use of CPNs. Parunak [25] introduces Dooley Graphs. Bradshaw [4] introduces the notion of a conversation suite as a collection of commonly-used conversations known by many agents. Labrou [21] uses definite clause grammars to specify conversations. While each of these works makes contributions to our general understanding of conversations, more work needs to be done to facilitate the sharing and use of conversation policies by agents.

2.4   Defining Common Agent Services via Conversations

A significant impediment to the development of agent systems is the lack of basic standard agent services that can be easily built on top of the conversation architecture. Examples of such services are: name and address resolution; authentication and security services; brokerage services; registration and group formation; message tracking and logging; communication and interaction; visualization; proxy services; auction services; workflow management; coordination services; and performance monitoring. Services such as these have typically been implemented as needed in individual agent development environments. Two such examples are an agent name server and an intelligent broker.

3   Colored Petri Nets

Petri Nets (PN), or Place Transition Nets, are a well known formalism for modeling concurrency. A PN is a directed, connected, bipartite graph in which each node is either a *place* or a *transition*. *Tokens* occupy places. When there is at least one token in every place connected to a transition, we say that transition is *enabled*. Any enabled transition may *fire*, removing one token from every input place, and depositing one token in each output place. Petri nets have been used extensively in the analysis of networks and concurrent systems. For a more complete introduction, see [1].

CPNs differ from PNs in one significant respect; tokens are not simply blank markers, but have data associated with them. A token's *color* is a schema, or type specification. Places are then sets of tuples, called *multi-sets*. *Arcs* specify the schema they carry, and can also specify basic boolean conditions. Specifically, arcs exiting and entering a place may have an associated function which determines what multi-set elements are to be removed or deposited. Simple boolean expressions, called *guards*, are associated with the transitions, and enforce some constraints on tuple elements. This notation is demonstrated in examples below.

CPNs are formally equivalent to traditional PNs; however, the richer notation makes it possible to model interactions in CPNs where it would be impractical to do so with PNs.

CPNs have great value for conversational modeling, in that:

- They are a relatively simple formal model, with an intuitive graphical representation.
- They support concurrency, which is necessary for many non-trivial interactions.
- They are well researched and understood, and have been applied to many real-world applications.
- Many tools and techniques exist for the design and analysis of CPN-based systems.

CPNs are not new, and they have been used extensively for a broad range of applications (see [19] for a survey of current uses). Since their target domain is distributed systems, and the line between that domain and MASs is vague at best, there is much work on which to build. Some of the more directly related research endeavors include Holvoet and Kielmann [15, 16], Fallah-Seghrouchni and Mazouzi [12], Moldt and Wienberg [31, 23], Billington et al. [3], and Purvis and Cranefield [28].

4   Putting Colored Petri Nets to Work

Currently, we are investigating the value of CPNs in a general framework for agent interaction specification. Within this scheme, agents use a common language, Protolingua, for manipulating CPN-based conversations. Protolingua itself is very sparse, and relies on the use of a basic interface definition language (IDL) for the association of well known functions and data types with a CPN framework. Agents use Protolingua interpreters to execute various protocols. Protolingua itself is simple in order to facilitate the porting of interpreters to many different platforms.

This approach allows the use of very lightweight, universal interpreters without restricting the expressiveness of the protocols used. Note that the purpose of the IDL in Protolingua however is the identification and retrieval of executable modules, not the interaction of distributed components. If types and actions are appropriately specified, they should be suitable for analysis, or translation into some analyzable form. For example, we are using Design/CPN, a tool from Aarhus University, Denmark, for high level design and analysis of protocols. This system uses an extension of ML, CPN-ML, as its modeling language. We plan to translate developed protocols into Protolingua and Java extensions, and restrict modification in such a way that CPN-ML equivalents of the extensions can be used to facilitate analysis of the protocols. As such, CPN-ML has played a major role in influencing the development of Protolingua. For the remainder of this paper, we will focus on the abstract application of CPNs to conversations, rather than their specification in Protolingua.

5   Example: Conversation Protocol

From its inception, Jackal has used JDFA, a loose Extended Finite State Machine (EFSM), to model conversations [8, 26]. The base model is a DFA, but the tokens of the system are messages and message templates, rather than simply characters from an alphabet. Messages match template messages (with arbitrary match complexity, including recursive matching on message content) to determine arc selection. A local read/write store is available to the machine.

CPNs make it possible to formalize much of the extra-model extensions of DFAs. To make this concrete, we take the example of a standard JDFA representation of a KQML Register conversation and reformulate it as a CPN. Note that this simplified Register deviates from the [21] specification, in that it includes a positive acknowledgment, but does not provide for a subsequent 'unregister' event. The graphic depiction of this JDFA specification can be seen in Figure 1.

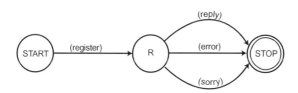

Fig. 1. Diagrammatic DFA representation of the simplified KQML Register conversation

There are a number of ways to formulate any conversation, depending on the requirements of use. This conversation has only one final, or accepting, state, but in some situations, it may be desirable to have multiple accepting states, and have the final state of the conversation denote the *result* of the interaction.

In demonstrating the application of CPNs here, we will first develop an informal model based on the simplified Register conversation presented, and then describe a complete, working CPN-ML model of the full Register conversation.

Some aspects of the model which are implicit under the DFA model must be made explicit under CPNs. The DFA allows a system to be in one state at a time, and shows the progression from one state to the next. Hence, the point to which an input is applied is clear, and that aspect is omitted from the diagrammatic representation. Since a CPN can always accept input at any location, we must make that explicit in the model.

We will use an abbreviated message which contains the following components, listed with their associated variable names: performative(p), sender(s), receiver(r), reply-with(id), in-reply-to(re), and content(c).

We denote the two receiving states as places of the names **Register** and **Done** (Figure 2). These place serve as a receipt locations for messages, after processing by the transitions **T1** and **T2**, respectively. As no message is ever received into the initial state, we do not include a corresponding place. Instead, we use a a source place, called **In**. This is implicit in the DFA representation. It must serve as input to every transition, and could represent the input pool for the entire collection of conversations, or just this one. Note that the source has links to every place, but there is no path corresponding to the flow of state transitions, as in the DFA-based model.

The match conditions on the various arcs of the DFA are implemented by transitions preceding each existing place. Note that this one-to-one correspondence is not necessary. Transitions may conditionally place tokens in different places, and several transitions may concurrently deposit tokens in the same place.

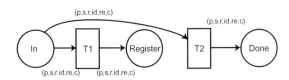

Fig. 2. Preliminary CPN model of a simplified KQML register conversation.

Various constants constrain the actions of the net, such as performative (Figure 3). These can be represented as color sets in CPN, rather than hard-coded constraints. Other constraints are implemented as guards; boolean conditions associated with the transitions. Intermediate places **S**, **R** and **I** assure that sender, receiver and ID fields in the response are in the correct correspondence to the initial messages. **I** not only ensures that the message sequence is observed, as prescribed by the message IDs, but that only one response is accepted, since the ID marker is removed following the receipt of one correct reply. Not all conversations follow a simple, linear thread, however. We might, for example, want to send a message and allow an arbitrary number of asynchronous replies to the same ID before responding (as is the case in a typical Subscribe conversation), or allow a response to any one of a set of message IDs. In these cases, we allow IDs to collect in a place, and remove them only when replies to them will no longer be accepted. Places interposed between transitions to implement global constraints, such as alternating sender and receiver, may retain their markings; that is implied by the double arrow, a shorthand notation for two identical arcs in opposite directions.

We add a place after the final message transaction to denote some arbitrary action not implemented by the conversation protocol (that is, not by an arc-association action). This may be some event internal to the interpreter, or a signal to the executing agent itself. A procedural attachment at this location would not violate the conversational semantics as long as it did not in turn influence the course of the conversation.

This CPN is generally equivalent to the JDFA depicted in Figure 1. In addition to modeling what is present in the JDFA, it also models mechanisms implicit in the machinery, such as message ordering.

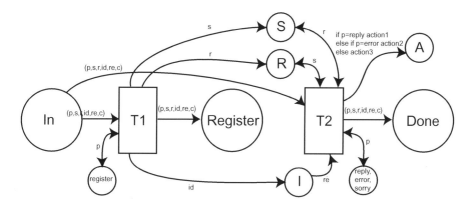

Fig. 3. Informal CPN model of a simplified KQML register conversation.

5.1   Register Implemented in CPN-ML

We further illustrate this example by examining a full, executable CPN implementation of the complete Register conversation. Register as given in [21] consists of an initial 'register' with no positive acknowledgment, but a possible 'error' or 'sorry' reply. This registration may then be followed by an unacknowledged 'unregister', also subject to a possible 'error' or 'sorry' response. This Register conversation (Figure 5) has been extracted from a working CPN model of a multi-agent scenario, implemented in CPN-ML, using the Design/CPN modeling tool. The model, a six agents scenario involving manufacturing integration, uses a separate, identical instance of the register conversation, and other KQML conversations, for each agent. They serve as sub-components to the agent models, which communicate via a modeled network. The declarations (given in Figure 4) have been restricted to only those elements required for the register conversation itself. The diagram is taken directly from Design/CPN. The full model uses concepts for building hierarchical CPNs, such as place replication and the use of sub-nets, which are beyond the scope of this paper. The interested reader is encouraged to refer to [17, 18, 19].

The declarations specify a message format **MES**, a six-tuple of performative, sender and receiver names, message IDs, and content. For simplicity, performative and agent names in the scenario are enumerated, and IDs are integers. For the content, we have constructed a special **Predicate** type, which will allow us to represent content in KIF-like expressions. The **Reg** type is used for registry entries, and encodes the name and address of the registrant, the name of the registrar, and the ID of the registration message. Finally, the **Signature** type is used to bind the names of the sender and receiver with the ID for a particular message.

The model is somewhat more complex than our informal sketch (Figure 3) for several reasons, which will become clear as we look more closely at its operation. For one thing, it is intended to model multiple concurrent conversations, and so must be able to differentiate among them. Also, it implements the complete registration operation, rather than simply modeling the message flow. All messages are initially presented in the **In** place, and once processed by each transition are moved to the **Out** place. Messages from the **Out** place are moved by the agent to the model network, through which they find their way to the **In** place of the same conversation in the target agent. The first transition (**T4**) accepts the message for the conversation, based on the performative 'register', and makes it available to the **T1** transition. **T1**, accepts the message if correct, and places a copy in the **Out** place. It also places an entry in the registry (**Reg**), and a message signature in **Sig1**. This signature will be used to make sure that replies to that message have the appropriate values in the sender and receiver fields. Message ID is included in the signature in order to allow the net to model multiple Register conversations concurrently. Note that because KQML does not provide for an acknowledgment to a 'register' message, the registration is made immediately, and is then retracted later if an 'error' or 'sorry' message is received.

Transition **T2a** will fire if an 'error' or 'sorry' is received in response to the registration. It unceremoniously removes the registration from **Reg**. The message signature constrains the names in the reply message. It is also possible for the initiating agent to send a subsequent 'unregister'; in that case **T2b** will fire (again, contingent on the constraints of the message signature being met), also removing the registration. However, since it is possible for an 'unregister' to be rejected (by an 'error' or 'sorry'), **T2b** archives the registration entry in **Arc**, and constructs a new signature for the possible reply. Such a reply would cause transition **T3** to restore the registration to **Reg**.

6   Example: Negotiation Model

In this section we present a simple negotiation protocol proposed in [7]. The CPN diagram in Figure 6 describes the pair-wise negotiation process in a simple MAS, which consists of two functional agents bargaining for goods. The messages used are based on the FIPA ACL negotiation performative set.

The diagram depicts three places places: **Inactive**, **Waiting**, and **Thinking**, which reflect the states of the agents during a negotiation process[1]; we will use the terms state and place interchangeably. Both agents in this simple MAS have similar architecture, differing primarily in the number of places/states. This difference arises from the roles they play in the negotiation process. The agent that begins the negotiation, called the *buyer* agent, which is shown on the left side of the diagram, has the responsibility of handling message failures. For this, it has an extra 'wait' state (**Waiting**), and timing machinery not present in the other agent, *seller*. For simplicity, some constraints have been omitted from this

---

[1] It is not always the case with such a model that specific nodes correspond to states of the system or particular agents. More often the state of the system is described by the combined state of all places.

```
color Performative = with register | unregister | error | sorry;
color Name = with ANS | Broker | AnyName;
color ID = int;
color Address = with ans | broker | anyAddress;
color PVal = union add:Address + nam:Name;
color PVals = list PVal;
color PName = with address | agentName;
color Predicate = product PName * PVals;
color Content = union pred:Predicate + C;
color MES = product Performative * Name * Name * ID * ID * Content;
color Reg = product Name * Name * Address * ID;
color Signature = product Name * Name * ID;

var c : Content;
var message : MES;
var s, r, anyName, name : Name;
var i, j : ID;
var p : Performative;
var a : Address;
```

Fig. 4. Declarations for the Register Conversation.

diagram; for example, constraints on message types, as depicted in the previous examples.

In this system, both agents are initially waiting in the **Inactive** places. The buyer initiates the negotiation process by sending a call for proposals ('CFP') to some seller, and its state changes from **Inactive** to **Waiting**. The buyer is waiting for a response ('proposal', 'accept-proposal', 'reject-proposal' or 'terminate'). On receipt, its state changes from **Inactive** to **Thinking**, at which point it must determine how it should reply. Once it replies, completing the cycle, it returns to the **Inactive** state. We have inserted a rudimentary timeout mechanism which uses a delay function to name messages which have likely failed in the **Timeout** place. This enables the exception action (**Throw Exception**) to stop the buyer from waiting, and forward information about this exception to the agent in the **Thinking** state. Timing can be handled in a number of ways in implementation, including delays (as above), the introduction of timer-based interrupt messages, or the use of timestamps. CPN-ML supports the modeling of time-dependent interactions through the later approach.

Note that this protocol models concurrent pairwise interactions between a buyer and any number of sellers.

7   Verification

The ability to verify the properties of a specification is one of the important benefits of applying formal methods. These benefits can be derived in two ways:

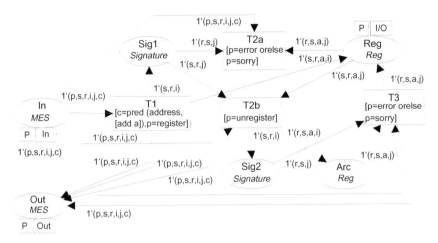

Fig. 5. KQML Register.

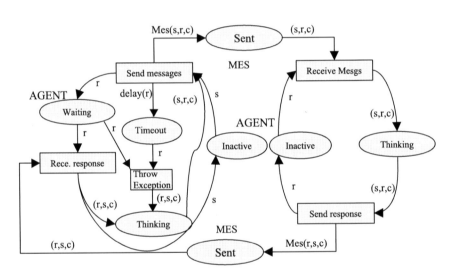

Fig. 6. Pair-wise negotiation process for a MAS constituted of two functional agents.

Verification of conversation policies directly, and verification of agents/MASs that are based on such protocols.

In addition to 'proof by execution', CPNs can be checked for a variety of properties. This is done by way of an Occurrence Graph (OG) [9]. Each node in an OG consists of a possible marking for the net. If another marking (B) can be reached by the firing of a transition, the graph contains a directed arc from the node representing the initial marking to B. All nodes in an OG are therefore derived from some initial marking of the net.

The properties subject to verification are:

1. Reachability Properties: This relates to whether or not the marking denoted by node B is reachable by some sequence of transition firings from node A.
2. Boundedness Properties: The upper or lower bound on the contents of place X in the net, over all possible markings.
3. Home Properties: The marking or set of markings which are reachable from all other markings in the OG define a homespace.
4. Liveness Properties: A marking from which no further markings can be derived is 'dead'. Liveness, then, relates to the possible progressions from a given node in the OG.
5. Fairness Properties: Relates to the degree to which certain transition instances (TI) will be allowed with respect to other TIs.

Many of these properties have different value depending on whether we are regarding a CP or a MAS, and also on the complexity of the net. CPs describe/operate on a message stream, which in most cases is finite; they are themselves static. One can imagine analyzing a CP in the context of (1) a single message stream, or (2) in the presence of a generator for all or many representative streams. In that sense, we may be interested in boundedness or home properties, and possibly reachability or fairness, but not liveness. On the other hand, liveness and fairness will often be more important in the analysis of a system as a whole.

It is possible to verify properties even for very large and complex nets. The version of Design/CPN used in this research supports the computation and analysis of OGs of 20,000 - 200,000 nodes and 50,000 to 2,000,000 arcs.

8 Summary

The use of conversation policies greatly facilitates the development of systems of interacting agents. While FSMs have proven their value over time in this endeavor, we feel that inherent limitations necessitate the use of a model supporting concurrency for the more complex interactions now arising. CPNs provide many of the benefits of FSMs, while allowing greater expression and concurrency. Using the Jackal agent development platform, we hope to demonstrate the value of CPNs as the underlying model for a protocol specification language, Protolingua.

References

1. Tilak Agerwala. Putting Petri Nets to work. *Computer*, pages 85–94, December 1979.
2. Mihai Barbuceanu and Mark S. Fox. COOL: A language for describing coordination in multiagent systems. In Victor Lesser, editor, *Proceedings of the First International Conference on Multi–Agent Systems*, pages 17–25, San Francisco, CA, 1995. MIT Press.

3. J. Billington, M. Farrington, and B. B. Du. Modelling and analysis of multi-agent communication protocols using CP-nets. In *Proceedings of the third Biennial Engineering Mathematics and Applications Conference (EMAC'98)*, pages 119–122, Adelaide, Australia, July 1998.

4. Jeffrey M. Bradshaw. KAoS: An open agent architecture supporting reuse, interoperability, and extensibility. In *Tenth Knowledge Acquisition for Knowledge-Based Systems Workshop*, 1996.

5. Jeffrey M. Bradshaw, Stuart Dutfield, Pete Benoit, and John D. Woolley. KAoS: Toward an industrial-strength open agent architecture. In Jeffrey M. Bradshaw, editor, *Software Agents*. AAAI/MIT Press, 1998.

6. Deepika Chauhan. JAFMAS: A Java-based agent framework for multiagent systems development and implementation. Master's thesis, ECECS Department, University of Cincinnati, 1997.

7. Ye Chen, Yun Peng, Tim Finin, Yannis Labrou, and Scott Cost. A negotiation-based multi-agent system for supply chain management. In *Working Notes of the Agents '99 Workshop on Agents for Electronic Commerce and Managing the Internet-Enabled Supply Chain.*, Seattle, WA, April 1999.

8. R. Scott Cost, Tim Finin, Yannis Labrou, Xiaocheng Luan, Yun Peng, Ian Soboroff, James Mayfield, and Akram Boughannam. Jackal: A Java-based tool for agent development. In Jeremy Baxter and Chairs Brian Logan, editors, *Working Notes of the Workshop on Tools for Developing Agents, AAAI '98*, number WS-98-10 in AAAI Technical Reports, pages 73–82, Minneapolis, Minnesota, July 1998. AAAI, AAAI Press.

9. Department of Computer Science, University of Aarhus, Denmark. *Design/CPN Occurrence Graph Manual*, version 3.0 edition, 1996.

10. Ian Dickenson. Agent standards. Technical report, Foundation for Intelligent Physical Agents, October 1997.

11. Renée Elio and Afsaneh Haddadi. On abstract task models and conversation policies. In *Working Notes of the Workshop on Specifying and Implementing Conversation Policies*, pages 89–98, Seattle, Washington, May 1999.

12. Amal El Fallah-Seghrouchni and Hamza Mazouzi. A hierarchial model for interactions in multi-agent systems. In *Working Notes of the Workshop on Agent Communication Languages, IJCAI '99*, August 1999.

13. Tim Finin, Yannis Labrou, and James Mayfield. KQML as an agent communication language. In Jeff Bradshaw, editor, *Software Agents*. MIT Press, 1997.

14. FIPA. FIPA 97 specification part 2: Agent communication language. Technical report, FIPA - Foundation for Intelligent Physical Agents, October 1997.

15. Tom Holvoet and Thilo Keilmann. Behavior specification of active objects in open generative communication environments. In Hesham El-Rewini and Yale N. Patt, editors, *Proceedings of the HICSS-30 Conference, Track on Coordination Models, Languages and Systems*, pages 349–358. IEEE Computer Society Press, January, 7–10 1997.

16. Tom Holvoet and Pierre Verbaeten. Using petri nets for specifying active objects and generative communication. In G. Agha and F. DeCindio, editors, *Advances in Petri Nets on Object-Orientation*, Lecture Notes in Computer Science. Springer-Verlag, 1998.

17. K. Jensen. *Coloured Petri Nets. Basic Concepts, Analysis Methods and Practical Use*, volume Volume 1, Basic Concepts of *Monographs in Theoretical Computer Science*. Springer-Verlag, 1992.

18. K. Jensen. *Coloured Petri Nets. Basic Concepts, Analysis Methods and Practical Use*, volume Volume 2, Analysis Methods of *Monographs in Theoretical Computer Science*. Springer-Verlag, 1994.

19. K. Jensen. *Coloured Petri Nets. Basic Concepts, Analysis Methods and Practical Use*, volume Volume 3, Practical Use of *Monographs in Theoretical Computer Science*. Springer-Verlag, 1997.

20. Kazuhiro Kuwabara, Toru Ishida, and Nobuyasu Osato. AgenTalk: Describing multiagent coordination protocols with inheritance. In *Proceedings of the 7th IEEE International Conference on Tools with Artificial Intelligence (ICTAI '95)*, pages 460–465, 1995.

21. Yannis Labrou. *Semantics for an Agent Communication Language*. PhD thesis, University of Maryland Baltimore County, 1996.

22. Fuhua Lin, Douglas H. Norrie, Weiming Shen, and Rob Kremer. Schema-based approach to specifying conversation policies. In *Working Notes of the Workshop on Specifying and Implementing Conversation Policies, Third International Conference on Autonomous Agents*, pages 71–78, Seattle, Washington, May 1999.

23. Daniel Moldt and Frank Wienberg. Multi-agent-systems based on coloured petri nets. In *Proceedings of the 18th International Conference on Application and Theory of Petri Nets (ICATPN '97)*, number 1248 in Lecture Notes in Computer Science, pages 82–101, Toulouse, France, June 1997.

24. M. H. Nodine and A. Unruh. Facilitating open communication in agent systems: the InfoSleuth infrastructure. In Michael Wooldridge, Munindar Singh, and Anand Rao, editors, *Intelligent Agents Volume IV – Proceedings of the 1997 Workshop on Agent Theories, Architectures and Languages*, volume 1365 of *Lecture Notes in Artificial Intelligence*, pages 281–295. Springer-Verlag, Berlin, 1997.

25. H. Van Dyke Parunak. Visualizing agent conversations: Using enhanced dooley graphs for agent design and analysis. In *Proceedings of the Second International Conference on Multi-Agent Systems (ICMAS '96)*, 1996.

26. Y. Peng, T. Finin, Y. Labrou, R. S. Cost, B. Chu, J. Long, W. J. Tolone, and A. Boughannam. An agent-based approach for manufacturing integration - the CIIMPLEX experience. *International Journal of Applied Artificial Intelligence*, 13(1–2):39–64, 1999.

27. Jeremy Pitt and Abe Mamdani. Communication protocols in multi-agent systems. In *Working Notes of the Workshop on Specifying and Implementing Conversation Policies*, pages 39–48, Seattle, Washington, May 1999.

28. M. Purvis and S. Cranefield. Agent modelling with petri nets. In *Proceedings of the CESA '96 (Computational Engineering in Systems Applications) Symposium on Discrete Events and Manufacturing Systems*, pages 602–607, Lille, France, July 1996. IMACS, IEEE-SMC.

29. Yoav Shoham. Agent–oriented programming. *Artificial Intelligence*, 60:51–92, 1993.

30. James White. Mobile agents. In Jeffery M. Bradshaw, editor, *Software Agents*. MIT Press, 1995.

31. Frank Wienberg. *Multiagentensysteme auf def Basis gefärbter Petri-Netze*. PhD thesis, Universität Hamburg Fachbereich Informatik, 1996.

32. Terry Winograd and Fernando Flores. *Understanding Computers and Cognition*. Addison-Wesley, 1986.

A Schema-Based Approach to Specifying Conversation Policies

Fuhua Lin[1], Douglas H. Norrie[1], Weiming Shen[1], and Rob Kremer[2]

[1] Department of Mechanical & Manufacturing Engineering, The University of Calgary, 2500
University Dr., NW, Calgary, AB, Canada, T2N 1N4
{fhlin, norrie, wshen}@enme.ucalgary.ca
[2] Department of Computer Science, The University of Calgary, 2500 University Dr., NW,
Calgary, AB, Canada, T2N 1N4
kremer@cpsc.ucalgary.ca

Abstract. This paper proposes a schema-based specification method for conversation policies in multi-agent systems. Conversation schemata are modeled through investigating conversational interactions among agents to exchange information. Information to be exchanged in a conversation interaction is specified through a set of "conversation topics". Schemata are conversational patterns implementing this information exchanged and detailed by conversation acts. Colored Petri Nets are used as a specification and verification tool for conversation schemata at the design stage. Examples in agentbased manufacturing systems are used to illustrate the concepts and method proposed.

1 Introduction

To facilitate multi-agent coordination and collaboration, it is vital that agents exchange information via communication about goals, intentions, results, and state to other agents. One challenge is to ensure reliable and flexible communication among heterogeneous agents in the sense that

- there are no possible inconsistencies and deadlocks,
- conversations end with the expected acts and the expected beliefs in memory of each agent, and
- the burden of inferring which communication acts are possible for the next message in a conversational sequence is lessened. (For this, a MetaMorph architecture was earlier proposed [1], which facilitates multi-agent coordination by minimizing communication and processing overheads.)

As conversation is the most effective and direct means for communication, conversation modeling is fundamental to the generation of collaborative activities in multi-agent systems.

Conversations are sequences of messages involving two or more agents intended to achieve a particular purpose [2]. To simplify the design of agent communications modules, it is desirable to derive a set of policies, called conversation policies (CPs). Due to the inherent complexity of the conversation problem and the particularity of

F. Dignum and M. Greaves (Eds.): Agent Communication, LNAI 1916, pp. 193-204, 2000.
© SpringerVerlag Berlin Heidelberg 2000

application domain, there are still many theoretical and technical problems to be solved. The main problems are how to represent, specify, verify, and implement CPs. To deal with this problem, many fundamental researches have been made. These will be briefly reviewed in next section.

In this paper, we define a *conversation policy* as a set of specification for information exchange among agents, which facilitates a specified change in the agents' states. Agents can rely on the patterns in the world to make their problem solving more efficient. When communicating with others, agents can also rely on communication patterns and group behavior [3]. Based on the notion of patterns, a conversation schema (schema, for short) based method for specifying CPs is presented.

We define a conversation schema as a pattern of conversation interactions specifying CPs centered on one or more conversation *topics*. Topics are extracted from application domain at the domain analysis stage. A goaldirected schema is a schema in which the pattern of interaction is directed towards achieving a specified goal of participating agent(s). We use Colored Petri Nets (CPN) [4] as a schema specification tool at the design stage because of the advantages of formal specification and executability. A schema is detailed by speech acts [5] and conversation acts [6].

In this paper, we focus on concepts in the schemabased conversation modeling approach. Some examples from agentbased systems in manufacturing enterprise are given to illustrate the concepts and approach. Section 2 of the paper reviews some related work. Section 3 details the definitions, and representation of conversation schemata. Section 4 briefly discusses the control mechanisms for conversation process. Finally, section 5 rounds up the paper with a conclusion and a discussion of ongoing work.

2   Related Work

Agents use some form of structured Agent Communication Language (ACL) for conversation. Supporting research for ACLs has involved *speech acts* [5] and *conversation acts* [6]. The notion of conversation act theory is more general than that for speech act theory, encompassing not only the traditional speech acts but turn taking, grounding, and higherlevel argumentation as well.

Many ACLs, based on *speech-acts*, such as KQML [7], COOL [8], AOP [9], and software agent architecture KAoS [10], framework such as JAFMAS [11], or Java Package such as JATLite [12], to name only a few, have been developed. Other ACLs include FIPA ACL [13] and AgenTalk [14]. Agent systems designers want to know when to use a protocol, what information to transmit, and how to describe the structure of interactions and exchange [15]. This problem is thought as being the hard part of for designing multiagent systems [16].

Communication act semantics based on the joint intentions theory (CL theory) [2], which involves the mutual adoption of beliefs, intentions, and goal, provides a basis for deriving semantics of CPs. Planbased or protocolbased theory for agent conversation scenario modeling is a wellknown approach that attempts to formulate conversations in multiagent systems [17], [18]. Turner *et al.* (1991) proposed schemabased approach and schemabased reasoning for cooperative problem solving, incorporating both problem solving and communication. What this approach lacks is a mechanism for constructing and specifying a schema and verifying that a schema has actually been successful.

The state transition diagram (STD) has been extensively used for conversation protocol specification due to its clarity. The weakness is that it does not reflect the asynchronous character of the underlying communication [19]. Furthermore, it is not easy to represent integration of protocols. The Dooley Graph [20], [21] is an alternative formalism for visualizing agent interrelationships within a conversation. Object-oriented methods like UML [22] offer a way to reduce the gap between users and analyst when considering message transfers, yet they only address the dynamic behavior of individual objects and are informal.

Colored Petri Nets [4] are a powerful model for protocol specification. They are particularly well-suited for systems that consists of processes which communicate asynchronously and concurrently. More importantly, the unique advantages of CPNs are (1) that they are a formal specification approach in which CPN-represented schema can be mathematically analyzed through occurrence graphs and place invariants; (2) they are executable models so that the models can be verified in simulation; (3) dynamic behaviors of the system can be represented by representing all dynamic components as 'colored tokens' carrying information represented by data structure. CPN's arcs expressions representing preconditions and postconditions can be used to define flexible and adaptive control mechanisms.

3   Conversation Schemata

Designing CPs is an evolutionary process that requires abstract thinking and expertise in both the application domain and software design. The process of conversation schema construction will begin with agentification and defining conversation topics. Individual conversation acts can be then aggregated to create more complex structures called "schema", which describes the (goaldirected) collective behaviors of agents. Schemata can be represented by CPN for checking possible inconsistency and deadlocks. By following objectoriented methodologies, the schema instances (models) can then be constructed. Fig. 1 gives an overview of the conversation schema construction procedure.

3.1   Conversation Topics

A conversation always centers on one or more "*topics*", each of which is associated with a set of attributes. Therefore, once we know the goal or task of an agent, we can conceptually specify its conversation behavior by defining the topics for relevant conversational interaction with other agents.

A *conversation topic* (TP) defines a unit of information exchanged by participating agents, without reference to the conversational implementation of the information or the control mechanisms of information exchanged. A TP can be described by a set of *variables* that have certain values to be agreed upon by the agent involved. Topics are used to convey the essence of relationships within an agent society concerned and in relation to its environment. The following gives the definition of a conversation topic:

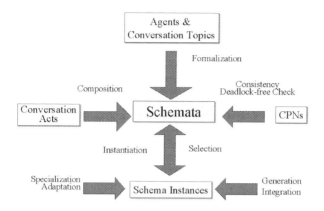

Fig. 1: Proposed conversation schema construction procedure.

Definition 1: A conversation topic (TP) can be defined as a 3-tuples
$$TP: (TP\_ID, AGENTS, ARGUMENTS) \qquad (1)$$
Here, *TP_ID* is the identity of a TP;
AGENTS lists the agents involving in this topic; and
ARGUMENTS lists all arguments in the topic.

Example 1: In "maketoorder" manufacturing system, to achieve common agreement about the indexes of a production order, such as due date, price, delivery location, a Logistics Agent (*LOA*), Production Planning Agent (*PPA*), and Factory Agent (*FAA*) need to conduct several conversations with different topics. The following are the examples of relevant TPs:
$$TP1: (Prod\_Tar, (LOA, PPA), (Cust\_order, Cust, Loc, DD, Price)), \qquad (2)$$
$$TP2: (Mfg\_Cost, (PPA, FAA), (Factory\_order, DD, Cost)), \quad (3)$$
Here, the TP *Prod_Tar* in (2) will be the focus of a conversational interaction between the *LOA* and the *PPA* about the production target: 'to ship products *Prod* to a customer *Cust* at a location *Loc,* duedate *DD* and price *Price*. The product parameters can identify unique product types, or groups of product types. The values of the parameters are shared by both the *LOA* and the *PPA*. TP *Mfg_cost* in (3) is the focus of conversational interaction between the *PPA* and the *FAA* about the manufacturing cost for the factory order with due date *DD*. These TPs abstract possible negotiations via a suite of conversations to determine feasible production targets and optimal due date.

We can see from the above that TPs define the exchange of information at a high level of abstraction, but do not discuss refined specification and do not describe the *timing* of the interactions. TPs do not describe the individual constraints of the systems, but provide the links for deriving conversation schemata.

3.2   Conversation Schemata

A schema can be constructed by identifying the conversation acts, the internal state changes, and the external information exchange related to the TP(s).

A conversation schema is defined at two levels: schema class and schema instance. The schema instances are created using schema classes as their templates. Schema classes are used for modeling schema libraries.

Definition 2: A conversation schema in a multi-agent system, *Conv-schema,* consists of 4-tuples

$$Conv\text{-}schema = (Agents, Acts, States, Arcs, TPs), \tag{4}$$

where $Agents = \{Agt_1, Agt_2, ..., Agt_m\}$ ($m>0$) are the set of agents participating in the conversation; $Acts = \{Act_1, Act_2, ..., Act_n\}$ ($n>0$) are packets of conversation acts performed together by each agent in *Agents* in some situation; $States = \{Sta_1, Sta_2, ..., Sta_l\}$ ($l>0$) are corresponding state changes respectively, of each agent in *Agents*; *Arcs* $= Acts \times States \cup States \times Acts$ are the relations between *Acts* and *States*; $TPs = \{Tp_1, Tp_2, ..., Tp_k\}$ ($k>0$) are the set of conversation topics relevant for the agents in the conversation.

Notes: (1) In a similar way, to the concept *suite* was proposed by Bradshaw *et al.* (1997) [10], which provides a convenient grouping of conversation policies that support a set of related services, schemata can be classified as *atomic schemata* and *composite schemata*. Composite schemata can be composed of several schemata, while atomic schemata can not. For example, *INFORM, OFFER,* and *REQUEST* can be modeled as atomic schemata. Further, *REQUEST* from agent *A* to agent *B* can be represented as a schema according to conversation act theory [20]: Schema *REQUEST*: ((A, B), (request, continue, repair, req_ack, req_repair, acknowledge, cancel), (submitted, failed, succeeded), (content)). (2) A conversation always has an initiator who starts the conversation by performing a communicative act. A goal-directed schema is a schema for conversation to achieve the agents' collective goal, or initiator's goal. (3) *Schemata* can have optional steps, *alternatives* that are chosen based on a particular situation and *variables* represented in *TPs* that allow the schema to be adapted.

Example 2: In a agentbased system in manufacturing, after receiving a customer order, the Logistics Agent (LOA) needs to find collaborators who can assisting (or commit to) this order, the agent would request local area coordinator (LAC) to obtain information about "how to collaborate". Then the LAC would request some knowledge agent (KA) to help find some suitable collaborator(s). Replying actions will occur in a reverse order. For LOA, *Agents* = {LOA, LAC1, KA1}, TP = "who to collaborate with". This schema is also suited for a Production Planning Agent (PPA) when it receives a factory order and for a Factory Agent (FAA) to form a virtual team to execute a manufacturing order, in which *Agents* = {PPA, LAC2, KA2}, TP = "part information of product" and *Agents* = {FAA, LAC3, KA3), TP = "feature information of part", respectively. They have same *Acts* = {REQUEST, REPLY}. REQUEST and REPLY here are atomic schemata.

Example 3: A "Due date negotiation schema" in agentbased manufacturing systems can be constructed from *TP1* and *TP2* in Example 1. Schema: *Agents* = (LOA, PPA, FAA), *TPs* = (TP1, TP2), *States* and *Acts* will be detailed later in this section.

Fig. 2: Example for goal-directed schema: Due-date Negotiation

3.3   Representation of Schemata

The choice of CPN as formalism was guided by natural support for concurrency, synchronization, and its use of "colored" tokens crucial in schema abstraction and integration. The hierarchical CPN, perhaps the most widely used highlevel Petri net formalism in industry, has been successfully used to model and analyze application systems. CPN's tokens can be arbitrary color (type) and complexity. Because CPN notations are based on a functional programming language SML [23], arc expressions allow concise specification of complex token manipulations. To support modularity, CPN provide such features as substitution transitions and fusion places. Substitution transitions, a notational convenience designed to allow modular representation of large and complex models, utilize the port concept. When a substitution transition is declared, its input and output places are considered as ports. The substitution transition is then further expanded on another page and additional (and internal) places and transitions can be declared as needed. However, all "atomic" transitions model communicative acts at the same level of abstraction, although they may appear on different and hierarchically organized pages. Fusion places are used to avoid the clustering of too many input and output arcs. Fusion places appearing on different pages are considered the same and the firing semantics of CPN are unaffected.

3.3.1   Atomic Schemata Construction

Conversation acts in a schema are represented as 'transitions' in CPN. The *state* of a schema is mapped in a combination of CPN *places* and structured *token* holding *messages*. The construction of schemata can be realized via instantiation, specialization, adaptation, integration, and alteration. Arc expressions are of two types: (1) input arc expressions determine which and how many tokens are removed from the input places; (2) output arc expressions determine which and how many tokens are created and input in the output places.

The following are the steps to construct an "atomic" conversation schema.

Step 1: For every agent, each communicative act in the schema is depicted by a transition in CPN. The transitions representing the acts performed by the same agent are aligned horizontally.

Step 2: Places and arcs are added between the transitions and connected to them. In this way, the implicit information exchanges that take place between the successive communicative acts performed by each agent are modeled.

Step 3: The information exchange represented by collective places that occur among the agents for the TPs are added.

Example 4: The CPN representation of the atomic schema REQUEST (A, B) is showed in Fig. 3 (the arc expressions are omitted).

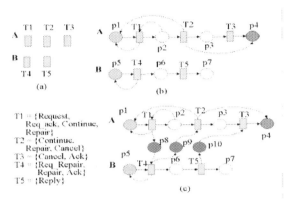

Fig. 3: CPN-represented atomic schema:REQUEST(A, B). (a) Drawing the transitions; (b) Adding places and arcs between transitions for each agent; (c) Adding collective state places that take place among the agents for information exchange.

3.3.2   Composite Schemata Construction

For composite schemata, the hierarchical CPN formalism and object-oriented methodologies facilitate the construction. We can use aggregation, classification, instantiation, and inheritance as main means for composite schema construction. Fig.4 shows an example of composite schema "infoobtaining" by aggregating atomic schema REQUEST, REPLY, and ACK. Three cases in example 2 are compacted (folded) into a CPN by placing color sets in the places and transitions of the net. X, Y, Z are the variables of the participating agents.

To make schema reusable, maintainable and conversation flexible, the synchronization constraints are separated from the internal part of each schema. Thus, every schema has an interface (*INTERFACE*) and a body (*BODY*). Fig. 5 shows an example of schema class and its instances. The interfaces are used to connect two or more schemata during the conversation execution and to facilitate combination of several subnets representing subschemata to a complex one. A schema class is instantiated to create actual schemata during execution. For example, from schema class "*info-obtaining*" schema class with three agent variables X, Y, Z, and topic *TP*, as well as order *O*, then three schemata in Example 2, *collaborator-finding* schema; *part-info-obtaining* schema; and *feature-info-obtaining* schema can be instantiated when needed. We can represent the commonalties among schemata in the form of an abstract schema from which more concrete schema can inherit.

Conversation schema classes are CPNbased descriptions of what a group of agent does in certain situations. A conversation schema class specifies the available conversation policies, their control mechanism and the local knowledge base that maintains the state of the conversation. A *conversation schema* can be "manufactured" by instantiating a schema class. Schema classes are used to structure

200   F. Lin et al.

a conceptual schema into modules by encapsulation. A schema library of an agent (*SCHEMA_LIB*) consists of a set of well-defined CPN-represented schemata and their possible relationships. We are developing a set of enabling algorithms and control mechanisms to help designers to construct conversation schemata.

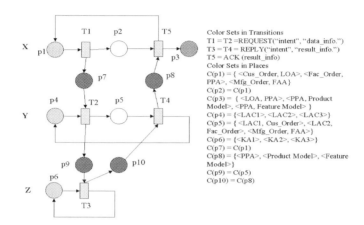

Fig. 4: Example of CPN-represented Schemata.

(a)	(b)

SCHEMA Info-obtaining;
INTERFACE:
INPORTS: p1, p4, p6
OUTPORTS: p3
ARCS: Pre(p1, T1) = <X, O, TP>, Pre(p4, T2) = <Y>,
Pre(p6, T3) = <Z>, Post(P3, T5) = <O, TP>
BODY:
  PLACES: p2, p5, p7, p8, p9, p10;
  TRANSITIONS: T1, T2: REQUEST; T3, T4: REPLY;
T5: ACK;
  ARCS: Post(T1, p2) = <O>, Post(T1, p7) = <O, TP>,
Pre(p1, T2) = <O>, Post(p5, T2) = <O>, Post(p9, T2) =
<O, TP>, Pre(p9, T3) = <O, TP>, Post(p6, T3) = <Z>,
Pre(p5, T4) = <O>, Pre(p10, T4) = <TP>, Post(p4, T4) =
<Y>, Post(p8, T4) = <O, TP> , Pre(p2, T5) = <O>,
Pre(p8, T5) = <O, TP>, Post(p1, T5) = <X>.
END SCHEMA
	INSTANCES Collaborator-finding;
	INSTANCE OF info-obtaining;
	INITIAL-MARKING: M(p1) = <Logistics Agent,
	Customer order, Collaborator-finding>, M(p4) = (LAC1),
	M(p6) = <KA1>
	END INSTANCE Collaborator-finding
	INSTANCES Part-info-obtaining;
	  INSTANCE OF info-obtaining;
	  INITIAL-MARKING: M(p1) = <Production Planning
	Agent, Factory order, Part-info-obtaining>, M(p4) =
	(LAC2), M(p6) = <KA2>
	END INSTANCE Part-info-obtaining
	INSTANCES Feature-info-obtaining;
	  INSTANCE OF info-obtaining;
	  INITIAL-MARKING: M(p1) = <Factory Agent,
	Manufacturing Order, Feature-info-obtaining>, M(p4) =
	(LAC3), M(p6) = <KA3>
	END INSTANCE Feature-info-obtaining

Fig.5: (a) Example for (simplified) textual specification of CPN representation of schema "Infoobtaining"; (b) Instances of the schema " *Info-obtaining*".

Consistency and deadlock checking. The derived CPN representation of schemata allows the verification for logical consistency, completeness, and deadlock-freedom through simulation and S-invariant analysis. After specifying an initial marking, which will put one token in each source, the CPN can be simulated for refining the logical consistency of requirements and to assess the behavior of schemata designed.

4 Control Mechanism

A conversation can be thought of as a set of *activities* of two or more agents in which information is transmitted. The ultimate result of a conversation is a change of state in the participants. Depending on the components of state of the particular agents, this could be a change in the agent's knowledge, goals, or other attributes.

A CPNbased conversation schema can be selected and adapted as the result of the beliefs, desires, and intentions of agents and the status of resource. The schema matching process is triggered when an agent receives a request to execute a new goal (with its associated task). This request can come from several sources: the user, via the mission description; unanticipated events that must be responded to; other agents, via requests or commands; and from the agent's own reasoning (e.g., subgoals). When a new goal arises, it is placed on a ``todo'' list called an *agenda*.

An agent can have several active conversations at the same time. A conversation control mechanism is provided to allow agents to suspend current conversations while waiting for others to reach certain stages. As a sequence, conversation scenarios form a conversation hierarchy dynamically. If an agent with an intention initiates a conversation with others by choosing a schema, then the other agent(s)' pattern of response is also limited to that schema. Control mechanism will only perform the *"Intra-schema decisions"* by executing CPN transitionfiring rules.

In CPNrepresented schemabased conversation model, intentions and situations of agents involved in a conversation are represented "tokens" with different types named by "colors". Conversation occurrence processes are modeled by *"recognize-trigger-act"* pattern according to current intentions and situations of the agents.

Step 1: [Initializing] (Initiator Agent) Select a goal (or task) from the agenda.

Step 2: [Reaching a Joint Intention]

(1) (Initiator Agent) Present an intention for the task (goal);

(2) (Partner Agent(s)) according to the intention provided by the initiator agent and its goal, accept the schema or reject the intention or propose some additional condition to the initiator agent.

Step 3: [Reaching a Collective Schema]

(1) (Initiator Agent) Propose a schema for the task to the partner agent(s);

(2) (Partner agent(s)) According to the schema provided by the initiator agent and its knowledge, accept the schema or reject the schema. If reject, back to (1) of this step.

Step 4: [Executing a schema] (Initiator Agent and partner Agent(s)) According the A-schema and M-schema, execute the schema by the firing rules.

If an agent is initiating a conversation by using an individual communicative act, then the receiving agent is "free" to select how he wishes to respond. In this case, the control mechanism will do *"active schema selection"* by searching an intention schema table (*INTENT_SCHEMA_TABLE*) from an appropriate schema class. After selecting a schema class, it creates an instance of the conversation schema class. An actual conversation maintains the current state of the conversation, a set of conversation variables whose values are manipulated by conversation rules, and various historical information accumulated during conversation execution. Each conversation schema class describes a conversation from the viewpoint of the agent group, rather than the individual agent.

In a CPNrepresented schemabased conversation model, intentions and situations of agents involved in a conversation are represented by "tokens" with different types named by "colors". Conversation occurrence processes are modeled by "*recognize-triggeract*" pattern according to the current intentions and situations of the agents. Control mechanism will only perform "*Intra-schema decisions*" by executing CPN transitionfiring rules. A transition is enabled if there is a consistent binding for its associated variables. Each of these consistent bindings defines a different *firing mode*. A transition firing may occur if the transition is enabled by some mode. The state change happens when the firing mode occurs. Fig.6 shows the dynamic execution of CPNrepresented schema in "Duedate negotiation" including "*production-target*" conversation schema and "*manufacturing cost*" conversation schema.

In collaborative agents systems, generating a solution to a problem is a multistep and incremental process involving a conversation among agents using information at multiple levels of abstraction. Designing a flexible and robust computational conversation model is fundamental. It is a challenge to keep the conversation coherent and to enhance efficiency in related reasoning.

A conversational interaction can be thought of as a set of *activities* of two or more agents in which information is transmitted. The ultimate result of an interaction is a change of state in the participants. Depending on the components of state of the particular agents, this could be a change in the agent's knowledge, goals, or other attributes.

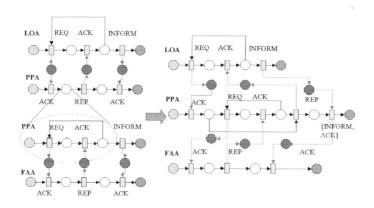

Fig.6: Dynamic execution of CPNrepresented schemata: "Due Date Negotiation"

5   Conclusions

In this paper, we have proposed a new approach to specifying conversation policies for agent communication and cooperation in multiagent systems. The specification processes for these conversation policies start with defining conversation topics in the realworld problem domain and follow objectoriented methodologies. Then we use conversation schemata to *link* the conversation topics and low-level conversation acts. "Conversation topics" allow us to understand and specify their related conversational interactions using schemas completely despite its formidable complexity. The goal oriented schemata are used to capture taskdriven and goaloriented conversation scenarios in a multiagent system. Domainspecific and welldefined conversation schemata can be used to capture interaction patterns in the agent's world and in its behavior. By using the schemata, the agent can quickly determine what to do without resorting to lengthy reasoning and reduce communication overheads. Schemata represent agents' communication knowledge and cooperation protocol during conversation.

We use Colored Petri Nets both to represent and to verify conversation schemata. Using this approach, it can be verified whether a schema has been successful. Flexibility is realized by incorporating decisionmaking units and control mechanism via arc expressions and tokens of nets. The initial markings of CPNs representing schema are used to represent the kinds of situation the agent will likely encounter. Therefore, they provide a possibility for incorporating *learning* mechanisms into conversation schemata for optimization.

A complementary part of this research is using lowlevel conventions named interaction protocols to offer a reliable and efficient transmission of messages [24].

6 Acknowledgement

Our thanks to researchers at the Collaborative Agents Group at the University of Calgary, especially to Dr. Mihaela Ulieru, Dr. Bob Brennam, Dr. Niek Wijngaards, Roberto FloresMendez, Sudong Shu, Bin Zhou, Prof. Matsumoto Tsutomu, and Dr. Xiaokun Zhang and for their comments and suggestions for improving the material presented in this paper.

References

1. Maturana, F. and D. H. Norrie (1996). Multi-Agent Mediator Architecture for Distributed Manufacturing. *Journal of Intelligent Manufacturing*, Vol.7, pp.257-270.
2. Smith, I. A., P. R. Cohen, J. M. Bradshaw, M. Greaves, & H. Holmback, (1998), Designing conversation policies using joint intention theory, *Int. Joint Conf. on Multi-Agent Systems* (*ICMAS-98*), Paris, France, 2-8 July 1998.
3. Turner, E. H. and R. M. Turner, A schema-based approach to cooperative problem solving with autonomous underwater vehicles, *Proc. of the IEEE Oceanic Engineering Society OCEANS'91 Conf.*, Honolulu, Hawaii. *http://cdps.umcs.maine.edu/Papers/1991/oceans/unhcopy.html*
4. Jensen, K. (1992) *Colored Petri Nets: Basic Concepts, Analysis Methods and Practical Use*, vol. 1, Springer-Verlag, New York.
5. Austin, J. L., *How to do things with words*. Oxford University Press, 1962.
6. Traum, D. R. and Allen, J. F., 1994, Discourse Obligations in Dialogue Processing. *Proc. of the 32th Annual Meeting of the ACL*, Las Cruces, NM, 1-8.
7. Labrou, Y. & T. Finin, 1994, A semantics approach for KQML --- A General Purpose Communication Language for Software Agents. *Paper presented at the third int. conf. on information and knowledge management* (*CIKM'94*), Washington, D. C.

8. Barbuceanu M. & M. S. Fox, The Specification of COOL: A Language for Representation Cooeration Knowledge in Multi-Agent Systems. EIL, Univ. of Toronto, Internal report, 1996

9. Shoham, Y., 1993, Agent-Oriented Programming, *J. of Artificial Intelligence* **60** (1): 51-94

10. Bradshaw, J. M., Dutfield, S., Benoit, P. & Woolley, J.D. (1997). KAoS: Toward an industrial-strength open agent architecture. In J.M. Bradshaw (Ed.) *Software Agents.* AAAI/MIT Press, pp.375-418.

11. JAFMAS: A Java-based Agent Framework for Multiagent Systems Development and Implementation, Deepika Chauhan, ECECS Department, University of Cincinnati, USA, 1997, *http://www.ececs.uc.edu/~abaker/JAFMAS/*

12. JATLite, Stanford University, http://java.stanford.edu */java_agent/html/*

13. FIPA ACL: *http://www.fipa.org/spec/fipa97.html*

14. Kuwabara, K., T. Ishida, and N. Osato, "AgenTalk: Describing Multiagent Coordination Protocols with Inheritance", *Tools for AI Conf.*, 1995.

15. Lesser, Victor R., 1998, Reflections on the nature of multiagent coordination and its implications for an agent architecture. *Autonomous agents and multi-agent systems*, **1**, pp89111

16. Russell, S. & P. Norvig, 1995, *Artificial Intelligence*: *A Modern Approach*, Prentice Hall, Inc.

17. Barbuceanu M. & M. S. Fox, 1997, Integrating Communication Action, Conversations and Decision Theory to Coordinate Agents. *Proc. of Autonomous Agents'97*, pp.4758.

18. Haddadi, A., *Communication and Cooperation in Agent Systems*: *A Pragmatic Theory*, LNAI 1056, SpringerVerlag Berlin Heidelberg, 1995

19. Martial, F. von, (1992), *Coordinating Plans of Autonomous Agents*, LNAI 610, Springer Verlag

20. Dooley, R. A., "Appendix B – Repartee as a graph", *An Anatomy of Speech Notions*, pp.345358, 1976

21. Parunak, H. V. D., 1996, Visualizing Agent Conversations: Using Enhanced Dooley Graphs for Agent Design and Analysis (8/96), *Proceedings of the 1996 International Conference on Multi-Agent Systems, http://www.erim.org/~van/papers.htm*

22. Booch, G., J. Rumbaugh, and I. Jacobson, The unified modeling language for object oriented development. *Document set version 1.0*, Jan. 1997. Rational Software Corporation, Santa Clara, CA.

23. Ullman, J., *Elements of ML Programming*, Prentice Hall, 1994.

24. Flores, R.A. and Wijngaards (1999) Primitive Interaction Protocols for Agents in a Dynamic Environment. Proceedings of the 12th Workshop on Knowledge Acquisition, Modeling and Management (KAW'99), B.R. Gaines, R.C. Kremer and M. Musen (Eds.), Banff, Canada, October, 1621, 1999.

Constructing Robust Conversation Policies in Dynamic Agent Communities

Marian H. Nodine and Amy Unruh

Microelectronics and Computer Technology Corporation (MCC)
Austin, Texas
{nodine, unruh}@mcc.com

Abstract. Conversation policies codify allowable exchanges of speech acts among agents as they execute specific types of tasks. Both the set of agents in a community, and the nature of those agents may change over time; however, these agents must conform to a common set of conversation policies that are robust to change and failure. We describe aspects of the implementation of conversation policies in InfoSleuth, including the integral use of finite-state automata for defining those policies. We identify features of those automata and the underlying performatives that are necessary for their robust and correct execution in an operational community. We describe the construction of new conversation policies from simpler underlying components using two mechanisms, extension and concatenation. In this way, we can ensure that the specification of these new policies is easily sharable, and that certain shared characteristics of multiple conversation policies are enforced consistently.

1 Introduction

Agent communication languages such as KQML [1,2] and FIPA [3] define message types (*speech acts*) that are exchanged among agents in an agent community during the execution of specific tasks. An agent communication language may be specified at several different semantic levels. A first level of specification enumerates the allowable message types or *speech acts*. A second level specifies the *policies*, or allowed orderings, of the speech acts during a specific message exchange, or "conversation". A third level defines intensional semantics for the message types, from which conversation policies emerge.

InfoSleuth™ [4,5,6] is an agent system which provides information retrieval, monitoring, and analysis at multiple levels of abstraction and aggregation. For InfoSleuth, it has become increasingly apparent that the interactions among agents in a community must be dealt with in a principled, consistent, manner by all of its agents, regardless of their capabilities or level of "intelligence". Many agents in an information-gathering system can not provably implement and adhere to a conversational semantics from which different types of conversation may emerge. Therefore, it has been useful to define a base set of conversation policies that are used by all agents in the system.

F. Dignum and M. Greaves (Eds.): Agent Communication, LNAI 1916, pp. 205–219, 2000.

We have developed a *generic agent shell* that defines and enforces the conversation policies that InfoSleuth uses. In implementing conversational support for the shell, we have had to deal not only with issues of correct conversational behavior, but also operational issues such as agents entering and leaving the community, communication failures, agent interrelationships, and others not currently considered within the scope of agent communication languages. Because this shell is used in an agent system that must be continually running, e.g. in its use by the EDEN project [7], robustness and resilience to failure are important issues in our conversational design.

This paper describes some ideas that have grown from our experience in constructing and modifying state-based conversation policies, including starting with a set of basic, correctly functioning policies; building in consistent extensions to handle unexpected situations; and showing how these basic conversations can be concatenated into richer conversation sets.

1.1   Conversations and Tasks

There are two different meanings for the word "conversation" in the literature. The first, a more focused definition, is a dialog among a specific set (usually two) of agents pertaining to some subtask of the current agent community. For instance, almost every activity in InfoSleuth that involves retrieving information from different information sources requires at least one conversation per information source requesting the specific information that pertains to the query and/or must be fed into the analysis. This is the meaning of "conversation" that is most commonly referred to in the literature.

The second use of "conversation" encompasses the collective set of message exchanges among agents in a community that are required to execute a given task. Thus, such an interaction in InfoSleuth would involve the agents that interface with the user, the agents that contain the requested information, and the agents that fuse, analyze, and filter the information to meet the user's request. For the purposes of this paper, we refer to this type of interaction as a "task".

How do we draw the line between *conversations* and *tasks*? Consider a community where every agent is built upon a generic shell that is the same in all agents and handles communication with other agents. Upon that shell sits the agent-specific, or "application" part of the agent, which is specialized to execute the services that the agent offers. Consider a performative that starts some activity, such as `achieve`. There is a well-specified interaction associated with communicating about the `achieve` that can be enforced within the generic shell. During the course of conversation execution, information may be passed up into the agent-specific code, which in turn may respond by initiating related actions with other agents. These new actions are new conversations, because they are not under the control of any existing conversations being enforced by the generic shell. However, they are part of the same task, because they are initiated in response to the original conversation.

From this perspective, it is evident that a task contains an interrelated set of conversations initiated (directly or transitively) in response to the task request.

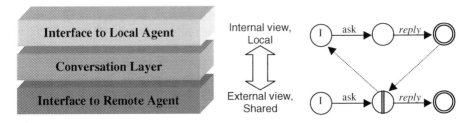

Fig. 1. Conversation Layer as an Intermediary Between the Remote and Local Agents

In a dynamic agent community, where different agents may enter or leave an agent system at any time, a specific task request may result in different sets of interrelated conversations in different contexts. However, a small set of conversation policies can potentially be used as building blocks for many diverse tasks. This suggests that it may be useful to view conversations, rather than messages, as the "unit of emergence" in task construction. However, if conversations are to be combined by an agent, then additional information about the constraints on and the effects of a policy must be made explicit [8].

In the remainder of this paper, we focus on interactions within the InfoSleuth system at the conversation rather than task level.

2   Conversation Implementation

2.1   The InfoSleuth Agent Shell's Conversation Layer

The InfoSleuth agent system implements its generic agent shell as an extensible, layered infrastructure that provides structured support for the rapid creation and easy deployment of agents. Crisp, plug-and-play layering facilitates the integration of application and/or third-party software. At the core of this infrastructure is the *conversation layer*. Conversations structure the message-passing interactions between pairs of agents into standard interaction protocols, or *conversation policies*. Our conversation layer currently embeds specific conversation policies as finite-state automata. These automata define and enforce the correctness of specific interactions between two agents. Each such interaction pertains to some specific subtask required during the execution of a task. Currently, InfoSleuth supports only pairwise conversations.

The conversation layer and its conversation policies act as an intermediary between the local agent and the remote agent, governing the correctness of the interactions between them. We currently have a state machine defined for each end of the conversation - the initiator end and the responder end. This is because the conversation layer is managing both the interactions with the remote agent (sending and/or receiving of a message) and interactions with the "local" agent (the application built upon the shell). Each end of the conversation has different interactions with the local agent, so the two state machines are different.

In Figure 1, we show the state machine associated with an *ask* conversation. The interactions with the remote agent are shown as "external view, shared". However, when the conversation is actually in the middle state, internally the agent that received the ask is itself holding a "sub-conversation" with its application level. This we label "internal view, local". In fact, the state machine we support replaces this middle state in the external view with the state machine in the internal view.

2.2 Conversation Policies

Many exchanges of messages reduce at the agent communication level to exchanges of requests (*asks*) and assertions (*tells*) [9]. However, the basic communicative acts may have different nuances of meaning depending on the semantics of the activity associated with the conversation; and thus it is often useful to develop a richer set of speech acts (e.g., *recommend, subscribe*).

A relatively small number of different conversation types are required to support the diverse and rich set of tasks that InfoSleuth can do. InfoSleuth supports three equivalence classes of conversation policies, shown in Figure 2. In these state machines, we have only represented the part of the state machine that is dealing with the transmission and receipt of messages between the two agents. Additionally, the state machines describe only the subset of the conversation policy that describes correct operation. We handle unexpected situations using *extensions*, described in the next section.

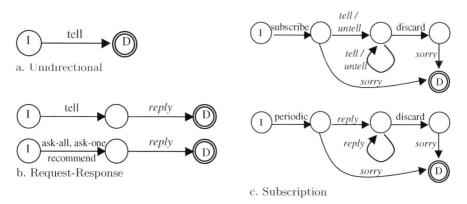

Fig. 2. Conversation types. In these figures, the start state is denoted by an "I", and the final state is denoted by a double circle and a "D". Other states are empty circles. Transmission of a message from the conversation initiator to a responder is denoted by the name of the performative type in standard font. The transmission of a message back to the conversation initiator is denoted by the name of the performative, in italics.

Unidirectional (Fig. 2a): This conversation type consists of a single message from the initiator to the responder. This is a non-robust transmission, useful for logging and monitoring.

Request-Response (Fig. 2b): This conversation type consists of a single message transmitted from the requester to responder, and a single response being returned as an acknowledgment, answer, or notification.

Subscription (Fig. 2c): This conversation type consists of a single request, followed by a stream of responses. It is terminated with a discard.

These three conversation classes show some of the different issues associated with conversation policies. Are the two request-response automata representative of the same conversation policy? How about the two subscription conversations? In InfoSleuth, conversations are represented as finite-state automata, where the initial performative determines the conversation policy to use [10]. Thus, the request-response conversations follow the same policy, because the only difference between the two automata is the initiating performative. The two subscription automata, however, must be expressed as different policies, because in one case, each reply can be either a `tell` or an `untell`, while in the other case it must be a `reply`. The two subscription conversation policies must be distinguished by the initiating performative. This may be accomplished by defining a distinct speech act for each type of subscription, but may also be accomplished by augmenting the performative with distinguishing information. For InfoSleuth we prefer the latter approach, as it does not require a different message type for each conversation policy.

2.3   Conversation Policy Requirements

During the implementation of conversation policies in InfoSleuth, specific definitional requirements have emerged.

Deterministic: The finite state automaton must have a single start state and only one arc leading from a single state for a single receipt or transmission of a given performative type.

Semantically meaningful: Different states must be used where the semantics of the conversation differ, even if structurally the states would be the same. In particular, conversations must distinguish the different types of correct and error end states.

Correct: The finite state automaton must admit only the message exchanges that are correct and no others. We note that, for instance, [11] contains some automata that do not follow this rule.

Robust to errors: To be robust to errors, the conversation policy must allow error information to be passed at any time. It must have a locally-generated error state and a remotely-generated error state, as the response to each is different. These error states must also be distinct from the correct end state for the conversation. We will discuss errors further in the next section.

Robust to premature termination: The conversation policy must be robust to communication or agent failure. When there is a communication or agent failure, all members of the conversation should be able to detect where in the conversation the failure occurred, and have a deterministic recovery path (either forwards or backwards).

The issues associated with robustness to premature termination arise when an agent community must take into account its operating environment and/or community. One distinguishing feature of agent communities is the potential for agents to enter and leave, even in the midst of conversations with other members in the community. The issues associated with preliminary and unexpected termination of conversations also arise if the underlying communications infrastructure has the potential to fail.

Clearly, when an agent ceases to participate in a conversation, there must be some mechanism within the agent system to detect this situation, figure out the specifics of the failure, and effect a recovery. There are two basic approaches:

1. Assume that the community has a conversation monitoring and control center, that can examine all of the conversations as they are being executed, note any failures, and notify the remaining agents of the state of the conversation at the time of the failure.

2. Ensure that the conversation policies encode enough communication that each agent in the conversation has a notion of the global state of the conversation at all times. Then, when there is a possibility of a failure in the conversation, the agents involved in the conversation can follow a predetermined policy for locating and recovering from the failure.

Since we believe that no approach to conversations that is geared towards having interoperable agent communities should make assumptions about the composition of an agent community, we prefer the second approach. Therefore, the robustness requirements will have an impact on the structure of the finite state automaton. Specifically, we believe that the minimum requirement is that all agents must know about all other agents that are participating in the conversation, and their roles. Thus, if the conversation is expanding beyond two agents, then each of the agents currently involved in the conversation must be notified of the new agent entering the conversation, before the agent can actually enter the conversation. Consider, for instance, the structure found in Figure 3, where the "smiley faces" represent agents and the arrows represent messages:

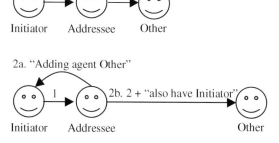

Fig. 3. Non-robust and robust conversation structures among more than two agents

On the left-hand side, if the Addressee (receiver of the initial message) fails, the Initiator has no means to contact Other and vice versa. Similarly, if message 2 is the last message of the Addressee, and Other fails, the Initiator cannot locate the point of failure. On the right-hand side, Addressee first notifies Initiator that it is adding Other to the conversation, then as it passes on message 2 it notifies Other if the identity of the Initiator. In case of the failure of any agent, they all know who the other agents are in the conversation, so they can query the other agents for the information needed to pinpoint the failure and effect a recovery.

2.4   Conversation Individuation and Enforcement

When a set of agents starts a conversation, it is important that they all agree on exactly what conversation policy they are using. Once this has been done each agent then needs to enforce the correctness of the actual execution of the conversation against the policy. An implementation of conversation management must meet the following requirements to support correct individuation and enforcement of conversations.

Conversation Policy Identification: With respect to prescriptive conversations, the initial performative in the conversation should define to the other agents what policy is being used. In the past, we used the speech act, or message type itself, to define this policy. This approach requires defining the speech acts in terms of the conversations they initiate. It requires a different message type for each conversation, which may not be semantically intuitive. Alternatively, the initial performative for a conversation may be annotated with the name of the policy being used.

Conversation Identification: Conversation identification is an issue that is usually ignored in ACLs. For example, KQML supports the chaining of messages using the `:reply-with` and `:in-reply-to` fields, which are predicated on a request-response model. Therefore, one would have trouble chaining together messages in conversations that do not follow that model. In InfoSleuth, we use the `:reply-with` field of the conversation-initiating performative as the conversation id. The FIPA specification also supports a `conversation-id` slot.

Message Ordering: Conversations with multiple messages add complexity and versatility to communication between agents but it creates the problem of message ordering. To determine if a particular conversation is legal given a policy it should follow, the agent receiving a stream of messages for that conversation should validate and process them in the order that they were sent. Thus, for conversation policies to be enforced properly in a system where lower layers of an agent architecture do not guarantee the preservation of ordering during the transmission of messages, the messages themselves must contain sufficient information to recreate that order as they are received.

3   Extending Conversations

In the previous section, we presented a set of requirements for conversation policies. In this section, we discuss the use of a set of state-based components to extend basic conversation policies. The components are useful in specifying how to handle premature, deviant, or extended interactions between agents.

We believe that a component-based approach to extending conversation policies is a good one for several reasons. First, applying the same extension to multiple conversations gives their response a similar "look and feel" in a similar situation (e.g., the same unexpected event occurs). Second, desirable properties of the components will carry over easily into the extended conversation. Third, an agent community with a common set of basic building blocks can declare how these are put together in a specific conversation without having to hard-code all of the potential variants.

Our basic building blocks are the unidirectional, request-response and subscription conversation policies described in the previous section. We describe two methods of extending conversations, *extension* and *concatenation*. In extension, a single conversation policy is composed with a specific and correct conversation fragment. This fragment may be used to extend multiple conversations in a consistent manner, usually by defining new transitions from internal states. For example, extensions are used for discarding a conversation when the initiator wants to terminate it before its natural conclusion. In concatenation, two conversations are put together back-to-back to form a larger conversation, with a single correct end state of the first conversation being identified with the initial state of the second conversation. For example, an agent in a market-based community may require a conversation in which it negotiates over a price before it asks for some information, effectively preceding an *ask* conversation by a *negotiate* conversation. We have experimented with extensions in our current work, and plan to investigate the use of concatenation in the future.

3.1   Conversation Extension

Extension is the process of expanding the scope of a conversation by enriching the transitions that can occur in the middle of a conversation. We foresee extensions as a useful way to codify the generic handling of unexpected or deviant conditions across classes of conversation policies. There are several types of standard extensions that appear to hold across multiple conversation policies. These include:

1. Handling of locally-generated errors by sending an error message to the other agent.
2. Handling of remotely-generated errors by receiving an error performative.
3. Discarding a conversation, e.g. when an agent does not want to wait for a reply.

InfoSleuth handles errors and discards by defining a standard set of extensions that can be added to conversations for these specific functions. Extensions enrich the transitions that can happen from the internal (non-initial and non-terminal) states of the finite-state automaton associated with the conversation. For example, the error extension enforces that any agent can send or receive an error performative at any time, and that these will put the conversation into the local or remote error states. An example showing the discard and error extensions is given in Figure 4.

Given our assumption that extensions are used to specify the common handling of unexpected or deviant occurrences across multiple conversation policies, we do not believe that conversations such as the "discardable ask conversation with error" should be captured as an explicit conversation policy in an agent community. Rather, we believe that these extensions should be added "on the fly" by the agents' conversation management layer as the differing situations arise. This belief is enhanced by the observation that, in the example above, the explicit extension process is not commutative.

Given that two agents that can extend conversations start out with the base conversation and adapt as needed, the question arises as to how the agents can know whether both agents can handle a specific extension. Clearly, in a specific conversation instance, the set of allowable extensions is the intersection of the set the initiator can handle and the set the responder can handle. One approach is to have the initiating agent specify its allowable extensions in the conversation-initiating performative. The responder can then determine if it can handle all of those extensions, and respond accordingly. Alternatively, and given the assumption that the error extension is handled by all agents in the community, one can assume that if one of the agents tries to extend the conversation using an extension that cannot be handled by the other agent, it returns an error. A third approach would be to assume that the community has a broker that knows which extensions each agent can handle, and both reasons over and returns extension information. We have yet to experiment with these alternatives enough to understand the practical ramifications of each.

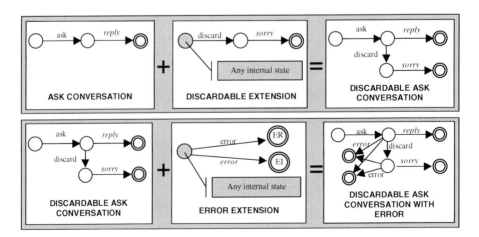

Fig. 4. Conversation Extension: ASK + DISCARDABLE + ERROR

Extension differs from the inheritance methods proposed by [12], in that the extensions are predefined and applicable to multiple other conversations. One merely begins with a complete conversation, and the additions necessary to make it a new, complete conversation. Extending a conversation to allow it to be discardable, for instance, is an activity applicable to any type of conversation that can extend over a long period of time.

3.2   Conversation Concatenation

Conversation concatenation is the gluing together of two conversations by identifying the (single) correct final state of the first conversation with the initial state of the second conversation. With concatenation, the agent that is the addressee of the message that causes the conversation to enter the correct done state is the same as the initiating agent in the second conversation. An example of this is shown in the Figure 5, where a *negotiation* conversation is initiated, which leads directly into an *ask* conversation if a proposal is accepted. The final state of the negotiation, entered on accepting the proposal, becomes the begin state of the ask conversation. A second example is shown for a *standby* conversation that leads into a *stream-all*, similar to the one described in [11].

The following guidelines are appropriate for a conversation that can have another conversation appended to it:

– The first conversation must have a unique final state indicating success.
– The conversations that are to be concatenated must be represented in the initiating message of the first conversation.

With respect to the second point, given the approach that the initiating performative defines the conversation policy being used, concatenation naturally corresponds to the nesting of that performative. For instance, in the example of the *negotiated ask*, the `cfp` performative initiating the conversation has a nested `ask` performative, defining the request that is being negotiated over (and, consequently, the conversation being concatenated on the end of the negotiate). Similarly, the `stream-all` nested within the `standby` request defines the *stream-all* conversation that is being concatenated onto the end of the *standby* conversation.

3.3   Expanding Beyond Initiator-Responder Conversations

In InfoSleuth, as our supported set of task types increases, "initiator-responder" conversations have proved limiting, and we have explored the following ways to expand our supported conversation types. All of the following conversation structures are currently being experimented with.

Multicast and Broadcast: Multicast is the ability to specify multiple responders for a single conversation. This can be handled as m initiator-responder conversations, one for each of the m responders.

Broadcast is the ability to send a conversation to an unknown set of responders. In this case, the initiator broadcasts the conversation-initiating performative, waits for a period of time to collect all the timely responders (say there are

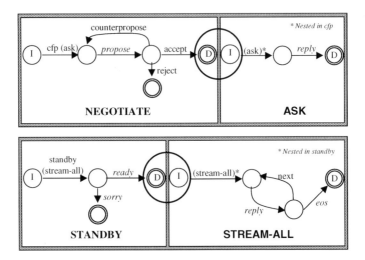

Fig. 5. A negotiated ask conversation, and a standby stream-all conversation

n of them), then holds n initiator-responder conversations from that point on. Thus, conversations are effectively individuated when the responder responds to the initial broadcast, as opposed to when the initiator sends the first message.

Forwarding and Delegation: Delegation allows an agent to respond to an initiating performative by recommending a different agent to respond to the conversation. Forwarding allows the responder to reroute the initiating message to another agent that might handle the message better. Figure 6 describes the delegation pattern and two different forwarding patterns. In this figure, the "smiley faces" represent agents and the arrows represent speech acts. The order in which the arrows are numbered indicates the sequences in which the messages are sent. Note that the three different delegation and forwarding conversation structures in Figure 6 correspond to the conversation structures used in facilitation for matchmaking, recruiting, and brokering, respectively.

Delegation is useful, for instance, if the initial responder is overloaded or is going down. In this case, the *ask* conversation with the first addressee is a distinct conversation from the *ask* conversation to the second addressee. However, to allow delegation, we need to add a delegatable extension to our list of conversation extensions. This is shown in Figure 7. This approach, which allows an addressee to end an *ask* conversation with a `delegate` response, also allows agents in the community to delegate multiple times, as needed.

The forwarding pattern shown in the center box of Figure 6 is not robust to failure, as it does not meet the robustness criteria described in the previous section. Therefore we do not use it. The forwarding pattern in the right-hand box is more robust, though it still does not meet the criteria unless one considers messages 1 and 4 to form one conversation, and messages 2 and 3 to form a second conversation. Concatenation does not work here. This is consistent with the distinction between tasks and conversations made in the Introduction, because the decision to forward probably cannot be done in the generic shell in any general way.

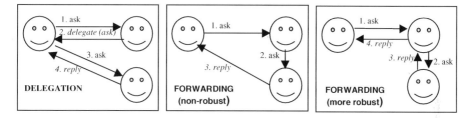

Fig. 6. Delegation and forwarding methods

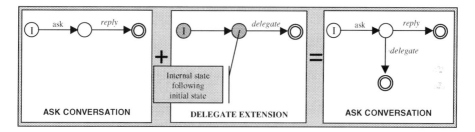

Fig. 7. Delegated ask conversation

Monitoring and Logging: In a system where agents can monitor and/or log traffic from other agents, a monitoring agent serves as an additional listener to the conversation traffic. In this case, information about the messages being sent is forwarded to the monitoring agent, but we do not assume that the transmission of monitoring messages must be robust. Monitoring agents may request status about a conversation, but this activity is adjunct to the actual execution of the conversation. Because of the adjunct and non-robust nature of these interactions, we do not recommend that these activities be a part of an actual conversation policy.

4   Related Work

4.1   Structural Support for Conversations

The use of finite state machines to define conversation policies has been described previously, for instance Barbuceanu and Fox [13,14], Kuwabara et. al. [12,15], Winograd and Flores [16], Nodine and Unruh [10], and Bradshaw et.al. [17].

FIPA [3] is incorporating structural support for conversations as well as speech acts into its standardization effort.

There are two separate models of state-based conversation policies. One, exemplified by Barbuceanu and Fox [13], uses the arcs to represent transmission or receipt of a message. This approach requires two different agents engaging in different ends in the same conversation to use two different finite state automata. However, it does not constrain who sent/received the message beyond the local view, so different agents may participate in the conversation at the other end. This makes delegation easier. The second, exemplified by Bradshaw et al. [18], represents the conversation from an external view, where each agent takes a role and the conversations are expressed in terms of the roles. For example, the state machine might imply, "the requester sends an ask-all message to the responder". This approach has the advantage that the same state machine can be used by all agents involved in the conversation. In AgenTalk, Kuwabara et al. [12] uses inheritance as a mechanism for extending a finite state automaton to support new conversations. A conversation is specified as a set of states with a distinguished initial state, a set of state transition rules, a set of local script functions which are invoked when certain events occur (such as entry into a new state), and a conversation that you inherit from. The conversation extends the one it is inherited from by adding new states and/or new transitions, and/or overriding existing states and transitions with new ones.

Other approaches include the use of enhanced Dooley graphs [19] to describe conversational structure. Dooley graphs capture some unique relationships among speech acts, and span both conversations and tasks as we have defined them in the paper. Cost et al. [20] describe an agent shell for which conversation policies may be declaratively specified, and then interpreted. They have also explored the use of colored petri nets to specify conversations [21]. Smith et.al. [22] show how to use joint intention semantics to analyze conversation policies for consistency, and to suggest how policies may be combined.

4.2   Message Support for Enforcing Conversation Structure

KQML [2] provides some basic message support for conversations. KQML performatives have an implied "message layer" that encodes the speech act as well as :reply-with and :in-reply-to fields that enable it to be linked to earlier performatives that participated in the same conversation. There is also an implied "communication layer" that encodes useful parameters such as :sender and :receiver. FIPA [3] also covers this message support.

Barbuceanu and Fox [13] further propose extending messages to contain an :intent slot to define which conversation structure to use in understanding the message. Nodine and Chandrasekara [23] propose a :conversation-id slot for identifying the messages pertaining to a specific conversation, especially needed when the conversation does not follow a request-reply paradigm. A similar mechanism is proposed within FIPA.

5   Conclusions

This paper discusses the robust construction of conversation policies for dynamic agent communities. We discuss conversation implementation in InfoSleuth, including the incorporation of a *conversation layer* in the agents' *generic shell*; and the separation of conversation management with the remote agent from conversational interactions with the local agent. InfoSleuth separates tasks from conversations, using the algorithm that continuance of a conversation is controlled by the generic agent shell, while starting a new conversation for a task in response to some other conversation requires decisions on the part of the agent-specific code.

InfoSleuth uses finite-state automata to represent conversation policies, and augments the first performative in a conversation (the "conversation-initiating performative") with information sufficient to determine which policy to use. We define classes of conversation policies that share the same basic structure, and differ only in that they have different speech acts in their conversation-initiating performative. In addition to supporting specific policies, we require each conversation to be identifiable, and the messages in the conversation to be explicitly reorderable in case of ordering problems during transport.

In this paper, our basic conversation policies define only correct operation. We have implemented a mechanism for composing a conversation with an appropriate *extension* when deviant or unforeseen events happen that affect the conversation. Examples of extension include `errors`, `discards`, and *delegation*. We also support a notion of composing different basic conversations together into a more complex conversation using *concatenation*. This allows us, for instance, to do negotiated asks, achieves, tells, etc. It also allows us to do a standby with respect to some other conversation, such as an ask. Both extension and concatenation can be described formally, based on the underlying finite-state representation of the conversation.

There are a number of directions in which we plan to extend this work. These include support for declaratively-specifiable conversation policies; further work on conversation concatenation; and exploration of the types of knowledge required to do task planning based on conversational building blocks.

Acknowledgments. We would like to thank the InfoSleuth group, and in particular Damith Chandrasekara, for their contributions to the ideas and work in this paper.

References

1. T. Finin et al. Specification of the KQML agent communication language. Technical Report 92-04, Enterprise Integration Technologies, Inc., 1992.
2. T. Finin et al. KQML as an agent communication language. In J.M. Bradshaw, editor, *Software Agents*. AAAI Press, 1997.
3. FIPA. <http://www.fipa.org>, 1998.

4. M. Nodine, J. Fowler, and B. Perry. Active information gathering in InfoSleuth. In *Proc. Int'l Symposium on Cooperative Database Systems for Advanced Applications*, 1999.
5. R. Bayardo et al. Semantic integration of information in open and dynamic environments. In *Proc. ACM SIGMOD Int'l Conference on Management of Data*, 1997.
6. A. Unruh, G. Martin, and B. Perry. Getting only what you want: Data mining and event detection using InfoSleuth agents. Technical report, MCC, 1998.
7. J. Fowler, M. Nodine, B. Perry, and B. Bargmeyer. Agent-based semantic interoperability in InfoSleuth. *SIGMOD Record*, 28, 1999.
8. M. Greaves, H. Holback, and J. Bradshaw. What is a conversation policy? In *AA-99 Workshop on Specifying and Implementing Conversation Policies*, 1999.
9. I. Smith and P. Cohen. Toward a semantics for an agent communications language based on speech-acts. In *Proc. Thirteenth National Conference on Artificial Intelligence*, pages 24–31. AAAI, AAAI Press/The MIT Press, 1996.
10. M. Nodine and A. Unruh. Facilitating open communication in agent systems. In M. Singh, A. Rao, and M. Wooldridge, editors, *Intelligent Agents IV: Agent Theories, Architectures, and Languages*. Springer-Verlag, 1998.
11. Labrou Y. *Semantics for an Agent Communication Language*. PhD thesis, UMBC, Sep 1996.
12. K. Kuwabara, T. Ishida, and N. Osato. AgenTalk: Describing multiagent coordination protocols with inheritance. In *Proc. IEEE Conference on Tools with Artificial Intelligence*, pages 460–465, 1995.
13. M. Barbuceanu and M. Fox. COOL: A language for describing coordination in multi-agent systems. In *Proc. Int'l Conference on Multi-Agent Systems*, 1995.
14. M. Barbuceanu. Coordinating agents by role based social constraints and conversation plans. In *Proc. National Conference on Artificial Intelligence*, pages 16–21, 1997.
15. K. Kuwabara. Agentalk: Coordination protocol description for multi-agent systems. In *Proc. Int'l Conference on Multi-Agent Systems*, 1995.
16. T. Winograd and F. Flores. *Understanding Computers and Cognition*. Addison-Wesley, 1996.
17. J. M. Bradshaw et al. Mediating representations for an agent design toolkit. In *Proc. Knowledge Acquisition Workshop*, 1998.
18. J. M. Bradshaw. Kaos: An open agent architecture supporting reuse, interoperability, and extensibility. In *Knowledge Acquisition for Knowledge-Based Systems Workshop*, 1996.
19. H. V. D. Parunak. Visualizing agent conversations: Using enhanced dooley graphs for agent design and analysis. In *Proc. Int'l Conference on Multi-Agent Systems*, pages 275–282, 1996.
20. R. S. Cost et al. Jackal: a java-based tool for agent development. In *AAAI-98 Workshop on Software Tools for Developing Agents*, 1998.
21. R. S. Cost et al. Modeling agent conversations with colored petri nets. In *AA-99 Workshop on Specifying and Implementing Conversation Policies*, 1999.
22. I. Smith et al. Designing conversation policies using joint intention theory. In *Proc. Int'l Conference on Multi-Agent Systems*, pages 269–276, 1998.
23. M. Nodine and D. Chandrasekhara. Agent communication languages for information-centric agent communities. In *Proc. Hawaii Int'l Conference on System Sciences*, 1999.

Conversation Oriented Programming
for Agent Interaction

Mihai Barbuceanu and Wai-Kau Lo

Enterprise Integration Laboratory
University of Toronto,
4 Taddle Creek Road, Rosebrugh Building,
Toronto, Ontario, Canada, M5S 3G9
{mihai, wklo}@eil.utoronto.ca

Abstract. Conversations are an agent programming abstraction intended to represent models of interaction among agents and to support the execution of these models in multi-agent environments. In this paper we review a conversational coordination language we have designed and used in the past few years, to characterize its main assumptions, strengths and limitations. Based on this analysis we discuss a number of major new features and extensions for our next generation conversational coordination language.

1 Introduction

It has recently been argued that *coordination knowledge* is a specific form of knowledge dealing with the social know-how that enables agents to interact successfully in collective problem solving [Jennings 92]. If this is true, agent research needs to come up with models, formalisms and languages able to represent coordination knowledge, use coordination knowledge in problem solving and acquire coordination knowledge, statically and dynamically, during agent interaction.

In our previous work [Barbuceanu & Fox 96,Barbuceanu & Fox 97] we have proposed *conversations* as an *agent programming abstraction* addressing the above issues, and we have tried to consolidate the conversation concept into a practical language design and implementation (the language is named COOL, from COOrdination Language). In this paper we review the current state of this conversational technology and on this basis propose a number of substantial improvements to it.

2 Review of Current Technology

The most important concept of our conversational coordination language is the *conversation plan* (CP). Conversation plans describe and guide the interaction among agents by specifying the *process* by which agents exchange messages and change their state. A CP specifies a number of composing conversation rules, their control mechanism and the local data-base that maintains the state of

F. Dignum and M. Greaves (Eds.): Agent Communication, LNAI 1916, pp. 220–234, 2000.
© Springer-Verlag Berlin Heidelberg 2000

```
(def-conversation-plan 'customer-conversation
  :content-language 'list
  :speech-act-language 'kqml
  :initial-state 'start
  :final-states '(rejected failed satisfied)
  :control 'interactive-choice-control-ka
  :rules '((start cc-1)
           (proposed cc-13 cc-2)
           (working cc-5 cc-4 cc-3)
           (counterp cc-9 cc-8 cc-7 cc-6)
           (asked cc-10 )
           (accepted cc-12 cc-11)))
```

Fig. 1. Customer-conversation.

the conversation. The latter consists of a set of variables whose persistent values (maintained for the entire duration of the conversation) are manipulated by conversation rules. Conversation rules are indexed on states, allowing a graph representation where nodes represent states and arcs rule-driven transitions amongst states.

Figure 1 shows the textual representation of a CP for a Customer's agent interaction with a Logistics agent in one supply chain application. Figure 2 shows the same customer conversation in graph form, on the left side, and, on the right, a matching CP executed by the Logistics agent while talking to the Customer. The graph G corresponding to a CP is $G = (S, T)$, where S is a set of CP states and $T \subset S^2$ is the set of transitions. $(v, t) \in T$ iff there exists a conversation rule with v as the current state and t as the next state. CPs must be connected in that all states must be reachable through directed edges from the (single) initial state.

Each of these CPs describes the interaction from the viewpoint of its agent. There is no central plan holding the moves of all interlocutors. The interaction process starts with the Customer proposing an order for Logistics to execute, after which it goes to state proposed. Logistics receives the order, acknowledges it and goes to order-received. The acknowledgment makes the Customer go to state working. From state order-received, Logistics starts working on the requested order by first decomposing it into sub-activities (order-decomposed), then retrieving and ranking the manufacturing agents (contractors) that may take over the execution of different sub-activities (in state contractors-ranked) after which it starts negotiating with the contractors the execution of the work.

This negotiation takes place in separate conversations between Logistics and each contractor. These conversations are spawned from the shown conversation (see later), and are run while the Customer is waiting in state working. If the negotiation ends successfully (Logistics has been able to assemble a team of contractors for the order) Logistics informs the Customer that it will accept the order. When receiving this message, the Customer goes to state accepted.

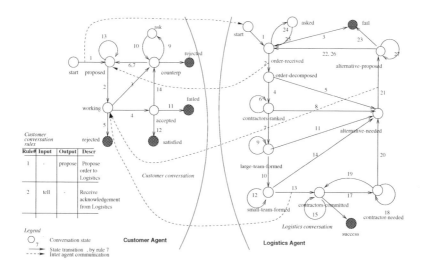

Fig. 2. Interacting Customer and Logistics conversation plans.

`Logistics` then continues with kicking off the execution of work by contractors (`contractors-committed`) and with monitoring the work. If all contractors finish their work, `Logistics` goes to state `success` and informs `Customer` about the successful termination of the work, which determines the `Customer` to go to state `satisfied`. If one or more contractors can not finish their work, `Logistics` tries first to replace it (`contractor-needed`) and, if this is not possible, renegotiates the work with the customer. Work renegotiation with the customer also takes place when the team of contractors can not be formed (`alternative-needed` and `alternative-proposed`). In the case of work renegotiation, after receiving the new work proposal from `Logistics`, the `Customer` goes to state `counterp` where it decides whether to reject it, ask clarification questions about it or accept it (in this case going to `proposed` from where a new cycle starts).

The execution state of a CP is maintained in *actual conversations*. An actual conversation is an object that stores the current state of the conversation, the actual values of the conversation's variables and historical information accumulated during conversation execution. Each agent taking part in a conversation owns and has sole control of an actual conversation representing the execution of the agent's CP in that conversation. Since different agents that take part in a conversation may use different CPs, the structure of each actual conversation may be different for each agent.

Conversation rules describe the actions that can be performed when the conversation is in a given state. In figure 1, when the conversation is in the `working` state, rules `cc-5`, `cc-4` and `cc-3` can be executed. Which of them actually gets executed and how depends on the matching and application strategy of the conversation's control mechanism (the `:control` slot). Typically, we execute the

```
(def-conversation-rule 'lep-1
  :current-state 'start
  :received '(propose :sender customer
                      :content (customer-order
                                 :has-line-item ?li))
  :next-state 'order-received
  :transmit '(tell :sender ?agent
                   :receiver customer
                   :content '(working on it)
                   :conversation ?convn)
        :do '(update-var ?conv '?order ?message))
```

Fig. 3. Conversation rule.

first matching rule in the definition order, but this can be changed by plugging another rule interpreter.

The rule in figure 3 states that when Logistics, in state start, receives a proposal for an order, it informs the sender (Customer) that it has started working on the proposal and goes to state order-received. We use pattern matching in the :received slot, which makes the coordination language *independent* on the syntactic details of the communication language, as long as communication language expressions can be described in the pattern language. This is why we can use liberal forms of KQML [Finin et al 92] or the FIPA ACL [FIPA] for communication. Other components include:

1. *Error recovery rules* (not illustrated) specifying how incompatibilities (caused by planning errors or unexpected execution events) among the state of a conversation and the incoming messages are handled: by changing the state, discarding inputs, changing the plan, starting new conversations, etc.

2. *Dynamic vertical composition* This is a control mechanism allowing a conversation to be suspended (with preserved state), other conversation to proceed and the suspended conversation to be resumed when certain conditions related to the agent environment and conversations are satisfied. It is up to the CP of the suspended conversation to inform the partner(s) that the conversation has been suspended. This form of dynamic spawning of a sub-conversation gives us a first form of conversation *composition* from sub-conversations. The mechanism is equivalent to having a conversation execute inside a state of another conversation. We call this *vertical composition*, to distinguish it from a form of horizontal composition to be described later on.

3. A *hierarchical organization* of conversations (rooted in an *initial conversation* every agent starts in) and allowing parent conversations to control the execution of child conversations.

4. A more complex *typology of rules* including various forms of event/condition triggered rules. In particular *time-out* rules are automatically triggered at given time intervals, and *on-entry* and *on-exit* rules are triggered whenever states are entered or exited.

5. A notion of *incomplete* conversation rule. This contains incomplete specifications of conditions, actions or both. The system does not try to apply incomplete rules itself. Rather, upon encountering such rules, it pops up a visual interface providing tools for the users to decide themselves if and which rules should
be applied and also to edit rules on the fly, for example by specifying a message to
be transmitted or a different condition to be tested [Barbuceanu & Fox 96]. This
is in the same time a debugging and an acquisition aid, allowing users to take
over the execution of critical segments of conversations and refine coordination
knowledge dynamically, in the execution context.

To conclude the above discussion we can now give a formal definition of the
main components of the framework. A conversation plan P is a tuple:

$P = < S, T, s_0, F, L, R, D, A >$ where

- S is a set of states.
- $T \subset S^2$ is the set of transitions.
- $s_0 \in S$ is the initial state, from which all states are accessible following the
  transitions.
- $F \subset S$ is the set of final states.
- R is a set of rules.
- $L \subset R \times T$ is the transition labeling relation, associating rules with the
  transitions they apply to.
- $D = D_1 \times D_2 \times ...D_n$ represents the data base of the conversation. The data
  base consists of n variables, D_i is the domain of the ith variable.
- A is the set of actions available to rules. A^* is the set of all finite sequences
  of actions from A.
- $r \in R$ (a rule) is described as a function $r : D_r \times S \rightarrow A^* \times S$ where $D_r \subset D$.

3   Horizontal Componentization

Human conversations are very flexible. If a message can not be understood, e.g.
due to unknown terms, humans can easily start clarification sub-dialogues. If
expected messages are delayed, parties find ways of signaling this and/or acting
on default assumptions. The current architecture can handle these problems in
a limited fashion. Timeout rules can deal with delays, and error handling rules
can deal with incomprehensible or unexpected messages. The limitation stems
from the fact that with the current architecture these problems can be addressed
only by adding special timeout and/or error rules to all states that need them -
practically to many or even all states in a CP.

For example, if a message contains a term that is not known to the recipient, a clarification sub-conversation can be created for dealing with this term.
The term must be sent to the clarification sub-conversation in an explicit message, together with any necessary context information. After the clarification
sub-conversation terminates, a known term, replacing the unknown one, has to
be sent back with another explicit message. Since unknown terms may appear
anytime in a conversation, the conversation plan needs to have rules for spawning the clarification sub-conversation and for communicating with it from any

of its states. This results in CPs that are unnecessarily complex, hard to write, understand and maintain.

A simpler way to address problems like the above, without adding the above complexity, is to extend the notion of conversation in a manner allowing several conversation plans to be simultaneously used within a single conversation. For example, suppose we have a special CP for carrying out a word clarification conversation. This should be available to any other CP in the context of which such a problem may arise, with minimal overhead for explicitly testing for the problem, spawning the clarification CP and synchronizing with its termination.

To allow for this capability, we extend the system in the following ways. First, we define a new relation between CPs. A CP P1 has another CP P2 as a *friend* if P2 may be needed during P1's execution. As friends, P1 and P2 have read and write access to some of each other's variables and they share the same message queue. To define which local variables can be shared we extend the CP specification to allow for specifying *private* variables - to which only the CP has access, *protected* variables - to which all friend CPs have access, and *public* variables - to which all CP-s have access. (This is similar to visibility rules in OO languages like Java and C++).

Second, (actual) conversations are extended to hold the execution state of a CP and of all its friends (included in the transitive closure of the *friend* relation).

Another way to look at this is to consider all CPs that are friends with each other as forming an extended CP. If $\{G_1, ...G_n\}$ are the graphs representing each CPs friendly with each other, the extended CP behaves as if described by the sum of G_1 to G_n, $ExtendedCP = (S_1 \cup S_2... \cup S_n, T_1 \cup T_2... \cup T_n)$. In an extended CP, the current state is a subset of the Cartesian product of S_1 to S_n. At execution, if the current state is $s = (s_1, ...s_j, ...s_n)$, the system will try to activate (in an unspecified order) one rule indexed on any of the states $\{s_1, ...s_n\}$. If the successfully activated rule is doing the transition (s_j, s'_j) in the jth component, then the new current state becomes $s' = (s_1, ...s'_j, ...s_n)$.

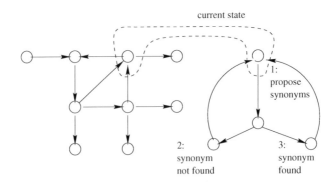

Main CP: *Customer conversation*   Secondary CP: *Word clarification*

Fig. 4. Extended CP with main and secondary components.

Suppose now (figure 4) that we have an extended CP composed of a main CP dealing with the main purpose of the interaction and a secondary CP devoted to handling clarification dialogues. When the main CP can not understand a term, it will set a special protected data base variable to the term itself. Having this variable set is part of the condition of a rule in the initial state of the secondary CP - this is why they need to be declared as friends, to access each other's variables. When the variable is set, a secondary CP rule is activated and starts the clarification dialogue, for example by determining if any of a list o synonyms represents the unknown term. When done, the special variable is set to the discovered synonym or to *nil* if none was found and the secondary CP goes back to its initial state (ready for another clarification round). The discovered synonym allows the main CP to continue the conversation using the new term. In this arrangement the two aspects work together seamlessly. The main conversation only signals the problematic term, without explicitly spawning any other conversation or synchronizing with it. The clarification conversation does its work behind the scene to reestablish consistency.

By defining the *friend* relation, the system knows which other CPs can be included in the execution of a given CP (and can statically check references to variables). As all friendly CPs share variables at run time, communication and synchronization overheads are minimized. The existence of friends simplifies a CP's definition because the problem resolution strategy does not have to be discovered and explicitly activated by the main CP. (E.g. the above example would work the same with more than one clarification CP, and the main CP would not need be aware which clarification CP has done the job). From the efficiency perspective, if the friends relation is implemented in a *lazy* (least commitment) way, only the needed friends of a CP would be active at any time, so no unnecessary run time overhead would be incurred.

The friend relation partitions a set of CPs into a disjoint collection of extended CPs. At execution, each extended CP has an associated actual conversation. This organization defines our second composition mechanism called *horizontal composition*. Here we do not execute a conversation *inside* a state of another conversation (as for *vertical composition*) but rather allow many CPs to be active in the same time, at the same level and sharing the same context.

4   Interface Definitions

A major design decision was to have individual and separate conversation plans for each agent rather than common plans prescribing all the possible moves of all participants, as done for example in [Medina-Mora et al 92].

The main advantage is the elimination of the middle agents that would have been required to manage the conversation moves of the participating agents. Such centralized management would be a problem in our language for several reasons. From the performance viewpoint, features like dynamic sub-conversation spawning and extended CPs would have to be supported by the middle agent for *all* participating agents. Moreover, as conversation rules make decisions based on

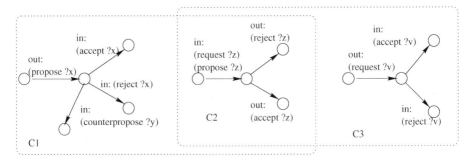

Compatible: C1 and C2, C2 and C3.   Incompatible: C1 and C3

Fig. 5. Interfaces showing compatibility and incompatibility of CPs.

the local state of agents and change it, the local state would have to be continuously passed to the middle agent and changes to it passed back to every participating agent (in particular, dealing with exceptions is heavily based on local state information). Both of these would create performance bottlenecks in a centralized implementation, affecting the scalability of the architecture.

From the expressiveness viewpoint, individual plans in our language allow for the number and identity of partners in a conversation to be determined dynamically. In our supply chain applications for example, the agents willing to participate in the execution of an order are dynamically determined. In our system, CPs involving dynamically determined partners often have the same code no matter how many participants are involved or who they are. Common plans as in [Medina-Mora et al 92] do not support this level of expressiveness. To add it would further complicate the implementation of the middle agents given the performance and scalability requirements they are subject to.

Finally, individual plans can be directly distributed over the Internet to the agents that need them. Web sites can be created to contain sets of compatible CPs for the various roles that agents need to play when interacting in business processes. Agents can download the CPs they need (e.g. vendors of some product types would download vendor specific CP-s and buyers of that product type buyer specific CPs) and then immediately start to interact on this basis. In a mediated architecture with common plans, agents would first have to find a mediator providing the desired plans for all participants, or have the mediator obtain them, only after that being able to interact.

One limitation of individual conversation plans is the impossibility to check in advance the compatibility of different conversation plans. Two CPs that two agents may use in a conversation are compatible if any message sent by one would find the other in a state where the message is expected and thus can be processed. If CPs are incompatible, agents may unexpectedly get stuck in the middle of an interaction without any hope of continuing the conversation. The current fix for the problem involves checking at the beginning of a conversation that both agents agree on the purpose of the conversation, which hopefully means they are using compatible CPs. This is done by having the initiating agent send a token identifying the conversation's purpose, which is checked by the accepting rule of the recipient's conversation. This solution works if there is prior agreement between agents about a set of conversation purposes.

A better solution is to introduce interface definitions for CPs. An interface definition is a CP *signature* computed from a CP by eliminating all edges (s_i, s_j) between which no messages are exchanged with another agent, and then merging the pairs of nodes between which there is no edge. The remaining edges are labeled with all the message patterns that can be received or transmitted during the transition represented by the edge. Given two such interface definitions of two CPs, it can be determined if every message sent from one CP will find an accepting state in the other one. Figure 5 gives examples of both compatible and incompatible CPs. This is not a proof of compatibility (rules contain procedural elements that make such proofs impossible), but offers a level of verification that is still useful, especially when agents have altered the CPs downloaded from consistent sources.

As shown by [Smith & Cohen 96], with a formally defined semantics of the communication language and a common plan representation it is possible to verify inter-agent communication. This is equally possible with signatures, because signatures can reconstruct common plans.

5   Group Conversations

Often we want to carry out conversations in a group, where any message sent by any member reaches every other member of the group. Some types of auctions for example are best viewed in this way. Groups may be created by a group leader, may be open to others to join or may be restricted in terms of who can join by explicit approval of the leader or in other ways (e.g. by limited group size). Members may temporarily leave the group conversation and may rejoin later on. When rejoining, members are updated as to the content of the conversation that took place in their absence. An agent rejoining an English auction for example may be updated about the bids that were made during its absence. Participation in groups may be subject to authentication. The exchanges occurring in group conversations may require group specific levels of security.

The introduction of these features require a number of extensions both at the level of the communication language and at the conversation level. The communication language needs to be extended with new message types for creating groups, leaving and (re)joining groups. At the conversational level, we need to support recording histories of interactions, secure communication, and authentication. A critical aspect of group communication is the ability to *guarantee* that any message sent to the group will reach *all* members, for which recent methods developed by distributed systems research can be used [CACM 96].

6   Adaptive Execution and Learning

The actions taken during a conversation have different *values* (according to various criteria) and different probabilities of success. If long duration of a conversation is costly, actions that take less time are more valuable. If obtaining a low price in a negotiation is important, then actions like choosing small increments for the offered price are more valuable. By estimating these values and considering the likelihood of success of actions, we can dynamically choose or order the next conversation move to improve on the desired effect of the conversation.

We can introduce a capability for such adaptive behavior by using decision theoretic mechanisms in our CPs. The basic element here is that conversations can be mapped to fully-observable, discrete-state Markov decision processes (MDP) [Bellman 57]. In this mapping, conversation states become MDP states and conversation rules become MDP actions. Let S be the set of states and A the set of actions of a conversation plan. For each action (rule) $a \in A$ we define the probability $P(s, a, t)$ that action a causes a transition to state t when applied in state s. In our framework, this probability quantifies the likelihood of the rule being applicable in state s and that of its execution being successful. For each action (rule), its reward (a real number) denotes the immediate utility of going from state s to state t by executing action a, and is written as $R(s, a, t)$. Since conversation plans operate for indefinite periods of time, we use the theory of infinite horizon MDPs. A (stationary) policy $\pi : s \to A$ describes the actions to be taken by the agent in each state. We assume that an agent accumulates the rewards associated with each transition it executes. To compare policies, we use the *expected total discounted reward* as the criterion to optimize. This criterion discounts future rewards by rate $0 \le \beta < 1$. For any state s, the value of a policy π is defined as:

$$V_\pi(s) = R(s, \pi(s), t) + \beta \sum_{t \in S} P(s, \pi(s), t) V_\pi(t)$$

The value of π at any state s can be computed by solving this system of linear equations. A policy π is optimal if $V_\pi(s) \ge V_{\pi'}(s)$ for all $s \in S$ and all policies π'. A simple algorithm for constructing the optimal policy is value iteration [Bellman 57], guaranteed to converge under the assumptions of infinite horizon discounted reward MDPs.

The application of this theory to conversation plans is illustrated in figure 6. With each rule number we show the probability and the reward associated to the rule. We use value iteration to actually order the rules in a state rather than just computing the best one. The result is the reordering of rules in each state according to how close they are to the optimal policy. Since the rules are tried in the order they are encountered, the optimal reordering guarantees that the system will always try the better behavior first. Of course, there are several reward structures corresponding to different criteria, like *solution accuracy* or *execution time*. To account for these, we produce a separate ordering for each criterion. Then a weighted combination of criteria is used to produce the final ordering. For example, if we have spent too much time in the current plan,

230   M. Barbuceanu and W.-K. Lo

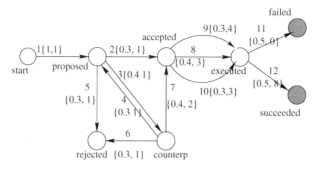

Ordering produced by value iteration: proposed: 2,3,5 accepted: 9, 8, 10
counterp: 7,4,6 executed: 12, 11

Fig. 6. Using value iteration to reorder rules.

when entering a new state we modify the global criterion giving *execution time* a greater weight. This dynamically reorders the rules in the current state, giving priority to a rule that saves time and thus achieving adaptive behavior of the agent. Finally, the same framework can be used in a learning mode, where the probabilities of transitions can be learned by Q-learning [Watkins &Dayan 92] methods from interactions. Agents can use this to learn the preferences of other agents and then adapt to these preferences.

7   Conversations on the Web

Conversations should be equally usable as a mechanism for interaction between human users and their agents. In such a setting, human users should be able to send messages to agents and receive replies within conversations, in the same way other agents can send and receive messages. Moreover, the Web should be the general medium for exchanging such messages. A user with a Web browser should be able to converse with an agent according to CP-s that the agent understands. On the human size, this interaction should look like any other Web based interaction - humans will not compose KQML or other agent communication language expressions. On the agent side, messages coming from humans should be like any message coming from any other agent.

We have already prototyped this sort of interaction in our new Java-based implementation of COOL, named JCOOL. The main idea is to introduce *user agents*, a type of agent that mediates the interaction between human users and functional agents in the system. User agents communicate with functional agents via conversations, as usual. For human interaction, they dynamically generate HTML pages and manage the interaction through Web browsers.

One of the applications we have built that illustrates the approach is a system that supports the QuickData Evaluation and QuickData Protocol specifications developed by the Electronic Component Information Exchange (ECIX)

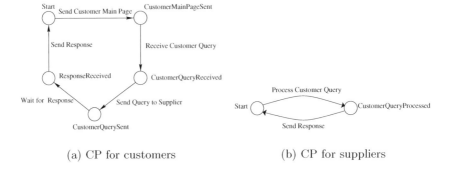

(a) CP for customers   (b) CP for suppliers

Fig. 7. Conversation plans for customers and suppliers

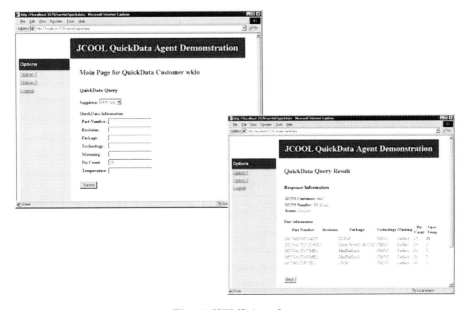

Fig. 8. HTML interfaces

project [Quickdata], designed to facilitate the creation, exchange and evaluation of electronic components information between supply chain partners. Using this system, (1) a consumer agent can send messages to relevant suppliers asking for information (such as package format and operating temperature) about specific electronic components, and (2) a supplier agent can reply to the query messages received from consumer agents.

To illustrate how human users can carry out conversations using Web browsers with other agents, let us describe in more detail the sequence of steps taken by a human customer to send a query message to a supplier agent using a browser. As mentioned, every human user that needs to interact with agents has an associated user agent. In this case the human customer has an associated user agent that runs a conversation according to the plan depicted in figure 7(a).

To query some agents, the human customer first directs the browser to an URL where the user agent resides. Then the user agent requires a login name and password to authenticate the user. If authentication succeeds, the user agent will send back an HTML form for the user to fill in all relevant information required for the query. This is shown in the left screen dump of figure 8. The user fills the form and submits it back to the user agent, which in turn translates the query into a KQML message and forwards it to the supplier agent specified in the form. In figure 8 the user is interested in all components supplied by `MotLogic` that have `Pin Count = 20`. The supplier agent, `MotLogic`, processes the received query (according to the simple CP shown in figure 7(b)) and generates a response message, which is then sent to the user agent. Upon receiving the response message, the user agent generates an HTML page for presenting the information contained in the response message. The right screen dump in figure 8 illustrates the resulting presentation seen by the human user in the browser.

The user agents are implemented as Java servlets. The information content is represented in XML, with XSL used to generate the final HTML presentations seen by humans.

This system demonstrates how the conversational coordination approach can be integrated with current Web technology to support interactive dialogues bet-ween human users and agents on the Web. We are using it both in applications and as an administration tool allowing users to set up, inspect and direct the work of their agents no matter where users and agents are located.

8   Conclusion

Conversations are programming abstractions able to capture complex peer to peer interactions between autonomous entities. The need for such abstractions naturally occurs in agent systems where dynamically changing roles and social behavior require agents to exhibit more complex and more dynamic patterns of interaction than in the current state-of-the-practice multi-tiered client server architectures. Objects, the main abstraction employed in current object oriented architectures, are better suited to client server interactions because method ba-sed interfaces model more faithfully this sort of uniform, multi-level client-server relations.

Conversational solutions to agent interaction are important from at least two perspectives. First, because knowledge about cooperation and coordination is a necessary type of knowledge for any multi-agent system. Conversational struc-tures offer representation and execution mechanisms for this type of knowledge. Second, from a more fundamental perspective, recent research has begun to inve-stigate more powerful models of computation than Turing machines [Wegner 97]. Although this work is in an early stage, it appears that interactive models of computation based on 'interaction machines' strictly more powerful than Turing machines provide a better understanding of today's open systems like airline reservation systems, global manufacturing or service provisioning systems, etc. It would be interesting to see how conversational structures of the kind we have presented are related to the transducer based models investigated by this work [Wegner 97].

In this paper we have presented a specific conversational interaction technology based on notions like conversation plans, conversation rules, conversation executions, etc. This technology is embedded into a conversational agent programming language that has been used in a variety of applications, from puzzles [Barbuceanu & Fox 95] to supply chain simulation [Barbuceanu, Teigen & Fox], auctions and service provisioning in telecommunications [Barbuceanu 99]. Our experience to date shows that the conversational model of interaction is natural and expressive and can reduce the development time for multi agent applications, especially when supported by appropriate programming tools. Some of our users have been persons without a computer background who were still able to quickly build complex multi-agent applications in their domain of interest.

We have also shown that the conversational approach can be developed along new avenues, including advanced componentization, group conversations, better interface specifications, decision theoretic execution and learning and full integration with the Web. We are now in the process of building a second generation conversational architecture implementing these extensions on a Java platform, JCOOL.

Acknowledgments. This research is supported, in part, by the Manufacturing Research Corporation of Ontario, Natural Science and Engineering Research Council, Digital Equipment Corp., Micro Electronics and Computer Research Corp., Spar Aerospace, Carnegie Group and Quintus Corp.

References

[Barbuceanu 99] M. Barbuceanu. Negotiating Service Provisioning. In *Multi-Agent Systems Engineering*, Francisco J. Garijo and Magnus Boman (eds), Lecture Notes in Artificial Intelligence 1647, Springer Verlag (Proceedings of MAAMAW'99), Valencia, Spain, July 1999, 150-162.

[Barbuceanu, Teigen & Fox] M. Barbuceanu, R. Teigen, and M. S. Fox. Agent Based Design And Simulation of Supply Chain Systems. *Proceedings of WETICE-97*, IEEE Computer Press, Cambridge, MA, pp 36-43.

[Barbuceanu & Fox 97] Barbuceanu, M. and Fox, M. S. 1997. Integrating Communicative Action, Conversations and Decision Theory to Coordinate Agents. *Proceedings of Automomous Agents'97*, 47-58, Marina Del Rey, February 1997.

[Barbuceanu & Fox 96] M. Barbuceanu and M.S. Fox. Capturing and Modeling Coordination Knowledge for Multi-Agent System. *International Journal of Cooperative Information Systems*, Vol. 5, Nos. 2 and 3 (1996) 275-314.

[Barbuceanu & Fox 95] M.Barbuceanu and M. S. Fox. COOL: A Language for Describing Coordination in Multi-agent Systems. Proceedings of ICMAS-95, San Francisco, CA, AAAI Press/MIT Press, pp 17-25.

[Bellman 57] Bellman, R. E. 1957. *Dynamic Programming*. Princeton University Press, Princeton.

[Finin et al 92] T. Finin et al. Specification of the KQML Agent Communication Language. The DARPA Knowledge Sharing Initiative, External Interfaces Working Group, 1992.

[CACM 96] Communications of ACM: Special issue on group communication. Volume 39, April 1996.

[FIPA] FIPA. http://drogo.cselt.stet.it/fipa/

[Jennings 92] N. R. Jennings. Towards a Cooperation Knowledge Level for Collaborative Problem Solving. In *Proceedings 10-th European Conference on AI*, Vienna, Austria, pp 224-228, 1992.

[Medina-Mora et al 92] R. Medina-Mora, T. Winograd, R. Flores, F. Flores. The Action Workflow Approach to Workflow Management Technology. In *CSCW 92 Proceedings*, pp 281-288, 1992.

[Quickdata] www.si2.org/ecix

[Smith & Cohen 96] Smith, I., Coehn, P. Toward a semantics for an agent communication language based on speech-acts. Proceedings of AAAI-96, pp 24-31, Portland, OR, 1996.

[Watkins &Dayan 92] Watkins, C.C.J.C.H. and Dayan, P. Q-Learning. *Machine Learning* 8, 279-292 (1992)

[Wegner 97] Wegner, P. Why Interaction is More Powerful than Algorithms. *Communications of the ACM*, May 1997.

Conversation Protocols: Modeling and Implementing Conversations in Agent-Based Systems

Francisco J. Martin, Enric Plaza, and Juan A. Rodríguez-Aguilar

IIIA - Artificial Intelligence Research Institute
CSIC - Spanish Council for Scientific Research
Campus UAB, 08193 Bellaterra, Catalonia (Spain)
Vox: +34 935 809 570, Fax: +34 935 809 661
{martin,enric,jar}@iiia.csic.es
http://www.iiia.csic.es

Abstract. We present Conversation Protocols (CPs) as a methodological way to conceptualize, model, and implement conversations in agent-based systems. CPs can be thought of as coordination patterns that impose a set of rules on the communicative acts uttered by the agents participating in a conversation (what can be said, to whom, and when). Our proposal relies upon *interagents*, autonomous software agents that mediate the interaction between each agent and the agent society wherein this is situated. Thus, Interagents employ conversation protocols for mediating conversations among agents.

1 Introduction

Interaction among agents can take place at several levels: *content level*, concerned with the information content communicated among agents; *intentional level*, expressing the intentions of agents' utterances, usually as performatives of an agent communication language (ACL); *conversational level*, concerned with the conventions shared between agents when exchanging utterances; *transport level*, concerned with mechanisms for the transport of utterances; and *connection level*, contemplating network protocols.

So far, much effort in agent research concerning agent interaction has focused on the semantic and pragmatic foundations of different agent communication languages (ACLs) based on speech act theory [3], [26], [7], [11], [12], [16]. However, new works in speech act research, exemplified by efforts such as KAoS [5], Dooley Graphs [22], COOL[4] and MAGMA [9], attempt at representing and reasoning about the relationships within and among conversations, or groups of utterances. A number of formalisms have been proposed for modeling conversations: FSMs [4,13], Dooley graphs [22], colored Petri Nets [8], etc.

In this work we present Conversation Protocols (CPs) as the methodological way to conceptualize, model, and implement conversations in agent-based systems. Our approach proposes a new model based on a special type of Pushdown

F. Dignum and M. Greaves (Eds.): Agent Communication, LNAI 1916, pp. 249–263, 2000.

Transducers (PDTs) that allows to store the context of ongoing conversations, and, in contrast with other approaches, that provides a mapping from specification to implementation. Moreover, as a distinctive feature from other approaches, we provide our model with a detailed analysis that studies the properties that conversation protocols must exhibit in order to ensure protocol compatibility, and therefore the soundness of agent conversations.

We view conversations as the means of representing the conventions adopted by agents when interacting through the exchange of utterances[27,4] — "utterance suggests human speech or some analog to speech, in which the message between sender and addressee conveys information about the sender"[22]. More precisely, such conventions define the *legal* sequence of utterances that can be exchanged among the agents engaged in conversation: what can be said, to whom and when. Therefore, *conversation protocols* are coordination patterns that constrain the sequencing of utterances during a conversation.

Our proposal relies upon *interagents*[19] [18], autonomous software agents that mediate the interaction between each agent and the agent society wherein it is situated. Interagents employ conversation protocols for mediating conversations among agents.

Interagents are responsible for posting utterances of its *customer*[1] to the corresponding addressee and for collecting the utterances that other agents address to its customer. Each interagent has a collection of relevant conversation protocols (CP) used for managing its customer conversations. When its customer intends to start a new conversation with another agent the interagent instantiates the corresponding conversation protocol. Once the conversation starts, the interagent becomes responsible for ensuring that the exchange of utterances conforms to the CP specification.

Before setting up any conversation the interagent must perform a *CP negotiation* process with the interagent of the addressee agent. The goal of CP negotiation is to reach an agreement with respect to the conversation protocol to be used. Moreover, before starting a conversation, the interagent performs a *CP verification* process. This process checks whether the CP to be used verifies the necessary conditions (liveliness, termination, deadlock and race condition free) for guaranteeing the correct evolution of an interaction. Finally, an interagent allows its customer to hold several conversations at the same time. This capability for *multiple conversations* is important because, although in the paper we consider only conversations with two participants (dialogues), conversations with any number of participants are built as a collection of simultaneous CP instances. In other words, the agent views a conversation as involving n participants while its interagent views such conversation as a collection of simultaneous dialogues represented as multiple CP instances.

The remainder of this article is organized as follows. Section 2 introduces a conceptual model of CPs. Next, in Section 3 the formalism underpinning our model is presented. Section 4 explains the way of instantiating CPs. Next, in Sec-

---

[1] We call customer the agent exploiting and benefiting from the services offered by an interagent

tion 5 we introduce the notion of CP compatibility, in order to ensure the correct exchange of utterances during a conversation. In Section 6 we describe two ways of negotiating the attributes of a CP instance. Finally, Section 7 presents some concluding remarks.

2   Conceptual Model

A Conversation Protocol (CP) defines a class of legal sequences of utterances that can be exchanged between two agents holding a conversation. We model and implement a CP as a special type of Pushdown Transducer (PDT), which can be seen in turn as a combination of a Finite-State Transducer (FST) and a Pushdown Automaton (PDA):

- An FST is simply a Finite State Automaton (FSA) that deals with two tapes. To specify an FST, it suffices to augment the FSA notation so that labels on arcs can denote pairs of symbols[23];
- A PDA is composed of an input stream and a control mechanism —like an FSA— along with a stack on which data can be stored for later recall[2,6].

Therefore, a PDT is essentially a pushdown automaton that deals with two tapes. A PDA can be associated to a PDT by considering the pairs of symbols on the arcs as symbols of a PDA. The choice of PDTs as the mechanism for modeling CPs is motivated by several reasons: i) analogously to other finite-state devices a few fundamental theoretical basis make PDTs very flexible, powerful and efficient [23]; ii) they have been largely used in a variety of domains such as pattern matching, speech recognition, cryptographic techniques, data compression techniques, operating system verification, etc.; iii) they offer a straightforward mapping from specification to implementation; iv) PDTs, unlike other finite state devices, allow us to store, and subsequently retrieve, the contextual information of ongoing conversations; and, finally, v) the use of pairs of symbols to label arcs adds expressiveness to the representation of agent conversations.

Conceptually, we decompose a CP into the following elements (see Figure 1): a finite state control, an input list, a pushdown list, and a finite set of transitions.

First, the *finite state control* contains the set of states representing the communication state of the interagent's customer during an ongoing conversation. We shall distinguish several states based on the communicative actions that they allow: *send*, when only the utterance of performatives is permitted, *receive*, when these can be only received, and *mixed*, when both the utterance and reception are feasible.

The utterances heard by an interagent during each conversation are stored into an *input list*. In fact, this input list is logically divided into two sublists: one for keeping the utterances' performatives, and another one for storing their predicates. The input list is continuously traversed by the interagent in search of a (p/d) pair (where p stands for a performative, and d stands for a predicate) which can produce a transition in the finite state control. Notice that the continuous traversing the input list differs from the one employed by classic FSAs

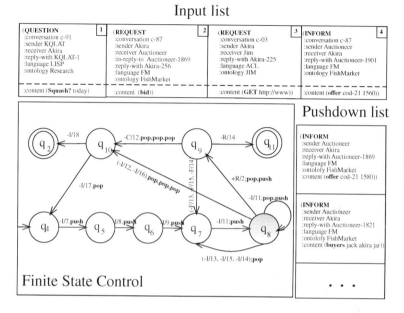

Fig. 1. Partial view of the CP DBP used by trading interagents in the Fishmarket.

whose read only input tapes are traversed from left to right (or the other way around).

Let us consider a particular CP related to an ongoing conversation. We say that an utterance is *admitted* when it is heard by the interagent and subsequently stored into the input list. Admitted utterances become *accepted* when they can cause a state transition of the finite state control. Then they are removed from the input list to be forwarded to the corresponding addressee, and thereupon the corresponding transition in the finite state control takes place. Notice that all utterances are firstly admitted and further on they become either accepted or not. Therefore, the input list of each CP keeps admitted utterances that have not been accepted for dispatching yet. From now on, these criteria will be taken as the message sending and receiving semantics used in Section5.

The context of each conversation can be stored and subsequently retrieved thanks to the use of a *pushdown list*. Such context refers to utterances previously sent or heard, which later can help, for example, to ensure that a certain utterance is the proper response to a previous one. For instance, an utterance in the input list —represented in a KQML-like syntax— will be processed only if its sender, receiver and the value of the keyword *:in-reply-to* match respectively the receiver, sender and value of the keyword *:reply-with* of the topmost message on the pushdown list.

Finally, each transition in the *finite set of transitions* of a CP indicates: i) what utterance can be either sent or received to produce a move in the finite state control; and ii) whether it is necessary to store (push) or retrieve (pop) the context using the pushdown list.

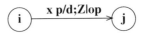

Fig. 2. Transition

Each arc of the finite state control is labeled by one or more transition specifications. The structure of a transition specification is shown in Figure 2: a transition from state i to state j occurs whenever an utterance with polarity x, performative p, and predicate d is found in the input list and the state of the pushdown list is Z. In such a case, the chain of stack operations indicated by op is processed. In order to fully specify a transition, the following definitions and criteria must be observed:

- the polarity of an utterance u, denoted as $polarity(u)$, can take on one of two values: $+$, to express that the utterance is sent, or $-$, to indicate that the utterance is received. Moreover, for a given CP c we define its *symmetric view* $\bar{c}$ as the result of inverting the polarity of each transition;
- the special symbol $p/^*$ represents utterances formed by performative p and any predicate, whereas the special symbol $^*/d$ stands for utterances formed by any performative and predicate d;
- when several transitions label an arc, $p_1/d_1; Z|op, .., p_n/d_n; Z|op$, they can be grouped into a compound transition as $(p_1/d_1|\ldots|p_n/d_n); Z|op$;
- our model considers the following stack operations:
  push pushes the utterance selected from the input list onto the stack;
  pop pops the stack by removing the topmost utterance; and
  nop leaves the stack unchanged. Usually this operation is omitted in specifying a transition;
- when the state of the pushdown list is not considered for a transition, it is omitted in the transition specification. In CPs, *e*-moves, i.e. moves that only depends on the current state of finite state control and the state of the pushdown list, are represented using the transition specification $Z|op$.

For instance, Figure 1 depicts the CP employed by the interagent used by a buyer agent to bid for items presented by an auctioneer agent who calls prices in descending order —the downward bidding protocol (DBP). Each item is adjudicated to the buyer that stops the descending sequence of prices called by the auctioneer following the rules of the DBP implemented in FM[25]. Notice that the performatives of the utterances considered in the figure follow the syntax of Table 1, and the predicates within such utterances belong to the list in Table 2. Such performatives and predicates belong to the FM communication language and ontology. This simple example illustrates the use of the pushdown list: i) for saving the state of the bidding round (round number, good in auction, list of buyers, etc.); and ii) for ensuring that whenever a request for bidding is dispatched, the bid conveyed to the auctioneer will be built by recovering the last offer pushed by the trading interagent onto the pushdown list.

Table 1. Types of performatives following Cohen and Levesque[7] (extracted from Parunak[22])

ID	Speech Act	Description
Q	QUESTION	SOLICIT the addressee to INFORM the sender of some proposition
R	REQUEST	SOLICIT the addressee to COMMIT to the sender concerning some action
I	INFORM	ASSERT + attempt to get the addressee to believe the content
C	COMMIT	ASSERT that sender has adopted a persistent goal to achieve something relative to the addressee's desires
F	REFUSE	ASSERT that the sender has not adopted a persistent goal to achieve something relative to the addressees desires

Table 2. Trading Predicates

#Message	Predicate	Parameters
1	admission	buyerlogin password
2	bid	[price]
3	exit	
4	deny	deny_code
5	accept	open|closed auction_number
6	open_auction	auction_number
7	open_round	round_number
8	good	good_id good_type starting_price resale_price
9	buyers	{buyerlogin}*
10	goods	{good_id good_type starting_price resale_price}*
11	offer	good_id price
12	sold	good_id buyerlogin price
13	sanction	buyerlogin fine
14	expulsion	buyerlogin
15	collision	price
16	withdrawn	good_id price
17	end_round	round_number
18	end_auction	auction_number
19	going	{single|multiple} + {1,2}
20	gone	
21	tie_break	buyerlogin
22	closed_market	

3   Formal Definition

Now it's time to formally capture the conceptual model introduced above in order to be later able to reason about the properties that we must demand from CPs. Therefore, formally we define a conversation protocol as an 8-tuple $CP = \langle Q, \Sigma_1, \Sigma_2, \Gamma, \delta, q_0, Z_0, F \rangle$ such that:

- Q is a finite set of state symbols that represent the states of the finite state control.
- Σ_1 is a finite alphabet formed by the identifiers of all performatives that can be uttered during the conversation.
- Σ_2 is a finite input list alphabet composed of the identifiers of all predicates recognized by the speakers.
- Γ is the finite pushdown list alphabet.
- δ is a mapping from $Q \times \{+, -\} \cdot \Sigma_1 \times \Sigma_2 \times \Gamma^*$ to the finite subsets of $Q \times \Gamma^*$ which indicates all possible transitions that can take place during a conversation.
- $q_0 \in Q$ is the initial state of a conversation.
- $Z_0 \in \Gamma$ is the start symbol of the pushdown list.
- $F \subseteq Q$ is the set of final states representing possible final states of a conversation.

CPs only contemplate a finite number of moves from each state that must belong to one of the following types:

Moves using the input list. These moves depend on the current state of the finite state control, the performative/predicate pair of a message into the input list, and the state of the pushdown list. For instance, the move expressed by the following transition: $\delta(q_8, +\mathsf{REQUEST}, \mathsf{bid}, \mathsf{offer}Z) = \{(q_9, \mathsf{bid}Z)\}$ allows a trading interagent to convey to the auctioneer a request for bidding received from its customer (a buyer agent) whenever an offer, received from the auctioneer, has been previously pushed upon the pushdown list.

e-moves. These moves depend exclusively on the current state of the finite state control and the state of the pushdown list. *e*-moves are specifically employed to model and implement time-out conditions within CPs, so that interagents can handle expired messages and automatically recover from transmission errors. For instance, the following transition $\delta(q_9, e, e, \mathsf{bid}Z) = \{(q_8, Z)\}$ could allow a trading interagent to roll back to a previous state.

It should be noted that we are only interested in deterministic CPs (DCP): a CP is said to be deterministic when for each state $q \in Q$, $p \in \Sigma_1$, $d \in \Sigma_2$ and $Z \in \Gamma^*$ there is at most one possible move, that is $|\delta(q, p, d, Z)| \leq 1$.

4   Instantiation

CPs can be defined declaratively and stored into conversation protocol repositories open to interagents. Each CP is identified by a unique name anonymously set by the agent society. When an interagent is requested by its customer to start a conversation with another agent it must retrieve the appropriate CP from a conversation repository, and next proceed to instantiate it. In fact, the CP must be instantiated by each one of the interagents used by the agents intending to talk.

We say that a CP becomes fully instantiated when the interagent creates a CP instance, i.e. after setting the values for the following attributes:

CP name. CP class to which the CP instance belongs;

speakers. identifiers of the agents to engage in conversation. Notice that we shall restrict a CP instance to consider exactly two speakers: the agent that proposes to start a conversation, the *originator*, and its addressee, the *helper*. In spite of this limitation, we are not prevented from defining multi-agent conversation, since these can be created by means of multiple CP instances;

conversation identifier. a unique identifier created by the originator;

polarity. this property indicates how to instantiate the polarity of each transition of the CP: if the instance polarity is positive, each transition is instantiated just as it is, whereas if it is negative each transition polarity is inverted. Notice that the helper must instantiate the symmetric view of the originator's CP in order to ensure protocol compatibility as shown in Section 5.

transport policies. such as time-out or maximum time allowed in the input list. These can be altered during the course of a conversation whereas the rest of attributes of a CP instance remain fixed. The use of transport policies require to extend the CP being instantiated with *e*-moves that enable to roll back to previous conversation states.

From the point of view of interagents the conversations requested to be held by its customer agent can progress through several states:

pre-instantiated after retrieving the requested CP from the originator's conversation repository;

instantiated a CP becomes instantiated when the originator creates a CP instance, and subsequently asks the helper for starting a new conversation accepting the terms (attributes) of the interaction expressed by the CP instance;

initiated this state is reached when both speakers agree on the value of the attributes of a new conversation, as a result of the negotiation phase described in Section 6;

running state attained after the first utterance;

finished a conversation is over whenever either the final state of the CP is reached, the helper refuses to start it, or an unexpected error comes about.

4.1 Instantaneous Description

An instantaneous description formally describes the state of a CP instance at a particular time. An *instantaneous description* of a CP instance p is a 7-tuple: $\langle o, h, p, t, q, l, \alpha \rangle$ such that: o is the originator agent; h is the helper agent; p is the polarity of the CP instance; t is the current setting of transport policies; q is the current state of the finite state control; l represents all utterances currently kept by the input list; and α is the current state of the pushdown list.

Figure 1 depicts a partial instantaneous description for an instance of the CP DBP employed by a trading interagent to allow its customer (a buyer agent) to participate in a bidding round open by the auctioneer agent. We identify buyer *Akira* as the originator, the *auctioneer* as the helper, and the colored node q_8 as the state of the finite state control.

A deterministic CP has at most —without taking into account possible e-moves for dealing with expired utterances— one possible move from any instantaneous description. However, continuously traversing the input list in search of an utterance that causes a transition can lead to *race conditions*. For instance, in the CP instance of Figure 1 the second and fourth utterances can originate a race condition since both utterances can cause a move in the finite state control. Thus, it is necessary to define criteria for deciding which utterance must be accepted —as we show in the next section.

5 Compatibility Semantics

In order to ensure the correct exchange of utterances during a conversation, there are important, desirable properties such as termination, liveliness, deadlock and race condition free that CPs must verify. In what follows we concentrate exclusively on the two last properties, since to guarantee both termination and liveliness it suffices to assume that every CP whose set of final states is non-empty does not remain forever in the same state.

First we formulate our notion of CP compatibility, following the notion of protocol compatibility proposed by Yellin and Strom in [28], whose work provides, in fact, the foundations of our analysis.

CPs can be assigned two different semantics: asynchronous or synchronous. Although asynchronous semantics may facilitate implementation, it makes generally harder reasoning about certain properties, such as *deadlock* which has proven undecidable under these semantics[28]. On the contrary, under synchronous semantics, reasoning about such properties is easier, though an implementation technique must map these semantics to a particular implementation. For our purposes, we have decided for a synchronous semantic for CPs and, consequently, for devising the adequate mechanisms for implementation. Such a type of semantic requires to assume that a speaker can send an utterance to the other speaker only if that is willing to receive the utterance. Therefore, we must assume that the finite state controls of both CP instances advance synchronously, and hence that sending and receiving an utterance are atomic actions. Upon this assumption, Yellin and Strom introduced the following notion of compatibility of protocols: "Protocols p_1 and p_2 are *compatible* when they have no *unspecified receptions*, and are *deadlock free*". On the one hand, in terms of CPs, the absence of unspecified receptions implies that whenever the finite state control of a CP instance corresponding to one of the speakers is in a state where a utterance can be sent, the finite state control of the CP instance of the other speaker must be in a state where such utterance can be received. On the other hand, deadlock free implies that the finite state control of both CP instances are either in final states or in states that allow the conversation to progress. Interestingly, the authors prove the existence of an algorithm for checking protocol compatibility. By applying such algorithm, it can be proved that under synchronous semantics a CP instance p and its symmetric view $\bar{p}$ are always compatible. From this follows that two CP instances are compatible if both belong to the same CP class, and both have the same speakers but different polarity. In this way, the complete agreement on the order of the utterances exchanged between the speakers is guaranteed.

Concerning the implementation, observe that the atomicity of sending and receiving utterances cannot be guaranteed. Nonetheless, when compatible CP instances lack mixed states, the unspecified receptions and deadlock free properties can still be guaranteed. But the presence of mixed states can lead to race conditions that prevent both speakers from agreeing on the order of the messages, and therefore unexpected receptions and deadlocks might occur. In order to avoid such situations, low-level synchronization mechanisms must be provided in accordance with the interpretation given to message sending and receiving in Section 2.

For this purpose, we consider that the speakers adopt different conflict roles —either *leader* or *follower*— when facing mixed states. The leader will decide what to do, whereas the follower will respect the leader's directions. By extending CP instances with a new attribute —which can take on the values *leader* or *follower*— we include the role to be played by each speaker in front of mixed states. Besides, we consider two special symbols —TRY and OK— that alter the interpretation of message sending. Thus, on the one hand when a message is sent under the TRY semantics, the receiver tries to directly accept the message without requiring previous admission. On the other hand, the OK symbol confirms that the TRY was successful. Then given a CP $\langle Q, \Sigma_1, \Sigma_2, \Gamma, \delta, q_0, Z_0, F \rangle$ for each mixed state $x \in Q$ the CP instance corresponding to the follower will be augmented in the following way:

$\forall p \in \Sigma_1, \forall d \in \Sigma_2, \forall Z \in \Gamma^*, \forall Z' \in \Gamma^*, \forall q \in Q$ such that $\exists \delta(x, +p, d, Z) = \{(q, Z')\}$ then a new state $n \notin Q$ will be added $Q = Q \cup \{n\}$ and the following transitions will be added:

1. $\delta(x, +TRY(p), d, Z) = \{(n, Z)\}$
2. $\delta(n, -OK, e, Z) = \{(y, Z')\}$
3. $\forall p' \in \Sigma_1, \forall d' \in \Sigma_2, \forall Z'' \in \Gamma^*$ then $\delta(x, -p', d', Z'') = \delta(n, -p', d', Z'')$

Therefore, when the leader is in a mixed state and sends an utterance, the follower admits it and subsequently accepts it. Conversely, when the follower is in a mixed state and sends an utterance, the leader, upon reception, determines if it is admitted or not. Figure 3 illustrates how the CP instance on the left should be augmented to deal with the mixed state q_8.

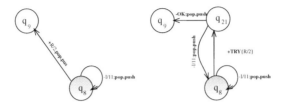

Fig. 3. Augmented CP instance

Notice that the conflict role played by each speaker must be fixed before the CP becomes completely instantiated. This and other properties of CP instances need be negotiated by the speakers as explained in the next section.

6   Conversation Protocol Negotiation

In Section 4 we introduced the attributes of a CP instance that have to be fixed before the conversation between the speakers becomes fully instantiated, and subsequently started. The value of each one of these attributes has to be mutually agreed by the speakers in order to guarantee conversation soundness. For this purpose, interagents have been provided with the capability of negotiating such values by means of the so-called *Handshake* phase, following the directions of their customers. During this process, the initial connection between the originator and the helper is established, and next the originator conveys its multi-attribute proposal (the set of attributes' values) to the helper. Then, we distinguish two models of negotiation based on the helper's response: one-step and two-step negotiation.

In one-step negotiation the helper either automatically accepts or refuses the originator's proposal. The sequence in Figure 4 depicts a typical exchange for this model of negotiation, where q values indicate the degree of preference over each proposal.

```
originator: START
            CP/DBP; id=21; polarity=+; leader=me; q=0.7
            CP/DBP; id=21; polarity=-; leader=you; q=0.3
helper:     OK
            CP/DBP; id=21; polarity=+; leader=me
```

Fig. 4. One-step negotiation. In this example the helper accepts the second proposal from the originator.

In two-step negotiation (see Figure 5), instead of directly accepting or refusing the originator proposal, the helper can reply with a a list of counterproposals ranked according to its own preferences. Then, the originator can either accept one of these proposals or cancel the process.

```
originator: START
            CP/DBP; id=22; polarity=+; leader=me; timeout=500; q=0.7
            CP/DBP; id=22; polarity=-; leader=you; timeout=1000; q=0.3
helper:     NOT
            CP/DBP; id=22; polarity=-; leader=me; timeout=200; q=0.4
            CP/DBP; id=22; polarity=+; leader=you; timeout=200; q= 0.6
originator: OK
            CP/DBP; id=22; polarity=+; leader=you; timeout=200
```

Fig. 5. Two-step negotiation. In this example the helper refuses the proposals of the originator, who finally accepts the first helper's counterproposal.

It should be noted here that the concrete conversation protocol to be instantiated can be negotiated too. For this purpose, we have introduced the CP type (e.g. the CP/DBP for the downward bidding protocol), analogously to MIME content types (text/html, image/gif, etc.). On the other hand, it makes no sense to negotiate certain attributes for some CPs. For instance, the polarity of the CP to be employed by an auctioneer attempting to open a DBP round is unnegotiable since the auctioneer cannot play the role of a buyer and vice versa.

7   Final Remarks

We have introduced conversation protocols as the methodological way to conceptualize, model, and implement conversations in agent-based systems. We have also explained the way of negotiating, instantiating and ensuring compatibility semantics of CPs. CPs allow to impose a set of constraints on the communicative acts uttered by the agents holding a conversation. Other finite state models have been largely used for network protocols, and subsequently adapted to speech act theory. Though valid for specifying the states through which a conversation may progress, they lack of mechanisms for maintaining contextual information valuable for tracking the evolution of the conversation in time. CPs, on the contrary, allow to store the context of an ongoing conversation.

Our proposal relies upon *interagents*[18], autonomous software agents that mediate the interaction between each agent and the agent society wherein this is situated. Interagents employ conversation protocols for mediating conversations among agents. We think that CPs together with interagents constitute a convenient *infrastructure* for easing the development of agent-based systems. Two major benefits are achieved by deploying our infrastructure from the point of view of the agent developer: on the one hand, their agents can reason about communication at higher levels of abstraction, and on the other hand they are released from dealing with interaction details, and so they can concentrate on the design of the agents' logics—from the agents' inner behavior (knowledge representation, reasoning, learning, etc.) to the agents' social behavior responsible for high-level coordination tasks (the selection, ordering, and communication of the results of the agent activities so that an agent works effectively in a group setting [15,14]).

We have materialized the conceptualization of interagents through the design and development of JIM: a java-based implementation of a general-purpose interagent capable of managing conversation protocols and capable also of dealing with agent interaction at different levels [20]. Although there is a large number of software tools for developing agents[1], not many of them happen to provide support for the specification of conversation protocols. AgentTalk[2], COOL[4], JAFMAS [13], Agentis[10], Jackal[8] and InfoSleuth[21], do offer conversation constructs. JAFMAS, for instance, provides a generic methodology for developing speech-act based multi-agent systems using coordination constructs similar to COOL. In addition to this, as far as our knowledge goes, none of them offers dynamically and incrementally specifiable conversation protocols except for InfoSleuth[21]. We attempt to make headway in this matter with respect to other agent building tools by introducing interagents, that permit both the dynamic and incremental definition of conversation protocols. We have chosen such conceptualization instead of an agent's built-in conversation layer as proposed in other agent architectures because of the need to separate the agents' logics from the agents' interactions —such separation has proven to be valuable in the development of a particular type of agent-based systems, namely electronic institutions such as FM.

JIM has been successfully applied in the development of FM[3][25,24], our current implementation of an agent-mediated electronic auction market. Additionally, JIM is being successfully employed by other ongoing research projects: the SMASH[4] project, that addresses the construction of prototype multi-agent systems with case-based reasoning capabilities that cooperate in the solution of complex problems in hospital environments; and in the multi-agent learning framework Plural[17] which tackles the problem of sharing knowledge and experience among cognitive agents that co-operate within a distributed case-based reasoning framework.

Acknowledgments. This work has been supported by the Spanish CICYT project SMASH, TIC96-1038-C04001 and the COMRIS project, ESPRIT LTR 25500; Juan A. Rodríguez-Aguilar and Francisco J. Martin enjoy DGR-CIRIT doctoral scholarships FI-PG/96-8490 and FI-DT/96-8472 respectively.

---

[2] http://www.cslab.tas.ntt.jp/at/
[3] http://www.iiia.csic.es/Projects/fishmarket
[4] http://www.iiia.csic.es/Projects/smash/

References

1. AAAI. *AAAI-98 Workshop on Software Tools for Developing Agents*, 1998.
2. A. V. Aho and J. D. Ullman. *The Theory of Parsing, Translation, and Compiling*, volume I: Parsing of *Series in Automatic Computation*. Prentice-Hall, 1972.
3. J. L. Austin. *How to Do Things With Words*. Oxford University Press, 1962.
4. M. Barbuceanu and W.-K. Lo. Conversation oriented programming in COOL: current state and future directions. In *Proceedings of the Agents-99 Workshop on Specifying and Implementing Conversations Policies*, 1999.
5. J. M. Bradshaw. Kaos: An open agent architecture supporting reuse, interoperability, and extensibility. In *Tenth Knowledge Acquisition for Knowledge Based Systems*, 1996.
6. J. G. Brookshear. *Theory of Computation, Formal Languages, Automata, and Complexity*. The Benjamin/Cummings Publishing, 1989.
7. P. R. Cohen and H. J. Levesque. Communicative actions for artificial agents. In *Proceedings of the First International Conference on Multi-Agent Systems (ICMAS-95)*, pages 65–72, Menlo Park, CA., jun 1995. AAAI Press.
8. R. S. Cost, Y. Chen, T. Finin, Y. Labrou, and Y. Peng. Modeling agent conversations with colored petri nets. In *Proceedings of the Agents-99 Workshop on Specifying and Implementing Conversations Policies*, 1999.
9. Y. Demazeau. From interactions to collective behaviour in agent-based systems. In *European Conference on Cognitive Sciences*, 1995.
10. M. d'Inverno, D. Kinny, and M. Luck. Interaction protocols in Agentis. In *Third International Conference on Multi-Agent Systems*, 1998.
11. T. Finin, Y. Labrou, and J. Mayfield. KQML as an agent communication language. In J. Bradshaw, editor, *Software Agents*. MIT Press, Cambridge, 1995.
12. FIPA-97. specification part 2: Agent communication language. Technical report, FIPA - Foundation for Intelligent Physical Agents, 1997.
13. A. Galan and A. Baker. Multiagent communication in jafmas. In *Proceedings of the Agents-99 Workshop on Specifying and Implementing Conversations Policies*, 1999.
14. N. R. Jennings. Commitments and conventions: The foundation of coordination in multi-agent systems. *The Knowledge Engineering Review*, 8(3):223–250, 1995.
15. V. R. Lesser. Reflections on the nature of multi-agent coordination and its implications for an agent architecture. *Autonomous Agents and Multi-Agent Systems*, 1:89–111, 1998.
16. R. MacEntire and D. McKay. KQML Lite Specification. Technical report, Lockheed Martin Mission Systems, 1998. Technical Report ALP-TR/03.
17. F. J. Martin, E. Plaza, and J. L. Arcos. Knowledge and experience reuse through communication among competent (peer) agents. *International Journal of Software Engineering and Knowledge Engineering* Vol. 9, No. 3, 1999.
18. F. J. Martin, E. Plaza, and J. A. Rodriguez. An infrastructure for agent-based systems: an interagent approach. *International Journal of Intelligent Systems*, to appear, 2000.
19. F. J. Martin, E. Plaza, J. A. Rodriguez-Aguilar, and J. Sabater. Java interagents for multi-agent systems. In *AAAI-98 Workshop on Software Tools for Developing Agents*, 1998.
20. F. J. Martin, E. Plaza, J. A. Rodriguez-Aguilar, and J. Sabater. Jim: A Java interagent for multi-agent systems. In *1r Congrés Català d'Intel.ligència Artificial*, pages 163–171, Tarragona, Spain, 1998.

21. M. Nodine, B. Perry, and A. Unruh. Experience with the InfoSleuth agent architecture. In *AAAI-98 Workshop on Software Tools for Developing Agents*, 1998.
22. H. V. D. Parunak. Visualizing agent conversations: Using enhanced dooley graph for agent design and analysis. In *Proceedings of the Second International Conference on Multi-Agent Systems*, 1996.
23. E. Roche and Y. Schabes. *Finite State Language Processing*. The MIT Press, 1997.
24. J. A. Rodriguez-Aguilar, F. J. Martin, P. Noriega, P. Garcia, and C. Sierra. Competitive scenarios for heterogenous trading agents. In *Second International Conference on Autonomous Agents*, 1998.
25. J. A. Rodríguez-Aguilar, F. J. Martín, P. Noriega, P. Garcia, and C. Sierra. Towards a test-bed for trading agents in electronic auction markets. *AI Communications*, 11(1):5–19, 1998.
26. J. Searle. *Speech Acts*. Cambridge University Press, 1969.
27. T. Winograd and F. Flores. *Understanding Computers and Cognition*. Addison Wesley, 1988.
28. D. M. Yellin and R. E. Strom. Protocol specifications and component adaptors. *ACM Transactions on Programming Languages and Systems*, 19(2):292–333, 1997.

Dialogue in Team Formation

Frank Dignum[1], Barbara Dunin-Kęplicz[2], and Rineke Verbrugge[3]

[1] Faculty of Mathematics and Computing Science
Technical University Eindhoven
P.O. Box 513, 5600 MB Eindhoven, The Netherlands
e-mail: `dignum@win.tue.nl`
Tel: +31-40-2473705, Fax: +31-40-2463992
[2] Institute of Informatics
Warsaw University
Banacha 2, 02-097 Warsaw, Poland
E-mail: `keplicz@mimuw.edu.pl`
Tel: +48 22 6584594, Fax: +48 22 6583164
[3] Cognitive Science and Engineering
University of Groningen
Grote Kruisstraat 2/1, 9712 TS Groningen, The Netherlands
E-mail: `rineke@tcw2.ppsw.rug.nl`
Tel: +31-50-3636334, Fax: +31-50-3636784

Abstract. The process of cooperative problem solving can be divided into four stages. First, finding potential team members, then forming a team followed by constructing a plan for that team. Finally, the plan is executed by the team. Traditionally, very simple protocols like the Contract Net protocol are used for performing the first two stages of the process. And often the team is already taken for granted. In an open environment (like in e.g. electronic commerce) however, there can be discussion among the agents in order to form a team that can achieve the collective goal of solving the problem. For these cases fixed protocols like contract net do not suffice. In this paper we present an alternative solution, using structured dialogues that can be shown to lead to the required team formation. The dialogues are described formally (using some modal logics), thus making it possible to actually prove that a certain dialogue has a specific outcome.

1 Introduction

Contract Net [12] is often proposed as a simple but effective and efficient way to distribute tasks over a number of agents in order to achieve a common goal. The reason of the success of this approach is the fact that it is completely fixed and thus easy to implement. In our opinion, however, the inflexibility is a disadvantage of this approach. Agents can either accept a task (by offering to perform it at a certain time and against a certain remuneration) or reject it.

[0] This research was supported by ESPRIT under the Grant CRIT-2 No. 20288.

F. Dignum and M. Greaves (Eds.): Agent Communication, LNAI 1916, pp. 264–280, 2000.
© Springer-Verlag Berlin Heidelberg 2000

It is hardly possible to negotiate about the tasks in this model. E.g. an agent might offer to retrieve some information before offering a certain time-limit and price. It offers a good response time-limit and price, because it already happens to know where the information is located. However, if it had known that it is the only agent that was responding (the other agent being too busy) it could have negotiated a much better price. Although some of these limitations have been remedied in [12] the Contract Net protocol remains very inflexible.

As an alternative to a completely fixed protocol like Contract Net, one could consider a situation in which the participants are free to respond in whatever way suits them best at each point during the team formation. It means that the agents have to deliberate constantly about every move. This will be very time consuming and maybe less practical. We would like to have something in between completely fixed protocols and totally free conversations. A good candidate to fill this position is the theory of dialogue [16]. The dialogue theory tries to give rules for appropriate moves within different types of dialogues. The rules direct the dialogue without completely fixing the order of the moves.

The overall goal of this paper is to give a first account of team formation by means of dialogue. In the next paper [3], we give a generic account of team formation. In [7] a general framework is developed for using dialogues in collective problem solving ([6]). In this framework four stages are distinguished inspired by [17].

The first stage is *potential recognition*. In this stage the agent that takes the initiative for cooperative problem solving tries to find out which agents are potential candidates for achieving a given overall goal and how these can be combined in a team. The second stage is *team formation*. The result of this stage is a collective intention among a team to achieve the overall goal to solve the problem. This is the team that will try to actually achieve the goal. The third stage is *plan formation*. Here the team divides the overall goal into subtasks, associates these with actions and allocates these actions to team members (including a temporal structure). In terms of motivational attitudes the end result of this stage is a collective commitment to perform the social plan that realizes the overall goal. The last stage is *plan execution*. In this stage the team members execute the allocated actions and monitor the appropriate colleagues. If necessary a reconfiguration of the plan can be constructed [8], [9]. In [7] it is shown which types of dialogues play a role in each of these stages and in which way they can be embedded into each other. Also the results in terms of informational and motivational attitudes are given. In the present paper we will refine the theory and indicate all the steps necessary for the first two stages of the process. Thus we will show how the collective intention that is the result of team formation is built up during the dialogues.

The paper is structured in the following manner. Section 2 presents a brief typology of dialogue in CPS. Sections 3 and 4 investigate different dialogue types during potential recognition and team formation, respectively. Finally, in section 5 conclusions and further research are discussed.

2   Typology of Dialogue in CPS

Dialogue can be defined as the communication among two or more agents. The agents speak in turn, for example asking questions and giving replies, and take into account, at each turn, what has occurred previously in the dialogue.

Krabbe and Walton [16] provide a typology of dialogue types between two agents, with an emphasis on the persuasion dialogue. They create a so called *a normative model*, representing the ideal way reasonable, cooperative agents participate in the type of dialogue in question. For each type of dialogue, they formulate *an initial situation, a primary goal*, and *a set of rules*. Below, their typology is briefly explained and adapted to the CPS perspective. In the course of communication among agents, there often occurs a shift from one type of dialogue to another, in particular *embedding* occurs when the second dialogue is functionally related to the first one.

A persuasion dialogue arises from a conflict of opinions. It may be that one agent believes φ while some others either believe a contrary proposition ψ_i (where $\varphi \wedge \psi_i$ is inconsistent) or just have doubt about φ. The goal of a persuasion dialogue is to resolve the conflict by verbal means, in such a way that a stable agreement results.

The initial situation of *negotiation* is a conflict of interests, together with a need for cooperation. The main goal is to make a deal. Thus, the selling and buying of goods and services, that is often described in the MAS-literature, is only one of the many contexts where negotiation plays a role in MAS. Negotiation and persuasion are often not distinguished adequately.

The initial situation of *inquiry* is one where all agents are ignorant about the solution to some question or open problem. The main goal is the growth of knowledge, leading to agreement about the conclusive answer of the question. This goal is attained by a incremental process of argument which builds on established facts in order to prove conclusions beyond a reasonable doubt. Both information retrieval and reasoning are used in this process.

The initial situation for *deliberation* is a need for action performance. The main goal is to reach a decision on how to act, for the time being. The kind of reasoning that is central to deliberation is practical reasoning.

The initial situation of *information seeking* occurs when one agent is ignorant about the truth of a certain proposition and seeks information from other agents in order to gain more knowledge.

The last type of dialogue i.e. *eristics* (verbal fighting between agents) has been left out as we focus on cooperative teams.

3   Potential Recognition

Potential recognition is about finding the set of agents that may participate in the formation of the team that tries to achieve the overall goal. These agents are grouped into several potential teams with whom further discussion will ensue during the team formation. Important starting point of the cooperative problem solving process is the overall goal that should be achieved in this process. This goal describes the solution of the problem (in an abstract way). It can arise in different ways. It can be a goal that is given from outside the system boundaries. E.g. a built in goal of the complete system such as "control the flights of all planes in a certain area" for an air traffic control system. The overall goal can also be formed by one agent that is interested in achieving that goal but does not have the abilities or desire to achieve it by itself. In this case this agent has to announce the goal as a possible collective goal for a group of agents. E.g. an agent tries to gather all possible information about some topic, but has only limited knowledge about the (possible) resources. It might at that moment ask for help of other agents to collectively gather all information.

In this paper both ways to form collective goals can be taken as point of origin. However, we restrict ourselves to the situation with one fixed overall goal and one agent that takes the initiative to achieve that goal. In future work we will also look at the process of collective goal formation, but we leave it out here because it would draw to much attention from the main goal of this paper and is an interesting subject in its own right.

The agent that takes the initiative to start the process of potential recognition can either be appointed or be the agent that is most interested to achieve the goal. The first usually is the case when the goal is given from outside. In that case there is usually one agent whose role it is to check this goal and to organize the team. In the air traffic control system this might be the air traffic coordinator. The most important difference between the two cases is that in the case of an appointed initiator this agent usually does not have a self-interest in achieving the goal (more than any of the other agents). Consequently it does not have a predetermined role in the process for achieving the goal in mind for itself (except as being the initiator). Of course, often, the initiator will also be the responsible agent for achieving the overall goal, which means it will at least check whether the other agents fulfill their role.

In case the initiating agent is the agent that is most interested to achieve the goal, this agent usually also has a certain role in the process of achieving the overall goal. This role will lead to the achievement of one of its private goals that it finds important and that might coincide partly with the overall goal.

3.1   The End Result of Potential Recognition

The first task of the initiator is to form a partial (abstract) plan for the achievement of the overall goal. On the basis of the (type of) subgoals that it recognizes it will determine which agents might be most suited to form the team. In order to determine this match the initiator tries to find out the properties of the agents. The initiator is interested in three aspects of the agents that can be approached for team formation.

1. their abilities
2. opportunities
3. their willingness to participate in the team formation

The first aspect considers whether the agents are suitable to participate in the team in a practical way (i.e. whether they can perform the right type of tasks, etc.). This deals with the subjective perspective of agent behaviour. It does not depend on the situation, but may be viewed as some kind of inherent property of the agent itself. The second aspect takes into account the possibilities of an action performance in the present situation. It involves resources and commitment strategies and possibly other such properties. This way the objective aspect of agent behaviour is expressed. The third aspect considers their mental attitude towards participating in the team. Very capable agents that do not want to do the job are of no use, neither are blindly committed agents that are already pursuing other goals.

The components of the agent's suitability are represented as follows:

1. the individual ability of agent b to achieve a goal ψ is denoted by $able(b, \psi)$.
2. the resources available to agent b are reflected by the opportunity that agent b has to achieve ψ denoted by $opp(b, \psi)$
3. the commitment strategy of an agent is denoted by *blind* (the agent is blindly committed to achieve its goals), *single-minded* (it can drop a goal only if it believes it can no longer achieve the goal) or *open-minded* (it can also drop a goal if it does no longer desire the goal).
4. the willingness to participate in team formation is denoted by $willing(b, \varphi)$.

We take Rao and Georgeff's semantics as a basis for our semantics, and refer the reader to [14,15] for details, especially completeness and decidability proofs. However, we give a short description here, providing the background needed to follow this paper.

As a reminder, the temporal structure is a discrete tree branching towards the future, as in Computation Tree Logic CTL, [10]. The different branches in such a time tree denote the optional courses of events that can be chosen by an agent. Primitive events are those events that an agent can perform and that determine a next time point in the tree. The branch between a point and the next point is labeled with the primitive event leading to that point. For example, if there are two branches emanating from a single time point, one labeled "go to dentist" and the other "go shopping", then the agent has a choice of executing either of these events and moving to the next point along the associated branch. The temporal operators include $inevitable(\varphi)$ (in all paths through the point of reference φ holds), $optional(\varphi) \equiv \neg inevitable(\neg\varphi)$, $\Diamond\varphi$ (somewhere later on the same path, φ holds) and $\varphi \, \mathbf{U} \, \psi$ (φ *until* ψ, i.e. either φ holds forever on this path, or, as soon as it stops holding, ψ will hold). Formulas are divided into state formulas (which are true in a particular state) and path formulas (which are true along a certain path).

As to Kripke semantics, we consider each possible world to be a temporal tree structure as described above. Evaluation of formulas is with respect to a world

w and a state s, using ternary accessibility relations B_i, D_i and I_i corresponding to each agent's beliefs, goals (or desires), and intentions, all of which lead from a pair of a world and a state in it to a world. Evaluation of formulas at world-state pairs is defined in the obvious manner inspired by CTL and epistemic logic.

able(b, ψ) if ψ is in a pre-given set of agent b's abilities.

opp(b, ψ) is true in a world and a state if there is a branch through that state such that at a later point on that branch, agent b has just seen to it that ψ. In [11] more formal definitions are given for ability and opportunity based on dynamic logic. The spirit of these definitions is captured in the ones given above except that we use states instead of actions.

As to commitments strategies, COMM(a, b, φ) stands for: agent a is socially committed towards agent b to fulfil φ (see [6,9]). Note that these social commitments are weaker than collective commitments, the strongest motivational attitude discussed in [6,9,8]. Let us stress that they are also different from the similar concept used in [16]. The strongest commitment is followed by the *blindly committed* agent, who maintains its commitments until it actually believes that they have been achieved. Formally,

$$\text{COMM}(a, b, \varphi) \rightarrow inevitable(\text{COMM}(a, b, \varphi) \textbf{ U } \text{BEL}(a, \varphi))$$

Single-minded agents may drop social commitments when they do not believe anymore that the commitment is realizable. However, as soon as the agent abandons a commitment, some communication and coordination with the other agent is needed. For open-minded agents, the situation is similar as for single-minded ones, except that they can also drop social commitments if they do not aim for the respective goal anymore. As in the case of single-minded agents, communication and coordination will be involved as expressed by the axiom:

$$
\begin{aligned}
&\text{COMM}(a, b, \varphi) \rightarrow \\
&inevitable[\text{COMM}(a, b, \varphi) \textbf{ U} \\
&\{\text{BEL}(a, \varphi) \vee \\
&(\neg\text{BEL}(a, optional \Diamond\varphi) \wedge \\
&done(communicate(a, b, \neg\text{BEL}(a, optional \Diamond\varphi))) \wedge \\
&done(coordinate(a, b, \varphi))) \\
&\vee(\neg\text{GOAL}(a, \varphi) \wedge \\
&done(communicate(a, b, \neg\text{GOAL}(a, \varphi))) \wedge \\
&done(coordinate(a, b, \varphi)))\}].
\end{aligned}
$$

The willingness to participate in the team formation is modeled as the agent's belief that it is optional that it is possible that it will have the individual intention to reach the overall goal. Formally *willing*(b, φ) stands for BEL$(b, optional \Diamond$ INT$(b, \varphi)))$

This does not conflict with the agent having different intentions INT(b, ψ), even if ψ is inconsistent with the overall goal φ. Note that the agent's willingness to participate in team formation does not mean that the agent will necessarily be a member of the resulting team. Agents can be more or less willing to participate in the team formation. If they have the overall goal already as their private intention, they are completely willing to participate in the team formation. On the other hand, if they do not want to participate at all, they believe never to intend to achieve the overall goal. Different intermediate positions are also possible. Metrics could be constructed in order to measure its willingness to participate. The metric could for instance be based on the percentage of branches in which the intention arises at some point and how far in the future these points lie.

3.2   Towards a Potential of Cooperation

In the previous section we have described what type of information the initiating agent tries to gather in order to start the team formation. In this section we will describe the formal outcome of this potential recognition stage, how the information is collected, and how this leads to this outcome.

The output at this stage is the "potential for cooperation" that the initiator a sees with respect to φ, denoted as $\text{POTCOOP}(a, \varphi)$, meaning that φ is a goal of a ($\text{GOAL}(a, \varphi)$), and there is a group G such that a believes that G can collectively achieve φ ($\text{C-CAN}_G(\varphi)$) and that they have the right distribution of commitment strategies to do so ($\text{STRAT}(\varphi, G)$) and are willing to participate in team formation. This is expressed by the following definition (of which the refined version may be found in [8]):

$$\text{POTCOOP}(a, \varphi) \leftrightarrow \text{GOAL}(a, \varphi) \wedge$$
$$\exists G \subseteq \text{TBEL}(a, \text{C-CAN}_G(\varphi) \wedge \text{STRAT}(\varphi, G)) \wedge \forall i \in G\, willing(i, \varphi))$$

$\text{POTCOOP}(a, \varphi)$ is derived from the information collected from the individual agents. To derive $\text{C-CAN}_G(\varphi)$ the initiator compares the information obtained about the other agents against a partial abstract plan for the overall goal φ. For this purpose the overall goal φ is split into a number of subgoals $\varphi_1, \ldots, \varphi_n$. These subgoals can be viewed as instrumental to the overall goal. Together they *constitute* φ and are compared with the individual abilities and opportunities that the agents are believed to have. Formally:

$$\text{C-CAN}_G(\varphi) \leftrightarrow \exists \varphi_1, \ldots, \exists \varphi_n (constitute(< \varphi_1, \ldots, \varphi_n >, \varphi) \wedge$$
$$\forall i \leq n \exists j \in G(able(j, \varphi_i) \wedge opp(j, \varphi_i)))$$

Unfortunately we cannot define the right distribution of commitment strategies ($\text{STRAT}(\varphi, G)$) in the same way in terms of individual commitment strategies. The reason is that this notion is not compositional. In fact we have to take the overall distribution of commitment strategies as primitive and regard it as a kind of constraint on individual commitments. Whenever the set of individual commitment strategies of the members is a suitable distribution for the whole group then the individual commitment strategies are also suitable. See [7] for a formal definition of suitable individual commitment strategies.

3.3 Information Seeking Dialogue

The initiator can find out the above properties of the agents by asking them or by using past experience or a database containing part of this information. The questions in this stage form part of an *information seeking* dialogue. The initiator has to form beliefs about the abilities, opportunities, commitment strategies and willingness of the individual agents in order to derive $\text{POTCOOP}(a, \varphi)$. This can be done by asking every agent about its properties and the agent responding with the requested information. Formally this can be expressed as follows:

$$[REQ_{a,i}(ASS_{i,a}(able(i, \varphi_i)) \cup ASS_{i,a}(\neg able(i, \varphi_i)))]$$
$$[ASS_{i,a}(able(i, \varphi_i))]\text{BEL}(a, (able(i, \varphi_i)))$$

The above formula is based on the formal theory on *speech acts* developed in [13] and [5]. This is based on a dynamic logic formula of the form $[\alpha_1][\alpha_2]\psi$, meaning that if α_1 is performed then always a situation arises such that if α_2 is performed then in the resulting state φ will always hold.
In the above case α_1 is the complex action
$REQ_{a,i}(ASS_{i,a}(able(i, \varphi_i))) \cup ASS_{i,a}(\neg able(i, \varphi_i)$ where $REQ_{a,i}(\alpha)$ stands for agent a requesting agent i to perform the action α. The action it requests i to perform is to either assert that it is able to achieve φ_i or to assert that it is not.
After this request i has three options.

1. It can simply ignore a and not answer at all.
2. It can state that it is not willing to divulge this information (formally expressed as
   $ASS_{i,a}(\neg(ASS_{i,a}(able(i, \varphi_i)) \cup ASS_{i,a}(\neg able(i, \varphi_i)))))$.
3. it can either assert that it is able to achieve φ (as is described in the formula above) or that it is not, in which case a believes that i is not able to achieve the goal:
   $[ASS_{i,a}(\neg able(i, \varphi_i))]\text{BEL}(a, (\neg able(i, \varphi_i))$.

Only in the last two cases will a have a resulting belief about the ability of i. Of course in the case that i does not want to divulge the information a can already derive that i is not willing to achieve φ as part of a team.
The same sequence as is shown above to seek information about the abilities of agents can be followed for the opportunities, commitment strategies and willingness of agents to participate in team formation.
We conclude this section with three remarks on some practical aspects on the above procedure of information seeking.
The first is a technical point about the exact questions that are asked by a. In the formulas above, a asks for the ability to achieve a specific goal φ_i. In principle, using this scheme, a should repeat this question for all the subgoals it distinguished to every agent. Of course it is more practical for agent a to ask each agent i about all the abilities it has with respect to achieving this set of goals. This can also be expressed formally in our logic, but is quite complex, and not very readable. Therefore we leave out this sophistication here.

A second point is about the case when agent i simply does not respond to the question. To avoid agent a waiting indefinitely for an answer, we assume that every speech act has an implicit deadline for reaction incorporated. The modeling of these type of deadlines is described in e.g. [4], but is not further pursued here.

Finally, the formal result of the potential recognition stage is that agent a has the belief that it is possible to form a team to achieve the overall goal or not. It would be useful for the other agents to know this fact as well, in order to revise their motivational and informational attitudes. In case no team could be formed or the agent is not considered as part of such a team formation, the agent can pursue other tasks again.

This information might be divulged to all agents by using a broadcast message of a stating the formal outcome of this stage.

4   Team Formation

At the start of this stage, the initiator has a sequence of groups in mind that could be suitable to form a team for achieving the overall goal. The sequence may be created arbitrarily or based on the properties of the agents involved. Although we do not go into details here, the organization of the groups into a sequence is important for the case that the most desirable group can not be formed.

All agents in these potential teams have expressed their willingness to participate in team formation, but do not necessarily have the individual intention to contribute towards achieving that goal yet. In this situation, the initiator tries to persuade all agents from a potential team to take on the intention to achieve the overall goal as well as to perform its own role within the team. This role corresponds to one of the temporary subgoals from a sequence $\varphi_1, \ldots, \varphi_n$ found during potential recognition, of which the initiator believes that $constitute(< \varphi_1, \ldots, \varphi_n >, \varphi)$.

The first decision the initiator has to make is with whom to start a *persuasion dialogue*. This decision could be based on a partial preferential ordering among agents, based on the initiator's information about their relevant abilities and degree of willingness to participate in team formation. It seems logical to start with an agent who has many relevant abilities and is highly willing to participate.

In the allocation of subgoals to agents, a process similar to constraint satisfaction takes place. In this case, the variables may take values that fall within the range corresponding to each agent's abilities and willingness. The aim of constraint satisfaction is to assign a value to each variable without depleting the domains of other variables. In our case we try to assign a temporary subgoal to each agent. However, in this case the values that can be assigned per agent are not fixed from the start: they may be the subject of negotiation. Techniques to find a proper order of agents with whom to start the persuasion dialogue and the preliminary subgoal about which to persuade them may be derived from well-known techniques from constraint satisfaction[1]. For example, the most constrained agent, e.g. the agent who is the only one able to achieve a certain crucial subgoal, might be a good starting point. Also, once the agent has been selected, the first subgoal about which to start persuading it could be the most crucial one.

4.1   The End Result of Team Formation

The end result that the initiator wants to achieve during this stage is a collective intention (C-INT$_G(\varphi)$ among a team G to reach the overall goal φ. A necessary condition for this is that all members of the group have the associated individual intention INT(i, φ), and that all members of the group are aware of this. That is, they have a collective belief about their intentions (C-BEL$_G$(E-INT$_G(\varphi)$). Moreover, to exclude the case of competition, all agents should *intend* the other members to have the associated individual intention, and it should be a collective belief in the group that this is so. In order to formalize the above two conditions, E-INT$_G(\varphi)$ (standing for "everyone intends") is defined by E-INT$_G(\varphi) \leftrightarrow \bigwedge_{i \in G}$ INT(i, φ). Formally:

$$C\text{-INT}_G(\varphi) \leftrightarrow E\text{-INT}_G(\varphi) \wedge C\text{-BEL}_G(E\text{-INT}_G(\varphi)) \wedge$$
$$E\text{-INT}_G(E\text{-INT}_G(\varphi)) \wedge$$
$$C\text{-BEL}_G(E\text{-INT}_G(E\text{-INT}_G(\varphi)))$$

The above formula makes evident that a crucial step for the initiator is to persuade all members of a potential team to take the overall goal as an individual intention. In practice this will mean that the initiator also persuades them to be willing to take on an appropriate temporary subgoal (this is much less strong than an intention [14]). To establish the second part of the above formula, the initiator also persuades each member to take on the intention that all other members of the potential team intend to contribute to the overall goal, in order to foster cooperation from the start. When all the individual motivational attitudes are established within the team, the initiator broadcasts the fact E-INT$_G(\varphi)) \wedge$ E-INT$_G(E\text{-INT}_G(\varphi))$, by which the necessary collective beliefs are established and the collective intention is in place.

4.2   Persuasion Dialogue

During the persuasion dialogue the initiator has to convince the other agent to form an intention to reach the overall goal as part of a team of agents that intend to achieve that goal. According to [16] the persuasion dialogue consists of three main stages: information exchange, rigorous persuasion and completion. In our case the information exchange already started in the potential recognition stage during which abilities, opportunities and willingness of the agents are exchanged.

Information exchange. During the information exchange the agents make clear their initial stand with respect to the overall goal, the willingness to take on a certain subgoal and to form part of a certain team to achieve the overall goal. These issues are expressed partly in the form of intentions and beliefs. Other beliefs supporting or related to the above issues might also be exchanged already. Only when a conflict arises about these issues a persuasion dialogue has to take place. In each persuasion there are two parties or roles; the proponent (P) and the opponent (O). In our case the proponent is the initiator and the opponent the other agent.

The stands the other agents take about the above issues are seen as its initial *concessions*. Concessions are beliefs and intentions that an agent takes on for the sake of argument, but need not be prepared to defend. The agents will also have private attitudes that may only become apparent later on during the dialogue. The stand of the initiator is seen as the initial thesis that it is prepared to defend during the dialogue.

The initial conflict description consists of a set of O's initial concessions and P's initial thesis.

Rigorous persuasion. During the rigorous persuasion stage the agents exchange arguments to challenge or support a thesis. The following rules can be used to govern these moves adapted from [16]:

1. Starting with O the two parties move alternately according to the rules of the game.
2. Each move consists of either a challenge, a question, a statement, a challenge or question accompanied by a statement, or a final remark.
3. The game is highly asymmetrical. All P's statements are assertions, and called theses, all O's statements are called concessions. P is doing the questioning and O all the challenging.
4. The initial move by O challenges P's initial thesis. It is P's goal to make O concede the thesis. P can do this by questioning O and thus bridge the gap between the initial concessions of O and the thesis, or by making an assertion to clinch the argument if acceptable.
5. Each move for O is to pertain to P's preceding move. If this move was a question, then O has to answer it. If it was an assertion, then O has to challenge it.
6. Each party may give up, using the final remark $ASS_{a,i}(quit)$ for the initiator, or
$ASS_{i,a}(\text{INT}(i,\varphi) \wedge willing(i,\varphi_i) \wedge \bigwedge_{j \in G} \text{INT}(i, \text{INT}(j,\varphi)))$. If O's concessions imply P's thesis, then P can end the dialogue by the final remark: $ASS_{a,i}(won)$. In our system we assume that we have the following rule:

$$[ASS_{a,i}(won)]O(ASS_{i,a}(\text{INT}(i,\varphi) \wedge$$
$$willing(i,\varphi_i) \wedge \bigwedge_{j \in G} \text{INT}(i, \text{INT}(j,\varphi)))$$

which means that agent i is obliged to state that it gives up and will play its role in the team. This does not mean that i will actually make this assertion!

Just that there is an obligation (according to the rules of the persuasion "game").

7. All challenges have to follow logical rules. E.g. A thesis $A \wedge B$ can be challenged by challenging one of the two conjuncts. For a complete set of rules for the propositional part of the logic we refer to [16].

In the completion stage the outcome is made explicit, such that the agents either have a collective belief and/or intention or they know that they differ in opinion.

Goal formation through speech acts. In this section we discuss goals and intentions and their relation. Although we do not give a formal semantics and/or definition, we assume that goals do not necessarily have to be consistent, but intentions do have to be consistent (leading to a K_n system for goals and a KD_n system for intentions). Also we assume that for each intention there is a goal that generated it and thus we have: $INT(x, \varphi) \rightarrow GOAL(x, \varphi)$.

Intentions are formed on the basis of beliefs and previously formed goals of a higher abstraction level by a number of formal rules (see [2]). E.g. the built-in goal can be to obey the law, or avoid the punishment. The (instrumental) belief is that driving slower than the speed limit is instrumental for obeying the law. Together with the rule the new goal of driving slower than the speed limit is derived.

The general intention generation rule is represented as follows:

$$GOAL(x, \varphi) \wedge BEL(x, INSTR(\psi, \varphi)) \rightarrow INT(x, \psi)$$

It states that if an agent x has a goal φ and it believes that ψ is instrumental in achieving φ then it will have the intention to achieve ψ. If ψ is instrumental in achieving φ then it means achieving ψ gets the agent "closer" to φ in some abstract sense. We do not define this relation any further, but leave it as primitive.

We acknowledge that the above rule is an oversimplification of reality. In most cases it will be too strong. But we see it as an example of a possible rule that links goals and intentions and do not explore more realistic, but also more complex, rules in this paper.

This very general rule for generating intentions can be combined with more specific ones, e.g. goal adoption, in which case an agent adopts the goals of another agent. One more specific rule for goal adoption can be given by:

$$GOAL(x, helped(x, y)) \wedge$$
$$BEL(x, [GOAL(y, \varphi) \rightarrow INSTR(OBT(y, \varphi), helped(x, y))]$$

Agent x has as abstract goal to help y. It believes that if y has a goal φ then it is instrumental for x to achieve its abstract goal to help y if it helps y obtain its goal. Where

$$OBT(y, \varphi) \equiv \varphi \wedge GOAL(y, \varphi) \, \mathbf{U} \, \varphi$$

So, agent y obtained φ if φ is true and it had the goal φ until the moment φ became true.

Together with the general intention generation rule we can now directly derive $INT(x, OBT(y, \varphi))$ whenever $BEL(x, GOAL(y, \varphi))$.

The above sketched mechanism can be used in our setting during persuasion. In this case the initiator tries to get the other agent to concede to higher level goals and instrumental beliefs that together with the general intention generation rule imply the intention to achieve the overall goal of the system. Here follows an example move of the initiator.

$$ASS_{a,i}(\forall j(GOAL(j, \psi)) \rightarrow INSTR(\varphi, \psi))$$

After this speech act agent i knows that the initiator believes that if an agent has the goal ψ then the overall goal φ is instrumental to this goal. Formally (see also [5]):

$$[ASS_{a,i}(\forall j(GOAL(j, \psi)) \rightarrow INSTR(\varphi, \psi))]$$
$$BEL(i, BEL(a, (\forall j(GOAL(j, \psi)) \rightarrow INSTR(\varphi, \psi))))$$

Let us assume that i has only two rules for answering. If i does not have a belief that is inconsistent with a belief of a then i will concede. If, on the other hand i does have a belief to the contrary it will challenge the assertion. Formally:

$$\neg BEL(i, \neg\gamma) \wedge BEL(i, BEL(a, \gamma)) \rightarrow DO(i, CONCEDE_{i,a}\gamma)$$

$$BEL(i, \neg\gamma) \wedge BEL(i, BEL(a, \gamma)) \rightarrow DO(i, CHALLENGE_{i,a}\gamma)$$

where the operator $DO(i, \alpha)$ indicates that α is the next action performed by i. We do not give a formal definition of the $CONCEDE$ and $CHALLENGE$ actions, but will only give their intuitive meaning here. The concede action has as effect that the agent is willing to assume the assertion during the dialogue. The challenge is a combination of a denial and a request to prove. We will come back to it shortly.

Suppose that i did not have a contrary belief then i concedes the above belief by the speech act

$$CONCEDE_{i,a}(\forall j(GOAL(j, \psi)) \rightarrow INSTR(\varphi, \psi))$$

The effect of this speech act is the same as for the ASS, except that a can only assume that i believes the formula during the dialogue and might retract it afterwards.

$$[CONCEDE_{i,a}(\forall j(GOAL(j, \psi)) \rightarrow INSTR(\varphi, \psi))]$$
$$BEL(a, BEL(i, (\forall j(GOAL(j, \psi)) \rightarrow INSTR(\varphi, \psi))))$$

Now the formula is a belief of both a and i. In this case, the initiator's next aim in the persuasion will be to get i to concede to the belief that ψ is a goal of i by the question

$$REQ_{a,i}(CONCEDE_{i,a}(\mathrm{GOAL}(i,\psi))).$$

The effect of this request is given formally through:

$$[REQ_{a,i}(CONCEDE_{i,a}(\mathrm{GOAL}(i,\psi)))]$$
$$O(CONCEDE_{i,a}(\mathrm{GOAL}(i,\psi) \cup ASS_{i,a}(\neg\mathrm{GOAL}(i,\psi)))$$

That is, i is obliged to either concede it has the goal ψ or assert the negation of it. After i's response the initiator knows whether or not i believes it has the goal ψ.

If i does not concede to the initiator's first speech act, it may instead counter with a challenge by first asserting that it doesn't share the initiator's belief and then asking the initiator to argue for the belief. This is done by the complex speech act $CHALLENGE$. This action can be described as follows:

$$CHALLENGE_{i,a} \ (\forall j(\mathrm{GOAL}(j,\psi) \rightarrow INSTR(\varphi,\psi))) \equiv$$
$$\neg ASS_{i,a}(\forall j(\mathrm{GOAL}(j,\psi) \rightarrow INSTR(\varphi,\psi)));$$
$$CONCEDE_{i,a}(\mathrm{GOAL}(j,\psi))$$
$$REQ_{i,a}(ASS_{a,i}(PROOF(INSTR(\varphi,\psi))))$$

The complete effects of this speech act are quite complex to describe formally, so, we leave it out here. The example gives an idea how the intention to achieve the main goal may be formed by persuasion. For intentions with respect to subgoals and with respect to cooperation with other potential team members, the process is analogous. In the latter case, the initiator tries to get the other agent to form beliefs that will trigger the formation of the intention that all other potential members also intend to achieve the overall goal. The final result of the team formation stage is reached when for one potential team all the persuasion dialogues have been concluded successfully.

Negotiation embedded in the persuasion dialogue. Krabbe and Walton ([16]) do not allow for embeddings of negotiations in persuasion dialogues. However, we feel that in contrast to persuasion with respect to informational attitudes, bargaining may be appropriate within a persuasion dialogue with respect to motivational attitudes (intentions). Thus, during team formation the initiator may persuade other agents to take on the overall goal by offering them return favors. Also, an agent may offer willingness to take on a subgoal and trade this for a promise of the initiator to take care during the later stage of plan formation that this will be the (only) subgoal for the agent. A prospective member may even negotiate by trading its membership for the inclusion or exclusion of certain other agents. However, negotiation about the overall goal is not possible in our setting.

Although the topic is too complex to give a complete account on how the negotiation is translated in logical terms, we still will show informally how this process works within the logic underlying our theory.

At the start of the negotiation both agents have a number of possible future courses of action which are preferentially ordered. That is, they have a preferred course of action which they will try to realize first. If the agent notices that this course of action is no longer realizable or preferred it might switch to another branch.

The preferential ordering of the courses of action is based on the beliefs of the agent. E.g. we believe that writing this paper will make us famous. The goal of the negotiation is to change the beliefs of the other agent such that the preferential orders change so that they fit with each other. Not all beliefs of an agent can be changed at will by speech acts of another agent. This depends on the situation and status of the agents. Therefore, it might be that the agents are unsuccessful in their attempts to change the preferential ordering of the other agent sufficiently (cf. "the bottom line").

In our case the initiator knows at the start of the negotiation that the other agent believes that the overall goal will be its intention during some course of action at some future time. The initiator tries to change the beliefs of the agent in such a way that this branch becomes the preferred course of actions for the other agent. Of course there might be several branches on which the agent adopts the goal, in that case the initiator tries to find its most preferred one.

We will not give a precise set of rules for negotiation, but give some examples of the differences with persuasion. The situation in negotiation is more symmetrical than in the case of persuasion. Both agents may propose theses as well as concessions, so the opponent O has more options than a fixed reaction to the previous move of the proponent. An agent is obliged not to retract its concessions (e.g. to take on a subgoal). The successful end result of negotiation is not that one agent wins, but that a deal is constructed to which both agents agree.

Termination of the negotiation dialogue. Because the negotiation dialogue is more symmetrical and both agents can propose new theses and concessions the termination of this type of dialogue is much less clear than that of the persuasion dialogue. Also the end of the negotiation does not imply a winner. Both parties might agree that no deal can be formed and end the negotiation. We assume in our situation that the initiative for this move lays with the initiator. As soon as it finds out that the negotiation cannot be concluded successfully it will stop not only the negotiation but also the persuasion dialogue in which it is embedded. The negotiation dialogue can thus be concluded in three ways.

1. A successful fit of the courses of actions of the two agents has been found. The initiator announces this by asserting the achieved deal (i.e. common intention).
2. A repetition of moves by one of the two parties is seen as a signal that the relevant beliefs of this party are not to be changed anymore. The initiator then announces the assertion $ASS_{a,i}(quit)$, which also concludes the persuasion dialogue.
3. The second agent i announces $ASS_{i,a}(quit)$; in this case the initiator replies with the assertion $ASS_{a,i}(quit)$, which again also concludes the persuasion dialogue.

In the case of successful termination of negotiation, the agents return to the persuasion dialogue where the deal may be used by the initiator as a concession of the other.

5   Conclusions

In previous work ([8] and [9]) it was shown how Cooperative Problem Solving can be divided into four stages, each of them resulting in specific motivational attitudes that can be formally described. Then in [7] the stages were related to specific types of dialogue (possibly embedded into each other) by which these motivational attitudes can be formed. In this paper, finally, we have shown for the first two stages of potential recognition and team formation which rules govern these dialogues and how the moves within the dialogues can be expressed by formally represented speech acts. The complete description of all elements of the dialogues in a formal logic has thus been made possible. However, many elements of the logic still have to be expanded and improved upon, before one can state that the dialogue has been described formally. Once this is done it will be possible to prove that in given circumstances the dialogue results in a certain outcome. This is of prime importance if you want to construct a MAS for automated cooperative problem solving.

It is clear that, even though the dialogues are governed by strict rules, the reasoning needed to find an appropriate move is highly complex. This implies that the agents also have to contain complex reasoning mechanisms in order to execute the dialogues. It means that, although the result is much more flexible and refined than using a protocol like Contract Net, the process is also more time consuming. For practical cases one should carefully consider what carries more weight and choose the method of team formation accordingly.

A final result of this ongoing research should contain a complete set of formal rules for all the types of dialogue and indicate how these are implemented through formal speech acts. This would make it possible to extend the framework to the next stages of cooperative problem solving (plan formation and execution).

It also should expand on several aspects of the internal reasoning of the agents. One example is the concept of giving a proof as defense of an assertion during the rigorous persuasion. Another is the actual formation of intentions based on previous beliefs and goals.

Another issue for further research is to investigate the consequences of not having a fixed overall goal, but an emerging goal. Another point is to check what should be done in case there is not one initiating agent (but possibly many or none).

Finally it should be investigated how actual proofs can be constructed in an efficient way to prove that the end results of a dialogue are formed through the speech acts given the rules of the dialogue.

References

1. R. Dechter. Enhancement Schemes for Constraint Processing: Backjumping, Learning and Cutset Decomposition. *Journal of Artificial Intelligence*, vol 41, 1990, pp. 273–312.

2. F. Dignum and R. Conte. Intentional agents and goal formation. In M. Singh et.al., editor, *Intelligent Agents IV (LNAI 1365)*, Springer Verlag, 1998, pp. 231-244.
3. F. Dignum, B. Dunin-Kęplicz and R. Verbrugge. *Creating Collective Intention through Dialogue.* Technical Report of Cognitive Science and Engineering, TCW-1999-16, University of Groningen, 1999.
4. F. Dignum and R. Kuiper. Combining dynamic deontic logic and temporal logic for the specification of deadlines. In Jr. R. Sprague, editor, *Proceedings of thirtieth HICSS*, Wailea, Hawaii, 1997.
5. F. Dignum and H. Weigand. Communication and deontic logic. In R. Wieringa and R. Feenstra, editors, *Information Systems, Correctness and Reusability*, World Scientific, Singapore, 1995, pp. 242-260.
6. B. Dunin-Kęplicz and R. Verbrugge. Collective Commitments. In *Proc. Second International Conference on Multi-Agent Systems, ICMAS'96*, IEEE Computer Society Press, Kyoto, 1996, pp. 56-63.
7. B. Dunin-Kęplicz and R. Verbrugge. The Role of Dialogue in Collective Problem Solving: Part I. To appear in *Proceedings of the Agent Day*, Krakow, 1999.
8. B. Dunin-Kęplicz and R. Verbrugge. A Reconfiguration algorithm for distributed problem solving. To appear in *Engineering Simulation: An International Journal of Electrical, Electronic and other Physical Systems*, special issue about distributed systems, 1999.
9. B. Dunin-Kęplicz and R. Verbrugge. Collective motivational attitudes in cooperative problem solving. In V. Gorodetsky et al. (eds.), *Proceedings of The First International Workshop of Central and Eastern Europe on Multi-agent Systems (CEEMAS'99)*, St. Petersburg, 1999, pp. 22-41.
10. E.A. Emerson. Temporal and Modal Logic. In J. van Leeuwen, editor, *Handbook of Theoretical Computer Science*, North-Holland, Amsterdam, 1989, pp. 995-1072.
11. B. van Linder, W. van der Hoek, and J.-J. Ch. Meyer. Formalising abilities and opportunities of agents. *Fundamenta Informaticae* 34 (1998) pp. 53-101.
12. T. Sandholm and V. Lesser. Issues in automated negotiation and electronic commerce: extending the contract net protocol. In *Proceedings First International Conference on Multiagent Systems (ICMAS95)*, San Francisco, AAAI Press and MIT Press, 1995. pp. 328-335.
13. J.R. Searle and D. Vanderveken. *Foundations of Illocutionary Logic*, Cambridge, Cambridge University Press, 1985.
14. A.S. Rao and M.P. Georgeff. Modeling rational agents within a BDI architecture. In R. Fikes and E. Sandewall (eds.) *Proceedings of Knowledge Representation and Reasoning (KR&R-91)*, San Mateo, Morgan Kaufmann, 1991. pp.473-484.
15. A.S. Rao and M.P. Georgeff. Formal Models and Decision Procedures for Multi-agent Systems. Technical Note 61, Carlton (Victoria), Australian Artificial Intelligence Institute, 1995.
16. D. Walton and E. Krabbe. *Commitment in Dialogue*, SUNY Press, Albany, 1995.
17. M. Wooldridge and N.R. Jennings. Cooperative Problem Solving. *Journal of Logic and Computation* 9 (4) (1999), pp. 563-592.

On Abstract Models and Conversation Policies

Renée Elio[1] and Afsaneh Haddadi[2]

[1]Department of Computing Science, University of Alberta,
Edmonton, Alberta Canada, T6G 2H1
ree@cs.ualberta.ca
[2] DaimlerChrysler, AG Alt-Moabit 96A,
10559 Berlin, Germany
afsaneh.haddadi@daimlerchrysler.com

Abstract. It is possible to define conversation policies, such as communication or dialogue protocols, that are based strictly on what messages and, respectively, what performatives may follow each other. While such an approach has many practical applications, such protocols support only "local coherence" in a conversation. In a mixed-initiative dialogue between two agents cooperating on some joint task, there must be a "global coherence" in both the conversation and in the task they are trying to accomplish. Recognition of agent intentions about the joint task is essential for this global coherence, but there are further mechanisms needed to ensure that both local and global coherence are jointly maintained. This paper presents a general yet practical approach to designing, managing, and engineering agents that can engage in mixed-initiative dialogues. In this approach, we promote developing abstract task models and designing conversation policies in terms of such models.

1 Introduction

Cooperation between agents denotes a kind of interaction required when each of the agents has some, but not all, the information and abilities required to accomplish a task. This requires specifying the semantics and pragmatics of a "conversation"—a sequence of messages—that enable two agents to bring a task to completion. Most definitions of a conversation implicitly or explicitly appeal to the notion of "task accomplishment" or "goal achievement," although what constitutes a task or goal is interpreted quite broadly. Recently, there has been considerable interest in specifying conversation policies, which speak to a range of matters in managing lengthy conversations, from turntaking and message timeout conventions to responding to dynamic constraints imposed by the environment [9]. Our concern here is what some researchers [3] claim is a crucial function of a broadlydefined conversation policy, which is: constraining "the messages that appear on the wire." It is argued that this need arises from the manytomany mapping between an intention an agent might have and the specific agent communication language (ACL) primitive used to convey that intention. The call for conversation policies stems from a belief that the solution to these matters will not be found at the level of individual message primitives or performatives within an agent communication language, such as KQML or FIPA's

F. Dignum and M. Greaves (Eds.): Agent Communication, LNAI 1916, pp. 301-313, 2000.

ACL [2,7]. However well-specified the semantics for a performative might be, they are under constrained with respect to the full illocutionary force of the communicative act. For example, an "inform" ought sometimes to be interpreted as a "suggestion" but in another context, as a "command." This in turn has given rise to a more protocol oriented view of ACL semantics, i.e., the specification of semantics for conversational sub-units as ways of structuring multi-message sequences between two agents [2, 6, 10,15]. This approach builds on the notion of representing dialogues and conversations among humans or software agents as state transition diagrams, a perspective which dates back at least to Winograd and Flores [16].

The continuing dilemma over identifying semantics for both primitive message types and message protocols is motivated, of course, by the need to have a clear, unambiguous message exchange. If we can cram all the nuances and distinctions into different primitive messages and protocols, then perhaps any run-time recognition and handling of intentions can be avoided. But we see several limitations to putting all hopes at these two levels alone. First, the run-time recognition and handling of intention seems essential for human-agent cooperation and communication. For while we may design a software agent that follows some particular communication protocol, we cannot assume that the human knows that protocol or would be inclined to abide by it, at least in cases where user messages cannot be directly constrained (as in, say, via menu choices on a graphical interface). This makes the problem of understanding and structuring even limited conversations for cooperation more complex. Second, elevating the level of analysis from the individual performative to protocols (which we think is a crucial step) only moves the set of problems back a level. As Greaves, Holmback & Bradshaw [3] note, there is no consensus here either on what the primitive protocols are, let alone their semantics. Although this matter is in principle resolvable, protocols can only maintain what we call *local coherence*—some unity between very short sequences of messages. When a dialogue expands beyond 23 message sequences, there must be some way to ensure *global coherence* to the entire conversation, i.e., a coherence to the way in which very short message sequences are, crudely put, patched together. And this leads to what we see as the third matter. Focusing on protocols alone will not fully address the primary function of a conversation policy as motivated in [3]: to constrain the messages that are sent. While protocol definitions do this locally, they do not do this globally. After one protocol completes, what constrains the next protocol? And in what sense does the concatenation of any sequence of protocols constitute a globallycoherent message exchange?

The appeal to global coherence as a feature of a conversation is implied by Grice's [4] maxim of relation, which states that speakers aim to make their contributions relevant to the ongoing conversation. In other words, each speaker's contribution to the conversation relates to the utterances that come before and follow it, so that the whole conversation is about something [12]. Under our view, that "something" is what we call an abstract task model. While we fully believe that precise semantics are crucial for individual performatives and protocols, the full illocutionary force of a message sequence will be under constrained without some appeal to an abstract task specification. Simply put, the only way to constrain messages is to constrain and delimit intentions. For us, an abstract task is something like "scheduling," "negotiation", "database search", or "diagnosis." Similar notions of generic tasks and task models had been developed to support domainindependent methodologies and architectures for developing knowledge-based problem-solving systems [1]. Further, the notion of a "shared plan" has a prominent role in models of human discourse processing [e.g., 5]. We think that it is reasonable to assume that two agents come to a cooperative venture knowing that their (abstract) task is one of search, negotiation, diagnosis, or whatever. Regardless of what the actual domain content and domain ontology is, two cooperating agents must share an ontology for the abstract task they are jointly solving, and this ontology is different from the ontology for the actual domain.

We adopt a pragmatic approach to specifying an abstract task specification that begins with a problem formulation using a traditional statespace representation. This representation defines and delimits a set of task intentions, which in turn defines and delimits discourse intentions. Discourse intentions are advanced by discourse protocols—standards for message sequences. The content of the individual performatives that comprise the protocols is also specified by the abstract task specification. The resulting analysis supports a flexible and pragmatic handling of "unexpected" messages. In this respect, while a message may be unexpected in the context of some protocol, its associated intention cannot be undefined in the context of the abstract task specification that is jointly held by the two agents.

As one component of a publicly posted conversation policy, an abstract task model addresses two elements of a broadlydefined conversation policy [3]: specific goal achievement policies and some aspects of conversation management policies. We illustrate the features of this approach by showing its application to a simple and well understood agentassistant task.

2   Successive Refinement Search as an Abstract Task

In this section, we briefly outline aspects of an application domain that led us to the perspectives described above. The problem called for a system, which we here call the database agent (DBA), that would assist a human (e.g., a driver in an automobile) in a variety of tasks, which included location and retrieval of information from various databases. Generally speaking, the DBA must identify one or more database entities that satisfy a set of constraints specified by the user. The database entities are defined by featurevalue tuples. Using a database of restaurants as an example, a particular database entry corresponds to a collection of featurevalue specifications like *:name Rangoon :location Palo Alto :ethnic-type Burmese :cost moderate etc.*

We assume that the database is so that the user cannot specify a single, simple database query (e.g., "Where is the closest gas station?") We also assume that the user may not necessarily have a definitive set of constraints in mind when starting the task. It may be more accurate therefore, to characterize the process as one of exploration. This was the motivation for viewing the DBA and the user as two agents cooperating in a successive refinement search, where the goal is to identify one or more database entries that satisfy a particular set (or possibly different sets) of constraints. The following example dialogue illustrates the nature of the task, where U designates the user.

DB-1:   What type of location do you want to locate?
         Lumber stores? Pharmacies?

U-2:   I want inexpensive food in San Francisco.
DB-3:   O.K.. There are several hundred inexpensive restaurants in San Francisco.
DB-5:   What type of food do you want?
U-6:   What do you mean?
DB-7:   I mean ethnic type such as Hungarian or French.
U-8:   Italian.
DB-9:   O.K. Do you want a take out or sit-down place?
U-11:   What about on the Peninsula?
DB-12: O.K. We'll leave San Francisco for a moment.
DB13:   There are 35 Italian restaurants on the Peninsula.
DB14:   A particular place or city will rapidly narrow
        down this set most rapidly.
U15:   Redwood City or Menlo Park.

There are many user interface systems and applications that support some or all elements of this interaction. Putting aside matters of speech input and processing, we use a few features of this task to motivate key aspects of an abstract task model specification for a conversation policy, particularly when communication is limited to simple message exchange (and not, say, enabled via a visual interface, as in [13]). First, in viewing the above dialogue to be about successive refinement search (and not about restaurant advising or locating), it appears there are a few generic objects of discourse that comprise the message content:(i) a *domain*: a particular domain database in which entities are defined by features and values; (ii) a *constraint*: any feature that has a particular value assigned to it; (iii) a *search space*: a set of database entities that satisfy a set of constraints; (iv) *search-space members*: particular entities within a particular search space.

From our perspective, the semantics underlying the messages being exchanged in the example dialogue are defined by the ontology of successive refinement search as an abstract task. What these objects of discourse are and what can be said about them are intimately defined with what actions can be taken to advance the task. In our analysis these actions are limited to: (i) *loading* a database to be searched, which defines the initial search space, (ii) *contracting*, or reducing the search space by specifying additional constraints that members must satisfy, and (iii) *expanding* that search space by relaxing one or more constraints. These are traditional database operations. There may be other capabilities that are unique to each agent (e.g., an agent might also compute the most-discriminating feature for a given search space.)

Another key aspect about the sample dialogue above is that either agent can take the initiative in advancing the task in a new direction. Therefore, the DBA must respond effectively to these "unexpected" messages. For example, in utterance U11, the user does not provide an answer to the question posed in utterance DB10, and instead shifts the direction of the search task. Intention recognition serves to support this mixedinitiative aspect of cooperation. Intentions that an agent can have about the task (and presumably express during the conversation) are limited by the objects of discourse, what can be done with them, and therefore what can be said about them. This is crucial to having a pragmatic but somewhat flexible approach to posting and recognizing intentions, for these objects of discourse serve to circumscribe the intention set.

3   The Abstract Task Defines Objects of Discourse

The semantics underlying the language primitives used in our framework borrow from general speech-act theory and the semantics are based on a number of pragmatic principles discussed in Haddadi [6]. A message consists of a specific message type (which we will call a performative type), specific object of discourse, and partially specific content. It has the format *(performative $agent-name1 $agent-name2 $object-of-discourse $content)*. For brevity's sake, we have omitted many message parameters such as feature keywords and others for protocol administration.

Table 1 presents the set of performatives defined for the DBA. The outermost performatives represent the general class of an utterance. In the DBA, we make use of the classes request, query, and inform. The inner performatives given in Table 1 further specialize the class, by supplying information related to the result of the task action that has been performed, the task itself or the action the speaker intends/expects the hearer to perform. The *$agent-name1* parameter refers to the speaker, sender or generally the actor of the performative, while *$agent-name2* refers to the hearer, receiver or generally the agent that would be effected by the performative.

Table 1. Performatives and their Combination

Outer Performative	Inner Performative	Immediately Expected Reply
Request	Provide	Inform
	Suggest	Inform + Accept/ Reject
Query	Provide	Inform
	Confirm	Inform + Confirm/Deny
	Suggest	Inform + Accept/Reject
Inform	Provide	
	Confirm	
	Deny	
	Accept	
	Reject	

The third column of Table 1—the immediately expected reply—designates the performative that would "complete" the dialogue initiated by the performative in column 1. Put another way, the information in Table 1 defines a basic statetransition definition for subdialogues.

Inform. Inform messages take on the outer and inner objectsofdiscourse, and a content specification, that occur in the request or query dialogue that they complete. *Request.* A request performative is tightly coupled with advancing the search task. The objects of discourse associated with request are (i) a system *action* that enables a search task to begin or terminate, such as loading a particular database for searching and (ii) a *constraint*, which specifies a featurevalue vector according to which database entities can be identified. Most request performatives concern constraints.

Following [6], we view a request as having an associated level of commitment. When a request is made by the DBA, the system is making a pre-commitment to how the progress on the search task might be accomplished and it prompts the user for information in order to do this. System requests thus take *suggest* as an inner performative. A suggestion refers to a possible task strategy and it must be accepted or rejected by the other agent, in this case, the user. By supplying the information asked for, the user is committing to this computation. When a request is made by the user, the user is simultaneously committing to a computation on the search space and delivering the information necessary to execute it. User requests thus take *provide* as an inner performative. We note that the abstract task model is the place to specify agent roles with respect to functionality and this in turn can be used to derive the appropriate nuances of message types such as "command" versus "suggest." Some examples of request messages, with their English gloss, include the following (where U means useragent and S means systemagent)

    (i) ReqU: Lets look for a restaurant in Mid-Peninsula.
                    (request U S :constraint (provide U S :value (fv-pairs :feature location:value Mid-peninsula)))
    (ii) ReqS: How about Chinese?
                    (request S U :constraint (suggest S U :value (fv-pairs :feature rest-type:value Chinese)))
    (iii) ReqS: What kind of price range?
                    (request S U :constraint (provide U S :value (fv-pairs :feature price :value ?)))

Query. A query is not about advancing a task but about exchanging information indirectly related to advancing the task. An abstract task model defines an ontology of what each agent knows about as well what each agent may be *allowed* to know about. This circumscribes to some extent the message content of queries; for the successive refinement task, the objects of discourse are: (i) system *functionality*, that is in what domains it can assist the user with the search task (ii) the *domain knowledge base*, which includes domainspecific information, such as the range of values on a particular feature, (iii) the *database*, which includes queries about the availability of information about particular entities in the database, and (iv) *task-information*, information relevant to the current state of the task. Queries may take either provide, suggest, or *confirm* as an inner performative. A confirm expresses the truth or falseness with respect to a property of some objectofdiscourse and it must be confirmed or denied. When a query is sent by the user agent, the system must respond with an *inform* followed by an appropriate inner performative. System queries often take the form of suggestions, in which case the user response must be interpreted as providing (at least) an acceptance or rejection of the suggestion. The objectsof discourse that may accompany the inner performatives associated with queries are restricted to (i) the *domain* (e.g., restaurants, hospitals); (ii) the current *search space* (i.e., the set of members defined by the current set of constraints); and (iii) a particular *member* in the current search space or database. Examples of query messages with English correspondences include the following:

(i) QueU: Do you have menus for restaurants?
               (query U S :knowledge-base (confirm S U :domain
               (describe-domain :domain $domain (has-feature :feature menu)))
(ii) QueU: Do you have the menu for Maxine's?
               (query U S :database (confirm S U :member (hasattribute :member
               $member :feature menu)))
(iii) QueU: What do you mean by (the descriptor) restaurant type?
               (query U S :knowbase (provide S U :domain (describefeature
               :domain $domainid featurelist :feature resttype :attribute range))

We now have a representation and semantics for the abstract task model of successive refinement search and have covered all possible task intentions (i.e., intentions in the sense of illocutions associated with speech acts) that agents can express when communicating about the search task.

We cannot overemphasize the role of the abstract task model in specifying the ontology for these performatives. The successiverefinement task model defined a semantics for the general performatives in terms of what could be talked about. A more general theory of semantics for performatives in terms of what messages must or may follow each other is found in [6]. However, the content of the performatives, i.e., the objects of discourse and what can be said about them, can only follow from the joint commitment to a shared abstract task model. What we have developed here is an abstract task analysis for cooperative successive refinement search, and let that abstract task model define these objects, their relations, and the set of methods that allow progress to be made on the task.

4   Abstract Tasks Define Intentions and Global Coherence

At this point, we have only covered utterances and their associated intentions in communication (i.e., the illocution of an utterance). Table 1's specifications about what performatives may or must follow each other ensure some local coherence at the level of 23 message sequences, but they do not structure how short message sequences can be patched together in a globally coherent way. We now consider how intentions are internalized for reasoning about the next course of action (progress on the task vs. progress in the discourse) and how to maintain a coherent dialogue between agents (i.e., coherent perlocutions). We assume a turntaking dialogue. The abstract task model we apply here allows (i) that both the agents can take the initiative in directing the task and (ii) the user's initiative always has priority over the system's initiative. While the user may change the direction or other aspects of the search at any time, the abstract task model defines that the system would do so only if the current direction could not be pursued further. In this case, the system takes initiative in suggesting a new course of action. The abstract task model, by specifying strategies for task progress (such as identifying the most discriminating feature to reduce a search set), also defines a larger set of intentions that the either agent can have,

There must be (i) a means for deciding or recognizing that a particular message is relevant to advancing either the task, the exchange of information about the task, or switching to a completely new task, and (ii) a means for representing how the semantics of the performative pairs in Table 1 actually advance these goals. The first is accomplished by relating agent intentions about the task or the discourse to specific performatives. The second is accomplished by protocols, which explicitly map sequences of messages to the fulfillment of a particular intention, and indicate what must happen when an unexpected message is received. We now turn to a more detailed discussion of intentions and protocols, and how they are represented.

4.1   The Interplay of Task Space and Discourse Space

In previous sections, we have underscored that the DBA must reason about both the task of successive refinement search and about the task of structuring the discourse with the user in an intelligent way. These two tasks are not only related, but at different times, one supports the other. Here, we introduce the conceptual distinction between "task space" and "discourse space", and indicate how intentions and protocols define elements of these two spaces.

Let a state in the discourse space correspond to shared information held by both the DBA and the user. A transition between one state into another is made by making an utterance (e.g., "Where do you want to eat?"). When an utterance is correctly interpreted, its intention is understood and that intention becomes part of the shared information between the two agents. For the abstract task of successive-refinement search, the problem at the task level is to identify a set of entities in a database that meet certain constraints. A state in this task space is a set of database entities and the constraints that define them. There are two legal transitions or operators at this level: the contract operator, which means adding a new constraint, or the expand operator, which means relaxing an existing constraint. When either of these operators are applied within a particular state, a new state results, defined by a new set of database entities and the feature-value specifications that uniquely define them. The goal state in the task space is the set of database entities that the user deems to be sufficient for his or her purposes.

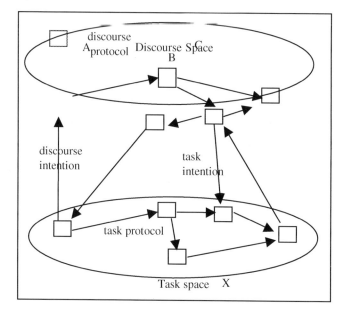

Fig. 1. Schematic Relation between Task and
Discourse State Spaces

Under this perspective, an intention is commitment to act to achieve a particular state in one of these spaces. A protocol is the realization of operators in each of these two state spaces. The interplay of task space and discourse space is summarized in Figure 1. The crucial feature is this: whenever an agent cannot proceed in one space, it must form an intention to make a transition in the other space. Thus, the failure to move ahead in the task space (e.g., contract the search space of entities) requires an intention to make a transition in the discourse space (e.g., a request for or suggestion about possible constraints, schematically illustrated as transitions ABC in Figure 1). Conversely, a transition in the discourse space may require movement in the task space (e.g., some new computation on domain objects to identify the answer to a query, schematically illustrated as transition X in Figure 1). We argue for a clean separation between discourse and task spaces, believing that it clarifies, using Moore's [8] distinction, what the "local" and "extended" effects of a message exchange are. For us, local effects of sending a message or completing a message exchange via a successful protocol are effects on the discourse space. The extended effects are those changes in shared knowledge—in discourse space— that impact the general task the agents are trying to accomplish in the task space

4.2   Intentions and Protocols as Plans

An intention to achieve a goal is represented as a general plan to advance either the task (in which case it is a task intention) or the exchange of information (in which case it is a discourse intention. We have adopted a generic beliefintentiondesire framework, in which an intention is represented via (i) an invocation condition, which returns true if the intention is applicable to the current task context; (ii) a completion condition, (iii) a methodtoadvance plan; and (iv) a resumption condition. The completion condition determines whether there is enough information in the current (task or discourse) state to satisfy the intention. If there is, a transition is made in the current space by executing one of the protocols specified in the completion routine which is appropriate in the current task context. Otherwise, the methodtoadvance— the plan body— is invoked. This leads to the adoption of an intention which is often an intention to move in the other, The resumption condition determines whether the intention, if it had been suspended, can be resumed. We will return to this later.

A protocol defines a structured exchange of information between two agents. Task protocols correspond to task operator for computing a successor state. (In our application they also represent communication between an agent that collects information from the user (agent) and an agent that performs computations). A task protocol is defined as a set of input parameters, that include a given state, and a set of output parameters, which fully define the successor state. We hasten to add that in most cases, this can be modeled as a simple function call, but we adopt the protocol terminology for consistency in our view of information exchange to promote state transitions. Discourse protocols advance discourse intentions and move the agents through discourse space, which includes shared knowledge. They specify temporal and contextual conditions on what message performatives, defined in some ACL, may follow each other. In our case, discourse protocols implement the semantics for adjacencypairs of performatives, as given in Table 1.

Protocols are also represented as plans within the belief-desires-intention framework we have adopted, whose representation has the form of (i) an invocation condition, which is the name of its invoking intention, and (ii) a plan body which we conceptually divide into invocation portion and an assimilation portion. The invocation portion of the plan body creates a message of the appropriate type and sends it. The assimilation portion of the protocol's defines the expected message and the associated state updates that would occur, if the protocol were successfully completed. After the protocol's plan sends its message and identifies its expected response, it is suspended.

It is in the realization of this assimilation routine that we allow for *locally* unexpected messages. In the case that the next arriving message is not the one expected by the most recently suspended protocol, that protocol remains suspended and the message is mapped to the intention plan library, where it triggers the recognition of a user intention. This is the manner in which the DBA can switch to a state in the task space that is not a predefined transition from its current task state. the DBA's modest amount of "reasoning" allows unexpected performatives (i) to be recognized as unexpected, (ii) to trigger the recognition of user intention and (iii) to pass control to responding to that intention. Exactly what new task intention is being signaled by the unexpected message requires a scheme for intentionmatching on the part of the DBA. But the crucial role of the abstract task model, in conjunction with the current task context, is to define a small set of possibilities.

A suspended intention (which is functionally suspended if its associated protocol is suspended) may never be resumed, if a new intention causes a state change in task or discourse space, such that the suspended intention has become irrelevant. Here is where the distinction we make between request and query performatives play an important role. Requests are directly associated with transitions in the task space and a commitment to making those transitions. Hence a user request causes adoption of a new task intention. If the completion condition of this task intention is true, the course of the current task context will change and this will be reflected in the task context variables. The resumption condition of a suspended intention checks these variables to determine if the intention may be resumed or abandoned. We require that a new direction in the search task results in abandoning a suspended task intention and its associated protocol. If the user performative, however, was a query (causing a transition in discourse space), the suspended intention (in task space) may be resumed.

4.3   Conversation Management

We have implemented the above design in PRS [see 11], a beliefdesiresintention architecture, in which both intentions and protocols are implemented as plans. Some aspects of conversation and task management are implicitly handled by the architecture itself, such as the passing of control from one plan to another. Other aspects of task and conversation management are a realized as plans as well. On the abstract level, given the turntaking assumption in dialogue, the general task and discourse management algorithm follows the following priority scheme: (i) recognize the need to set or respond to discourse intentions, (ii) react to any user intentions, and (iii) set and pursue the DBA task intentions. DBA task intentions are set and pursued through the combination of an intention priority scheme (defined by the abstract task model) that indicates how features of the current task context trigger certain types on intentions. We note that this sort of dialogue (or conversation) management algorithm characterizes much of the work in the discourse processing area. What is new here is our reliance on formalizing an abstract task model to implement the crucial aspects of run-time intention recognition in a practical and domain independent way.

5   Discussion

The framework we have described could be viewed as a two-level state-transition model: the abstract task model defines transitions at the level of task intentions and the discourse protocols define transitions at the level of shorter sub-conversation messages. Task intentions essentially structure the problem solving process and in turn, the dialogue that can ensue about the problem solving process. However, we allow that certain task intentions may be forever abandoned, as the initiative between agents shifts during the problem solving process. Hence, we allow for transitions as well as "jumps" between intentional states. It is through this sort of approach that we aim to realize a pragmatic implementation of notions such as beliefs and intentions. While mixed initiative dialogues are currently mostly studied in relation to interacting with users, we envision mixed initiative dialogues between software agents to be an important requirement for many applications systems of the future. In particular, in complex settings such as agent to agent negotiation, where protocols as they are typically employed simply cannot provide sufficient flexibility needed by agents for exploring the negotiations space.

Pitt and Mamdani [10] present protocol-level semantics that includes what they call an "add function"—an agent's procedure for computing the change in its information state from the content of an incoming message using a particular performative uttered in the context of a particular protocol. We would include the extended effects of such an update to include changes into task space. They also envision a realization of their framework in a BDI architecture, much like we have implemented for the DB agent described here. Specifically, they call for the representation of conversations (what we call protocols) as plans, and the notion that beliefs and desires (goals) would initiate a conversation by starting an instance of the appropriate protocol. We have pragmatically realized many aspects of their protocolbased semantics via our abstract task specification, which designates the relationship between task intentions, discourse intentions, and ultimately, wellstructured communication acts.

The matter of adopting the idea of abstract tasks to subtasks within a larger task needs further consideration. The first point is whether our notion of a protocol "violation" is too restrictive a mechanism for signaling an intention change and thus moving to some different subtask within the problem. When a subtask is completed, the agents will have to naturally move onto some new intention to make further progress. We do not intend that protocol violations are the only means of shifting attention. A violation merely means that the current intention may need to be dropped. In our brief discussion of conversation management, we noted that the algorithm follows a threestep priority scheme—the last step is "set and pursue intentions." Those intentions in turn are specified by a strategy that might be viewed as a meta plan. This intentionordering scheme is somewhat like a plan of attack that sets intentions as a function of they dynamic task context. A hierarchical task network planning approach is likely to provide further structure for very complex tasks. We use protocol violations merely as a way to signal something about the current intention: a message that cannot be resolved in the context of the currently active protocol must be signaling a different intention.

A second issue concerns the dominance of the user in the approach we have advocated here. On the one hand, we are calling this a 'mixed initiative approach', which makes it seem as if both agents have equal status. On the other hand, the DBA's intentions take back seat to any user intention. Note that this is defined strictly within the discourse management algorithm and not within the abstract task model. If both agents are software agents, then the question naturally arises about which agent steers the conversation, or whether they both would be searching inefficiently for sub-conversations. Two agents have to cooperate because they each have access to different sorts of knowledge and different capabilities. Even if the two agents shared the same abstract task model (and by definition, this would include the same strategy or plan of attack outlined in the previous paragraph), one of them must know something or be able to do something the other cannot. (In our case, the human agent has the constraint information and the goal information, and the DB agent has the database access and system functionality to compute the results). However, we believe that the abstract task model is the place for defining agent roles and functionality, thus clarifying the range of task management and discourse intentions for each agent.

The critical, more general issue concerns how to assess the pragmatic advantage that may be gained by specifying the semantics for abstract tasks as the semantics that are required to support flexible multiagent communication. Within the knowledge-based system arena, Chandrasekaren and his colleagues advanced the notion that complex tasks could be decomposed into sub-tasks that were, in some sense, generic, such as classification, data retrieval, plan selection and refinement, and so forth. If there are generic ontologies associated with generic tasks, then that ontology can be the foundation for intentions that in turn can structure the conversation and the content of the individual performatives. Thus, a crucial area for further work is assessing whether and how this abstract (or generic) task approach can be leveraged to define semantics for a core set of objects-of-discourse to be used in the evolution of some standard task languages for agents.

Acknowledgments

Aspects of this work were developed while A. Haddadi was seconded to the Adaptive Systems Laboratory, Daimler-Benz Research and Technology Center, Palo Alto, California, where R. Elio spent part of a sabbatical during 1997-1998. The support of that group, the University of Alberta, and NSERC Grant A0089 to R. Elio is gratefully acknowledged.

References

1. Bylander, T., Chandrasekaren, B.: Generic tasks for knowledge-based reasoning: The "right" level of abstraction for knowledge engineering. International Journal of Man-Machine Studies **26** (1987) 231-243

2. FIPA-99 specifications, see www.fipa.org/spec

3. Greaves, M., Holmback, H., Bradshaw, J.: What is a conversation policy. In this volume.

4. Grice, H.P.: Logic and conversation. In Cole, P. & Morgan, J.L. (eds.): Syntax and Semantics, Vol 3: Speech Acts. Academic Press, New York (1975) 225-242

5. Grosz, B.J., Sidner, C.L.: Plans for discourse. In Cohen, P., Morgan, J.L., Pollack, M.E. (eds.): Intentions and Communication. MIT Press, Cambridge (1990) 417-444

6. Haddadi, A.: Communication and cooperation in agent systems: A pragmatic theory. Lecture Notes in Computer Science, Vol.1056 Springer-Verlag, Berlin Heidelberg New York (1996)

7. Labrou, Y., Finin, T.: Semantics and conversations for an agent communication language. In Huhn, M. N., Singh, M. P. (eds.): Readings in Agents. Morgan Kaufmann, San Francisco, (1998) 235-242

8. Moore, S.: On conversation policies and the need for exceptions. In this volume.

9. Phillips, L., Link, H.: The role of conversation policy in carrying out agent conversations. In this volume.

10. Pitt, J., Mamdani, A.: Communication protocols in multi-agent systems. In this volume.

11. Rao, A.S., Georgeff, M.P.: BDI agents: From theory to practice. Tech. Rep. 56, Australian Artificial Intelligence Institute, Melbourne, Australia, (1995)

12. Reinhart, T.: Pragmatics and linguistics: An analysis of sentence topics. Philosophica **27** (1981)53-94

13. Rich, C., Sidner, C. L.: COLLAGEN: When agents collaborate with people. In: Huhns, M.N. , M. P. Singh (eds.): Readings in Agents. Morgan Kaufmann, San Francisco (1998) 117-124

14. Singh, M.P.: Agent communication languages: Rethinking the Principles. IEEE Computer **31** (1998), 40-49

15. Smith, I. A., Cohen, P.R., Bradshaw, J. M., Greaves, M., Holmback, H.: Designing conversation policies using joint intention theory. In Proceedings of the Third International Conference on Multi-agent Systems. IEEE Press, (1998) 269-276

16. Winograd, T., Flores, F.: Understanding computers and cognition. Ablex Press, New Jersey (1987)

Investigating Interactions between Agent Conversations and Agent Control Components*

Thomas Wagner, Brett Benyo, Victor Lesser, and Ping Xuan

Department of Computer Science
University of Massachusetts, Amherst, MA 01003
{wagner,bbenyo,pxuan,lesser}@cs.umass.edu

Abstract. Exploring agent conversation in the context of fine-grained agent co-ordination research has raised several intellectual questions. The major issues pertain to interactions between different agent conversations, the representations chosen for different classes of conversations, the explicit modeling of interactions between the conversations, and how to address these interactions. This paper is not so ambitious as to attempt to address these questions, only frame them in the context of quantified, scheduling-centric multi-agent coordination research.

1 Introduction

Based on a long history of work in agents and agent control components for building distributed AI and multi-agent systems, we are attempting to frame and address a set of intellectual questions pertaining to agent conversation. *Interaction* lies at the heart of the matter; the issue is interaction between different agent conversations, that possibly occur at different levels of abstraction, but also interaction between the machinery for holding a conversation with other agents and the underlying machinery for controlling the individual agent. Henceforth we will use the term *coordination protocol* to describe the specification for a dialogue between one or more agents that is held for the purpose of coordinating their activities; a *conversation* is an instantiation of a protocol. A *coordination mechanism*, in contrast, denotes a larger grouping of concerns – it is the way in which an agent reasons about interactions, plans to resolve them, and carries out communication activities to do so. We return to the issue of coordination mechanisms in Section 2.3, however, the notion of a mechanism is intertwined in the following intellectual issues:

- Assuming a model where agents are engaged in multiple conversations concurrently, and asynchronously, what are the ramifications of interactions between the different conversations?

* Effort sponsored by the Department of the Navy and Office of the Chief of Naval Research under Grant number N00014-97-1-0591 and by the National Science Foundation under Grant number IIS-9812755. The U.S. Government is authorized to reproduce and distribute reprints for Governmental purposes notwithstanding any copyright annotation thereon. Disclaimer: The views and conclusions contained herein are those of the authors and should not be interpreted as necessarily representing the official policies or endorsements, either expressed or implied, of the Department of the Navy and Office of the Chief of Naval Research, the National Science Foundation, or the U.S. Government.

Should interactions be accounted for at the conversational level or by the underlying agent control components? For example, if an agent is engaged in dialogues with two other agents in an attempt to contract-out two different tasks, e.g., x and y, and the tasks are mutually exclusive, what happens if both tasks are contracted at the same time? Or one is contracted while the other is being negotiated? In our work, recovery would generally take place via decommitment [1], possibly with some penalty involved, but, this response is generally triggered by the agent control components, not the conversation machinery itself.

– Conversations held to coordinate multiple agents generally entail the exchange of task or goal information and temporal constraints. This information may be viewed as particular bindings on variables that are used by the conversation machinery. Using this view, one can envision the conversation machinery querying an oracle (temporal belief-base, truth maintenance system, agent scheduler, etc.) for particular bindings that should be used during the dialogue, e.g., "I can provide you the result by time 10." However, what if multiple candidate tasks are being negotiated that require the same resource(s)?[1] The conversations are clearly interdependent, however, the underlying agent control mechanisms that identify the constrained situation and enumerate possible responses is also part of the interaction. In other words, the involved conversations must query the underlying oracle for information, and in this case, the oracle needs the information from all the conversations in order to make decisions about priorities and what can be accomplished. As soon as one of the conversations results in a committed or intended course of action, the other conversations are impacted. The question is what is the appropriate interface between the conversation machinery and the lower level control components?

– Consider another situation that approaches the same issue from a different perspective. Let α be an agent that has a hard deadline looming and lacks sufficient time to coordinate over all *soft* task interactions (optional coordination points), it must thus modulate the conversation machinery to reflect the upcoming deadline. Options include curtailing conversational activities, i.e., ending existing dialogues or refraining from starting new dialogues, or modifying conversations to reflect the need for haste. The first case involves simply terminating standard dialogues, the second case, however, requires dialogues that are parameterized or include branches that have different temporal requirements (possibly anytime [7,18,42] in nature). However, the problem is not that neat – it is actually cyclical. Non-local information obtained via communication influences the agent's beliefs and thus impacts its intentions or planned actions. Thus, continuing a dialogue and gaining more information might actually change the choices that an agent has made and thus result in the agent having more time for conversations. Conversely, time spent conversing may simply detract from domain problem solving. The question is whether or not we must address the issue and if so, what are the implications to the conversational machinery of the agent? Certainly, one can argue that for agents to address real-time and real-resource concerns, the issue must be addressed.

Attempting to frame these questions leads one to consider the implications of agents having multiple, asynchronous, conversations pertaining to different matters and dealing with activities at different levels of abstraction. As discussed in Section 5, intra-level and inter-level interaction in conjunction with interactions between conversations and agent control components pushes harder on the issue of interaction.

These questions are the outcome of an effort to modify our agent coordination technology, namely GPGP [26] and Design-to-Criteria [37,35], to support openness, situation

---

[1] The issue is more clear if resources are not simple objects that require exclusive access, but are instead sharable, e.g., network bandwidth, where the performance of an action using the resource may degrade based on the state of the resource – and the degrees of degradation vary.

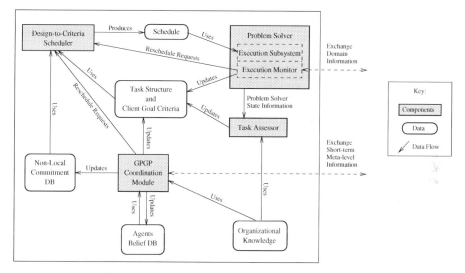

Fig. 1. A Portion of the Prototypical Agent Architecture

specificity, and adaptation to different application domains. For example, in a current project we are interfacing our agent control technology with a higher-level process view [21] of the task of sending robot teams into hazardous environments to perform unmanned exploration (e.g., damaged buildings to access structural conditions). This application requires different protocols and different behaviors than applications such as the coordination of agents in an intelligent environment [25], or information gathering agents [8]. In an effort to open GPGP for different applications and to adapt its protocols, we redesigned and reimplemented the important concepts from GPGP and created $GPGP^2$ [40].

It is important to note that while our view of agent control differs from others in the community, from the perspective of the agent conversation, the questions we have posed are relevant to other agent technologies. Perhaps the overall question is the role of agent conversation research and work in multi-agent coordination. On one hand conversational work often focuses on structuring the dialogue between agents [24,23,13], or the formal models, motivations, and implications of information exchange [6,30,31]. On the other hand, coordination work [29,33,34,19,14,9] generally pertains to making decisions about what an agent should do, when, and how it should be done. These two areas of research are related (interdependent?) and we believe both can benefit from cross fertilization and exploring our research ideas, and these conversational issues, in context. Work akin to this has begun using abstractions of the underlying agent machinery or simplified agent task models [13,30].

Additional context is required to properly frame and understand our questions about interactions and the agent conversational machinery. In some sense, interactions stem from the complexity of the agent control problem. In our work, agents have multiple interacting goals or tasks and multiple different ways to perform them. Agents are also resource bounded and must address real-time and real-resource limitations. The combination of resource limitations and alternative different goals to perform, and alternative different ways to perform them, results in agent control as an optimization style problem rather than a satisfaction style problem, i.e., the issue becomes evaluation of trade-offs of different alternative courses of action. The interdependencies and the optimization problem view mean that decisions rarely have limited or local scope but instead may impact all of the other choices/decisions made by the agent. In the following sections we clarify by describing our particular view of agent control and our domain independent architecture. We also discuss the finite-state machine approach for coordination protocol specification used in *GPGP2* and return to the questions posed this section.

2   Agent Control Components

We frame the general agent control problem as an action-selection-sequencing activity. Agents have multiple tasks to perform, different ways to perform the tasks, and the control problem is to choose subsets of these for scheduling, coordination with other agents, and execution. The objective of agent control problem solving is to enable agents to meet real-time and real-resource constraints, and to facilitate agent coordination through islands of predictable or stable agent activity.

We approach the control problem from a domain independent perspective, i.e., our research focus is on the construction of generalized agent control components that can be coupled with domain problem solvers, planners, or legacy systems to construct agents suitable for deployment in a multi-agent system. This generalization is achieved by abstracting away from the agents internals. In our work, domain problem solvers describe or translate their problem solving options, their candidate tasks and the primitive actions used to accomplish them, into a task modeling language called TÆMS [11]. The TÆMS models are then passed to generic control components, such as the Design-to-Criteria (DTC) agent scheduler and the (GPGP/*GPGP2*) agent coordination module. Other components include a learning module [32,20] and a module for system diagnosis [17,22].

With respect to other approaches to agent control, e.g., BDI-based [28,4] problem solvers, our tools operate at a different level of detail. We return to this issue in Section 4, though the general idea is that the DTC/GPGP tools perform detailed *feasibility analysis* and *implementation* of high-level goals and tasks selected by other components, like a BDI problem solver. The DTC/GPGP control model assumes that some other component is producing the high-level tasks that the agent is to achieve, either as the result of local-only domain problem solving or as the result of communication (at higher levels) with other agents. A subset of the larger generic agent architecture is shown in Figure 1. In this paper, we describe agent control in the context of the two primary control components, namely the Design-to-Criteria scheduler and the GPGP coordination module.

2.1   TÆMS Task Models

TÆMS (Task Analysis, Environment Modeling, and Simulation) is a domain independent task modeling framework used to describe and reason about complex problem solving processes. TÆMS models are used in multi-agent coordination research [10,38]

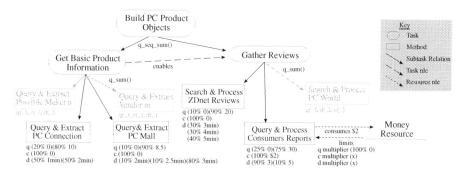

Fig. 2. Simplified Subset of an Information Gathering Task Structure

and are being used in many other research projects, including: cooperative-information-gathering [27], collaborative distributed design [12], intelligent environments [25], co-ordination of software process [21], and others [5,36,3,9]. Typically a problem solver represents domain problem solving actions in TÆMS, possibly at some level of abstraction, and then passes the TÆMS models on to agent control problem solvers like the multi-agent coordination modules or the Design-to-Criteria scheduler.[2]

TÆMS models are hierarchical abstractions of problem solving processes that describe alternative ways of accomplishing a desired goal; they represent major tasks and major decision points, interactions between tasks, and resource constraints but they do not describe the intimate details of each primitive action. All primitive actions in TÆMS, called *methods*, are statistically characterized via discrete probability distributions in three dimensions: quality, cost and duration. Quality is a deliberately abstract domain-independent concept that describes the contribution of a particular action to overall problem solving. Duration describes the amount of time that the action modeled by the method will take to execute and cost describes the financial or opportunity cost inherent in performing the action. Uncertainty in each of these dimensions is implicit in the performance characterization – thus agents can reason about the certainty of particular actions as well as their quality, cost, and duration trade-offs. The uncertainty representation is also applied to task interactions like enablement, facilitation and hindering effects, [3] e.g., "10% of the time facilitation will increase the quality by 5% and 90% of the time it will increase the quality by 8%." The quantification of methods and interactions in TÆMS is not regarded as a perfect science. Task structure programmers or problem solver generators *estimate* the performance characteristics of primitive actions. These estimates can be refined over time through learning and reasoners typically replan and reschedule when unexpected events occur.

To illustrate, consider Figure 2, which is a conceptual, simplified sub-graph of a task structure emitted by the BIG [27] information gathering agent; it describes a portion of

---

[2] In the process work, a translator transforms and abstracts process programs into TÆMS task structures for scheduling and coordination.

[3] Facilitation and hindering task interactions model soft relationships in which a result produced by some task may be beneficial or harmful to another task. In the case of facilitation, the existence of the result, and the activation of the nle generally increases the quality of the recipient task or reduces its cost or duration.

the information gathering process. The top-level task is to construct product models of retail PC systems. It has two subtasks, *Get-Basic* and *Gather-Reviews*, both of which are decomposed into methods, that are described in terms of their expected quality, cost, and duration. The *enables* arc between *Get-Basic* and *Gather* is a non-local-effect (nle) or task interaction; it models the fact that the review gathering methods need the names of products in order to gather reviews for them. Other task interactions modeled in TÆMS include: *facilitation*, *hindering*, *bounded facilitation*, *sigmoid*, and *disablement*. Task interactions are of particular interest to coordination research because they identify instances in which tasks assigned to different agents are interdependent – they model, in effect, implicit joint goals or joint problem solving activity. Coordination is motivated by the existence of these interactions.

Returning to the example, *Get-Basic* has two methods, joined under the *sum()* quality-accumulation-function (*qaf*), which defines how performing the subtasks relate to performing the parent task. In this case, either method or both may be employed to achieve *Get-Basic*. The same is true for *Gather-Reviews*. The qaf for *Build-PC-Product-Objects* is a *seq_sum()* which indicates that the two subtasks must be performed, in order, and that their resultant qualities are summed to determine the quality of the parent task; thus there are nine alternative ways to achieve the top-level goal in this particular sub-structure. In general, a TÆMS task structure represents a family of plans, rather than a single plan, where the different paths through the network exhibit different statistical characteristics or trade-offs.

TÆMS also supports modeling of tasks that arrive at particular points in time, individual deadlines on tasks, earliest start times for tasks, and non-local tasks (those belonging to other agents). In the development of TÆMS there has been a constant tension between representational power and the combinatorics inherent in working with the structure. The result is a model that is non-trivial to process, coordinate, and schedule in any optimal sense (in the general case), but also one that lends itself to flexible and approximate processing strategies.

2.2 Design-to-Criteria Scheduling: Local Agent Control

The Design-to-Criteria (DTC) scheduler is the agent's local expert on making control decisions. The scheduler's role is to consider the possible domain actions enumerated by the domain problem solver and choose a course of action that best addresses: 1) the local agent's goal criteria (its preferences for certain types of solutions), 2) the local agent's resource constraints and environmental circumstances, and 3) the non-local considerations expressed by the GPGP coordination module. The general idea is to evaluate the options in light of constraints and preferences from many different sources and to find a way to achieve the selected tasks that best addresses all of these.

The scheduler's problem is framed in terms of a TÆMS task structure emitted by the domain problem solver. Scheduling problem solving activities modeled in the TÆMS language has four major requirements: 1) to find a set of actions to achieve the high-level task, 2) to sequence the actions, 3) to find and sequence the actions in soft real-time, 4) to produce a schedule that meets dynamic goal criteria, i.e., cost, quality, duration, and certainty requirements, of different clients. TÆMS models multiple approaches for achieving tasks along with the quality, cost, and duration characteristics of the primitive actions, specifically to enable TÆMS clients to reason about the trade-offs of different courses of action. In other words, for a given TÆMS task model, there are multiple approaches for achieving the high-level task and each approach has different quality, cost, duration, and certainty characteristics. In contrast to classic scheduling problems, the TÆMS scheduling objective is not to sequence a set of unordered actions but to *find and sequence* a set of actions that *best* suits a particular client's quality, cost, duration, and certainty needs. Design-to-Criteria is about examining the current situation, the current options before the agent, and deciding on a course of action – it is about targetable contextual decision making.

Design-to-Criteria scheduling requires a sophisticated heuristic approach because of the scheduling task's inherent computational complexity ($\omega(2^n)$ and $o(n^n)$) it is not possible to use exhaustive search techniques for finding optimal schedules. Furthermore, the deadline and resource constraints on tasks, plus the existence of complex task inter-relationships, prevent the use of a single heuristic for producing optimal or even "good" schedules. Design-to-Criteria copes with these explosive combinatorics through approximation, criteria-directed focusing (goal-directed problem solving), heuristic decision making, and heuristic error correction. The algorithm and techniques are documented more fully in [37,35].

2.3   GPGP Coordination: Managing Non-local Interactions

GPGP (Generalized Partial Global Planning) is the agent's tool for interacting with other agents and coordinating joint activity. GPGP is a modularized, domain independent, approach to scheduling-centric coordination. In GPGP, coordination *modulates* local control by posting constraints on an agent's local DTC scheduler. The GPGP coordination module is responsible generating communication actions, that is communicating with other agents (via their local communication modules), and making and breaking task related *commitments* with other agents. The coordination module is comprised of several modular coordination mechanisms, subsets of which may be applied during coordination depending on the degree of coordination desired. More specifically, GPGP defines the following coordination mechanisms (for the formal details see [10]):

1. **Share Non-Local Views** - This most basic coordination mechanism handles the exchange of local views between agents and the detection of task interactions. Exchanging local views is the only way in which agents can detect and coordinate over task interactions. The mechanism exchanges information, or not, according to three different exchange policies: *exchange none*, where no information is exchanged; *exchange some*, where only part of the local view is communicated; and *exchange all*, where the entire local view is communicated. This coordination mechanism is necessary for all other coordination mechanisms – without a local view of non-local tasks and an understanding of existing task interactions there is nothing to coordinate.

2. **Communicate Results** - This coordination mechanism handles communicating the results of method execution to other agents. It is governed by three different policies: the *minimal policy* where only the results necessary to satisfy external commitments are communicated; the *task-group policy* where all the minimal results plus the final results for a task group are communicated; and the *all* policy where all results are communicated. This mechanism is meaningless without mechanism 1 above or the following mechanisms that form commitments.

3. **Avoid Redundancy** - This mechanism deals with detected redundancy by picking an agent at random to execute the redundant method in question. The agent then becomes committed to performing the action and the other agents will have non-local commitments denoting that some other agent will carry out the task at a predetermined time. Note, the type of redundancy in question here is simple duplication of work, in contrast to the redundancy of being able to generate a similar result using different methods.

4. **Handle Hard Task Relationships** - The *enables* NLE pictured in Figure 2 denotes a hard task relationship. This coordination mechanism deals with such hard, non-optional, task interactions by committing the predecessors of the *enables* to perform the task by a certain deadline.

5. **Handle Soft Task Relationships** - Soft task interactions, unlike hard interactions like *enables*, are optional. When employed, this coordination mechanism attempts to form commitments on the predecessors of the soft interactions to perform the methods in question before the methods that are on the receiving end of the interaction.

As mentioned above, the GPGP coordination module modulates local control by placing constraints, called *commitments*, on the local scheduler. The commitments represent either deals that GPGP has made with other agents, e.g., agreeing to perform method M by time T, or deals that GPGP is considering making with other agents. The commitments fall into four categories:

Deadline Commitment This type of commitment denotes an agreement to execute a particular method by a particular time. Thus if agent A needs the results from a method execution being performed by another agent, agent B, and they form a deadline commitment, agent A can then plan other activities based on the expectation of receiving the results from B by the deadline T.

Earliest Start Time Commitment This commitment denotes an agreement not to start executing a particular method prior to an agreed upon time. This type of commitment is the converse of the deadline commitment. In the two agent scenario above, this commitment could be used to denote that while agent B should execute M by time T, it should also not start executing M before time T'.

Do Commitment This commitment is weak and simply denotes a commitment to execute a particular method at some time.

Don't Commitment This commitment denotes an agreement not to perform a particular method during a particular interval. It is particularly useful for coordination over shared resources.

Salient features of GPGP-based coordination include a domain independent approach to coordination, exchange of non-local information to construct a partial global view, a *worth* driven view of tasks and actions (from TÆMS), different information exchange policies for many of the coordination mechanisms, a subset of mechanisms that are independent and can be applied, or not, depending on the current context (e.g., looming deadlines).

Figure 3 shows a multi-agent problem solving situation in which an information gathering task structure (akin to Figure 2) is distributed across several agents. The high-level objective is to build product objects. The two subtasks are to build objects for PC software products, and to build objects for Mac products. Note that the actions used to perform tasks like *Gather-Reviews* are abstracted out of this figure. The entire PC related branch of the tree is contracted out to a single agent, *Task Agent A*, while the Mac related branch is broken down and contracted out to two other agents, *Task Agents B*

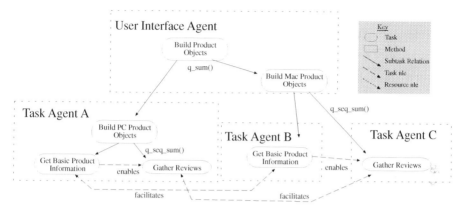

Fig. 3. Multiple Interacting Information Agents

and C. There are interactions between the *Get-Basic-Product-Information* tasks and the *Gather-Reviews* tasks, as well as interactions between the PC and Mac versions of these tasks (products may be multi-platform). Using GPGP, the agents coordinate as follows:

- Step 1: Exchange local views. Agents A, B, and C exchange their local views, i.e., they exchange portions of their task structures. This gives each agent a limited view of the activities being performed by the other agents.
- Step 2: Detect interactions. In this case, the interactions may be specified *a priori* by the *User Interface Agent*. However, if the interface agent did not have a complete view of the task beforehand, the agents will compare inputs and outputs of their different actions and match up relationships accordingly.
- Step 3: Coordinate over interactions. Agent A has mutual facilitations with agents B and C. Agent B has a mutual facilitation with agent A, as well as an enables relationship with C. C has a mutual facilitation with A, but also requires input from B in order to do its problem solving. The sequencing and interaction of coordination over these interactions is one of the issues of this paper, however, in general, the interactions are handled by:
    1. Agent B evaluating its intended course of action and offering agent C a deadline commitment that specifies the deadline by which it will produce a result so that agent C can execute.
    2. Agent A evaluating its intended course of action and offering a commitment to agent B that specifies when a portion of the results for A's *Get-Basic-Product-Information* will be available.
    3. Agent B evaluating its schedule and offering agent A a similar commitment about the partial results of its *Get-Basic-Product-Information* task.
    4. Agent A, after considering its schedule, will then offer agent C a commitment about when the partial results of its *Gather-Reviews* task will be available.
    5. Agent C will offer a similar commitment to agent A about its *Gather-Reviews* task's results.
- Step 4: Execute, recommit, and exchange. The agents will then perform their scheduled primitive actions, rescheduling and recommitting if necessary, and exchanging results as specified by the commitments they have formed.

As mentioned, coordination or agent conversation must rely on an underlying oracle or analysis procedures to determine bindings on particular variables that are exchanged during the agent dialogue. For example, an agent must have a good idea of when a particular result can be provided to another agent in order to propose a commitment to that effect. In the GPGP/DTC world view, this information is generally provided by the scheduler. However, GPGP also requires non-scheduler analysis code, for example, code to detect task interactions or to determine which information policy should be used. Thus, GPGP mechanisms embody both analysis aspects of the coordination problem and coordination protocol aspects. The problem is that this integration of concerns makes extending the protocols difficult – they are, in essence, built into the code and isolated from the outside world. *GPGP2* addresses this problem by separating the analysis procedures from the specification of the agent coordination protocol.

3   *GPGP2*

The *GPGP2* label on our current generation of agent coordination tools is primarily for historical reasons. The goal of the *GPGP2* project is to develop a new approach to specifying coordination *mechanisms* that separates the coordination protocol from the supporting analysis code so that coordination protocols may be easily modified and adapted for particular contexts. One step in the verification of the new tools is to reimplement the functionality of GPGP, including its fairly simple coordination protocols and one-shot coordination nature. However, the main objective is to take the work beyond the territory already covered by GPGP.

Whereas GPGP grouped analysis functionality and protocol specification into a single body of embedded code, *GPGP2* takes a very different approach. Coordination protocols are specified using an extended finite state machine (FSM) model where states denote conversational states and transitions are associated with calls to communication actions or analysis code. This approach to specification is widespread and akin to Agen-Talk [23] and COOL [2], but the work differs in the way in which conversations interact with the underlying agent control machinery. Implementationally, FSMs are specified via scripts that are processed by a java-based FSM interpreter. The interpreter emits java code that is then incorporated into a *coordination bean* which is integrated into the generic java agent framework [16]. The coordination bean interacts with the rest of the agent components through an event/registration mechanism and by direct invocation when using certain support features of the framework. Features of the FSM model / interpreter include:

- Support for multiple concurrent asynchronous conversations between a given agent and other agents in the environment.
- FSM variables enabling protocols to store information explicitly – in addition to the implicit information contained in each conversation state. For example, to store the commitment time last proposed by another agent.
- Shared FSM variables that enable different conversations (FSM instances) to interact. For example, conversations focused on a particular set of interrelated tasks (possibly sequentially dependent) might contain points of synchronization to serialize their efforts. The synchronization phase would entail a shared semaphore-like variable and the passing of particular bindings. This information could also be passed outside of the coordination bean via the standard agent data structures / knowledge bases, but, intuitively it seems more efficient to do this sort of operation inside the coordination machinery rather than through the general agent control structures. This is a design decision, but, it is the embodiment of the issue of handling

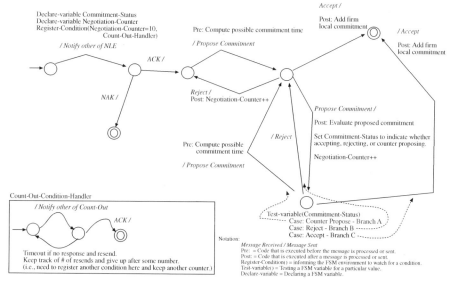

Fig. 4. Initiator FSM to Coordinate Hard Task Interaction

interactions between different conversations. It is unclear, at this time, which is the right approach and unclear as to whether or not a stronger, explicit, representation of conversation interaction is needed.

- Timers enable machines to set timers and then block, waiting for particular events to occur. The timers enable conversations to time-out if responses are not produced within a given window. The timeout duration can be specific to the conversation or a global default used by all conversations.
- Event registration and creation. Events may be generated from within the FSMs as well as from within the agent. In effect, each conversation is a first class object within the agent framework in terms of event generation and event catching. Conversations can thus interact even without explicit *a priori* knowledge of which other conversations are likely to interact.
- As part of the event mechanism, FSMs can initiate other conversations, i.e., one FSM may detect the need for a new dialogue and can fire-up a new FSM to handle the dialogue.
- Inheritance. Coordination protocols can be subclassed and specialized. This facilitates rapid protocol development and simple specialization of existing protocols.
- Pre and post conditions on transitions. Transitions may have a set of actions (including tests of FSM variables) that take place before the transition and sets of actions that take place as the transition completes.
- Exceptions. FSMs may throw and catch exceptions. This allows FSMs to handle timeout conditions and other events that drastically change the execution flow through the FSM, and to do so in a succinct fashion. The alternative is complete specification of all exceptions as transitions from each state.

Figure 4 show an example of an initiator FSM[4] to handle the coordination of a hard task interaction (the temporal sequencing of task performance). The FSMs in the figure

---

[4] Generally the responder is a reflected version of the initiator, in these cases, it is probably reasonable to specify a single FSM and then adapt the interpreter to output two versions. This would remove the need to analyze the FSMs for reachability and related issues.

are designed to handle the formation of a single commitment. One of the outstanding research questions is determining the appropriate grainsize for an agent conversation. We are currently using a model where conversations and task interaction coordination are 1:1. However, consider a case where there is an interaction from task α to β, and then from β to γ. Chains of such interactions may require one conversation to coordinate the chain of interactions, rather than multiple independent conversations or multiple conversations that interact via shared variables. Relatedly, consider a case where agent A and agent B have multiple different task interactions. With our current model, these will be handled by multiple concurrent and asynchronous conversations between the agents. However, they could also be handled by a single conversation that dealt with the multiple task interactions at once. In both cases, interactions between the FSMs are at issue. In the first case, the conversations are interdependent because the tasks over which they are coordinating are interdependent. In the second case, the conversations are interdependent because the tasks are associated with the same agents, i.e., the interdependence is not between the tasks per se, but, stems from the particular assignment of tasks to agents.

4   Interactions Revisited

The issue of interactions is potentially larger than described in Section 1. We have thus far identified the issue of interactions between different conversations, and interactions between the conversation machinery and the agent control machinery. However, we are currently considering new agent dialogues or coordination mechanisms that potentially operate at a higher-level than the conversations held to perform GPGP style coordination.

GPGP and *GPGP2* deal with the temporal sequencing of tasks and with exploring different tasks and constraints assigned to a set of agents. In some sense, this style of coordination is about feasibility analysis and solution enactment based on the assumption that tasks are generated dynamically during problem solving by the agent problem solver or by an external (possibly human) client. In other words, GPGP assumes that some other process is responsible for determining the set of candidate tasks to schedule and coordinate. Note that TÆMS models alternative different ways to perform tasks, and does so hierarchically, so the GPGP problem is not simply to coordinate and schedule a set of primitive actions that must be performed but instead to *choose* which actions to perform based on utility and feasibility. However, GPGP's (and DTC's) choices are limited to the set of tasks and actions emitted by the problem solver. All GPGP conversations pertain to the detection of interactions, the sequencing of activities to resolve interactions, and the sharing of results; they do not pertain to the determination of the high-level goals of the agent.

Our current work in integrating *GPGP2* with a process-level controller, however, requires that we address the issue of task allocation to agents and the determination of which tasks to perform from a more global perspective. Note that these are two separate, but similar, issues. Task allocation is the problem of assigning members of a set of tasks, say $\mathcal{T}$, to individual agents belonging to a set of candidate agents. This requires knowledge about the capabilities and resources of the agents and knowledge about the structure of the tasks (possibly a high-level view of interdependence or ordering). The determination of which tasks the overall agent network should pursue is a different matter

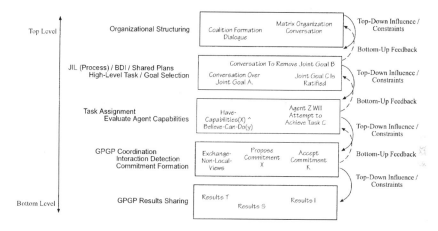

Fig. 5. Conversational Levels and Interactions

– this is the process of generating $\mathcal{T}$. Both of these activities require that agents be able to engage in conversations other than those required for GPGP-style coordination. These conversations must convey information such as the capabilities of the agents but also information pertaining to the state of the overall problem solving network. It appears that these conversations pertain to different concerns and operate at different levels of detail.[5] However, there is clearly an interaction between the production of $\mathcal{T}$, the assignment of members of $\mathcal{T}$ to agents, and the feasibility of the tasks, i.e., in this case we are faced with interactions between the conversations held to determine overall objectives, conversations held to determine task assignment, and conversations held to determine task feasibility and task performance. Additionally, these conversations are asynchronous; not just with respect to the different levels, but there might be different conversations at each level going on simultaneously. Figure 5 illustrates this idea. In some sense, decisions made at the upper levels set the policy for conversations at the lower levels. For example, deciding to pursue tasks α and β at the upper level determine that at the GPGP-level, conversations will be held toward that ends. However, there is also a feedback process in which the lower-level must explore the feasibility of the tasks selected by the upper levels. Consider a situation in which a set of tasks are selected but when the agents attempt to coordinate, sequence, and perform the required actions it is discovered that the agent network lacks sufficient resources to carry out the activities (recall, we address problems where task interactions and temporal constraints make it difficult to ascertain what is possible without actually going through the process of attempting to coordinate and schedule the activities). In this case, the choice of which

---

[5] We are currently also exploring the integration of our temporal/constraint based coordination with BDI approaches to agent control. We believe that a BDI framework can be used in the upper level of the agent control to determine which tasks to perform from a coarse-grained perspective (intentions). The fine-grained coordination and scheduling of the activities is then carried out by our tools.

tasks to pursue for the overall network must be modified.[6] Again, we return to the issue of interaction. Should these interactions be explicitly modeled and handled by the conversation machinery? Does this require a negotiation style interface [15] between the different conversational levels? Relatedly, should there be different conversational machinery for these different levels of conversation?

Once one begins regarding agent conversation as being stratified, other levels become obvious. Work in organizing the computation and organizing multi-agent systems obviously entails conversations that take place at yet another (higher) level of abstraction. In these conversations agents determine the structure in which the problem solving will take place. Again, conversations at this level appear to interact with the lower levels, and vice versa. Again, are new representations needed? Is new machinery needed to hold conversations of this type? We have recently developed new modeling constructs and reasoning tools for addressing local agent control at these higher levels [39,35], but the question of interaction and machinery remains.

The stratification also moves down the food chain. If we examine GPGP, there are clearly two different levels of conversation within GPGP itself. At one level, agents exchange local information to construct partial global views of the rest of the world. The agents then carry out dialogues to attempt to handle various task interactions. These activities fall under the general umbrella of feasibility and solution enactment. However, the act of communicating results can be viewed as a different type of activity. In *GPGP2*, the same machinery is used to communicate results as to carry out the other activities, but, the activities are inherently different. In this case it appears that new representations and machinery are not needed, possibly because the interactions between these levels are one way – results being communicated does not affect existing conversations, though the results may cause agents to engage in new conversations with other agents as their problem solving state evolves.

5 Conclusion

We have attempted to identify the issue of interactions in agent conversations and to provide the reasons that interactions are a research question worth addressing. In summary, we believe that both the agent conversation community and the coordination community could benefit from the integration of our technologies and that the meaningful integration of these technologies leads to the issue of interaction between the conversational level and the control level. Additionally, based on our work in coordination, we hypothesize that different levels of interacting, asynchronous, conversations are necessary to scale multi-agent systems for deployment in complex, open environments. The main issues are what representations or formalisms are useful and whether or not explicitly representing and reasoning about interactions is required.

---

[6] An alternative is to provide the lower-level feasibility and implementation tools with a larger view of the space of candidate tasks. In this model, the lower-level tools could provide guidance about which tasks should be pursued at the higher-levels based on the analysis. Note that in this case, the upper and lower-levels have essentially the same information, just at different levels of abstraction.

Stepping aside from the notion of levels and interactions – there is also the issue of uncertainty in conversations and uncertainty in agent coordination. In TÆMS we explicitly represent, and reason about, the certainty of actions. We have begun to reason about the role of uncertainty in GPGP-style coordination [41], but, it seems intuitive that the uncertainty question is ubiquitous and applies to all levels of agent conversation.

References

1. M. Andersson and T. Sandholm. Leveled commitment contracts with myopic and strategic agents. In *Proc. of the 15th Nat. Conf. on AI*, pages 38–44, 1998.
2. M. Barbuceanu and M.S. Fox. COOL: A language for describing coordination in multi agent syste ms. In *Proc. of the First Intl. Conf. on Multi-Agent Systems (ICMAS95)*, pages 17–25, 1995.
3. A.L.C. Bazzan, V. Lesser, and P. Xuan. Adapting an Organization Design through Domain-Independent Diagnosis. UMASS CS Technical Report TR-98-014, February 1998.
4. M.E. Bratman. *Intention Plans and Practical Reason*. Harvard University Press, Cambridge, MA, 1987.
5. N. Carver and V. Lesser. The DRESUN testbed for research in FA/C distributed situation assessment: Extensions to the model of external evidence. In *Proc. of the First Intl. Conf. on Multiagent Systems*, June, 1995.
6. P.R. Cohen and H.J. Levesque. Communicative actions for artificial agents. In *Proc. of the First Intl. Conf. on Multi-Agent Systems (ICMAS95)*, page 445, 1995.
7. T. Dean and M. Boddy. An analysis of time-dependent planning. In *Proc. of the Seventh Nat. Conf. on Artificial Intelligence*, pages 49–54, St. Paul, Minnesota, August 1988.
8. K. Decker, M. Williamson, and K. Sycara. Intelligent adaptive information agents. *Journal of Intelligent Information Systems*, 9:239–260, 1997.
9. K. Decker and J. Li. Coordinated hospital patient scheduling. In *Proc. of the Third Intl. Conf. on Multi-Agent Systems (ICMAS98)*, pages 104–111, 1998.
10. K. Decker. *Environment Centered Analysis and Design of Coordination Mechanisms*. PhD thesis, University of Massachusetts, 1995.
11. K. Decker. Task environment centered simulation. In M. Prietula, K. Carley, and L. Gasser, editors, *Simulating Organizations: Computational Models of Institutions and Groups*. AAAI Press/MIT Press, 1996.
12. K. Decker and V. Lesser. Coordination assistance for mixed human and computational agent systems. In *Proc. of Concurrent Engineering 95*, pages 337–348, McLean, VA, 1995. Concurrent Technologies Corp. Also available as UMASS CS TR-95-31.
13. M. d'Inverno, D. Kinny, and M. Luck. Interaction protocols in agentis. In *Proc. of the Third Intl. Conf. on Multi-Agent Systems (ICMAS98)*, pages 261–268, 1998.
14. E.H. Durfee and T.A. Montgomery. Coordination as distributed search in a hierarchical behavior space. *IEEE Transactions on Systems, Man, and Cybernetics*, 21(6):1363–1378, 1991.
15. A. Garvey, K. Decker, and V. Lesser. A negotiation-based interface between a real-time scheduler and a decision-maker. In *AAAI Workshop on Models of Conflict Management*, Seattle, 1994. Also UMASS CS TR–94–08.
16. B. Horling. A Reusable Component Architecture for Agent Construction. UMASS CS Technical Report TR-1998-45, October 1998.
17. B. Horling, V. Lesser, R. Vincent, A. Bazzan, and P. Xuan. Diagnosis as an Integral Part of Multi-Agent Adaptability. UMASS CS Technical Report TR-99-03, January 1999.

18. E.J. Horvitz. Reasoning under varying and uncertain resource constraints. In *Proc. of the Seventh Nat. Conf. on AI*, August 1988.
19. N.R. Jennings. Controlling cooperative problem solving in industrial multi-agent systems. *AI*, 75(2):195–240, 1995.
20. D. Jensen, M. Atighetchi, R. Vincent, and V. Lesser. Learning Quantitative Knowledge for Multiagent Coordination. *Proc. of AAAI-99*, 1999. Also as UMASS CS Technical Report TR-99-04.
21. S.M. Sutton Jr. and L.J. Osterweil. The design of a next-generation process language. In *Proc. of the Fifth ACM SIGSOFT Symposium on the Foundations of Software Engineering*, pages 142–158, September 1997.
22. G.A. Kaminka and M. Tambe. What is Wrong With Us? Improving Robustness Through Social Diagnosis. In *Proc. of the 15th Nat. Conf. on AI*, July 1998.
23. K. Kuwabara, T. Ishida, and N. Osato. Agentalk: Coordination protocol description for multi-agent systems. In *Proc. of the First Intl. Conf. on Multi-Agent Systems (ICMAS95)*, page 445, 1995.
24. Y. Labrou and T. Finin. A Proposal for a new KQML Specification. Computer Science Technical Report TRCS-97-03, University of Maryland Baltimore County, February 1997.
25. V. Lesser, M. Atighetchi, B. Horling, B. Benyo, A. Raja, Regis Vincent, Thomas Wagner, Ping Xuan, and Shelley XQ. Zhang. A Multi-Agent System for Intelligent Environment Control. In *Proc. of the Third Intl. Conf. on Autonomous Agents (Agents99)*, 1999.
26. V. Lesser, K. Decker, N. Carver, A. Garvey, D. Neiman, N. Prasad, and T. Wagner. Evolution of the GPGP Domain-Independent Coordination Framework. UMASS CS Technical Report TR-98-05, January 1998.
27. V. Lesser, B. Horling, F. Klassner, A. Raja, T. Wagner, and S. XQ. Zhang. BIG: A resource-bounded information gathering agent. In *Proc. of the 15th Nat. Conf. on AI (AAAI-98)*, July 1998.
28. A.S. Rao and M.P. Georgeff. Modelling rational agents within a BDI-architecture. In J. Allen, R. Fikes, and E. Sandewall, editors, *Proc. of the 3rd Intl. Conf. on Principles of Knowledge Representation and Reasoning*, pages 473–484. Morgan Kaufmann, 1991.
29. S. Sen and A. Biswas. Effects of misconception on reciprocative agents. In *Proc. of the 2nd Intl. Conf. on Autonomous Agents (Agents98)*, pages 430–435, 1998.
30. M. P. Singh. Developing formal specifications to coordinate heterogenous autonomous agents. In *Proc. of the Third Intl. Conf. on Multi-Agent Systems (ICMAS98)*, pages 261–268, 1998.
31. I. Smith, P.R. Cohen, J.M. Bradshaw, M. Greaves, and H. Holmback. Designing conversation policies using joint intention theory. In *Proc. of the Third Intl. Conf. on Multi-Agent Systems (ICMAS98)*, 1998.
32. T. Sugawara and V.R. Lesser. Learning to improve coordinated actions in cooperative distributed problem-solving environments. *Machine Learning*, 1998.
33. M. Tambe, J. Adibi, Y. Al-Onaizan, A. Erdem, G. Kaminka, S. Marsella, I. Muslea, and M. Tallis. ISIS: Using an Explicit Model of Teamwork in RoboCup'97. In *Proc. of the First Robot World Cup Competition and Conf.*, 1997.
34. M. Tambe. Towards flexible teamwork. *Journal of AI Research*, 7:83–124, 1997.
35. T. Wagner. *Toward Quantified Control for Organizationally Situated Agents*. PhD thesis, University of Massachusetts at Amherst, February 2000.
36. R. Vincent, B. Horling, T. Wagner, and V. Lesser. Survivability simulator for multi-agent adaptive coordination. In *Proc. of the First Intl. Conf. on Web-Based Modeling and Simulation*, 1998.
37. T. Wagner, A. Garvey, and V. Lesser. Criteria-Directed Heuristic Task Scheduling. *Intl. Journal of Approximate Reasoning, Special Issue on Scheduling*, 19(1-2):91–118, 1998. A version also available as UMASS CS TR-97-59.

38. T. Wagner and V. Lesser. Toward Ubiquitous Satisficing Agent Control. In *1998 AAAI Symposium on Satisficing Models*, March, 1998.
39. T. Wagner and V. Lesser. Relating quantified motivations for organizationally situated agents. In N.R. Jennings and Y. Lespérance, editors, *Intelligent Agents VI (ATAL-99)*, Lecture Notes in AI. Springer-Verlag, Berlin, 2000.
40. T. Wagner, V. Lesser, B. Benyo, A. Raja, P. Xuan, and S. XQ Zhang. GPGP2: Improvement Through Divide and Conquer. Working document, 1998.
41. P. Xuan and V. Lesser. Incorporating uncertainty in agent commitments. In N.R. Jennings and Y. Lespérance, editors, *Intelligent Agents VI (ATAL-99)*, Lecture Notes in AI. Springer-Verlag, Berlin, 2000.
42. S. Zilberstein and S. Russell. Efficient resource-bounded reasoning in AT-RALPH. In *Proc. of the First Intl. Conf. on AI Planning Systems*, College Park, Maryland, June 1992.

An Executable Model of the Interaction between Verbal and Non-verbal Communication

Catholijn M. Jonker, Jan Treur, and Wouter C.A. Wijngaards

Vrije Universiteit Amsterdam
Department of Artificial Intelligence
De Boelelaan 1081a, 1081 HV Amsterdam, The Netherlands
URL: http://www.cs.vu.nl /~{jonker,treur,wouterw}
Email: {jonker,treur,wouterw}@cs.vu.nl

Abstract. In this paper an executable generic process model is proposed for combined verbal and non-verbal communication processes and their interaction. The model has been formalised by three-levelled partial temporal models, covering both the material and mental processes and their relations. The generic process model has been designed, implemented and used to simulate different types of interaction between verbal and non-verbal communication processes: a non-verbal communication process that adds and modifies content to a verbal communication process, but also provides a protocol for the (control of the) verbal communication process. With respect to the communication protocol stimulus-response behaviour and deliberate behaviour have been modelled and simulated.

1 Introduction

Communication is often modelled exclusively as a process of information exchange, abstracting from the physical realisation of the communication process. This approach is based on the more general perspective that a strict separation between the level of *symbols* (symbolic processes) and the *material* level (physical processes) has advantages in modelling. Following this perspective, the communication process is not embedded in the physical environment. In particular, for the case of embodied non-verbal communication, for example on the basis of body language or gestures, a strict separation of communication processes from interaction at the material level can be rather artificial. On the other hand, describing communication processes only in physical terms may be too restrictive as well. In the model of communication presented in this paper both the material level and the level of information, as well as the interaction between the levels are taken into account in one generic process model.

At the symbolic level a distinction can be made between information representing the subject matter of the communication, and information that refers to the *process* of communication, for example, information on the communication protocol that is

F. Dignum and M. Greaves (Eds.): Agent Communication, LNAI 1916, pp. 331-350, 2000.
© Springer-Verlag Berlin Heidelberg 2000

followed, or the current stage of the communication process within the protocol. Thus, three semantic or representation levels are introduced:

- the *material level* (for the physical world),
- the *symbolic object level* (for symbolic manipulation of information on the physical world), and
- the *symbolic meta-level* (for symbolic manipulation of the dynamics and reflective aspects of the agents).

Each of these three levels uses representations of structures of one of the other levels: the symbolic object level uses representations of the material world, the symbolic meta-level uses representations of the symbolic object level, and the material level uses representations of the symbolic object level. The three levels are explained in more detail in Section 2; process semantics is defined by means of multi-levelled traces based on triples of three-valued states, formalised by partial models [10].

Next, in Section 3 an executable generic process model is introduced in which a number of processes within a communication process are distinguished. This process model is in accordance with the semantics given in Section 2. In Section 4 different types of interaction between non-verbal communication and verbal communication processes are identified; it is shown how the generic process model can be applied to model both verbal communication and non-verbal communication, as well as different types of interaction between these forms of communication, in one semantic framework. One example model is presented in which the communication protocol of a verbal communication process is modelled as reflex-based non-verbal communication (one gesture triggers another one by stimulus-response behaviour), and an alternative model in which the non-verbal communication in the communication protocol is guided by conscious deliberation. Section 5 summarizes and compares this approach with other work.

2 Semantic Levels in Communication

The semantic model is built by identifying the semantic levels involved, making the representation relations between them explicit, and by determining the state transitions at the different levels during the communication process. Three semantic levels are used in the semantic model of communication presented in this paper. The first is the *material level*: of the world itself, the physical reality. The second level is the level of symbolic representation of the world state: the *symbolic object level*. Within the agents, symbols are used to represent information regarding the world state. The third semantic level is the symbolic level where the agent reasons about aspects of its own state, e.g., its own knowledge and actions it intends to perform in the world: the *symbolic meta-level*. Symbolic expressions at this level do not represent information about world states, but instead are an explicit representation of information about the state of the process, of an agent's related mental aspects, such as its state of knowledge, its goals, and its intentions.

2.1 A Simple Example Communication Process

All examples in this paper are about a lecture, which is finishing. The chair person, agent A, puts up a slide expressing where to find tea and coffee. A thirsty person in the audience, agent B, interprets this information. However, the communication may be affected by an event in the material world, for example, somebody erroneously standing between the projector and the screen. In the example, agent A has a representation of the world information that pot 2 contains tea, represented at the symbolic object level by the symbolic expression contains(pot2, tea). By upward reflection to the symbolic meta-level it establishes that it has the positive belief that pot 2 contains tea. The agent A reasons at the symbolic meta-level and concludes that this world information should be communicated to agent B. Using knowledge of the meaning that can be associated to certain material configurations, it discovers that if at position p0 in the material world pattern 3 is visible then this world situation represents that pot 2 contains tea (e.g., a written text on a visible place). Moreover, still reasoning at the symbolic meta-level, it finds out that an action 'put slide 3' exists, which has as an effect that pattern 3 is at position p0. Therefore it concludes at the symbolic meta-level that the action 'put slide 3' has to be performed. The action is performed, and the intended effect is realised in the world state at the material level. In the example, the two agents are assumed to have a common ontology on the world including the names of all objects in the world, like pot 2, pattern 3, and the names of the positions.

Agent B performs the observation that pattern 3 is at position p0 (which provides information at the symbolic meta-level, namely the meta-fact that this has been observed), and represents the information acquired at the symbolic object level by at_position(pattern3, p0) (the agent B's world model). Note that agent B cannot observe directly the world information that pot 2 contains tea or that slide 3 is on the projector, but it can observe that pattern 3 is at position p0. Knowing at the symbolic meta-level that to this world situation the interpretation 'pot 2 contains tea' can be associated, it now concludes at the symbolic meta-level that it has been communicated that pot 2 contains tea. This information is then stored by B at the symbolic object level in its representation of the world state. Note that after this process, the representation of the world state at the symbolic object level includes information that was acquired by observation (pattern 3 is at position p0), and also information that was not obtainable by observation, but acquired by the communication process (pot 2 contains tea).

This example communication process can be described by tracing the states and state transitions at the different levels; see Figure 1. In this figure each cell describes a state, and state transitions are indicated by a line separating the two states in the transition. Time goes from top to bottom. In the figure only the relevant new information elements are represented. The first table gives the state of the external world (first column), and the states of the symbolic object level and meta-level of agent A (second and third column). The second table gives the same for agent B. The first table 'happens' before the second table. Note that not only the content but also events of the behaviour level and signal level (see [19]) are explitly modelled here.

External World material level	Agent A symbolic object level	symbolic meta-level
pot 2 contains tea	contains(pot2,tea)	belief(contains(pot2,tea),pos)
		has_verbal_material_rep(contains(pot2,tea),pos, at_position(pattern3,p0), pos)
		has_effect(put_slide3, at_position(pattern3,p0),pos)
		to_be_observed(I:INFO_ELEMENT)
		to_be_communicated(contains(pot2,tea),pos)
		to_be_achieved(at_position(pattern3,p0),pos)
		to_be_performed(put_slide3)
slide 3 at projector pattern3 at p0		

External World material level	Agent B symbolic object level	symbolic meta-level
pot 2 contains tea slide 3 at projector pattern3 at p0		to_be_observed(I:INFO_ELEMENT) has_verbal_material_rep(contains(pot2,tea),pos, at_position(pattern3,p0), pos)
		observation_result(at_position(pattern3,p0), pos)
	at_position(pattern3,p0)	
		belief(at_position(pattern3,p0), pos)
		has_been_communicated(contains(pot2, tea), pos)
	contains(pot2, tea)	
		belief(contains(pot2,tea), pos)

Figure 1. Multi-levelled trace of an example communication process

2.2 Formalisation of the Semantic Model

In the semantic formalisation a state-based semantics is chosen. Each of the states is formalised by a partial (or three-valued: with truth values *true*, *false* and *undefined*) model [2], [15]. The signature (the lexicon) for these partial models is partitioned according to the three semantic levels. To define semantics of the whole communication process, partial temporal models are used [10], [18]. Within this approach the semantics of a process is formalised by a set of (alternative) partial temporal models, i.e., sequences of partial models. For an example of such a partial temporal model, see Figure 1. Within each of the states in such a temporal model the three semantic levels can be distinguished. Representation relations are defined in the sense that symbolic expressions at the object level (such as contains(pot2, tea)) refer to the state of the material level, symbolic expressions at the meta-level (such as belief(contains(pot2, tea), pos)) refer to states of the object level, and the material level configurations (such as pattern 3) refer to object level information (that pot 2 contains tea).

Only the following types of transitions between two subsequent states are allowed in these temporal partial models:

Single Level Transitions
- *world change transition*
    A change in the state of the material level
- *object reasoning transition*
    A change in the state of the symbolic object level
- *meta-reasoning transition*
    A change in the state of the symbolic meta-level

Level Interaction Transitions
- *upward reflection transition*
    A change of the meta-level state under influence of the object level state.
- *downward reflection transition*
    A change of the object level state under influence of the meta-level state.
- *action execution transition*
    A change of the material level state under influence of the meta-level state
- *observation transition*
    A change of the meta-level state under influence of the material level state

A levelled transition is a transition of the overall (three-level) state which is induced by a transition of one of the types distinguished above. The transition types depicted in the first part of the trace are, subsequently:
- meta-reasoning; three times:
    - deciding that contains(pot2, tea) has to be communicated,
    - selecting the goal at_position(pattern3, p0) to be achieved,
    - determining the action put_slide3 to achieve the goal
- action execution.

The transition types depicted in the second part of the trace are, respectively,
- observation (of at_position(pattern3,p0)),
- downward reflection (including at_position(pattern3,p0) in B's world model),
- upward reflection (identifying at_position(pattern3,p0) as a belief),
- meta-reasoning (interpreting at_position(pattern3,p0) as a communication of the information contains(pot2,tea)),
- downward reflection (including contains(pot2,tea) in B's world model),
- upward reflection (identifying contains(pot2,tea) as a belief).

The formal definitions are given below. The elements used to describe the states (the ground atoms) are expressed in a language defined by an information type.

Definition 1 (Information State)

An *information type* Σ is a structure of symbols defining a set of *ground atoms* At(Σ). An *information state* for an information type Σ is a mapping $M : At(\Sigma) \rightarrow \{0, 1, u\}$ from the set of ground atoms At(Σ) to the set of truth values $\{0, 1, u\}$; i.e., a *(partial) model* . The set of all information states of information type Σ is denoted by IS(Σ). An information state $M : At(\Sigma) \rightarrow \{0, 1, u\}$ is called a *two-valued* information state if $M(a) \in \{0, 1\}$ for all $a \in At(\Sigma)$. The set of two-valued information states for Σ is denoted by $IS_2(\Sigma)$.

An example of a structure that defines an information type is a tuple of (sub-)sorts, constants, functions, and predicates of an order-sorted predicate logic. Each of the three levels has such an information type.

Description of Material Level and Symbolic Object Level
A world state at the material level can be formally described by a two-valued model (assuming that the world in principle can be described in a deterministic manner) for the language depicted in Figure 2. The textual description can be found on the left in Figure 3.

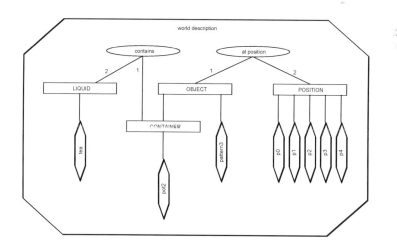

Figure 2. Information type **world_description**.

A state of the symbolic object level can be formally described by a three-valued model for the same language. The third truth value is used to express that some fact is not represented (e.g., not known to the agent).

Description of Symbolic Meta-level

The symbolic meta-level can be formally described by three-valued models for the language depicted in Figure 3. The textual description is on the right in Figure 3.

information type world_description
  sorts
    OBJECT, CONTAINER, LIQUID,
    POSITION
  subsorts
    CONTAINER: OBJECT
  objects
    pattern3: OBJECT;
    pot2: CONTAINER;
    p0, p1, p2, p3, p4: POSITION;
    tea: LIQUID
  relations
    contains: CONTAINER * LIQUID;
    at_position: OBJECT * POSITION;
end information type

information type meta-info
  sorts
    INFO_ELEMENT, ACTION, SIGN ;
  subsorts
    INFO_ELEMENT;
  meta-description
    world_description: INFO_ELEMENT;
  objects
    pos, neg : SIGN;
    put_slide3 : ACTION;
  relations
    to_be_observed: INFO_ELEMENT;
    observation_result, has_been_communicated,
    to_be_communicated, to_be_achieved, belief:
       INFO_ELEMENT * SIGN;
    to_be_performed: ACTION;
    has_effect: ACTION * INFO_ELEMENT * SIGN;
    has_material_rep: INFO_ELEMENT * INFO_ELEMENT;
end information type

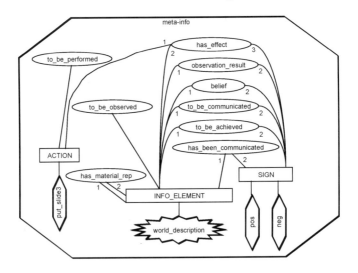

Figure 3. Information type meta-info.

The meta-description used in the information type of Figure 3 transforms all ground atoms specified by information type world description into ground terms of sort INFO ELEMENT. Formalising information states as partial models makes it possible to also model the reasoning behaviour of common inference mechanisms, such as chaining or unit-resolution, in terms of all ground literal conclusions that have been derived up to a certain moment in time: the third truth value unknown is used for information that has not (yet) been derived in the current state.

Definition 2 (Transition)

A *transition between information states* is a pair of partial models; i.e., an element $< S, S' >$ (also denoted by $S \to S'$) of $IS(\Sigma) \times IS(\Sigma)$. A *transition relation* is a set of these transitions, i.e., a relation on $IS(\Sigma) \times IS(\Sigma)$.

Behaviour is the result of transitions from one information state to another. If a transition relation is functional then it specifies deterministic behaviour. By applying transitions in succession, sequences of states are constructed. These sequences, also called traces (and interpreted as temporal models), formally describe behaviour.

Definition 3 (Trace and Temporal Model)

A *trace* or *partial temporal model* of information type Σ is a sequence of information states $(M^t)_{t \in N}$ in $IS(\Sigma)$. The set of all partial temporal models is denoted by $IS(\Sigma)^N$, or $Traces(\Sigma)$.

A set of partial temporal models is a declarative description of the semantics of the behaviour of a process; each temporal model can be seen as one of the alternatives for the behaviour. Next these notions are applied to the three levels distinguished in a communication process.

Definition 4 (Levelled Information State)

The *set of levelled information states* of the whole process is defined by:
$$IS = IS(\Sigma^{mat}) \times IS(\Sigma^{obj}) \times IS(\Sigma^{meta})$$

Levelled transitions and traces adhere to the levelled structure of the states: a levelled transition describes a levelled information state that changes in time. Following the levelled structure, only some types of transitions are allowed. For each of the levels a transition limited to this level (leaving untouched the other levels) is possible: a *world change*, an *object level reasoning* step, or a *meta-level reasoning* step. Two examples of transitions involving interaction between levels are *upward reflection* (information from the symbolic object level is lifted and incorporated in the symbolic meta-level), *downward reflection* (information from the symbolic meta-level influences the information at the symbolic object level). Other examples of transitions involving interaction between levels are *observation* (material level influences symbolic meta-level information), and *action execution* (symbolic meta-level information influences the material level). The following definition postulates that only these types of transitions are possible.

Definition 5 (Levelled Transition)

a) The following types of transitions are defined:

- *world change transition* $\qquad\qquad\qquad\qquad$ $IS_2(\Sigma^{mat}) \;\rightarrow\; IS_2(\Sigma^{mat})$
- *object reasoning transition* $\qquad\qquad\qquad$ $IS(\Sigma^{obj}) \;\rightarrow\; IS(\Sigma^{obj})$
- *meta-reasoning transition* $\qquad\qquad\qquad$ $IS(\Sigma^{meta}) \;\rightarrow\; IS(\Sigma^{meta})$
- *upward reflection transition* $\quad$ $IS(\Sigma^{obj}) \times IS(\Sigma^{meta}) \;\rightarrow\; IS(\Sigma^{meta})$
- *downward reflection transition* $\quad$ $IS(\Sigma^{obj}) \times IS(\Sigma^{meta}) \;\rightarrow\; IS(\Sigma^{obj})$
- *action execution transition* $\quad$ $IS_2(\Sigma^{mat}) \times IS(\Sigma^{meta}) \;\rightarrow\; IS_2(\Sigma^{mat})$
- *observation transition* $\quad$ $IS_2(\Sigma^{mat}) \times IS(\Sigma^{meta}) \;\rightarrow\; IS(\Sigma^{meta})$

b) A *levelled transition* is a transition: $IS \rightarrow IS$ which is based on a transition of one of the types defined in a).

Definition 6 (levelled Trace)

a) A *levelled trace* is a sequence of information states $(M^t)_{t \in N}$ in IS. The set of all levelled traces is denoted by IS^N, or Traces.

b) An element $(M^t)_{t \in N} \in$ Traces is called *coherent* if for all time points t the step from M^t to M^{t+1} is defined in accordance with a levelled transition. The set of coherent levelled traces forms a subset CTraces of Traces.

Note that in Figure 1 a coherent levelled trace is depicted. It is possible and sometimes necessary to define more constraints on the transitions. For example: physical laws for the material level, or: if an observation transition leads to meta-level information observation_result(a, pos), then a is true in the current world state, or: if an object reasoning transition adds information to the object level, then this information is in the deductive closure of the object level knowledge (consisting of the object level knowledge base and the information from the current object level information state).

3 The Generic Process Model for Communication

Within a communication process as described in Section 2 a number of more specific symbolic processes can be distinguished:

- observation generation
- information interpretation
- goal generation
- action generation
- maintenance of world information

Together with the physical processes in the material world that realise action and observation execution, these processes are used as building blocks to compose an executable generic process model of communication. Within the DESIRE approach each of the processes is modelled by a component (the boxes in Figure 4). Each component processes information as soon as it becomes available. The information is processed by applying knowledge rules to the input information, deriving conclusions that are the output information of the component. The interaction is modelled by information links (the arrows in Figure 4). By default information links transfer information from the source to the destination when it becomes available. Agent B is identical in composition to agent A.

The component observation generation determines the observations the agent initiates. In the example, agent B is initiating observation of the projection screen and agent A, and agent A observes agent B. The component information interpretation produces the information conveyed in the observation results, using specific interpretation knowledge (which involves, among others, knowledge on material representation of information). The component maintain world information constructs and maintains the agent's world model. The component communication initiation makes the decision to communicate and does some preparation of the communication; it uses knowledge about when to communicate information, and the selection of goals in relation to the material representation of information. The component action generation produces the actions to be performed, using knowledge of the effect of actions.

The component external world takes the observations and the actions initiated by the agents and produces the observation results for the agents. It maintains the state of the world and takes care of the changes to the world state.

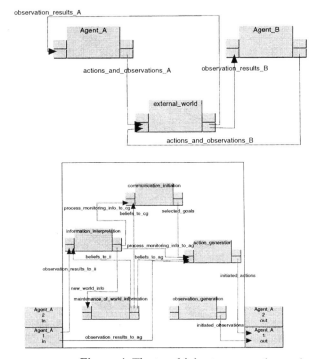

Figure 4. The two highest process abstraction levels

The reasoning of the agent is specified using a number of generic rules; for example, in the component information interpretation the following knowledge is used:

if   belief(R:INFO_ELEMENT,pos)
  and has_verbal_material_representation(C:INFO_ELEMENT,pos, R:INFO_ELEMENT,pos)
then has_been_communicated_by_modality(C:INFO_ELEMENT,pos, verbal)

This rule describes a meta-reasoning transition; it determines the content information that is communicated. It realises the state change depicted in Figure 1, from the 4th to the 5th row in the table depicting agent B's process. The other knowledge bases are specified in a similar way. In the model all components and information links in agents A and B process information when the input information changes, possibly in parallel.

4 Combining Verbal and Non-verbal Communication

During real-life communication processes several types of communication play a role, among them are verbal and non-verbal communication. Furthermore, combining verbal and non-verbal communication can sometimes be done in a stimulus-response manner in contrast to consciously. In Section 4.1 different types of interaction between verbal and non-verbal communication are distinguished and explained. In Section 4.2 it is shown how differences between reflex-based (also called direct stimulus-response) reactions and conscious reactions on non-verbal communication can be modelled.

4.1 Interaction between Verbal and Nonverbal Communication

The example communication process in Section 2 shows only verbal communication. The verbal type of communication is the type that is normally exclusively considered in research in multi-agent systems in which all agents are software agents. However, in real life situations, often the non-verbal communication is as important as verbal communication. In this section, non-verbal communication is addressed and classified into three different types of interaction with verbal communication. In the classification one of the distinguishing criteria is the nature of the processing of the communication: based on reflex reactions, or on conscious reactions. For each of the types of interaction between verbal and non-verbal communication an example is presented.

The following kinds of interaction between non-verbal and verbal communication are distinguished:

A. Interaction of non-verbal communication with the *content* of verbal communication:

1. non-verbal communication provides information additional to the content information transferred by the of the verbal communication:

   • the subject of the non-verbal communication has no connection with the subject of the verbal communication

   • the subject of the non-verbal communication is related to the subject of the verbal communication

2. non-verbal communication affects the interpretation of the contents of the verbal communication; modified interpretation

B. Interaction of non-verbal communication with the *process* of the verbal communication:

   1. the verbal communication process is affected by reflex-based reactions to the non-verbal communication

   2. the verbal communication process is affected by conscious reactions to the non-verbal communication

Notice that non-verbal communication of type A. will lead to conscious reactions of the recipient; as the interpretation of observations as being communicated information is a conscious process. Combinations of the different types of interaction can occur during one communication process. In the examples it is assumed that the agents share a common ontology for world information. Simple examples of the different types of non-verbal communication are:

A.   *Interaction of non-verbal communication with the content of verbal communication*:

1. *Additional information*

a) *No connection* Agent A communicates verbally to B that tea can be found in pot 2. Agent B observes that agent A smiles to him and concludes that agent A recognises him. This observation does not influence the communication process concerned with where the tea can be found. Furthermore, agent B does not change his interpretation of the verbal communication on account of noticing that agent A recognises him.

b) *Related*. Agent A communicates verbally to B that tea can be found in pot 2. During the communication Agent A points to position p3. Agent B observes the direction that agent A is pointing in and concludes that agent A is telling it that tea can be found in pot 2 that can be found at position p3.

2. *Modified interpretation*

Agent A communicates verbally to B that **fresh** tea can be found in pot 2. However, agent A makes a face that indicates she is disgusted at the moment the verbal communication process takes place. Agent B combines this non-verbal communication with the verbal one and, therefore, interprets the communication as follows: tea can be found in pot 2, but it is definitely not fresh. Modification of the interpretation of the verbal communication appeared to be necessary, based on the non-verbal part of the communication.

B.   *Interaction of non-verbal communication with the process of verbal communication*:

Agent A initiates the communication process by walking to position p1. She notices that agent B is looking at her and she starts her communication to agent B that tea can be found in pot 2, by putting the correct slide (slide 3) on the projector. However, after performing this action agent A observes that agent B is looking in another direction; in reaction (either by reflex or consciously) she breaks off the communication process by removing the slide, and (to get attention) starts tapping the microphone. Agent B observes the noise of the microphone and (either by reflex or consciously) reacts by looking at agent A with interest. Agent A waits until she observes that agent B is looking interested, and then resumes the verbal communication process by putting the slide on the projector again. In such a case the information transferred by verbal communication is not affected by the non-verbal communication, but (the control of) the process of communication is. An example communication process in which a combination of types of interaction occurs is the following:

Example 1 The Complete Tea Story

1.   Agent A wants to communicate to agent B that non-fresh tea can be found in pot 2 that is located at position p3.
2.   Agent A figures out how to perform the communication. She does not have a (verbal) slide that reflects all that she wants to communicate; she only has a slide that says that fresh tea can be found in pot 2. The rest of the communication will, therefore, have to be non-verbal. She finds the following solution: she will put the slide on the projector, point at position p3 and pull a disgusted face at the same time.
3.   Agent A attracts the attention of her audience (agent B) by going to position p1.
4.   Agent B observes this movement and responds by looking interested.
5.   Agent A observes that agent B is looking interested and performs the prepared actions.
6.   However, in the mean time, agent B's attention is distracted by a noise from outside. As a reaction to the noise from outside agent B looks away from agent A and stops looking interested.
7.   Agent A notices that agent B no longer is looking in her direction. Therefore, she removes the slide, stops pointing, and reverts her face to a neutral expression. Furthermore, in order to attract agent B's attention again, she taps the microphone.
8.   Agent B observes the noise inside the room and towards the front of the room (i.e., in the direction of agent A) and looks interested.
9.   Agent A waits until agent B looks interested again, and then communicates verbally to agent B that fresh tea can be found in pot 2 (she puts slide 3 on the projector). Agent A makes a face that indicates she is disgusted at the moment the verbal communication takes place. At the same time Agent A points to position p3.
10. Agent B observes:
     a) the pattern on projection screen that is caused by the slide

b) that agent A is pointing towards position p3
c) that agent A has a disgusted face
11.   and Agent B concludes:
a) tea can be found in pot 2: the interpretation of this part of the verbal communication of the pattern caused by the slide is not affected by any of the non-verbal communication of agent A.
b) the tea can be found at position p3: this additional information comes from interpreting the pointing gesture of agent A.
c) the tea is definitely not fresh: this interpretation is based on modification of the contents of the verbal communication (fresh tea) because of the non-verbal communication (disgusted face of
agent A) and the knowledge that tea has a taste.
12.   At the same time agent A looks questioningly towards agent B.
13.   Agent B observes the questioning face of agent A and puts his thumb up.
14.   Agent A observes that agent B's thumb is up and walks away from position p1.

4.2 Modelling a Communication Protocol: By Stimulus-Response or by Deliberate Behaviour

The next question is how much interpretation is needed to decide upon some action. The above example allows for three possible models:

1. Agent A observes that agent B is looking away and directly taps the microphone (a form a direct stimulus-response behaviour, also called behaviour by reflex).
2. Agent A observes that agent B is looking away, interprets this information as a belief of the form 'Agent B is not paying attention', and on the basis of this belief decides to tap the microphone
3. As in 2. Agent A generates the belief that Agent B is not paying attention, and realises that she needs to attract his attention (as a goal), and decides to tap the microphone (as an action to realise the goal. This is a form of goal directed behaviour based on conscious interpretations.

The generic process model described in Section 3 has been used to design and implement specific models for each of these three cases. An integral part of the communication process is the interpretation of the content information, which is assumed to be a conscious process. The knowledge to interpret information is the same for both agents and is used within the component information interpretation.

component information interpretation

(reflex-based and conscious)

generic knowledge:

if   belief(R:INFO_ELEMENT, SR:SIGN)
  and has_verbal_material_representation(C:INFO_ELEMENT, SC:SIGN,
          R:INFO_ELEMENT, SR:SIGN)
then has_been_communicated_by_modality(C:INFO_ELEMENT, S:SIGN, verbal);

if   belief(R:INFO_ELEMENT, SR:SIGN)
  and has_non_verbal_material_representation(C:INFO_ELEMENT, S:SIGN,
        R:INFO_ELEMENT, SR:SIGN)
then has_been_communicated_by_modality(C:INFO_ELEMENT,S:SIGN, non_verbal);

if   has_been_communicated_by_modality(C:INFO_ELEMENT,S:SIGN, verbal)
  and not concerns_taste(C:INFO_ELEMENT)
then has_been_communicated(C:INFO_ELEMENT, S:SIGN);

if   has_been_communicated_by_modality(C:INFO_ELEMENT,S:SIGN, non_verbal)
then has_been_communicated(C:INFO_ELEMENT, S:SIGN);

domain-specific knowledge:

if   has_been_communicated_by_modality(C:INFO_ELEMENT,pos,verbal)
  and concerns_taste(C:INFO_ELEMENT)
  and has_been_communicated_by_modality(tastes_good, neg, non_verbal)
then has_been_communicated(C:INFO_ELEMENT, neg);

Component maintenance of world information is used by the agent to maintain a (what he hopes to be correct) representation of the current state of the external world. It uses the following knowledge, if the agent behaves consciously.

component maintenance of world information

(conscious)

domain specific knowledge:

if   has_property(A:AGENT, looks_interested)
then has_property(A:AGENT, paying_attention);

if   **not** has_property(A:AGENT, looks_interested)
then not has_property(A:AGENT, paying_attention);

Within the component goal_generation the agent determines the goals that should be achieved if some information is to be communicated. Because of lack of space only the knowledge of agent A is given (that of agent B is similar).

component goal generation
(reflex-based and conscious)
generic part to choose modality and material representation
(similar knowledge is used for non-verbal communication):

if   to_be_communicated(C:INFO_ELEMENT, S:SIGN)
  and has_verbal_material_representation(C:INFO_ELEMENT, S:SIGN,
        R:INFO_ELEMENT, SR:SIGN)
then to_be_communicated_by_modality(C:INFO_ELEMENT,S:SIGN, verbal);

if   to_be_communicated_by_modality(C:INFO_ELEMENT,S:SIGN,verbal)
  and has_verbal_material_representation(C:INFO_ELEMENT,S:SIGN,
        R:INFO_ELEMENT,SR:SIGN)
then to_be_achieved(R:INFO_ELEMENT,SR:SIGN);

domain specific part to combine verbal and non-verbal communication:

if   to_be_communicated(C:INFO_ELEMENT, neg)
  and has_verbal_material_representation(C:INFO_ELEMENT, pos,
              RV:INFO_ELEMENT, SV:SIGN)
  and concerns_taste(C:INFO_ELEMENT)
  and has_non_verbal_material_representation(tastes_good, neg,
              RNV:INFO_ELEMENT, SN:SIGN)
then to_be_communicated_by_modality(C:INFO_ELEMENT, pos, verbal)
  and to_be_communicated_by_modality(tastes_good,neg,non_verbal);

In this case the difference between reflex-based and conscious behaviour can be easily modelled. The reflex-based agent uses the knowledge within component action generation in which all actions to be performed are guarded by conditions on available observation results. This means that as soon as these observation results become available the agent can react according to the goals set by (in this case) component goal_generation. A conscious agent does not react directly on observation results, it first interprets this information and decides what information it wants to believe. The conscious agent then reacts on its beliefs and not directly on its observation results. Therefore, the knowledge of the conscious agent with respect to action generation can be modelled by taking the following knowledge base and changing every relation observation_result into the relation belief. Because of lack of space only the knowledge of agent A is given (that of agent B is similar).

component action generation
(reflex-based)
generic communication action knowledge:

if   to_be_achieved(G: INFO_ELEMENT, S:SIGN)
  and possible action_effect(A:ACTION, G: INFO_ELEMENT, S:SIGN)
  and observation_result(has_property(agent_B, looks_interested), pos)
  and observation_result(at_position(agent_A, p1), pos)
  and observation_result(has_property(agent_A, disgusted_face), neg)
  and observation_result(has_property(agent_A, questioning_face), neg)
then to_be_performed(A:ACTION);

domain specific knowledge:

if   observation_result(there_is_noise_inside, pos)
  and observation_result(has_property(agent_B, looks_away), neg)
then to_be_performed(stop_tapping);

if   to_be_achieved(G: INFO_ELEMENT, SG:SIGN)
  and observation_result(has_property(agent_B, looks_away), pos)
  and observation_result(at_position(agent_A, p1), pos)
  and observation_result(has_property(agent_A, disgusted_face), pos)
then to_be_performed(tap_microphone)
  and to_be_performed(remove(S:SLIDE))
  and to_be_performed(do_not_point)
  and to_be_performed(pull_no_disgusted_face);

if   observation_result(has_property(agent_B, looks_interested), pos)
  and to_be_achieved(G:INFO_ELEMENT, S:SIGN)

and observation_result(G:INFO_ELEMENT, S:SIGN)
  and observation_result(has_property(agent_A, questioning_face), neg)
then to_be_performed(pull_questioning_face);

if   to_be_achieved(G:INFO_ELEMENT, S:SIGN)
  and observation_result(at_position(agent_A, p1), neg)
then to_be_performed(go_to(p1));

if observation_result(has_property(agent_B, thumb_up), pos)
  and observation_result(at_position(agent_A, p1), pos)
then to_be_performed(go_to(p2))
  and to_be_performed(pull_no_questioning_face);

Both agents always have knowledge in their symbolic meta-level information states:

Agent A always has the following knowledge at its symbolic meta-level:
has_verbal_material_representation(contains(pot2, tea), pos, at_position(pattern_3, p0), pos)
has_verbal_material_representation(has_property(tea, fresh), pos, at_position(pattern_3, p0), pos)
concerns_taste(has_property(tea, fresh))
has_non_verbal_material_representation(tastes_good, neg,
                    has_property(agent_A, disgusted_face), pos)
has_non_verbal_material_representation(at_position(pot2, p3), pos,
                    has_property(agent_A, points_to(p3)), pos)
possible_action_effect(go_to(p1), at_position(agent_A, p1), pos)
possible_action_effect(pull_disgusted_face, has_property(agent_A, disgusted_face), pos)
possible_action_effect(point_to(p3), has_property(agent_A, points_to(p3)), pos)
possible_action_effect(show(slide_3), at_position(pattern_3, p0), pos)
possible_action_effect(tap_microphone, there_is_noise_inside, pos)
possible_action_effect(pull_questioning_face, has_property(agent_A, questioning_face), pos)
has_non_verbal_material_representation(communication_succeeded, pos,
                    has_property(agent_B, thumb_up), pos)

Agent B always has the following knowledge at its symbolic meta-level:
possible_action_effect(look_interested, has_property(agent_B, looks_interested), pos)
has_verbal_material_representation(has_property(tea, fresh), pos, at_position(pattern_3, p0), pos)
has_verbal_material_representation(contains(pot2, tea), pos, at_position(pattern_3, p0), pos)
has_non_verbal_material_representation(tastes_good, neg,
                    has_property(agent_A, disgusted_face), pos)
has_non_verbal_material_representation(at_position(pot2, p3), pos,
                    has_property(agent_A, points_to(p3)), pos)
not concerns_taste(contains(pot2, tea))
concerns_taste(has_property(tea, fresh))
has_non_verbal_material_representation(message_understood, pos,
                    has_property(agent_B, thumb_up), pos)
possible_action_effect(put_thumb_up, has_property(agent_B, thumb_up), pos)

5 Discussion

In the area of agents, communication processes play an important role. In this paper a semantic model has been proposed for combined verbal and non-verbal communication processes and their interaction. The semantic model distinguishes three semantic or representation levels; it has been formalised on the basis of three-levelled partial temporal models [10], [18]. These partial temporal models formalise both the material and mental processes and their relations. The relations between the levels can be defined as (partly circular) representation relations, as in [14].

Moreover, using the compositional development method DESIRE [4], an executable generic process model has been designed that can be used to simulate different types of combinations of verbal and non-verbal communication processes. In an example it has been shown how a non-verbal communication process can be modelled that adds and modifies content to a verbal communication process, but also provides a protocol for the (control of the) verbal communication process. In this example different types of behaviour with respect to the communication protocol have been modelled: stimulus-response behaviour and variants of deliberate behaviour. The first type of behaviour has the advantage that it is very direct, but the second type of behaviour may be more flexible in unforeseen circumstances. The distinction made between stimulus-response behaviour and deliberate conscious reasoning in communication is also made in [6]. Three levels of cognitive control are distinguished, corresponding to the stimulus-response level, the conscious level and a heuristic-based level in between these two. The heuristic-based level, used in familiar, although not entirely routine, situations, can be expressed in the proposed model by rules guarded with beliefs and concluding actions.

The manner in which in the example the non-verbal communication process modifies the meaning of the verbal communication can be used as a more general approach to model irony; see, e.g., [16] for another approach to irony, based on an application of default logic to speech act theory.

The generic model for verbal and non-verbal communication presented here makes the communication process vulnerable to the effects of (other) causal patterns in the material world. This may occur as a negative aspect, as often communication is assumed ideal. However, in situations in which this assumption is not fulfilled, the approach introduced gives the possibility to explicitly model the interaction between the communication process and other material processes, and to take into account causality within the communication process, situated in the other processes; see also [9]. Moreover, this approach can be a starting point for simulations of the development of communication from an evolutionary perspective on communication; e.g., see [13].

A substantial part of research on communication (e.g., see [7],) takes speech act theory (cf. [1], [17]) as a point of departure. Agent communication languages such as KQML [11] have been proposed. Semantics of such languages is still an issue to be investigated further [8]. Speech acts are used to designate the effect an agent wishes to bring about in the world by communicating. Sometimes they are labelled as 'promise' or 'threaten', or more precisely 'put receiver clear about employer-employee relationship, and use this to force decision' or 'appeal to receiver to reconsider decision in light of new information'. Speech act theory treats these things in great detail. The theory, however, only considers the content of the communication, abstaining from the material realization. The limitation is that these approaches focus on communication at a verbal or symbolic level, and do not cover non-verbal communication processes in which the physical aspects play an important role. In conclusion, speech act theory aids us when determining the content of any communication, but when the material level is important (as in non-verbal interaction), it is less applicable.

In [5] a model is presented that does integrate verbal and non-verbal communication, however, the model is restricted to only gestures (with the arms). The gestures are modelled in a naturalistic fashion, as the authors take great care to generate realistic verbal and non-verbal behaviour. The interaction is limited to only one kind, type A1 (see section 4.1), where the non-verbal information content complements the verbal content. Several types of complementary gestures are distinguished, but the overall model is less refined and a formal semantics is not presented.

In comparison to [12], at the sender's side, our processes goal generation and action generation correspond to their 'goal formulation' and 'message formulation'. Moreover at the receiver's side, our processes observation generation information and interpretation correspond to their 'message deconstruction' and 'reception'. In principle our model could be extended to also include processes for their 'motivation' and 'elaboration' and 'message expectation'. A main difference is that our model explicitly treats verbal and nonverbal communication.

A demo has been developed which allows the user to view the process step-by-step. They can also take matters into their own hand and select the types of behaviour for each agent, or even select specific actions by hand, taking the role of one or both agents.

References

1. Austin, J.L., How to do things with words. Oxford University Press. London, 1962.
2. Blamey, S., Partial Logic. In: D. Gabbay and F. Günthner (Eds.), *Handbook of Philosophical Logic*. Vol. III, pp. 1-70, Reidel, Dordrecht, 1986
3. Bradshaw, J.M. (ed.), Software Agents. AAAI Press/MIT Press, 1997.
4. Brazier, F.M.T., Dunin-Keplicz, B.M., Jennings, N.R. and Treur, J., Formal Specification of Multi-Agent Systems: a Real World Case, In: Lesser, V. (Ed.), *Proceedings First International Conference on Multi-Agent Systems, ICMAS'95*, MIT Press, 1995, pp. 25-32. Extended version in: Huhns, M. and Singh, M. (Eds.), *International Journal of Co-operative Information Systems, IJCIS* vol. 6 (1), special issue on Formal Methods in Co-operative Information Systems: Multi-Agent Systems, 1997, pp. 67-94.
5. Cassell, J., Steedman, M., Badler, N.I., Pelachaud, C., Stone, M., Douville, B., Prevost, S. and Achorn, B., Proceedings of the 16th Annual Conference of the Cognitive Science Society, Georgia Institute of Technology, Atlanta, USA, 1994.

6. Chaib-draa, B., and Levesque, P., Hierarchical model and communication by signs, signals and symbols in multi-agent environments. In: J.W. Perram and J.P. Mueller (eds.), Distributed software agents and applications: 6th European Workshop on Modelling Autonomous Agents in a Multi-Agent World, MAAMAW'94, Lecture Notes in Computer Science, vol. 1069, Springer Verlag, 1994. Also in: Journal of Experimental and Theoretic Artificial Intelligence, vol. 8, pp. 7-20, 1996.

7. Cohen, P.R., J. Morgan, M. Pollack (eds.), Intentions in Communication. MIT Press, 1990

8. Cohen, P.R., Levesque, H.J., Communicative Actions for Artificial Agents. In: [3], 1997, pp. 419-436

9. Dretske, F.I., Knowledge and the Flow of Information. Oxford: Basil Blackwell, 1981.

10. Engelfriet J., Treur J., Temporal Theories of Reasoning; Journal of Applied Non-Classical Logics, 5, 1995, pp. 239-261.

11. Finin, T., Labrou, Y., Mayfield, J., KQML as an Agent Communication Language. In: [3], 1997, pp. 291-316.

12. Goldsmith, S., and Spires, S., Agent communication using Distributed Metaobjects. In: Dignum, F., Chaib-draa, B., and Weigand, H. (eds), Proceedings of the Agent Communication Languages Workshop 1999, ACL'99. Lecture Notes in AI, Springer Verlag, 2000. This volume.

13. Hauser, M.D., The Evolution of Communication. MIT Press, 1996.

14. Jonker, C.M., and J. Treur, Modelling an Agent's Mind and Matter. In: Proceedings of the 8th European Workshop on Modelling Autonomous Agents in a Multi-Agent World, MAAMAW'97, Lecture Notes in AI, vol. 1237, Springer Verlag, 1997, pp. 210-233.

15. Langholm, T. (1988). Partiality, Truth and Persistence. *CSLI Lecture Notes, No. 15.* Stanford University, Stanford, 1988.

16. Perrault, C.R., An Application of Default Logic to Speech Act Theory. In: [7], 1990, pp. 161-186

17. Searl, J.R. (1969). Speech Acts: an Essay in the Philosophy of Language. Cambridge University Press. New York, 1969.

18. Treur, J. (1994), Temporal Semantics of Meta-Level Architectures for Dynamic Control of Reasoning. In: L. Fribourg and F. Turini (ed.), Logic Program Synthesis and Transformation-Meta-Programming in Logic, Proceedings of the Fourth International Workshop on Meta-Programming in Logic, META'94. Springer Verlag, Lecture Notes in Computer Science, vol. 883, 1994. pp. 353-376.

19. Vongkasem, L., and Chaib-draa, B., Conversations are Joint Activities. In: Dignum, F., Chaib-draa, B., and Weigand, H. (eds), Proceedings of the Agent Communication Languages Workshop 1999, ACL'99. Lecture Notes in AI, Springer Verlag, 2000. This volume.

Author Index